John Henry Middleton

The Remains of Ancient Rome

Vol. 1

John Henry Middleton

The Remains of Ancient Rome
Vol. 1

ISBN/EAN: 9783337384128

Printed in Europe, USA, Canada, Australia, Japan

Cover: Foto ©ninafisch / pixelio.de

More available books at **www.hansebooks.com**

THE REMAINS

OF

ANCIENT ROME

BY

J. HENRY MIDDLETON

SLADE PROFESSOR OF FINE ART, DIRECTOR OF THE FITZWILLIAM MUSEUM, AND
FELLOW OF KING'S COLLEGE, CAMBRIDGE; AUTHOR OF 'ANCIENT
ROME IN 1888,' 'THE ENGRAVED GEMS OF CLASSICAL
TIMES,' 1891, ETC. ETC.

'Possis nihil urbe Roma
Visere majus.'—HOR. *Car. Sec.* 11.

VOL. I.

LONDON AND EDINBURGH
ADAM AND CHARLES BLACK
1892

PREFACE

THE present work is a revised and greatly enlarged version in two volumes of the former one-volume books entitled *Ancient Rome in 1885* and *in 1888*.

A great part has been rewritten, accounts of the recent discoveries have been added, and a large number of new illustrations have been introduced.

I have to thank Mr. John Murray for kindly supplying *clichés* of the cuts of the Colosseum and the Circus of Maxentius, and for allowing me to reprint part of the description of the Circus Maximus which I originally wrote for the new edition of Smith's *Dictionary of Antiquities*. I also have to thank Messrs. Swan Sonnenschein and Co. for the use of their cuts of the Pantheon, the Theatre of Marcellus, the Arch of Constantine, and the Coin of the Gens Scribonia. The Council of the Society of Antiquaries have been good enough to supply the cuts taken from Ligorio's Bodleian manuscript.

Unhappily the growth of the modern city, which has recently progressed with extraordinary rapidity, has led to the obliteration of many interesting features in the topography of the ancient city, and the destruction of a large proportion of its natural beauties.

The many lovely gardens and vineyards which were scattered throughout the Aurelian enclosure are now rapidly disappearing under the destructive hand of the speculating builder; the picturesque old streets are being rebuilt, frequently on wholly new lines, and Rome, which was once not only among the most interesting, but also one of the most beautiful cities in the world, is rapidly assuming the aspect of a third-rate Parisian suburb.

Thus, for example, the famous Ludovisi Gardens, one of the loveliest spots on the face of the earth, are now uprooted and made into a dreary quarter of "jerry-built" stuccoed boulevards.

The destruction of the beautiful avenue of ilex oak trees which led from the Lateran Church to the Basilica of S. Croce in Gerusalemme, in order to make room for a new row of stuccoed barrack-like houses, has for ever ruined what was formerly one of the most perfect views in Italy.

No less horrible is the conversion of the garden-like "prati," all round the Castle of S. Angelo, into a hideous waste of bricks and mortar, together with countless other outrages of the same kind.

One of the most serious injuries to the beauty of the city is the demolition of the picturesque old houses which skirted the Tiber banks, especially on the left side, and the formation of an ugly stone embankment. A number of interesting ancient river-side houses, very beautifully decorated, were exposed and then completely destroyed during the progress of the work.

The destruction of the *Ghetto*, and of much more of the most populous quarter of the *Campus Martius*, has obliterated a great portion of the mediaeval city, and destroyed much that was picturesquely beautiful, and full of real historical interest.

No words can adequately express the disgust which must be experienced both by the antiquary and by the lover of beauty in any form who now visits this unhappy city. The injury done in former periods of destruction was but superficial compared to the ruin which is being wrought by the present scheme of the *piano regolatore*, which aims and is partly succeeding in levelling the seven hills and filling up the intermediate valleys ; changing the very face of nature, and utterly destroying the character of the former Capital of the world.

It should, however, be remembered that a great proportion of the injury which has been done to the remains of ancient and mediaeval Rome and to the natural beauties of the place has been the unavoidable result of the fact that Rome has again become the Capital of Italy, and that in number of inhabitants it is now considerably more than double what it was in 1870.[1]

It would not be fair, therefore, to speak as if the Italians were a wantonly destructive race, inferior, for example, to the English in their respect for what is beautiful and historically interesting.

In England there was less to destroy, but proportionally the ravages of the last fifty years in old London and among the mediaeval buildings of Oxford and Cambridge and elsewhere have been no less lamentable than the changes which have gone so far to blot out the once unrivalled charm of the Eternal City.

J. HENRY MIDDLETON,

KING'S COLLEGE,
CAMBRIDGE.

[1] The population of Rome is now close on half a million

CONTENTS

PREFACE

INTRODUCTION

SOURCES OF INFORMATION; Classical writers; Inscriptions and coins; Mediaeval books and pictures; Modern books . . Pages xv-xxxiii

CHAPTER I

SITE OF ROME; physical aspect; building materials, stone, concrete, and brick; varieties of marble, granite, and porphyry; Architectural styles, Etruscan, Greek, and native Roman . . . 1-35

CHAPTER II

METHODS OF CONSTRUCTION; masonry, concrete, brick facing, opus reticulatum, concrete vaults, centering, lacunaria, stucco and cement made of pounded marble; mosaic for floors and walls; marble wall-linings; Metropolitan Building Act; the technical methods employed in Roman wall-paintings, encaustic and tempera; painter's colours and tools; paintings of the Republican period found in tombs on the Esquiline 36-103

CHAPTER III

PREHISTORIC AND REGAL PERIOD; early tombs with Phoenician imports; the Pomoerium; Tacitus on its circuit; Roma Quadrata and the so-called Wall of Romulus; existing remains; gates of Roma Quadrata; the Lupercal; Hut of Romulus; the Regal Period; four Regiones of Servius; their circuit wall and its gates; the Agger of

Servius, existing remains; the great cloacae, recent discoveries; the river embankment, the Curatores alvei; marble wharf by the Campus Martius; the "Mamertine prison" and the Scalae Gemoniae . . . . Pages 104-155

CHAPTER IV

THE PALATINE HILL; Prehistoric and Republican buildings; early temples and houses; Altar to the Unknown God; House of Livia; Palace of Augustus and the Area of Apollo; the Palace and Cryptoporticus of Caligula 158-198

CHAPTER V

THE PALATINE HILL (*continued*); the Flavian Palace; the "Domus Gelotiana"; the Palatine Stadium and the Palace of Hadrian; Palace of Severus; the Velia, the Germalus, the Velabrum; the Nova Via, the Sacra Via; late baths and other buildings skirting the Sacra Via 199-230

CHAPTER VI

THE FORUM ROMANUM; early development; its use for gladiatorial fights; the Comitium and the Curia; early ritual; the Rostra; the Ficus Ruminalis; the Basilica Aemilia; the bronze temple of Janus; the Sacra Via; existing remains of the Rostra and so-called Graecostasis; the Umbilicus and the Milliarium Aureum; the Temple of Saturn; the Arch of Tiberius; the Basilica Julia; the Temples of Augustus, of Castor, and of Divus Julius; the Rostra Julia 231-288

CHAPTER VII

THE FORUM ROMANUM (*continued*); the cult of Vesta; the Vestal Virgins; the Temple of Vesta; the Domus Publica; the Regia; the House of the Vestals; statues of the Vestales Maximae and their inscribed pedestals; the Arch of Fabius; the Temple of Faustina; the Temple of Concord; the Temple of Vespasian; the small aedicula; the Porticus of the Dii Consentes; the Schola Xanthi; the Arch of Severus; the central area of the Forum: sculptured plutei and other monuments 289-352

CHAPTER VIII

THE CAPITOLINE HILL; the Arx and Capitolium; the *flavissae* or treasure chambers; Temple of Jupiter Feretrius; Temple of Jupiter Capitolinus, its treasures and religious importance; the Temple of Juno Moneta, the early mint; other smaller temples; works of art on the Capitol; the Capitoline Tabularium; its existing remains of Republican date . . . . Pages 353-377

CHAPTER IX

THE ARCHITECTURAL GROWTH OF ROME; the development of the Campus Martius; the fourteen *Regiones* of Augustus and their principal contents; the *Res gestae* of Augustus from the Temple at Ancyra, his munificence in the improvement of Rome and his many benefactions to the Roman people; the Age of Severus; the accumulation in Rome of works of art 378-391

List of references to the Plan of the Forum Romanum   392-393

LIST OF ILLUSTRATIONS

COLOURED PLATES

I. Map of Ancient Rome, opposite p. 1.
II. Map of Modern Rome, showing the existing ancient remains and proposed new streets ; in a pocket at the end.
III. Plan of the Forum Romanum, showing the most recent discoveries ; in a pocket at the end.

ILLUSTRATIONS IN THE TEXT

FIG.		PAGE
1.	Doorway into the Forum Pacis . . .	41
2.	Arch opening into the Forum Augusti .	43
3.	Method of casting concrete walls .	48
4.	Opus incertum and reticulatum .	52
5.	Mixed opus reticulatum and brick	53
6.	Doorway in Caligula's Palace .	55
7.	Concrete wall faced with brick . .	56
8.	Perspective sketch of brick-faced wall	57
9.	Concrete arch faced with brick . .	59
10.	Concrete used like solid stone . .	64
11.	Centering used for concrete arch .	68
12.	Centering used for stone arch . .	69
13.	Lacunaria in a concrete vault . .	71
14.	Wall-lining of marble panels . . .	86
15.	Marble lining from the Temple of Concord	87
16.	Section of the Wall of Roma Quadrata .	113
17.	Elevation of the Wall of Roma Quadrata .	115
18.	Wall and Agger of Servius . .	136
19.	Early Masons' marks	138
20.	Part of the Servian wall on the Aventine .	140
21.	The Mamertine prison (Tullianum) . .	152

xiv LIST OF ILLUSTRATIONS

FIG.		PAGE
22. Plan of the Palatine Hill . .	to face	156
23. Early cistern by the Scalae Caci	.	160
24. Altar to the Unknown God .		174
25. Plan of the "House of Livia" .	.	177
26. A Roman shop-front, restored . .		193
27. The Curia (Church of S. Adriano) .		239
28. Ligorio's sketch of the Curia . .		240
29. The Temple of Janus on a coin of Nero		248
30. Early piece of paved road . . .		251
31. Plan of the Rostra and "Graecostasis" .		253
32. Section of the Rostra and "Graecostasis".		255
33. Front of the Rostra, restored	.	257
34. The Rostra shown on Constantine's relief . . .	.	259
35. Ligorio's sketch of the "Temple of Augustus" . .	.	275
36. Plan of the Temple of Castor	.	278
37. Details of the Podium of the Temple of Castor . .	.	280
38. The Puteal Scribonianum on a coin . . .		284
39. The Palladium on a coin of Antoninus Pius .		296
40. The Temple of Vesta, restored		298
41. Plan of the Atrium Vestae .	.	302
42. Section of the Atrium Vestae . .	.	308
43. Roman corn-mill	.	314
44. Statue of a Vestal wearing the suffibulum . .	.	320
45. The Temple of Concord on a coin of Tiberius .		337
46. The Temple of Capitoline Jupiter on a relief .		363
47. Sacrificial scene on the Capitol, from a coin .		364
48. Doorway of the Tabularium . .	.	376

INTRODUCTION

MUCH additional knowledge with regard to the Archaeology of Ancient Rome has recently been acquired owing to the fact that the last few years have been extraordinarily fertile in the discoveries of hitherto unknown remains, and in the new light that has been thrown on many of those that have for long been visible. To excavations made during the last fifteen years are due the complete exposure of the whole area of the *Forum Romanum* and much of the ground near it; the determination of the real form of the Rostra of Julius Caesar; the discovery of most important remains of the Temple of Vesta, the House of the Vestals, the Regia, the Domus Publica, and the line of the Nova Via. The great Servian Agger, with countless early tombs and houses of all dates, has, during the same period, been brought to light by the extensive excavations made in laying out a new quarter of modern Rome. Most important of all, in its relation to the early history of Rome, has been the discovery of a large Necropolis on the Esquiline Hill, the objects found in which show that at an early prehistoric period a settlement existed there in which the Etruscans were the predominant and civilising influence, and that the inhabitants were largely dependent upon Oriental, probably Phoenician traders for a great proportion of the objects both of use and ornament which they possessed. *Recent discoveries.* *Prehistoric cemetery.*

Moreover, in the following pages an attempt has been made to describe the buildings of ancient Rome with increased *Importance of details.*

attention to detail and methods of construction—points which are usually passed over too lightly by those antiquaries who are without any practical acquaintance with the actual processes and materials employed in building.

Existing evidence.   Great as must always be the value of documentary evidence, such as that which is supplied by inscriptions, coins, and the long list of classical writers mentioned below, yet it is of quite equal importance for the student to learn to read the story told by each building itself—a record by no means clear, and which requires long and careful study of what may at first sight appear to be matters of small moment.

It is not only the general design of a building, the contours of its mouldings, or the style of its sculpture, which supplies valuable evidence as to its history, but no less important help is often to be gained by the minute examination of such purely constructional points as the composition of the concrete, the form of the wood centering shown by its imprints on the vaults, and countless other technical details.

Measured plans.   It is hoped, too, that the plans and other illustrations may be of assistance to future students—especially the plan of the Forum, which has been measured and drawn by the author entirely afresh, and shows in a minute way the whole extent of the area of the Forum and most of its surrounding buildings.[1] The latest excavations are shown on the plan of the Palatine Hill and on that of the House of the Vestals.

References to Pliny.   The references to Pliny's *Historia Naturalis* are given in all cases according to the system of smaller subdivisions into paragraphs which has been adopted in all the best recent editions. This makes it much easier to find the passage referred to.

Before passing on to the subject in hand it may be well to give a list of the various sources of information on the Archaeology of Rome, with the names of the chief books and

[1] This plan of the Forum has been reproduced in more than one German work on Roman topography.

periodicals which should be consulted by those who wish to enter upon the study of this most fascinating subject.

The sources of information on the Archaeology of Rome may be classified in the following way:—

I. CLASSICAL WRITERS.

II. INSCRIPTIONS, COINS, AND OTHER EXISTING REMAINS.

III. THE REGIONARY CATALOGUES AND OTHER DOCUMENTS OF THE DECADENCE AND MIDDLE AGES.

IV. A NUMBER OF WORKS, MOSTLY ILLUSTRATED, DATING FROM THE REVIVAL OF INTEREST IN CLASSICAL ANTIQUITIES IN THE FIFTEENTH CENTURY DOWN TO THE PRESENT CENTURY, AND OLD PICTURES WHICH SHOW CLASSICAL BUILDINGS NOW DESTROYED.

V. MODERN WORKS.

I. The following are the chief classical writers who give information on the antiquities and topography of Rome:—

PLAUTUS, *Comic Poet*: b. c. 254 B.C.—d. 184 B.C. Wrote *Comedies*, of which twenty exist.

ENNIUS, *Poet*: b. 239—d. 169 B.C. Wrote *Satires* and *Tragedies*, of which only fragments exist.

POLYBIUS, *Greek Historian*: b. c. 204—d. c. 122 B.C. Wrote a *History of Rome, Greece, and other countries*, in forty books, of which the first five exist, and considerable fragments of others.

TERENTIUS AFER, native of Carthage, *Comic Poet*: b. 195—d. c. 159 B.C. Wrote *Comedies*, of which six exist.

M. TERENTIUS VARRO, *Antiquary and Philologist*: b. 116—d. 28 B.C. Wrote *De Lingua Latina, De Re Rustica, Antiquitatum Libri*, and other works.

M. TULLIUS CICERO, *Orator and Statesman*: b. 106—d. 43 B.C. Wrote *Orations, De Natura Deorum, De Legibus*, and many other works on *philosophy and theology*.

C. SALLUSTIUS CRISPUS, *Historian*: 86-34 B.C. Wrote on the *Jugurthine War* and *Catiline Conspiracy*.

VALERIUS (or QUINTUS) CATULLUS, *Poet*: 87-c. 47 B.C. Wrote *Odes*, of which 116 exist.

P. VERGILIUS MARO, *Poet*: 70-19 B.C. The *Aeneid* contains many references to Rome and its history. The very valuable commentary which passes by the name of *Servius* is mentioned below.

Q. HORATIUS FLACCUS, *Poet*: 65-8 B.C. His *Satires* especially contain passages illustrative of Roman topography.

TITUS LIVIUS, the chief *Roman Historian*: 59 B.C.-17 A.D. His *History of Rome*, which ends with the year 9 B.C., consisted of 142 books, of which 35 exist complete, with *Epitomes* of all the lost books except two.

SEXTUS AURELIUS PROPERTIUS, *Poet*: b. c. 50—d. c. 15 B.C. Wrote *Elegies*.

DIODORUS SICULUS, *Greek Historian*: reign of Augustus. Wrote *Bibliotheca Historica*.

P. OVIDIUS NASO, *Poet*: b. 43 B.C.—d. 18 A.D. His *Fasti* are especially valuable to the student of Roman archaeology.

STRABO, *Greek Geographer*: b. c. 54 B.C.—d. after 20 A.D. Wrote on the *Geography* of the known world, in seventeen books.

DIONYSIUS OF HALICARNASSUS, *Greek Historian*: died 7 B.C. Wrote on the early *History of Rome*.

M. VITRUVIUS POLLIO, *Architect and Military Engineer* in the reign of Augustus: probably born in the early part of the first century B.C., date of death unknown. Wrote *De Architectura*, dedicated to Augustus, a most interesting and valuable work.

C. VELLEIUS PATERCULUS, *Historian*: b. c. 20 B.C.—d. c. 31 A.D. Wrote *Historia Romana*, published in 30 A.D.

M. VALERIUS MAXIMUS, *Historian*: reign of Augustus and Tiberius. Wrote *De Factis Dictisque Memorabilibus Libri IX.*, a curious collection of historical anecdotes.

M. ANNAEUS LUCANUS, *Poet*: 39-65 A.D. Wrote the *Pharsalia*, a poem in ten books, descriptive of the struggle between Pompey and Caesar.

PLINY THE ELDER (*C. Plinius Secundus*): 23-79 A.D. Wrote an Encyclopaedia of general information, called *Historia Naturalis*, which contains much valuable information on the buildings of Rome and their works of art.

FLAVIUS JOSEPHUS, *Jewish Historian*: b. 37 A.D.—d. after 97. Wrote in Greek the *History of the Jewish Wars*, a book on *Jewish Antiquities*, and other works.

P. PAPINIUS STATIUS, *Poet*: c. 61-c. 96 A.D. Wrote *Silvae*, *Thebais*, and

INTRODUCTION

Achilleis. The first of these contains descriptions of various parts of Rome in the reign of Domitian.

M. VALERIUS MARTIALIS, *Poet*: b. 43 A.D.—d. after 104 A.D. Wrote *Epigrams*, fourteen books of which exist. One of these, entitled *De Spectaculis*, is of special archaeological interest.

DECIMUS JUNIUS JUVENALIS, *Satiric Poet*: end of the first century A.D. Wrote *Satires*, which contain many passages illustrative of Roman topography.

C. CORNELIUS TACITUS, *Historian*: b. c. 55 A.D.—d. after 117 A.D. Wrote *Annales* and *Historiae Romae*, and other works.

PLINY THE YOUNGER (*C. Plinius Caecilius Secundus*), b. 61—d. after 110 A.D., was the nephew of the elder Pliny; he practised as an advocate in the *Basilicae* of Rome, and wrote a *Panegyricus* and *Epistolae*; the latter are of special interest.

C. SUETONIUS TRANQUILLUS, *Historian*: second half of the first century A.D. Wrote *Lives of the Caesars* down to Domitian, of great value and interest, together with many other works now lost.

PLUTARCH, a *Greek Historian and Moralist*: second half of the first century A.D. Wrote *Lives of forty-six distinguished Greeks and Romans*, and a work called *Quaestiones Romanae*, which contains much curious information on Roman antiquities.

S. JULIUS FRONTINUS, *Curator of the Aqueducts* under Trajan. Wrote *De Aquaeductibus Romae*. See vol. ii. p. 314.

AULUS GELLIUS, *Essayist*: c. 117–180 A.D. Wrote *Noctes Atticae*, in which are many notes on Roman antiquities.

SEXTUS POMPEIUS FESTUS, a Roman lexicographer of not later than the second century A.D. His chief work, *De verborum significatione*, is an abridgment of a sort of encyclopaedia compiled by Verrius Flaccus, who was tutor to Augustus' grandchildren.

DION CASSIUS COCCEIANUS, *Senator and Historian*: b. c. 155 A.D.—date of death unknown. Wrote a *History of Rome* in Greek down to the reign of Caracalla; only parts of it now exist; it is of very great value.

Q. SEPTIMIUS TERTULLIANUS, the earliest of the Latin Fathers: c. 160– c. 220 A.D. Wrote a tract called *De Spectaculis*, on the wickedness of the cruel shows in amphitheatres; it contains some information on the details of the games.

HERODIANUS, *Greek Historian* of Rome: c. 180–240 A.D. Wrote the *History of his own Time*.

INTRODUCTION

The biographies of the Roman Emperors from Hadrian 117 A.D. to Carinus 284 A.D., entitled *Historiae Augustae*, were the work of six writers, *Aelius Spartianus, Julius Capitolinus, Vulcatius Gallicanus, Aelius Lampridius, Trebellius Pollio*, and *Flavius Vopiscus*, but it is impossible to attribute with certainty each biography to its real author. This work was compiled at different times towards the end of the third and beginning of the fourth century.

C. JUNIUS SOLINUS, *Historian and Archaeologist*: third century A.D. Wrote *Polyhistor*, a sort of Encyclopaedia.

CALPURNIUS SICULUS, *Roman Poet*: date doubtful, probably of the third century A.D. Wrote *Eclogues*, in one of which he describes shows in a Roman amphitheatre with much detail and vividness.

EUSEBIUS OF CAESAREA: c. 264–c. 340 A.D. Wrote *Historia Ecclesiastica* and the *Chronicon*.

AMMIANUS MARCELLINUS, *Roman Historian*: second half of fourth century A.D. Wrote *History of Rome* from Nerva 96 A.D. to Valens 378 A.D., of which only the latter part exists.

AURELIUS THEODOSIUS MACROBIUS, *Roman Writer*: first half of fifth century A.D. Wrote *Saturnaliorum Conviviorum Libri VII.*, an interesting archaeological work.

CLAUDIUS CLAUDIANUS, *Poet*: d. c. 408 A.D. Wrote *De Bello Getico* on Stilicho's victories over the Goths, and many other poems.

SIDONIUS APOLLINARIS, a *Latin Bishop*: 430–482 A.D. Wrote *Poems* and *Epistles*.

ZOSIMUS, *Greek Historian*: fifth century A.D. Wrote a *History of the Decline of the Roman Empire*, in six books, down to 410 A.D.

MAGNUS AURELIUS CASSIODORIUS, *Roman Statesman and Writer*: b. c. 468—d. c. 564. Wrote a *Chronicon* or *Abstract of Universal History*, an *Ecclesiastical History*, and many other works. He also compiled a series of contemporary State papers.

PROCOPIUS, *Byzantine Historian*: b. c. 500. Wrote a *History of his own Time*, containing an account of the wars of the Romans with the Persians, the Goths, and the Vandals.

II. INSCRIPTIONS.

These are frequently of the highest value in throwing light on Roman topography.

The most important existing inscription, as regards this

subject, is that cut on the walls of the Temple of Augustus at Ancyra, an account of which is given in vol. i. p. 384.   *Inscriptions.*

The *Consular Fasti*, inscribed on marble blocks, contained lists of Consuls and other State officials down to the time of Augustus. In the sixteenth century many fragments of this valuable record were found near the Temple of Vesta and the Regia, and are now preserved in the Palazzo dei Conservatori on the Capitol. It appears probable that the *Fasti* were originally cut on the walls of the *Regia*; see vol. i. p. 307. See Fea, *Frammenti dei Fasti*, Rome, 1820, and Reber, *Ruinen Roms*, p. 135.

The very important inscriptions from the Grove of the Fratres Arvales have been published more than once. The best and most complete edition is that of G. Henzen, *Arvalium fratrum acta quae supersunt*, Berlin, 1874.

The marble plan of Rome has been well published by Jordan, *Forma Urbis Romae*, Berlin, 1875-82. An interesting monograph on it was published by Professor Ant. Elter, Bonn, 1891.

The first important collection of Roman inscriptions was edited about 1480 by the Dominican Friar Fra Giovanni Giocondo of Verona, who was born about 1435. This wonderful man was one of the greatest architects of the Renaissance, a most enthusiastic antiquary and a learned scholar. His *Corpus Inscriptionum*, dedicated to Lorenzo de' Medici, contains more than 2000 inscriptions. It is incorporated in the collections of Maffei, Gori, and Muratori.   *Fra Giocondo.*

Fra Giocondo also edited the works of Pliny, Vitruvius, Frontinus, Varro, *De re rustica*, the epitome of Aur. Victor and Caesar's *Commentaries*. No other single man probably did so much to increase the knowledge and love of classical learning.

The Ancyrean inscription, *Res gestae Augusti*, has been edited by Zumpt, Berlin, 1845, and by Mommsen in 1883.

The other chief collections of inscriptions are published by the following writers :—

xxii   INTRODUCTION

Works on inscriptions.
Gruter, *Inscriptiones Antiquae Romanae*, 1690.
Muratori, *Thesaurus veterum inscriptionum*, Milan, 1739.
Orelli and Henzen, *Inscriptionum Latinarum collectio*, 1828–56.
Zumpt, *Commentationum Epigraphicarum volumen*, Berlin, 1850.
Garruccius, *Sylloge inscrip. Lat. aevi Romanae Reipublicae usque ad C. J. Caesarem*, Turin, 1877.
Mommsen and others, *Corpus Inscriptionum Latinarum*, 1863 — in progress ; and its Supplement, *Ephemeris Epigraphica*, 1872 — in progress. The earliest inscriptions are given by Ritschl as an Appendix to the Corpus, 1863–88.
A very valuable series of Roman inscriptions, including a large number which illustrate the topography of Rome, is published in the *Bull. Com. Arch. Mun. Rom.* 1879, and still in progress.
Cagnat's *Épigraphie Latine*, 1889, forms a useful guide to Latin epigraphy.

Coins and Medallions.

Evidence of coins.
The coins of Rome contain an immense number of records relating to the buildings of the city. The *reverses* of the *denarii* of the later Republic, after about 150 B.C., are very rich in this way. Under the Empire coins of all denominations very frequently have reverses with representations of buildings erected or restored by the emperors. These, as a rule, are treated in a conventional way—the number of the columns of the front is often reduced for want of space ; thus *hexastyle* temples are commonly shown as *tetrastyle*, and the statue of the god which was within the *cella* is often shown between the columns of the portico. The coins may, however, usually be trusted to give the general design of the buildings they commemorate, and some are treated with much minuteness and accuracy, showing not only the form of the temple but even the details and arrangement of its sculptured decorations; this is the case with the representation of the *Temple of Concord* on a coin of Tiberius, and that of the bronze *Temple of Janus* on a coin of Nero, both of which are carefully and accurately shown ; see vol. i. pp. 248 and 337.

Medallions.
The large bronze medallions of the Empire are even richer

than the current coins in carefully executed representations of *Medallions.*
the buildings and sculpture of Rome, and were frequently
struck to commemorate the completion of some important
architectural work. The chief examples which relate to this
class of subject begin with the reign of Antoninus Pius, and
continue till about the middle of the third century.

Many coins and medallions on which Roman buildings are *Works on coins.*
represented are illustrated by Canina in his *Indicazione*, 1830,
and by Donaldson, much enlarged, in his *Architectura Numismatica*, London, 1859; neither set of drawings are remarkable
for accuracy. Cohen's works on Roman coins of the Republic
and Empire; Froehner, *Médaillons de l'Empire*, Paris, 1878;
and Grueber, *Roman Medallions*, British Museum, 1872, are all
well and accurately illustrated.

III. REGIONARY CATALOGUES.

Urlichs in his *Codex Urbis Romae Topographicus*, Wurtz- *Ancient catalogues.*
burg, 1871, has published the *Regionary Catalogues*, called the
Notitia and *Curiosum*, which were compiled in the fourth
century, giving lists of the chief buildings and monuments
in each of the *regiones* of Augustus.

In the same work are printed the catalogue of the pseudo-
Publius Victor,[1] and the itinerary of the *Einsiedlen MS.*, so
called from its being preserved in the Benedictine monastery
of Einsiedeln in Switzerland; it was written by an unknown
visitor to Rome in the ninth century.

Also the *Mirabilia Urbis Romae*, a twelfth-century account *Mediaeval descriptions.*
of the marvels of the sacred city, drawn up for the use of
pilgrims, as a sort of guide-book to the principal objects of
interest.

The *Graphia Aureae Urbis Romae*, a similar list, founded on

[1] Publius Victor and the *Regionary Catalogue*, of which he is supposed
to have been the author, are inventions of some early mediaeval antiquary.

the *Mirabilia*, dating from the thirteenth century, is included in this *Codex*.

In the same valuable compilation are included many other extracts from mediaeval sources which relate to Roman antiquities.

Preller, *Regionen der Stadt Rom*, Jena, 1846, also gives the *Regionary Catalogues*; and they are printed in the works of Nardini, Jordan, and other antiquaries; see below.

The *Mirabilia* has also been edited by Parthey, Berlin, 1869; and the *Einsiedlen MS.* by Haenel, *Archiv für Philologie*, Berlin, 1837, v. 115.[1] A good English translation of the *Mirabilia* with valuable notes has been published by F. M. Nichols, London, 1889.

Scholiasts. Much information about Roman Antiquities is given by the various commentators on Virgil, who pass under the general name of SERVIUS, a grammarian of the fifth century. An excellent edition is that published by Thilo and Hagen, Leipsic, 1881-85.

Other early Scholiasts give valuable topographical notes, especially some commentaries on Cicero's works, written probably in the fifth century, but which have been wrongly ascribed to Asconius, a Roman writer of the first century A.D.

IV. EARLY WORKS ON ROMAN ANTIQUITIES.

Revival of learning. The revival of interest in classical archaeology, which naturally accompanied the revival of classical learning, began to dawn in Rome about the middle of the fifteenth century.

The antiquarian works which were produced at this early time, and for long after, are not of course remarkable for finished scholarship or power of accurate and critical research, but are frequently of the greatest value to the modern student

[1] On the *Einsiedlen MS.* see Lanciani in *Mon. Ant.* of the *R. Accad. dei Lincei*, Part iii., Milan, 1891.

both for their accounts of discoveries which were made, and would otherwise have been forgotten, and also for their numerous illustrations of buildings which have now either wholly or in part disappeared.

The Florentine Poggio and the Venetian Biondo were the first of that throng of students of pagan remains which in the succeeding century became so large. Poggio's work, *De Fortunae Varietate*, written about 1440 A.D. and dedicated by him to Eugenius IV., contains an interesting account of the ruins of Rome in his time. His MS. was printed at Basle in 1538, and several other editions appeared within a few years. Biondo's *Rome Restored* was written about the same time. Fra Giocondo of Verona, the chief antiquary of the fifteenth century, has been already mentioned; see p. xxi. He wrote an eloquent letter addressed to Lorenzo the Magnificent urging the importance of an organised scheme for the Preservation of Ancient Monuments; see *Mus. Class. Ant.* 1851, vol. i. p. 17. The great outburst of enthusiasm on this subject did not, however, occur till the beginning of the sixteenth century, in the Pontificate of Julius II., when fresh impulse was given to study of the classical remains of Rome by the discovery of the buried chambers of Nero's *Golden House* under the *Thermae of Titus*, with their rich store of decorations in colour and stucco reliefs. These at once became not only objects of interest to the antiquary, but also were copied and imitated by countless sculptors and painters, especially by Raphael and his numerous pupils, who reproduced them with varying degrees of imitation or originality on the walls and vaults of most of the magnificent palaces which sprang up with such wonderful rapidity during the first quarter of the sixteenth century.

The *loggie* and the bath-room of Cardinal Bibiena in the Vatican, the chamber of Clement VII. in the Castle of S. Angelo, and, most magnificent of all, the Villa Madama on the slopes of Monte Mario, built for Cardinal de' Medici (afterwards Clement VII.), are among the chief existing

Early antiquaries.

Discoveries in 1503-13.

Classic influence.

examples of the result of this study of classical methods of decoration by Raphael and his school.¹

Revival of classic style. Nor was the influence of ancient Rome confined to methods of decoration; the thoroughly pagan spirit of the sixteenth century brought with it a taste for the scholastic formalism of Roman architecture, and hence every important architect of that time measured and drew the then existing remains of ancient Rome as one of the chief parts of his professional training.

This has fortunately preserved to us a large number of drawings, from now destroyed buildings, by the hands of Raphael, Bramante, Bramantino, Baldassare and Sallustio Peruzzi, Andrea Sansovino, Palladio, Vignola, and many other great architects of the sixteenth century.

Raphael. Raphael's zeal as an archaeologist, not only in making drawings of ancient buildings but also in taking energetic measures for their preservation, is strongly shown by a report which he wrote to Leo X., describing (as Fra Giocondo had done more than thirty years before) the wholesale destruction that had been going on in Rome, and pleading for assistance from the Pope to prevent further injury.²

Early records. Some of these drawings by sixteenth-century architects exist only in MSS. preserved in the libraries of the Vatican, the Uffizi, Siena, Milan, and elsewhere. A valuable MS. by Ligorio exists in the Bodleian at Oxford; *Canonici MSS.* No. 138. The most important sketches in this have been published by the present writer in *Archaeologia*, vol. li., 1889,

---

¹ Another splendid example, rather later in date, is the Villa of Pope Julius III. built by Vignola, near Monte Parioli, a short way outside the Porta del Popolo. This is now one of the most interesting of the Roman Museums, containing a magnificent collection of objects of all dates from the tombs of Falerii.

² This was published by Visconti, *Lettera sull' Antichità di Roma . . . da Raffaello*, etc., Rome, 1834; see also Müntz, *Gaz. des Beaux Arts*, October and November 1880.

p. 489 *seq.* Palladio's very valuable work on the *Thermae of Rome* is well illustrated by plans, which show far more than now exists—some, such as the Thermae of Constantine, have almost wholly disappeared; this was first published in London in 1730 at the expense of Lord Burlington.

Paintings, especially those of the fifteenth and sixteenth centuries, often give representations of the remains of ancient Rome, supplying much that is now lost. These are frequently overlooked, as they are scattered about in various churches and palaces, and are usually of but little artistic value; moreover, the valuable bit of information which a painting supplies is often merely put in as an accidental accessory or background, and may easily be overlooked. All old pictures should, however, be examined by the student with this object in view. Among the most notable examples are the frescoes in the library of the Vatican, painted for Sixtus V.; those by Vasari in the Palazzo della Cancelleria; frescoes in the Caraffa Chapel in S. Maria Maggiore, and those in S. Martino ai Monti. The ancient monuments shown on the bronze door of S. Peter's are mentioned in vol. ii. p. 287.

Painted records.

One of the most important pictures to the student of Roman Archaeology is a large bird's-eye view of Rome, now in the gallery of Mantua, which was painted in oil in the sixteenth century, and shows all the then existing monuments of Rome with some minuteness. This has been published by De Rossi, in a work which contains much that is interesting of the same sort—*Piante di Roma anteriori al Secolo XVI.*, Rome, 1879. See also Müntz, *Un plan de Rome, au XVme Siècle*, Soc. Nat. des Antiquaires, Paris, April 1880; and *Bull. Com. Arch.* 1885, p. 63.

Mantuan picture.

The earliest view of Rome given in any printed book is a woodcut in the *Supplementum Chronicarum* of Foresti of Bergamo (Bergomensis), Venice, 1490, fol. 49.

V. LIST OF WORKS ON THE ARCHAEOLOGY OF ROME.[1]

WORKS OF THE FIFTEENTH AND SIXTEENTH CENTURIES.

Flavio Biondo, *Roma Instaurata*, MS. of 1430-40, printed at Verona in 1481.
Poggio, *De Fortunae Varietate*, MS. of about 1440, printed at Basle in 1538.
Bramantino, *Rovine di Roma*, 1503-13, with many sketches, printed by Mongeri, Milan, 1875, from the original MS. in the Ambrosian Library at Milan.
Albertini, *Opusculum de Mirabilibus Urbis Romae*, 1509.
Pomponius Leto, *De Vetustate Urbis Romae*, 1523.
Andrea Fulvio, *Antiquaria Urbis Romae*, Venice, 1527.
Calvus, *Antiquae Urbis Romae Simulachrum*, 1532.
Ant. Lafreri, *Speculum Romanae Magnificentiae*, 1540-86, has a large number of engraved plates of the buildings of ancient Rome; many of them are of great interest. Some of them are by Steph. Du Perac, the author of the *Vestigj* mentioned below; others are by Pirro Ligorio, the rest are mostly by Lafreri himself.
Marlianus,[2] *Urbis Romae Topographia*, 1520.
Serlio, *L'Architettura*, Venice, 1545; lib. iii. deals with the buildings of ancient Rome.
Fauno, *Antichità di Roma*, 1548.
Labacco, *Architettura ed Antichità di Roma*, 1557; a careful and well illustrated work, which has been much used by later antiquaries.
Lucio Mauro, *Antichità di Roma*, Venice, 1558.
Ligorio, *Effigies Antiquae Romae*, 1561.
Kock, *Operum antiquorum Romanorum Reliquiae*, 1562.
Gamucci, *Antichità di Roma*, Venice, 1565.
Andrea Palladio in his *Libri dell' Architettura*, lib. iv., first published in Venice in 1570, gives a number of very interesting woodcuts of many of the ancient buildings of Rome. His illustrations of the following buildings are specially valuable on account of their showing much more than now exists: *Basilica of Constantine, Forum of Augustus* and *Temple of Mars Ultor, Forum of Nerva* and *Temple of Minerva* (now wholly destroyed), *Temple of Faustina*, part of the *Thermae*

---

[1] All these books are printed in Rome unless otherwise described. Other works on special sections are mentioned in the text under their respective headings—Baths, Amphitheatres, etc.

[2] An edition of this work, printed in 12mo at Lyons by Seb. Gryphius in 1534, is of interest as having been edited by the famous Rabelais.

of *Constantine*, the so-called *Temple of Vesta* by the Tiber, and the *Pantheon*.

Palladio's *Terme dei Romani*, with plans of all the chief *Thermae* of Rome, was not printed till 1730; it was probably prepared before the *Architettura* of 1570.

Steph. Du Perac, *Vestigj di Roma*, 1575; this very valuable series of etched plates shows an immense quantity of what is now lost. The drawings appear to have been made soon after the middle of the century, though not published till 1575.

Fabricius, *Romae Antiquitates*, 1587.

Vacca, *Memorie di varie Antichità*, 1594; printed in Nardini, *Roma Antica*, ed. Nibby, vol. iv.

Theodoro de Bry, *Romae Urbis Topographia*, 1597-1602.

Franzini, *Palatia Romae Urbis*, 1596-99.

WORKS OF THE SEVENTEENTH CENTURY.

Crechi, *Antichità di Roma*, 1601.
Laurus, *Antiquae Urbis Splendor*, 1612.
Maggius, *Aedificia et Ruinae Romae*, 1618; a set of etchings.
Felini, *Alma Città di Roma*, 1625.
Scamozzi, *L'Antichità di Roma*, 1632.
Donati, *Roma vetus et recens*, 1638.
Franzini, *Roma Antica e Moderna*, 1653.
Desgodetz, *Edifices Antiques de Rome*, 1632; a valuable collection of measured plans and details.
Ciampini, *Vetera Monumenta*, 1690.
Bartoli, *Admiranda Romae Vestigia*, 1693.
De Rubeis, *Romae Magnificentiae Monumenta*, 1699.

WORKS OF THE EIGHTEENTH CENTURY.

Pinarole, *Antichità di Roma*, 1709, and *Vestigi di Roma*, 1744.

Piranesi's large and skilfully executed etchings are now of great interest for their record of buildings which have since been injured or destroyed. They are grouped in sixteen atlas folio volumes, entitled *La Magnificenza dei Romani*, 1761-66, *L'Antichità Romana*, 1756, and other works.[1]

---

[1] Piranesi's copper plates, though much retouched, are preserved and still printed from at the *Calcografia Camerale* of Rome; they are sold, either in sets or singly, at three lire each. The *Calcografia* also possesses the coppers of many other valuable old plates of Roman antiquities. It is now called the *Calcographia Regia* instead of *Camerale*, as it has ceased to be a Papal establishment.

INTRODUCTION

Bellori, *Ichnographia Veteris Romae*, 1764.
Venuti, *Vetera Monumenta*, 1778, and *Descrizione Topographica di Roma*, 1824.
Guattani, *Monumenta Antiqua*, 1784-89, and *Roma Descritta*, 1805.

WORKS OF THE NINETEENTH CENTURY (in addition to those named at p. xxxii.)

Valadier, *Le piu insigni Fabbriche di Roma*, 1810-26.
Rossini, *Antichità di Roma*, 1817.
Fea, *Ragionamento*, and other works, 1821-33.
Taylor and Cressy, *Architectural Antiquities of Rome*, London, 1821.
Romanis, *Vestigie di Roma Antica*, 1832.
Gell, *Topography of Rome*, London, 1834.
Donovan, *Rome, Ancient and Modern*, 1842.
Becker, *Die Römische Topographie*, Leipsic, 1844.
Zestermann, *De Basilicis*, Brussels, 1847.
Braun, *Die Ruinen und Museen Roms*, Berlin, 1854.
Ampère, *Histoire Romaine*, Paris, 1862-64.
Zinzow, *Das älteste Rom*, Pyritz, 1866.
Parker, *Photographs*, illustrating the Archaeology of Rome; a very valuable set, price half a franc each.[1]
Friedländer, *Sittengeschichte Roms*, Leipsic, 1869, and *Darstellungen aus der Sittenges. Roms*, Leipsic, 1881.
Gsell-Fels, *Romische Ausgrabungen*, Hildburghausen, 1870.
Jordan, *Forma Urbis Romae*, Berlin, 1875, with supplement of 1883; *Novae Questiones Topographicae*, Königsberg, 1868; and other works mentioned below.
Lanciani, *Dissertazioni Archaeologiche*, 1876-85, and other works on the *Aqueducts, Vestals, Curia*, etc.; and by the same author an interesting work in English, *Ancient Rome in the light of recent discoveries*, London, 1888.
De Rossi, *Note di Topografia Romana*, 1882.
Duruy, *Histoire des Romains*, Paris, 1878-84; well illustrated.
Dyer, *The City of Rome*, new edition, 1883.
Maps—Nolli's *Map of Ancient Rome*, 1748, has been largely followed by Canina in his large and fanciful plan of Rome in many plates, published in 1850.

---

[1] All students of Roman archaeology owe a great debt of gratitude to Mr. J. H. Parker for this large and well-selected set of photographs; unhappily, his numerous writings on this subject are rendered worse than useless to the student by their countless inaccuracies and baseless theories.

INTRODUCTION   xxxi

Moltke, *Carta Topographica di Roma*, Berlin, 1852.
Rieu, *Romae veteris ichnographia*, Leiden, 1863.
Burn, *Rome and the Campagna*, London, 1871, gives a good map of ancient Rome.

WORKS ON THE MUSEUMS AND SCULPTURE OF ROME.

Pistolesi, *Il Vaticano*, 1829-38.
Visconti, *Museo Chiaramonti, Pio Clementina*, and *Museo Gregoriano*, 1803-43.
Bottari, *Museo Capitolino*, Milan, 1821-22.
E. Q. Visconti, *Sculture della Villa Borghese*, 1796, and *Sculture del Pal. Giustiniani*, 1811.
Winckelmann, *Opere di*; best edition is in Italian, ed. Fea, Prato, 1830.
Vitale, *Marmi nel Pal. Torlonia*, n.d.
Benndorf, *Die Bildwerke des Lateran Museum*, Leipsic, 1867.
Wolff, *Bildwerke des Vaticans*, etc., Berlin, 1870.
Schreiber, *Antiken Bildwerke der Villa Ludovisi*, Leipsic, 1880.
De Montault, *Musées et Galeries de Rome*, 1880.
Matz and Von Duhn, *Antike Bildwerke in Rom*, Leipsic, 1881.
Bernoulli, *Romische Ikonographie*, Stuttgard, 1881.
See also Overbeck, *Geschichte der griechischen Plastik*, new ed., Leipsic, 1882, vol. ii.

Some of the most valuable information on Roman archaeology, and especially accounts of the recent discoveries, are contained in the following periodicals:—

The *Annali, Bulletino*, and *Monumenti dell' Instituto di Corrispondenza Archaeologica di Roma*, 1829—in progress. The title was altered in 1886 to *Bulletino dell' Imperiale Istituto Archeologico Germanico* or *Mittheilungen des Kaiserlich Deutschen archaeologischen Instituts, Roemische Abtheilung*. This publication takes the place of the former *Bulletino* and *Annali*; the *Monumenti* are still published as a separate work in atlas folio.
Atti dell Accademia Romana dei Lincei—in progress.
Bulletino della Commissione Archeologica Municipale di Roma, 1872—in progress.
Notizie degli Scavi, 1876—in progress.

The *Monografia di Roma*, 1878, by various writers, gives a list of works on Rome down to 1876, and contains valuable articles on the health, population, etc., of ancient Rome. See also Bonghi, *Bibliografia Storica di Roma Antica*, 1879.

The reader who wishes to study the subject of Roman archaeology in a fairly concise form, and without immediate reference to original sources, will find the following books the most useful:—

Nardini, *Roma Antica*, ed. Nibby, 1818-20.
Nibby, *Antichità di Roma*, 1830, and *Roma nell' Anno* 1838.
Becker, *Handbuch der Romischen Alterthümer*, Leipsic, 1843, edited by Mommsen, Leipsic, 1867 ; of special value from its numerous references to classical writers.
Bunsen and others, *Beschreibung der Stadt Rom*, Stuttgard, 1829-42 and its abridgment by Plattner and Uhlrichs, 1844.
Reber, *Die Ruinen Roms*, Leipsic, 1863.
Von Reumont, *Geschichte der Stadt Rom*, Berlin, 1867-70.
Nichols, *The Roman Forum*, London, 1877.
Jordan, *Topographie der Stadt Rom*, Berlin, 1878-86 ; a very useful work, but unfortunately incomplete at the time of the author's death in 1887.
Burn, *Rome and the Campagna*, London, 1871 ; this is by far the best general work in English.
Otto Gilbert, *Geschichte und Topographie der Stadt Rom*, Leipsic, 1890-92 ; this is a short but useful handbook.

The large and magnificently illustrated works by Canina must be used with great caution ; they contain highly imaginative restorations, often invented without a shadow of evidence. Even those parts of the drawings which profess to show the existing remains are rendered of little value by their numerous inaccuracies. The chief of Canina's works are *Indicazione di Roma Antica*, 1830 ; *Esposizione Topografica*, 1842 ; *Edifizj di Roma Antica*, 1840-56 ; *Foro Romano*, 1845 ; and *Architettura Antica*, 1834-44.

MUSEUMS OF ROME.

In addition to the old-established museums of the Vatican, the Capitol, and the Collegio Romano, three very important new museums have recently been established in Rome. One of these, in the Villa del Papa Giulio, outside the Porta del Popolo, contains a vast collection of antiquities from the great

Necropolis at Falerii, modern Civita Castellana; including native objects of prehistoric date, fine Greek imports, and again, objects of Greek style but of local workmanship.

Another large collection of statues and other works of art which have been found in Rome and Ostia is arranged in the Monastery of S. Maria degli Angeli, in the Thermae of Diocletian. Sculpture is arranged all along the four sides of the beautiful cloister, and by degrees this magnificent museum will be extended so as to occupy all that exists of Diocletian's Baths, with the exception of the church. This collection is now called Museo delle Terme.

A large storehouse for objects found in Rome has been established by the Municipality in the Gardens of SS. Giovanni e Paolo on the Caelian Hill, under the title *Magazzino Archeologico Municipale*. Unfortunately this collection is not yet available for purposes of study, but it will some day become one of the most interesting of the museums of Rome, rich in objects of prehistoric date and of the early period of Roman history.[1]

[1] A very useful work, in two small and portable volumes, on the contents of the Museums of Rome, has recently been prepared by W. Helbig, *Die öffentlichen Sammlungen klassischer Alterthümer in Rom*, Leipsic, 1891.

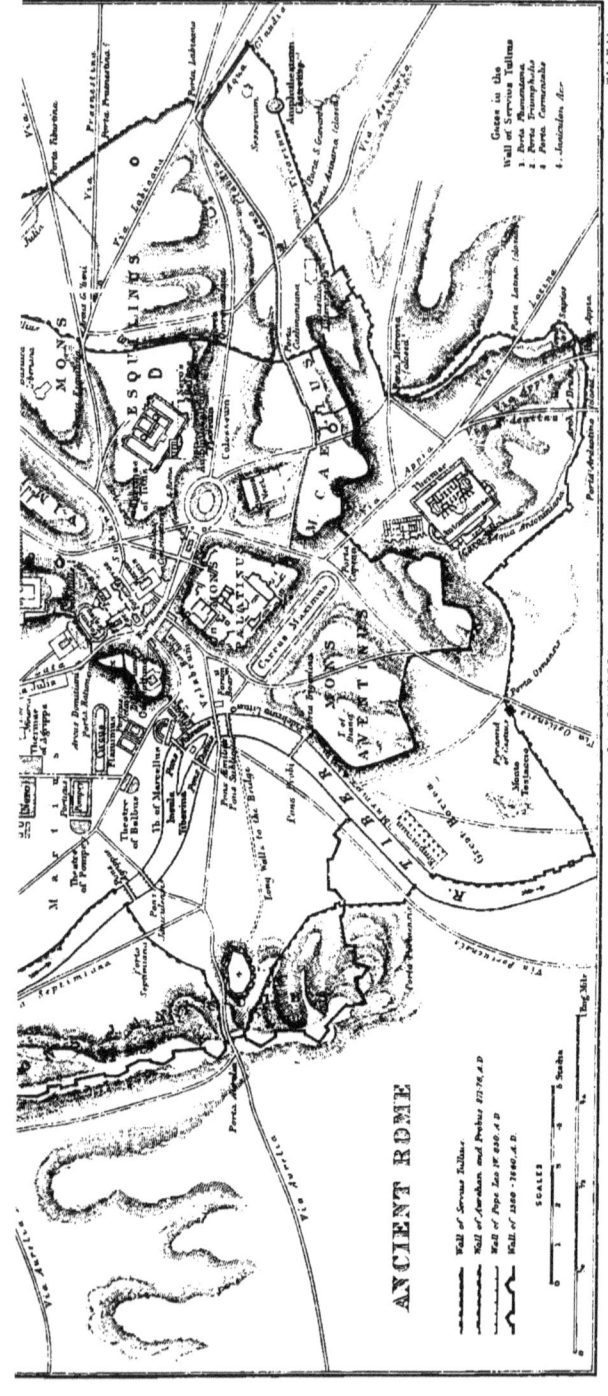

CHAPTER I

SITE OF ROME, AND ROMAN METHODS OF CONSTRUCTION.

THE city of Rome stands about fourteen miles from the present mouth of the Tiber, in a great plain of alluvial and marine deposit, broken into elevations by numerous masses of volcanic matter.

Site of Rome.

The nine or ten hills and ridges on which the city is built are formed of great heaps of tufa, or conglomerated ashes and sand thrown out of the craters of a number of volcanoes now extinct, but which were in an active state down to a comparatively recent period.

One group of volcanoes is that around the Lago Bracciano, while another, still nearer to Rome, is that which composes the Alban Hills.

That some at least of these craters have been in a state of activity at no very distant period has been shown by the discovery at many places of broken pottery of a primitive character and bronze implements, below the strata of tufa or other volcanic deposit. Traces of human life have even been found below that great flood of lava which, issuing from the Alban Hills, flowed towards the site of Rome, and only stopped short about three miles from the city. The tomb of Caecilia Metella was afterwards built on the very edge of this great lava stream.

Recent volcanoes.

The superficial strata on which Rome is built are of three kinds—*first*, the plains and valleys on the left bank of the Tiber, which are covered, as it were, by a sea of alluvial

Three kinds of strata.

deposit, in the midst of which, *secondly*, the hills of volcanic origin rise like so many islands; and *thirdly*, on the right bank of the Tiber, around the Janiculan and Vatican Hills, are extensive remains of an ancient sea-beach, conspicuous in parts by its fine golden sand and its deposit of pure greyish-white potters' clay. From its yellow sand the Janiculan Hill has been sometimes known as the *Golden Mount*, a name which survives in the title of the church at its summit, which is called *S. Pietro in Montorio* (*monte d' oro*).

Travertine. In addition to these chief deposits, at a few places, especially on the Aventine and Pincian Hills, under-strata of travertine crop out; this is a hard limestone rock, once in solution in running water, and deposited gradually, as the water by exposure to air loses its carbonic acid solvent— a process still rapidly going on at Terni, Tivoli, and other places in the neighbourhood of Rome along the course of the river Anio.

Tufa hills. The conditions under which the tufa hills were formed have been very various, as is clearly seen by an examination of the rock at different places. The volcanic ashes and sand, of which the tufa is composed, appear in parts to lie just as they were showered down from the crater; in that case the tufa shows but little or no sign of stratification, and consists wholly of igneous products.

In parts time and pressure have bound together these *scoriae* into a soft and friable rock; in other places they still lie in loose sandy beds, which can be dug out with the spade.

Other masses of tufa, again, show signs either of having been deposited in water or else washed away from their first resting-place and redeposited elsewhere with visible marks of stratification. This is shown by the water-worn pebbles and chips of limestone rock which form a conglomerate, bound together by the volcanic ashes into a sort of natural cement.

Palatine tufa. A third variety is that of which the Palatine Hill is composed. Here the shower of red-hot ashes has evidently fallen on a thickly-growing forest, the burning wood of which, partly smothered by the ashes, has been converted into charcoal, large lumps of which are embedded in the tufa rock. *Burnt forest.*

In some places charred branches of trees, their form and structure well preserved, can be easily distinguished. The so-called *Wall of Romulus*, and some others of the prehistoric buildings of the Palatine, are built of this curious conglomerate of tufa and charcoal. At one point—by the north side of the *Scalae Caci*—a very perfect section of the branch of a tree is visible on the face of one of the massive tufa blocks.

So great have been the physical changes in the site of Rome since the first dawn of the historic period that it is very difficult now to realise what its aspect once was.

The *Forum Romanum*, the *Velabrum*, the great *Campus Martius* (now the most crowded part of modern Rome), and other valleys, were once almost impassable marshes and pools of water— *Marshes.*

"*Hic, ubi nunc Fora sunt, udae tenuere paludes.*"
Ov. *Fast.* vi. 401.

And Dionysius (ii. 50) speaks of the site of the Forum having formerly been a marshy thicket owing to the depressed nature of the ground—διὰ τὸ κοῖλον εἶναι τὸ χωρίον. The draining of these valleys was effected by means of the great *Cloacae*, which were among the very earliest important architectural works of Rome; as Varro says (*Lin. Lat.* v. 149), . . . *lacum Curtium in locum palustrem, qui tum fuit in Foro, antequam cloacae factae sunt*; see below, vol. i. p. 231.

Moreover, the various hills and ridges of Rome were once more numerous and very much more abrupt than they are now. At an early period, when each hill was crowned by a separate village-fort, surrounded by hostile tribes, the great object of the inhabitants was to increase the natural steepness of the cliffs, and so render access more difficult and defence easier. In later years, when the various villages and races *Separate hills.*

which formed the city of Rome were united under one government, and the whole group of hills was surrounded by one extensive circuit wall, the very physical peculiarities which had originally made its hills so populous through their natural adaptability for defence became extremely inconvenient in a united city, where architectural symmetry and splendour were above all things aimed at. This later process was exactly the reverse of the earlier one, which had aimed at isolating, as far as possible, each of the hills. In Imperial times the chief object was to get rid of all that tended to separate and break up the city into different parts. Hence the most gigantic engineering works were carried out, with the object of obliterating as much as possible the natural unevenness of the site. Tops of hills were levelled, whole ridges cut away, and gentle slopes were formed in the place of abrupt cliffs. The levelling of the *Velia* and the excavation of the site for Trajan's Forum are instances of this.

Levelling process.

This work continued in the Middle Ages, as when in the fourteenth century an access was made to the Capitoline Hill from the side of the *Campus Martius*,[1] where up to that time a steep cliff had prevented all approach except from the side of the *Forum Romanum*.

Modern changes.

Under the present government an even more extensive plan, called the *Piano regolatore*, is being gradually carried out, with the object of reducing hills and valleys to one level, on which wide boulevards are being constructed on a formal plan, regardless of the ancient topography of the city. The constant fires which have devastated Rome have been an important agent in obliterating the natural contour of the ground. The accumulated rubbish from these and other causes has in some

---

[1] This approach was made by building the great flight of steps up to the church of Ara Coeli. These steps were built of marble taken from the so-called "Temple of the Sun" on the Quirinal Hill. In 1887-88 a great deal of the beauty and interest of this stately flight of steps was destroyed by restoration.

places covered the ancient levels to the depth of as much as 40 feet, especially at the bottom of the valleys.

BUILDING MATERIALS EMPLOYED IN ROME.

The rapid growth and the permanent stability of Rome were very largely due to the richness of its site and the immediate neighbourhood in a variety of excellent building materials, including several kinds of stone, and the different ingredients of the most durable concrete, cements, and mortar that have ever been produced.

The following is a list of the principal materials used in the buildings of ancient Rome :—

I. *Tufa*, the *ruber et niger tophus* of Vitruvius, ii. 7. This was the only stone used during the early prehistoric period of Rome.[1] Its manner of formation has been described above. It varies in colour from a dark brown, often reddish tint, to a light yellow; and in density from a deposit that can be cut with the spade to a firmly concreted mass about as hard as English Bath stone. It is usually a very bad "weather-stone," but the harder varieties are of ample strength for building purposes when protected from frost and wet. A simple coating of stucco was sufficient to protect exterior walls of tufa, and even in the earliest times it was probably never used externally without this protection; see vol. i. p. 78. Vitruvius, ii. 7, advises that tufa should be quarried in the summer, and allowed two years to season before being used;[2] and Pliny

Tufa.

Season for quarrying.

---

[1] Partly because the tufa was found close at hand, and also because it could be worked with tools of bronze.

[2] What stone-masons call the "sap" should always be allowed to dry out of stone before it is used; otherwise, frost and damp rapidly cause it to flake or split. When once the "sap" is got rid of, the stone can be soaked with wet without harm. The necessity of drying out the sap in timber is a somewhat similar case.

(*Hist. Nat.* xxxvi. 162) copies his remarks.[1] Quarries of tufa are mentioned by Strabo (lib. v.), as existing on the banks of the Anio, near the quarries of *travertine* and *peperino*.

Every hill in Rome consists mainly of tufa, and the materials for the early buildings appear usually to have been quarried on the spot. The quarries in the Aventine supplied the best and hardest kind.

Alban stone. II. *Lapis Albanus*, so called from its quarries in the Alban Hills, still worked at Albano and Marino. This also is of volcanic origin, and is a conglomerate of ashes, gravel, and other fragments of stone, all cemented together into a dense mass. It is a moderately good weather-stone and is quite fireproof. Its modern name is *peperino*, so called from the black *scoriae*, like peppercorns, which stud the stone. It is dark brown in colour, and is harder than the hardest kinds of tufa. It is used in parts of the Servian wall, and at the exit of the "*Cloaca Maxima*."[2]

Gabine stone. III. *Lapis Gabinus* (also called *peperino*) is a variety of the same stone found at Gabii, near the modern Lago di Castiglione. It is similar in formation to the Alban stone, but contains less mica, is harder, and stands the weather much better. It contains broken fragments of lava, the product of some earlier eruption; these lumps vary in size from about 2 to 12 inches across.

The *Tabularium* is faced with this stone, the inner walls being of tufa; see vol. i. p. 373. In the lofty circuit wall round the Forum of Augustus both the Alban and Gabine stones are used, and their different powers of resisting decay can be

---

[1] All the parts of Pliny's *Historia Naturalis* which relate to practical matters of construction appear to be taken from Vitruvius, and are incorporated by Pliny without acknowledgment of their source; this is specially the case with *Hist. Nat.* xxxvi. 166 to 189.

[2] Another volcanic stone (something like *peperino*), which is now called *sperone*, is found in the neighbourhood of Rome, but it does not seem to have been used in ancient times.

readily compared. The lower part of the wall is of Gabine stone, and is as fresh and sharp as ever; while the upper story of Alban stone shows considerable signs of surface decay; see fig. 2, in vol. i. p. 43.

The fire-resisting qualities of the *lapis Gabinus* are mentioned by Tacitus (*Ann.* xv. 43); and on account of this property the building Act of Nero, enacted after the great fire, directed that it should be used for the fronts of houses in the streets of Rome, in order to prevent the recurrence of so wholesale a conflagration; see vol. i. p. 90.

IV. *Lapis Tiburtinus* (modern *travertine*), so called from its chief quarries at Tibur (Tivoli), or rather on the road to Tibur, near the *Aqua Albula*, where the ancient quarries have recently been opened and re-worked; see Vitr. ii. 7. It is a pure carbonate of lime, very hard, of a beautiful creamy colour, which weathers into a rich golden tint. It is a deposit from running water, and is formed in a highly stratified state, with frequent cavities and fissures, lined with crystallised carbonate of lime. In it are frequently embedded bits of petrified stick and leaves. Great beds of it exist all along the river Anio and other streams near Rome. The hill just outside the Porta del Popolo, called *Monte Parioli*, is composed of a coarse variety of travertine. *Travertine.*

As Vitruvius remarks, *Lapis Tiburtinus* is an excellent weather-stone, but is easily calcined by fire.[1] If laid on its *Properties of travertine.*

---

[1] This stone when burnt produces excellent lime, and contributed greatly to the wonderful durability of the Roman concrete, cements, and mortar; see Vitr. ii. 5. The chemistry of mortar, concrete, and cements made with lime is not thoroughly understood, but to a certain extent the gradual hardening that takes place depends on an absorption of carbonic acid gas from the atmosphere. Limestone consists of a carbonate of lime. When it is burnt in the kiln the carbonic acid gas is driven off and pure lime or oxide of calcium is left behind. When this lime, made into mortar by the addition of sand, gravel, or other similar substances, is used in a building it slowly absorbs carbonic acid from the air, and thus

Laminated structure.

natural bed it is very strong, but if set upright its crystalline beds are a great source of weakness, and it splits into *laminae* from end to end. Neglect of this important precaution on the part of Roman masons frequently caused serious failures to occur in their buildings. This was notably the case in the *Rostra*; see vol. i. p. 254.

The exterior of the Colosseum is one of the most conspicuous examples of the use of travertine.

The finest close-grained kind of travertine, which occurs in thin beds among the coarser variety round Tivoli, was specially used for the earliest Roman mosaics in which the *tesserae* were not made of marble, but of dark grey lava and this fine cream-coloured limestone. The "House of Livia" on the Palatine Hill, and the Temple of Castor in the Forum, have examples of this earliest kind of mosaic.

Lava.

V. *Silex* (modern *selce*); this has no relation to what is now called *silex* or flint, but is simply *lava*, poured out from the now extinct volcanoes near Rome.

One great stream has very conveniently brought this useful material to within three miles of Rome. As is mentioned above, the tomb of Caecilia Metella stands on its very edge. It was used in great quantities for the paving of roads, and when broken into pieces and mixed with lime and pozzolana formed the hardest and most durable kind of concrete. It is dark gray in colour, very hard, and breaks with a slightly conchoidal fracture; see Pliny, *Hist. Nat.* xxxvi. 168, and Vitr. ii. 7.

Pozzolana.

VI. *Pulvis Puteolanus* (modern *pozzolana*), so called from the extensive beds in which it exists at Puteoli, near Naples. It also exists in enormous quantities under and all round the city of Rome, lying in thick strata just as it was showered down out of the neighbouring volcanoes. It is a chocolate

returns to its former state of carbonate of lime or limestone. The silica (sand) remains unchanged, and it is very doubtful what part is played in the mortar by the addition of this or other substances to the lime.

red in colour,[1] and resembles a clean sandy earth mixed with larger lumps about the size of coarse gravel. When mixed with lime it forms a very strong *hydraulic* cement—having the power, that is, of setting hard even under water. This peculiarity is mentioned by Vitruvius, who says (ii. 6. 1) *etiam moles quae construuntur in mare sub aqua solidescunt*, "even piers constructed in the sea set hard under the water," provided that cement made with *pozzolana* is used. Vitruvius devotes chapter six of his second book to this very important material, to which is mainly due the immense strength and durability of the Roman concrete and cements used alike for walls, vaults, and floors.

Hydraulic cement.

Concrete.

The fact is, this *pozzolana*, more than any other material, contributed to make Rome the proverbially "eternal city." Without it a great domed building like the *Pantheon* would have been impossible, as would also the immense vaulted *Thermae*, and a wide-spanned Basilica such as that of Constantine; especially as the Romans, like other classical races, were not in the habit of using massive, far-projecting buttresses, such as those which played so important a part in all large mediaeval buildings from the thirteenth century downwards.[2]

[1] An inferior sort is brown; the better red quality was nearly always used till the third century A.D. After then the brown pozzolana was very frequently used. This fact is sometimes a useful guide to the date of existing buildings.

[2] The architecture of the "Romanesque" or Norman period, from about the time of the Conquest to nearly the end of the twelfth century, in its system of building without buttresses, and in many other points both of detail and of general design, closely resembles the architecture of ancient Rome, alike in France, in Germany, and in Britain. It has not usually been realised to what an extent such structures as our great Norman Cathedrals were influenced in their design by the then existing remains of Roman buildings, which in the eleventh century were far more common in Britain than they are now. Even the details, such as the capitals of the pillars in the nave of Gloucester Cathedral and other buildings of that class, are clearly modifications of the Tuscan capitals of

Sand and gravel.   VII. Excellent sand (*arena*) and gravel (*glarea*) abound in and near Rome, and also contributed to the strength of the Roman mortar and cement. Vitruvius' remarks on sand are very sensible (see lib. ii. 4); he mentions the three kinds of sand—*arena fossitia* (pit-sand) being the best, and *arena de fluminibus* (river-sand) next best. No sand could be purer or better for building purposes than the golden pit-sand of the Janiculan Hill; while that which is deposited by the Tiber is not free from muddy impurities. *Arena marina* (sea-sand) is to be avoided on account of the salt it contains efflorescing out from the mortar or stucco. The best sort of sand is known, Vitruvius says, by its crackling when rubbed in the hand, and by its not staining a white dress—thus showing that it is both sharp and clean.

Lateres and testae.   VIII. Bricks were of two kinds—*lateres*, sun-dried bricks, and *testae* or *tegulae*, kiln-baked bricks. The remarks of Vitruvius, ii. 3, refer wholly to the *lateres* (*crudi*), and he never mentions the triangular bricks which were used in all the existing Roman walls which have brick facings. Vitruvius uses the words *testa* or *tegula* for baked brick; *later* always meaning the crude brick, except in one passage (i. 5. 8) where the phrase *lateres cocti* is used. This distinction is clearly brought out in the passage (ii. 8. 18) where Vitruvius gives directions for protecting walls of crude *lateres* by setting on the top of them, under the eaves of the roof, several courses of burnt brick, *structura testacea*, 18 inches deep, so as to prevent rain which has leaked through the roof from soaking into the crude brickwork below.

Crude brick.   The whole of Vitruvius' chapter on sun-dried bricks (*lateres*) is of great interest, as it records the methods used by the Greeks as well as by the Romans in the preparation of this very important early building material. The clay was to be carefully selected and exposed to the weather for

the Romans; and many other details were adopted by the Normans from what they saw among the ruins of classical times.

two years before being made into bricks. It was then to be thoroughly beaten, mixed with chopped straw, and then moulded into shape and put in the sun to dry. A very long time was allowed to elapse before the bricks were used.

At Utica, Vitruvius says, bricks had to be kept for five years and then approved by a magistrate before they might be used. Various sizes of brick were used; one called *Lydium* was 18 by 12 inches, and this was the size used in Rome.

As long as they were protected by a coat of fine, hard stucco these crude bricks were perfectly durable, but when once a building so constructed went to ruin its bricks rapidly crumbled away. For this reason it is only in the rainless climate of southern Egypt that any examples of buildings in crude brick still exist. *Stucco.*

The following important Greek examples of the use of crude brick are mentioned by Vitruvius (ii. 8. 9), the walls of Athens, and the palaces of the Attalid kings at Tralles and of Mausolus at Halicarnassus. *Greek use of crude brick.*

In the time of Vitruvius (reign of Augustus) and earlier, little but unburnt brick was used in Rome, and of this no examples are still in existence.

The existing examples of bricks in Rome are used merely as facing to concrete walls; no wall is ever of solid brick.[1] These facing bricks are not rectangular, but are equilateral triangles, varying in length from 4 to 14 inches. About 10 inches is perhaps the commonest size. *Brick triangles.*

Though the bricks are usually regular in point of size, yet their apparent length, when seen in the face of a wall, usually varies a good deal, owing to the fact that very frequently one or more of the sharp points of the triangle has been accidentally broken off before the brick was set in its place.

The courses of these brick triangles are carefully laid so as to "break joint"; the visible angles of each brick being

---

[1] Even walls which are only 7 inches thick are not built of solid brick, but are of concrete, faced with very small brick triangles; see vol. i. p. 59.

placed so as to come as nearly as possible over the centres of the triangles in the course below.

Square bricks. The facings of arches are nearly always made with large square tiles, about 2 Roman feet square,[1] the *tegulae bipedales* of Vitruvius. These are usually cut into three or four pieces so as only to tail a few inches into the concrete arch which they hide; at intervals in each arch a few of the complete squares are introduced to improve the bond; see fig. 8, vol. i. p. 57.

Tiles 12, 14, and 18 inches square also occur, but are less common: and there are also the small squares of only 8 or 9 inches, which were used specially for the *pilae* or short pillars of *hypocausts*, and also for laying over the wooden centering into which the fluid concrete to form vaults was poured. The *Colours of bricks.* bricks in Roman buildings are of many colours—red, yellow, and more rarely brown; they are nearly always well burnt, and comprise a great many varieties of clay.

Some of the finest facing bricks, like those used in the gateway of the Praetorian Camp,[2] are reddened on the surface with a fine red "slip," something like that used for the Roman "Samian" or Aretine pottery.

In some of the bricks, and frequently in those of best quality, a quantity of the red pozzolana has been worked up with the clay, probably to prevent warping.[3] A great many varieties of brick frequently occur in the same building; this is specially the case in part of Nero's Golden House, under the Thermae of Titus.

Brick stamps. The stamps (*sigilla*, mod. *bolli*) which occur on the bricks

[1] They really are rather less than that, probably owing to shrinkage in firing; they average about 1 foot 11 inches square.

[2] See fig. 89, vol. ii. p. 235.

[3] This can be seen in many of the bricks in the Flavian Palace on the Palatine, and in the finest bit of brick-facing in Rome, an archway with engaged columns, which has been included in the line of the Aurelian wall, near the *Porta Latina*; see vol. ii. p. 380.

of buildings of Imperial date in Rome are of great value in determining the dates of various structures. Though in other places in Italy brick stamps occur as early as the middle of the first century B.C., yet in Rome the complete series does not begin till after the first century A.D., and continues, though not without interruptions, till *circa* 500 A.D., in the reign of Theodoric. The later stamps are usually rectangular, but those of the second and third centuries are nearly always circular, with the inscription in two concentric rings. Various names and facts are recorded on these stamps, *e.g.* the names of the Consuls, though rarely; of much more frequent occurrence is the name of the owner of the brickfield from which the clay came, and that of the potter (*figulus*) who made the brick; after his name often comes the phrase *Valeat qui fecit*, "may the maker prosper"; see vol. i. p. 190.

Brick stamps.

Names on bricks.

The words *ex praediis* denote the estate where the clay was dug; after it comes the name of the owner—very often the Emperor. Severus appears to have owned many *praedia*, which supplied the bricks used in his great palace on the Palatine; see vol. i. p. 214. The potter's name comes after the words *opus doliare* or *opus figlinum*, meaning "clay-work," or else after *ex figlinis* or *ex officina*, meaning "from the pottery" or "manufactory."

The following is a good example of a tile-stamp inscription in concentric rings:—

EX · PRAE[DIIS] · DOMITIAE · LVCILLAE · EX · FIG[VLINIS] DOMIT[IANIS] · MINORIB[VS] · OP[VS] · DOL[IARE] · AELI · ALEXANDRI ; Descemet, *inf. cit.* No. 134.

The use of brick-stamps appears to have been enforced by law, probably in connection with a tax that was levied on bricks and tiles of all sorts.

Tax on bricks.

An immense number of these brick inscriptions exist,[1] and

[1] Similar stamps to those on the bricks occur on the handles of the large Roman *amphorae*; an enormous number of these stamped handles

are being published in the *Corpus Inscrip. Lat.*, Berlin; see also Marini, *Le iscrizioni antiche doliari*, Rome, 1884; and Descemet, *Inscrip. dol. latines*, 1886. For a further account of the use of brick in Rome see below, vol. i. p. 54 *seq.*

DECORATIVE MATERIALS USED IN ROME.

Marble in Rome. The use of marble, especially in private houses, was at first viewed with great jealousy, as savouring of Greek luxury or Regal pomp. Pliny (*Hist. Nat.* xxxvi. 47) suggests that marble slabs (*crustae*) for wall decoration were first used in the brick Palace of Mausolus at Halicarnassus in Caria, c. 350 B.C. In Rome marble was not used till the first century B.C., and then the earliest marble introduced into the city was an importation from Greece. The native marble from Luna, near Pisa, was not worked till the reign of Augustus. The house of the orator Crassus on the Palatine, built about 92 B.C., was the first which had marble columns, namely, six *Greek imports.* columns of Hymettian marble, 12 feet long, in the Atrium. For this he was severely blamed; and the stern republican, M. Brutus (the murderer of Caesar), nicknamed him the "Palatine Venus"; see Pliny, *Hist. Nat.* xxxvi. 7. A few years later, in 78 B.C., M. Lepidus was the first who used Numidian marble (*giallo antico*); he employed it not only for columns in his house, but even for thresholds of the doors, and L. Lucullus, who was Consul in 74 B.C., introduced the black marble that was called after him; Pliny, *Hist. Nat.* xxxvi. 49; see vol. i. p. 20. Wall-linings of marble sawn into thin slices (*crustae*) were first used in a Roman house by a knight named Mamurra, one of Caesar's officials in Gaul. Pliny states

help to make up the great mass of broken pottery of which *Monte Testaccio* consists. One of the circular bronze stamps used for marking tiles was dredged up in the Tiber in 1879. It has the name of a lady proprietor of brickfields, *Coelia Mascellina*; see *Bull. Com. Arch.* 1879, p. 198, and Tav. xxi.

this on the authority of Cornelius Nepos (*Hist. Nat.* xxxvi. 48). In this house were columns of Carystian (cipollino) and Luna marble.

It was, however, considered more excusable to use marble in a public building; and the magnificent temporary theatre, built in 58 B.C. by the aedile M. Aemilius Scaurus, had one story of its *scena* lined with marble, and 360 columns of solid Greek marble; Pliny, *Hist. Nat.* xxxvi. 5; see vol. ii. p. 63. In a very few years marble became very common under the rule of Augustus, who did all he could to make Rome splendid, not only by his personal munificence in building magnificent theatres, temples, and other public buildings, but also by urging and persuading other Roman citizens to follow his example. Suetonius (*Aug.* 29) gives a list of wealthy Romans who were induced by Augustus to embellish the city with magnificent temples and places of amusement, and he remarks that Augustus used to boast that he had found Rome of brick and left it of marble, *Urbem . . . marmoream se relinquere, quam lateritiam accepisset.* *Theatre of Scaurus.*

Boast of Augustus.

The word *later*, it should be remembered, means crude brick, which at that date was very largely used in Rome, together with a certain amount of *peperino* and *tufa*. Burnt brick had not yet come into general use, and the usual Roman wall-facings of the time of Augustus for the more important buildings were *opus quadratum* of peperino or tufa and *opus reticulatum* of tufa only. Most of the private houses of Rome were then built of unburnt brick and wood, the upper stories especially being constructed with timber framing filled in with plaited osiers and then covered with mud and stucco—what is now called "wattle and dab"; see Vitr. ii. 1. 7, and ii. 8. 20. *Early methods.*

As a rule, except in a few exceptionally costly buildings, marble was not used in Rome at any period in solid blocks, but merely in slabs (*crustae*) with which walls of concrete or stone were faced. Exceptions to this rule are mentioned *Crustae.*

below, vol. i. p. 307. At xxxvi. 50, Pliny mentions the *Temple of Jupiter Tonans* on the Capitoline as an example of the use of solid marble blocks (*solidis glaebis*). The various methods of sawing marble into veneering slabs are described by Pliny, *Hist. Nat.* xxxvi. 51 to 54.

Bond-courses of marble.   A link between the method of building with solid blocks of marble and thin facing slabs is that employed in the Temple of *Mars Ultor*; see vol. ii. p. 11. The cella walls of this temple have occasional courses of solid blocks, the spaces between them being faced with slabs.

VARIETIES OF MARBLE AND PORPHYRIES USED IN ROME.

Four kinds of white "statuary marble" were chiefly used, one being from Italian quarries, the other three imports from Greece:—

Luna marble.   (1) *Marmor Lunense*, from Luna, near the modern Carrara; Strabo, lib. v., and Pliny, *Hist. Nat.* xxxvi. 14. It is of many qualities, from the purest white, with a fine sparkling grain like loaf sugar, to the coarser sorts disfigured with bluish-grey streaks.

Example: The eleven Corinthian columns of the *Temple of Neptune* built into the old *Dogana*, near the column of Marcus Aurelius; see vol. ii. p. 207.

Hymettian.   (2) *Marmor Hymettium*, from Mount Hymettus, above Athens. This appears to have been the first foreign marble introduced into Rome. It resembles the inferior kinds of Luna marble, being rather coarse in grain and usually stained with bluish-grey striations; Strabo, lib. x. It is much used for the buildings of modern Athens.

Examples: The forty-two columns in the nave of S. Maria Maggiore, and the twenty columns in S. Pietro in Vincoli.[1]

Pentelic.   (3) *Marmor Pentelicum*, from Mount Pentelicus, a few miles

[1] These, and all the fine marbles in the churches of Rome (except some in S. Paolo fuori le mura), have been taken from ancient Roman buildings.

from Athens; Pausan. I. xxxii. 1. It is fine in grain, and of a pure white; some ancient sculptors, such as Scopas and Praxiteles, are said to have preferred it to any other marble. Its quarries are still largely worked, and the greater part of the hill appears to consist of it. It lies on a bed of schist.

Example: The statue of Augustus in the Vatican.

(4) *Marmor Parium*, from the isle of Paros: a very beautiful marble, though of a strongly crystalline grain; it is slightly translucent. When fractured its crystals catch the light and sparkle brightly; hence it was also called *lychnites*. Pliny, quoting Varro (*Hist. Nat.* xxxvi. 14), wrongly explains this name, by saying that its quarries were underground and were worked by lamplight. This is not the case: the quarries in Mount Marpesius (Strabo, lib. x.) were always worked, as they are now, from the surface; see Dodwell, *Journey in Greece*, 1740, i. p. 501.

Parian.

Examples: The so-called Eros of Praxiteles in the Vatican, and some of the statues of the Vestals in the *Atrium Vestae*.

Other statuary marbles, though to a less degree, were used by the Romans, especially a kind which Pliny (*Hist. Nat.* xxxvi. 132) calls *Porus*.[1] This is possibly the modern *grechetto*, very similar to Parian, but not so crystalline in grain. The torso of Heracles, by Apollonios, in the Vatican, is of this *grechetto*.

Other marbles.

Thasian, Lesbian, and Tyrian white marbles were also used in Rome; see Pliny, *Hist. Nat.* xxxvi. 44.

[1] Pausanias uses the word πῶρος to mean not marble but limestone, of various kinds. It is noticeable that the Greeks had no special word for marble. Pliny is certainly wrong (*Hist. Nat.* xxxvi. 46) in understanding a block of marble to be meant by Homer (*Il.* xvi. 735)—

ἑτέρηφι δὲ λάζετο πέτρον
Μάρμαρον ὀκριόεντα.

Pausanias always calls white marble λίθος λευκός, *white stone*.

Coloured Marbles, etc.

Giallo antico.
(1) *Marmor Numidicum* (modern *giallo antico*). Pliny (*Hist. Nat.* v. 22) mentions this as being, together with wild beasts for the amphitheatres, the principal export from Numidia and Libya in northern Africa; from the latter province it was also called *Marmor Libycum*. It is of a rich golden yellow, deepening in tint to orange and pink. Enormous quantities of it were used in Rome, especially for columns and wall-linings.

Examples: Six large fluted columns in the Pantheon, and seven on Constantine's Arch; the eighth has been taken to the Lateran Basilica. These eight columns originally belonged to the Arch of Trajan.

Cipollino.
(2) *Marmor Carystium* (modern *cipollino*), from Carystos, in the Island of Euboea (Strabo, lib. x.) It is a highly stratified marble, with alternate wavy beds of white and pale green—the "*undosa Carystos*" of Statius, *Silv.* I. v. 36. It is called *cipollino* from its layers like an onion—*cipolla*.[1]

Example: Columns of the *Temple of Faustina*.

Pavonazetto.
(3) *Marmor Phrygium* or *Synnadicum* (modern *pavonazetto*, or "peacock marble"), from Synnada in Phrygia; Strabo, lib. xii.; Juv. xiv. 307; Pliny, *Hist. Nat.* xxxv. 3; and Tibull. III. iii. 13. A slightly translucent marble, with rich purple markings—violet verging on crimson; according to the legend, it was stained with the blood of Atys; Stat. *Silv.* I. v. 36.

Examples: Twelve fluted columns in the nave of S. Lorenzo fuori le mura, and four large columns in the tribune of S. Paolo fuori le mura.

Porta Santa.
(4) *Marmor Iasense*, from the island or peninsula of Iasos, on the coast of Caria;[2] probably the modern *porta santa*, so

---

[1] Plutarch (*De defec. Or.* 42) says that in his time the marble quarries of Carystos were exhausted.

[2] Iasos used to be an island, but is now united to the mainland by a rocky ridge.

called because the "holy door" of S. Peter's is framed with this marble. It is mottled with large patches and veins of dull red, green, and brown, with some white.

Examples: The slabs in front of the "*Graecostasis*," and the four altar columns in S. Peter's, in the chapels of the Presentation and of S. Sebastian.

(5) *Marmor Chium*, from the island of Chios, probably the modern "*Africano*." It is similar in markings and colours to the *porta santa* marble, but the tints are more brilliant; see Pliny, *Hist. Nat.* xxvi. 46.   *Africano.*

Examples: A great deal of the pavement of the *Basilica Julia*, and two large columns in the façade of S. Peter's.

(6) *Rosso antico*, a Greek marble; its ancient name is unknown. As a rule it does not occur in large pieces, but was much used for small cornices, architraves, and other mouldings in the interiors of buildings. It is hard, very fine in grain, and of a deep red, like blood. It takes a very high polish, and is one of the most richly decorative marbles used in ancient Rome.   *Rosso antico.*

Examples: The largest known pieces are the fourteen steps to the high altar of S. Prassede, and two columns, nearly 12 feet high, at the Rospigliosi *Casino dell' Aurora*. During the period of decadence it was occasionally used for sculpture: *examples*, two statues of fauns in the Vatican and Capitoline Museums.

(7) *Nero antico* is probably the ancient *marmor Taenarium*, from Cape Taenarum, the most southern point of Laconia. It is mentioned by Tibullus (III. iii. 14) in conjunction with the Phrygian and Carystian marbles; see also Prop. *El.* III. ii., and Pliny, *Hist. Nat.* xxxvi. 158.   *Nero antico.*

Examples: Two columns in the choir of the church of Ara Coeli. It is of rare occurrence.

An immense number of other less common marbles, including many varieties of *breccia*, and fossil *madrepores*, have been found in the ruins of Rome; but their ancient names are unknown.   *Other varieties.*

Some of the classical names for marbles, also, cannot with certainty be identified—such as the *marmor Luculleum*, from the island of Melos; Pliny, *Hist. Nat.* xxxvi. 50. This was a black marble; it was so called because it was specially used in Rome by the Consul L. Lucullus, about the year 74 B.C.

Proconnesian. Another very decorative marble is the *marmor Proconnesium*, from the island of Proconnesos, with which the celebrated Palace of King Mausolus[1] at Halicarnassus was decorated; see Vitr. ii. 8, and Pliny, *Hist. Nat.* xxxvi. 47.

The great columns in the nave of S. Mark's at Venice are made of Proconnesian marble. They are ancient columns, and were brought in Venetian ships from some ruined city in the East, possibly from Halicarnassus, in the tenth century A.D.

A very rich and beautiful mottled red and white marble, *Marmor Molossium.* now called "*Fior di Persico*," may possibly be the *marmor Molossium*. A great part of the walls of the magnificent *Corsini Chapel*, in the Lateran Basilica, is lined with it.

Many varieties of the beautiful "precious serpentines" were used by the Romans; these are not *marbles* strictly speaking, not being calcareous stones.

Verde antico. The commonest is the *lapis Atracius* (*verde antico*), from Atrax on the Peneius in Thessaly; Livy, xxxii. 15. Like *rosso antico* it was mainly used for internal decoration. It has a brilliant green ground, mottled with white and dark brown. It seldom occurs in large pieces, but some columns of it were found by the *Temple of Castor* in the Forum, and are now set on its front flight of steps.

The finest examples in Rome are the twenty-four columns by the niches of the Apostles in the nave of the Lateran Basilica.

Ophites. Another variety of "precious serpentine" found in Rome is the *lapis ophites* of Pliny; *Hist. Nat.* xxxvi. 55. It is deep

---

[1] The correct spelling of this name is Maussollos; see Frochner, *Inscr. Grecques du Louvre*, pp. 185, 186.

green, with markings like the scales of a snake (ὄφις); hence its name. It was found near Thebes.

Example: A fine vase in the Vatican *Galleria dei candelabri*.

Alabaster: The hard Oriental varieties of alabaster are among the most magnificent materials used in ancient Rome.[1] This is the *onyx* or *alabastrites* of Pliny, *Hist. Nat.* xxxvi. 59.[2] Its chief quarries were in Arabia, in Syria near Damascus, and on the Nile near Thebes; these last quarries have been largely worked in the present century, to supply materials for the facing of the mosque of Mehemet Ali on the citadel of Cairo, and many blocks were imported into Rome for the rebuilding of the Basilica of *S. Paolo fuori le mura*. *Alabaster.*

When Pliny was writing (c. 70 A.D.) it was very rare; he mentions (*Hist. Nat.* xxxvi. 60), as an almost miraculous thing, four small columns of "*onyx*" which were placed in the Theatre of Balbus; see vol. ii. p. 74. This precious material had previously been mainly used for cups and perfume bottles, which were hence called *alabastoi*;[3] great numbers have been found in the tombs of Egypt, and of Cyprus and other Phoenician and Greek colonies. *"Onyx."*

In later times it was introduced in larger quantities, and many columns of it have been found in the Baths of Caracalla, on the Palatine, and elsewhere. It is a very beautiful semi-transparent stone, richly marked with concentric nodules and wavy strata, the result of its calcareous matter being usually deposited in the stalactite form.

An immense number of varieties of alabaster have been *Varieties of alabaster.*

---

[1] They are very different from the soft native alabasters of Italy, such as that quarried near Volterra, and much used by the Etruscans for their cinerary urns.

[2] It should be observed that Pliny (*Hist. Nat.* xxxvii. 90) uses the word *onyx* in quite another sense, meaning the stratified chalcedony which we now call *onyx*.

[3] The late Greek form of this word is *alabastron*, used in the New Testament.

found in Rome, some almost as transparent as rock crystal, and others marked with brilliant red and purple mottlings.

During the second and third centuries the more transparent and richly marked sorts were often used for drapery round the shoulders of marble busts, the natural markings having some resemblance to the stripes on woven stuffs. Many examples of this are preserved in the Capitoline Museum. Some of the finest specimens of the red variety are used to line the "font" at the end of the so-called Christian Basilica, by the side of the *Sacra Via*; see vol. i. p. 227.

Myrrhina.   *Fluor-spar.* Another even more sumptuous material was used in Rome, though it was apparently very scarce. This is *fluor-spar*, a translucent crystalline substance marked with blue, red, and purple.[1] A lump of it, found at the *Marmoratum* in the present century, has been cut into slabs to line the high altar of the Church of the Jesuits. A few other pieces have been found among the ruins of Rome.

Corsi, *Pietre antiche*, 1845, pp. 165 to 195, attempts, and apparently with success, to show that this is the substance of which the precious *myrrhine cups* were made, for which such fabulous prices were given by wealthy Romans; see Pliny, *Hist. Nat.* xxxvii. 18 to 22. It was certainly a natural stone, and not Chinese *porcelain*,[2] as has been suggested on the strength of a passage where Propertius (IV. v. 26) speaks of it as "*cocta focis*," "baked in the fire." The context shows that he may be speaking of *sham* myrrhine cups.

---

[1] Large quantities of this beautiful material are found near Matlock in Derbyshire, but these mines do not appear to have been worked by the Romans. The *myrrhina* of Pliny came from the East; *Hist. Nat.* xxxvii. 21.

[2] The fact is that Chinese porcelain was not made till several centuries after the Christian era. The small porcelain scent-bottles, which are said to have been found in Egyptian tombs, were all placed there in recent times by the Egyptian peasants. They are inscribed with sentences from Chinese poets of the tenth century A.D. and later.

The *Museo Kircheriano* possesses a small shallow cup made of fluor-spar, which appears to be antique.

Hard stones, such as *granites, basalts*, and *porphyries*, were first introduced into Rome in the latter part of the first century B.C., and were afterwards imported in enormous quantities, especially in the form of huge monolithic columns. The earliest existing examples of granite columns in Rome are those which support the portico of the Pantheon, 27 B.C. To bring columns such as these and the granite obelisks from Egypt, gigantic ships were specially built; see Pliny, *Hist. Nat.* xxxvi. 2 and 70.¹ *Granite and basalt.*

These granites and porphyries are all very refractory, and can only be worked by the help of emery or diamond dust. *Emery and drill.*

The former was got chiefly from the island of Naxos; see Pliny, *Hist. Nat.* xxxvi. 54. Drills worked with diamond dust are mentioned by Pliny, *Hist. Nat.* xxxvii. 200.

The *basalts* (*Basanites* of Pliny, xxxvi. 58) are of various colours—black, green, and brown, usually free from spots or markings. Examples of all three exist, but are comparatively rare. In the period of Decadence basalt and porphyry were used for statues, as for example that of the Nile in the *Temple of Peace*; see vol. ii. p. 14, and the existing statue of Minerva on the Capitoline steps. In many cases statues were made with the nude parts, such as the head and hands, of white marble and all the draped parts of porphyry. *Basalts.*

Pliny (*Hist. Nat.* xxxvi. 57) mentions that the first porphyry statue was sent from Egypt to Rome in the reign of Claudius, but in Rome, he says, this practice of cutting statues in porphyry was not imitated.

¹ The enormous ship, which had brought an obelisk from Egypt in the reign of Caligula, was sunk by Claudius at Ostia to form foundations for part of a new harbour; it was of such enormous size that it nearly equalled in length a whole side of the great harbour. Remains of it still exist; see Pliny, *Hist. Nat.* xxxvi. 70; and *ib.* 2; and Suet. *Claud.* 20.

Red porphyry. The red porphyry (*Porphyrites*) was brought from Egypt to Rome in enormous quantities, and was used chiefly for monolithic columns and pavements; many examples exist. It has a deep red ground, covered with small white specks of feldspar, and was hence called *Leptopsephos* or "white-spotted"; Pliny, *Hist. Nat.* xxxvi. 57.[1]

The chief quarries which supplied immense blocks of the finest red porphyry are in Upper Egypt, in the range of mountains which forms the watershed between the Red Sea and the Nile. In these quarries, which are about 25 miles from the sea and 96 from the Nile, considerable remains exist of the dwellings of the workmen and of paved roads, which appear to date from the time of the Roman Empire. An English marble merchant has recently begun to work the old quarries, but the very heavy expenses of transport will probably prevent any extensive import of this beautiful material.

Green porphyry. A rich green *porphyry* was also much used, but not in such large masses as the red sort.

This is the *lapis Lacedaemonius* (wrongly called *serpentino* by the modern Romans), so named from its quarries in the Lacedaemonian Mt. Taygetus, near the city of Sparta; Pausan. iii. 20 and 21; and Juv. xi. 173. Pliny (*Hist. Nat.* xxxvi. 55) describes it as *Lacedaemonium viride, cunctisque hilarius*.[2] It has a rich green ground, covered with rectangular greenish-white crystals of feldspar. It appears to have been mostly used for pavements and wall linings, as, for example, in the pavement of the *Triclinium* of the Flavian Palace.

Great quantities of it are used in the mediaeval church

---

[1] Porphyry, both red and green, consists almost wholly of feldspar, coloured by minute quantities of iron or copper. In structure it is mainly amorphous, but in some cases the porphyry is studded with small crystallised portions, as, for example, the *lapis Lacedaemonius* mentioned below.

[2] This beautiful green basalt is used for some of the earliest Greek gems of the lenticular type, probably cut by Peloponnesian engravers; see Middleton, *Ancient Gems*, 1891, p. 20.

floors which have mosaic of *opus Alexandrinum*. It does not as a rule occur in blocks large enough for columns.

The *granites* used in Rome came mostly from Syene, on the Nile, and other quarries near the first cataract; Pliny, *Hist. Nat.* xxxvi. 63.

Granites.

The red granite was called *lapis pyrrhopoecilus*, and the grey *lapis psaronius*. The columns of Trajan's *Basilica Ulpia* are a fine example of the latter. Both sorts are used for the columns of the Pantheon, and of the *Temple of Saturn* in the Forum Romanum.

One very rare variety of Egyptian granite is of a rich green colour. Among the very few examples of its use which now exist in Rome, are a colossal statue of a hound in the octagonal hall of the Palazzo dei Conservatori and a statue of the sacred Egyptian ape in the Museo Gregoriano in the Vatican.

The granites from Elba were also used in Imperial Rome, though much less than those from Egypt.

Methods of quarrying and working.—The quarries all over the Roman Empire were mostly worked by slaves and convicts, and were presided over by a number of officials— *praefecti marmorum, tabularii ad marmora, procuratores montium,* and other grades.[1] The selection of the beds and the general direction of the work were entrusted to a class of mining engineers called *machinarii*, under whom worked the *lapicidae* and the *metallarii*.

Quarries.

The blocks, before being shipped off, were usually numbered, and were frequently marked with the name of the reigning Emperor, and that of the *praefectus* or other official in charge of the quarry.[2]

[1] An interesting inscription was found by Belzoni in one of the Nile granite quarries, dedicating it to Jupiter Ammon in the name of Severus, his sons, and wife; it also records the names of the *praefectus operum* (see Corsi, *Pietre ant.* p. 23).

[2] A valuable paper on these quarry-marks was published by Bruzza,

Marble wharfs.   The blocks were brought up the Tiber, and landed at a special marble wharf—the *marmoratum*—below the Aventine Hill. Extensive remains of this massive stone wharf have been discovered, and also a very large number of blocks of marble which had been landed but never used. Most of these were used by Pius IX. to decorate the churches of Rome.

The other marble wharf, used to land marble for the Campus Martius, was above the *Pons Aelius*. It is described in vol. i. p. 149.

An eloquent description is given by Pliny (*Hist. Nat.* xxxvi. 1 to 5) of the enormous quantities of marbles of all kinds which were imported into Rome—a thing which he regards as a sign of excessive luxury and degeneracy from the old times of Republican simplicity.

Marble masons.   The marble and stone masons of Rome formed a very large body of workmen, divided into many classes:—*statuarii* or *fictores* (sculptors of statues), *sculptores* (carvers of foliage and architectural ornament), *lapidarii* (workers of mouldings and simple details in stone), *marmorarii* (do. in marble), *politores* (polishers), *characterarii* (cutters of inscriptions), *musivarii* (mosaic workers), *quadratarii* (blockers-out in the rough), *caesores* (sawyers).

ARCHITECTURAL STYLES OF ROMAN BUILDINGS.

The architecture of ancient Rome may be said to have *Three styles.* passed through three stages—*first* the Etruscan, *second* the Greek, and *third* the Roman or rather Graeco-Roman.

Ann. Inst. 1870, p. 106 *seq.* These marks are often of great value in determining the date of a building or statue. On the under part of the so-called "*Trophies of Marius*," which once stood in the *Nymphaeum of Severus Alexander*, and are now by the Capitoline steps, is this quarry-mark, showing that the block, which is of Athenian marble, was sent to Rome in the reign of Domitian by the freedman Chresimus.

```
IMP · DOM · AVG.
⁎ C ⋛ GERM · PER
      CHREZ · LIB
```

ARCHITECTURAL STYLES

I. *The Etruscan Period.* The Romans of all periods [1] appear to have been a thoroughly inartistic race, endowed with great powers of borrowing and adapting from various nations that proficiency in the fine arts in which they themselves were wanting. The Etruscans, on the other hand, whose country surrounded the primitive city of Rome, and who appear to have formed an important part of the ruling classes among the early Romans, were a nation highly skilled in the practice and technique of the fine arts, although without, as it seems, much real originality.[2]

Etruscan style.

Their architecture, painting, and sculpture, appear to have been an ingenious compound of these arts as practised in Greece, Assyria, and Egypt, a combination mainly due to the active commerce which was carried on between those countries and the shores of Etruria by a large fleet of Phoenician traders.

Complex style.

The same Etruscan tomb will contain wall paintings of Homeric scenes drawn with much of the true Hellenic grace and beauty, doors and cornices almost exactly resembling those of certain tombs in Egypt, and painted vases with the oft-repeated sacred symbol of the tree or the fire altar between two attendant genii or beasts—one of the oldest of Aryan symbols, and one which is repeated over and over in wall sculptures, cylinders, and other objects found in the ancient cities of Babylonia and Assyria,[3] but was quite unknown in Egypt, except in connection with Assyrian imports.

Greek and Assyrian styles.

---

[1] The inartistic character of the Romans lasted down to the end of the mediaeval period. Thus we find that the many beautiful works of art with which Rome was adorned in the fifteenth century, were nearly all the work of Florentine artists from Fra Angelico to Michelangelo, including especially the sculpture of Mino da Fiesole and his pupils.

[2] Their mechanical skill was very superior to their power of design; even among the Greeks Etruscan bronze work was celebrated.

[3] This symbol never occurs in pure Egyptian art, and, though common on early Hellenic pottery, it is clearly of Oriental origin.

28   ETRUSCAN STYLE   CHAP.

Etruscan style.   It was this strange Etruscan medley of the art of various Eastern countries that was adopted and imitated during the first few centuries of the existence of Rome. This is clear, not only from the scanty existing remains, but also from the universal agreement of the ancient Roman writers themselves as to the character of the early Roman buildings and their decoration. Even in the style of the early paintings executed by Roman artists there was a strong Etruscan element; see vol. i. p. 102.

Early temples.   The primitive Roman temple was either a simple *Cella*, such as we see on the Palatine near the *Scalae Caci*; or, if a more ambitious building, like the Temple of Jupiter on the *Capitolium*,[1] had a *peristyle* of widely spaced (*araeostyle*) columns, so that the architrave was necessarily of wood, owing to the intercolumniation being more than a stone lintel could span.

Etruscan decoration.   The architectural decorations of these early buildings were formed in gilt bronze, or painted terra-cotta, rather than in stone; and the pictures and statues they contained were not only Etruscan in style, but were usually the work of Etruscan artists. This was notably the case with the terra-cotta sculpture on the pediment of the *Temple of Capitoline Jupiter*; see vol. i. p. 359.

Pliny (*Hist. Nat.* xxxv. 154), quoting Varro, says that the painting and sculpture of the *Temple of Ceres*, near the *Circus Maximus*,[2] were the work of the first Greek artists employed in Rome, and that before then (c. 493 B.C.) "*all things in temples were Etruscan.*"

Use of clay and bronze.   Vitruvius (iii. 3. 5), speaking of Roman temples in the Etruscan style, says—*Ornantque signis fictilibus aut aereis inauratis earum fastigia, Tuscanico more: uti est ad Circum*

[1] Not only the architectural form of this ancient temple was purely Etruscan, but so also was its special triad of deities, whom the Romans called Jupiter, Juno, and Minerva.

[2] Remains of the temple are built into the *Church of S. Maria in Cosmedin*; see vol. ii. p. 194.

Maximum Cereris, et Herculis Pompeiani, item Capitolii, i.e. "The pediments of Tuscan (Etruscan) temples are adorned with statues of terra-cotta or of gilt bronze, in the Etruscan fashion; as is the case with the *Temple of Ceres* at the *Circus Maximus*, that of *Hercules Pompeianus*, and that (of Jupiter) on the *Capitolium*;" see also Vitr. iv. 7. 1, and vi. 3. 1.

II. *The Greek Style.* The Greek influence is even more *Greek style.* obvious. Nearly all the temples of the late Republican and earlier Imperial age are Hellenic in style, with modifications, not only in general design, but also in minute details and ornaments. Indirectly there was much Greek influence in the primitive Etruscan art of Rome, and possibly direct influence also. According to tradition Tarquinius Priscus was a Greek, the son of Demaratus of Corinth, who had been expelled by Cypselus in 665 B.C. The conquest of Magna Graecia and Sicily in the third century B.C., and the taking of Corinth by Mummius in 146 B.C., filled Rome with the spoils of Greek art. A great impulse was given to the taste for Greek works of art by the capture of Syracuse by Marcellus in 212 B.C. (Liv. xxv. 40), and by the sack of Tarentum (Livy, xxvii. 16). In 167 B.C. Aemilius Paullus, after his victories over King Perseus, sent to Rome 250 waggons' load of Greek spoils; see Plutar. *Paul. Aem.* 32.

Many Greek architects were employed in Rome, such as *Greek* the celebrated Apollodorus in the reigns of Trajan and *architects.* Hadrian; and those architects who were Romans by race, such as M. Vitruvius and C. Mutius (first century B.C.), Severus and Celer under Nero, and Rabinius under Domitian, were purely Greek by training, and in most cases obtained their professional education in Athens.

It is noticeable that as early as about 174 B.C. Cossutius, a Roman architect, was selected by Antiochus Epiphanes to design the magnificent Corinthian temple of Olympian Zeus in Athens. Cossutius' work is, however, purely Greek in style. Cossutius and C. Mutius are both mentioned by

Vitruvius as being the authors of books on architecture.[1] C. Mutius was the architect of the Temple of Honor and Virtus in Rome, dedicated by Marius. See Vitr. vii. *Praef.* 17 ; Hirt, *Gesch. der Bauk.* ii. p. 257 ; and Burn's *Rome*, p. 76.

Ionic and other styles.
The Ionic and Corinthian styles were adopted by the Romans with but little alteration ; while the Doric was usually merged into that modified form which had been adopted by the Etruscans, and was hence called Tuscan. Another Romanised form of Doric was also used, but its severe purity of form was but little appreciated by the splendour-loving Romans.

Composite style.
A specially tasteless invention of the Romans was the so-called *Composite* capital, a clumsy union of the beautiful Ionic and Corinthian capitals of the Greeks, which appears to have been invented during the Flavian period. The earliest existing example is on the *Arch of Titus.* In the second and third centuries A.D. it was very frequently used.

Roman temples.
The Roman tendency was to increase the size of the *Cella*, either by making the temple wider in proportion to its length than a Greek temple would have been, as is the case with the *Temple of Castor*, or by sacrificing the *peristyle* and building a large *Cella* with *prostyle Portico*, and, in some cases, engaged columns[2] along its walls; as, for example, the temple of "*Fortuna virilis*" (so called); see vol. ii. p. 189 ; and the *Temples of Saturn, Vespasian*, and *Faustina*. Another point in

---

[1] In 1889 a pedestal was found in the Olympieion in Athens inscribed with the words, "Decimus Cossutius the son of Publius, a Roman," spelt thus—ΔΕΚΜΟΣ ΚΟΣΣΟΥΤΙΟΣ ΠΟΠΛΙΟΥ ΡΩΜΑΙΟΣ. Possibly this refers to the architect of the temple.

[2] Engaged columns were used by the Greeks during the fifth century B.C., as in the Great Doric Olympieion of Agrigentum, the "lion-tomb" at Cnidus, and, in the next century, in the Corinthian *Choragic monument of Lysicrates*, and very commonly in the fronts of the *scenae* of theatres ; they were, however, used in temples less frequently by the Greeks than by their Roman imitators.

which the Roman temples differed from those of the Greeks was in the lofty *stylobate* or *podium* on which they were very frequently raised, examples of which are the *Temples of Castor, Divus Julius*, and *Saturn*, all in the *Forum Romanum*.

Another respect in which Roman temples differed from those of the Greeks is that the latter appear to have depended for light (other than that of lamps) on a hypaethral roof opening, or else on the open door at the end of the *cella*.[1] Roman temples, on the other hand, not unfrequently had large windows. The *Temple of Concord* in the Forum Romanum is an example of this; it had a large window in the *cella* on each side of the prostyle portico, as is shown on the coin of Tiberius which is illustrated in vol. i. p. 337.

Use of windows.

Windows in this and other Roman temples were specially necessary on account of their being used as museums of sculpture and as picture galleries to hold the rich spoils of Greek art which were brought in almost incredible quantities to Rome. A good existing example of a temple window is to be seen in the circular temple on the cliffs of Tibur (Tivoli).

Roman windows in temples appear to have been filled in with bronze screens, such as that which still exists in perfect preservation in the window over the door of the Pantheon, or else by thin slabs of marble pierced so as to form a simple pattern, the holes being in some cases filled in with pieces of glass.[2] Coloured glass was sometimes used in the pierced marble slabs; this method was the earliest example of the use of a "stained glass window." Windows in houses, which were usually on a much smaller scale, had very frequently glazed

Metal screens and glass.

See Pliny, Hist. Nat. xxxiii. 163.

---

[1] No example is known of a purely Greek temple with windows. Those which (till half a century ago) existed in the east front of the Athenian Erechtheum were additions of late Roman date, made when the temple was converted into a Christian church.

[2] Some of the windows in the upper story of the amphitheatre at Pola were filled in with slabs of marble pierced with a great variety of patterns, some of which were derived from the designs of bronze screens.

casements made either of bronze or of wood. Examples of both have been found at Pompeii.

Temples not for public worship. With regard to the use of Roman temples, it is important to notice that, like Greek temples, they were not so much places for public worship as dwellings for the deities and shrines to hold the *cultus* statue. What we call a temple was called by the Romans an *aedes sacra* or Holy House. Public worship, such as sacrifice and other ritual, was performed, not inside the *cella* of the temple, but at an altar in the open court or *temenus* of the temple, or in some cases under the portico in front of the chief doorway. This is shown on the coin which is illustrated in vol. i. p. 364.

Porticus for worshippers. When space would permit it was usual for the *temenus* or temple enclosure to be surrounded by a cloister-like colonnade which the Romans called a *porticus*.

An altar was commonly placed in this open court in front of the main entrance to the temple.

Pliny the younger, in one of his letters (*Ep.* ix. 39), clearly indicates this system, the temple being, as he says, for the god, and the *porticus* being built for the convenience of the worshippers; see also vol. ii. p. 248, where an inscription is quoted which distinguishes between the *aedes* which we should now call the "temple," and the *templum* which denotes the whole sacred precinct.[1]

Roman details. To return, however, to the stylistic peculiarities of the Romans, it was more in the architectural details that the Roman want of taste showed itself, and though they were at first content to copy the Greek mouldings and enrichments, almost with absolute fidelity, yet the Roman craving for richness of effect soon led them to cover all the various members of the *entablature* with elaborate surface ornament, a very great artistic mistake, as the plain flat *mouldings* and *fillets* (*coronae purae*), catching the light strongly, served a very important purpose in setting off by contrast the lines of dark

[1] Other meanings of the word *templum* are given in vol. i. p. 238.

hollows and delicate surface enrichments which the Greeks applied to a few of the members only.

The slight commencement of this decadence in taste can be seen even in the very splendid and well-designed cornice of the *Temple of Concord*; it has progressed further in the cornice of the *Temple of Vespasian*, in which one of the *coronae* is cut into short upright flutings, and the lower egg and dart member is covered with elaborate surface ornament. Later on, in the second and third centuries, this excessive use of ornament was carried further still, till every single member in a cornice was often covered with enrichments (*coronae caelatae*), leaving no plain surfaces to relieve the eye or to give bands of bright light. A remarkable example of this is the very beautifully executed cornice, taken from some much earlier building, which was used by Maxentius to decorate the door of the temple to his son Romulus; see vol. ii. p. 19. *Excess of ornament.*

The best period of Graeco-Roman art was during the reign of Augustus, an eclectic period, when the ablest Greek sculptors who were working in Rome imitated, and to some extent revived, the glories of ancient Greek architecture and sculpture. Not only the highly developed styles of Praxiteles and Lysippus were imitated by these Graeco-Roman artists, but they even produced archaistic imitations of the sculpture of the age of Pheidias and his predecessors. *Age of Augustus.*

During the reigns of the very inartistic Flavian emperors, Graeco-Roman art appears to have been in a state of serious decadence, but in the second century A.D., especially in the time of Hadrian, 117 to 138 A.D., there was a fresh revival of Hellenistic art of various styles; and then, for a brief period, architectural and plastic works were produced in Rome and its provinces which almost rival in beauty the finest works of the Augustan age. *Greek revival.*

As examples of this we may mention the well-known relief of Antinous in the Villa Albani in Rome, and the extraordinarily graceful and refined sculpture which decorates the marble throne of the High Priest of Dionysus in the great Theatre in Athens. The reliefs of Eros and Fauns on this throne might pass for good examples of the Praxitelean age, were it not that they are combined with dull, feebly executed designs of pseudo-Assyrian style.

Rapid decay. This brilliant period of revival did not last long. By the beginning of the reign of Sept. Severus, 193 A.D., a most complete and rapidly growing decadence had set in. Sculpture became feeble in design and clumsy in execution; and all architectural details grew to be coarse, heavy, and overloaded with badly executed ornament of the most utterly tasteless kind. Niebuhr, in his *Lectures on Ancient History*, vol. ii. p. 53, points out that the abnormally rapid decadence of art in the second half of the second century A.D. was largely due to *Great plague.* the great plague which, in the reign of Marcus Aurelius, destroyed a large proportion of the population of Europe.[1]

The lowest depths of degradation were reached in the time of Constantine and his sons; and this lasted without any signs of improvement till that wonderful outburst of a new and brilliant art-development took place in Byzantium in the early part of the sixth century, in the time of the Emperor Justinian.

Native style. III. *The Native Roman Style*; see vol. ii. p. 75, on the *Amphitheatres*. The Romans, though quite devoid of any artistic originality, or even power of refined appreciation, were the most able of engineers, and were remarkably skilful in contriving and planning so as to provide in the most complete way for all the practical requirements of their different buildings.

This purely utilitarian spirit led naturally and easily to the development of a new style, which had at least that beauty which *fitness* is supposed to bring with it, and fre-

[1] In a very similar way the Black Death, which devastated England in the middle of the fourteenth century, brought about a serious falling off in the excellence of most branches of English art.

quently possessed, even if it were by accident, much harmony of proportion and grandeur of effect from the stately vastness of the mass.

In their desire for large covered halls the Romans were led to throw aside the restrictions imposed by the Hellenic use of the stone lintel, and even the more elastic limits permitted by the use of the wooden beam; and making use of their strong natural cement (the *pozzolana*) constructed concrete domes and vaults of enormous span, cast in one solid mass of concrete, which covered the space like a metal lid without lateral thrust; having, that is, the *form* but not the principle of the arch. This allowed them safely to vault spaces so wide that the walls would have been pushed out if they had been covered with a true arched vault either in brick or stone.

Concrete vaults.

It is frequently supposed that the main characteristic of the native architecture of Rome was the great development of the principle of the arch: but that the chief Roman invention was rather the extensive and very skilful use of concrete I have attempted to show below; see vol. i. p. 44 *seq.*

CHAPTER II

ROMAN METHODS OF CONSTRUCTION AND DECORATION.

Practical skill. THE ancient Romans appear to have been a thoroughly inartistic race; but for many centuries, throughout the whole classic period, they certainly possessed an unrivalled knowledge of the best methods of construction, and were preeminently skilful in their use of various materials of all kinds—stone, wood, concrete, and metal. For this reason a careful examination of the many different modes of construction employed in ancient Rome is not only of interest to the student of archaeology, but may also supply many valuable lessons to the architect and engineer of modern days.

Probably no subject has had so much that is misleading written about it as this—partly because in many cases it has been treated by archaeologists who had no practical knowledge of building,—and also because the real methods of construction in ancient Rome are frequently hidden behind very deceptive modes of surface decoration.

Concealed construction.

For this reason it is necessary to warn the architectural student in Rome to trust little to existing works on the subject, however magnificently illustrated, and to use his own eyes with special care and thoughtfulness.[1]

The methods of building walls in Rome may be classified thus:—

[1] The richly illustrated folio volumes of Canina are simply works of imagination, and worse than useless to the real student.

I.—*Opus quadratum*, that is, rectangular blocks of stone set either with or without mortar. *Two classes of walls.*

II.—*Concrete*, either unfaced or faced.

These two main classes really include the whole systems of building employed in ancient Rome.

The usual classification, which makes *opus incertum*, *opus reticulatum*, and *opus testaceum* or brick, distinct methods of construction like *opus quadratum*, is wholly misleading, as they are merely used as thin facings to concrete walls.

Strange as it may sound, there is no such thing as a brick wall among the buildings of classical Rome; this will be explained below at greater length.

I. *Opus Quadratum*, that is, masonry of rectangular blocks, is the most primitive among existing methods of building in Rome. The earliest example, the prehistoric wall of *Roma Quadrata*, is described below; see vol. i. p. 112. *Opus quadratum.*

At first *tufa* was the only material used, and neither clamps nor mortar were used to bind the wall together. Soon the harder *peperino* was worked, as for example is seen in the wall of Servius Tullius; see vol. i. p. 137. *Tufa.*

Mortar was introduced at a very remote period both in Greece and in Rome; it occurs in the *Tullianum*, probably among existing buildings the next in date to the prehistoric fortifications of the Palatine; see vol. i. p. 152. Its purpose was not, however, like that of modern mortar, to bind the blocks together, but it was a mere skin about the thickness of cardboard, apparently of pure lime, introduced simply to give the joints and beds quite even and smoothly-fitting surfaces. This thin layer of lime occurs in the Servian wall on the Aventine; in the very early masonry of the so-called "*Temple of Jupiter Victor*" on the Palatine Hill; in the *peperino* wall of the front of the *Tabularium* (see fig. 48, vol. i. p. 376); and in the tufa walls of the Colosseum (see fig. 61, vol. ii. p. 94). In later times, towards the close of the Republic and under the Empire, the thin bed of lime was seldom used, as the beds and *Mortar.*

joints of the blocks were rubbed perfectly smooth, so that the junction of two blocks in well preserved examples is almost invisible.[1] Thus the use of mortar in Roman stonework is a sign of early rather than of late date.

Even the earliest blocks—those of the so-called wall of Romulus—were worked with metal tools, distinct marks of which exist in places where the surface is well preserved.[2]

Sizes of blocks. The sizes of the blocks, whether of *tufa* or *peperino*, from the earliest period till the time of the Empire, appear to have been almost always the same in two of their dimensions; that is, they were roughly 2 Roman feet deep (about $1' 11\frac{1}{2}''$), and the same across the ends.[3] In the ruder primitive work these dimensions can only be taken as an average, but under the Republic they were followed with much accuracy.

The lengths of the blocks as a rule vary, but in the finest specimen of *opus quadratum*, that of the front of the *Tabularium*, 78 B.C., the blocks are exactly the same in all their dimensions; the end is a square of 2 Roman feet, and the length exactly

---

[1] A wonderful example of the perfect jointing of *peperino* blocks can be seen in the recently exposed angle of the podium of the Temple of Faustina, near the bottom, where accumulations of earth have preserved the surface ever since its marble lining was torn away. Here the beds and joints are so close as to be imperceptible except with the closest examination. The Greek builders produced the most wonderful closeness of jointing, especially in the case of marble columns, by grinding together the two adjacent beds of the marble blocks or drums till the surfaces fitted with the perfect accuracy of a glass stopper in a bottle. It seems probable that a similar process was adopted by the Romans in their finest work.

[2] It has been more than once stated that these primitive tufa blocks were split with wooden wedges; that was never the case, and indeed it would be impossible to square tufa in this way, as it is not at all laminated in structure.

[3] The Roman foot appears to have been almost exactly a quarter of an inch shorter than a modern English foot; it is the usual unit used in all Roman buildings. The Greek foot was a fraction less. It appears to have been ·9708 of the English foot.

4 feet; so that one block set lengthways in the wall (*stretcher*) ranges exactly with two set endways (*headers*). They are arranged with a course of *headers* and then a course of *stretchers* alternately, all the way up.

This masonry with courses of regular depth is called by Vitruvius (ii. 8. 6) *isodomon*; and the bonding arrangement, with alternate courses of headers and stretchers, is called *emplecton* (from ἐμπλέκειν, to weave in), and the extra long "through stones," extending through the whole thickness of the wall, were called διατόνοι. *Isodomon.* *Emplecton.*

This solid kind of masonry, formed wholly of rectangular blocks, is described by Vitruvius as if it were peculiar to the Greeks, in spite of its having once been largely practised in Rome. In his time the Roman method was to make the bulk of the wall of concrete, and only face it with stone: he thus contrasts the two systems—*Graeci vero non ita; sed plana (coria) collocantes, et longitudines chororum alternis coagmentis in crassitudinem instruentes, non media farciunt sed e suis frontatis perpetuum et in unam crassitudinem parietem consolidant. Praeterea interponunt singulos perpetua crassitudine utraque parte frontatos, quos* διατόνους *appellant, qui maxime religando confirmant parietum soliditatem*: Vitr. ii. 8. 7. The meaning of this passage can only be given in a somewhat free translation: "The Greeks do not build thus, but they lay the blocks on level beds, setting them lengthways (as stretchers) throughout the whole thickness of the wall, so that the joints alternate (that is, so that the joints in one course come over the middle of the blocks in the next course). (Thus) they do not fill in the middle of the wall with concrete or rubble, but they build the wall quite solid from back to front. In addition (to the courses of stretchers) they set single blocks (as headers) reaching through the whole thickness of the wall. These through-stones, which they call διατόνοι, have each end showing on the face of the wall, and thus, by acting as bonders, they greatly increase the solidity of the masonry." *Greek masonry.* *Description of Vitruvius.*

Clamps and dowels. Great care was taken by the Romans in the close fitting of the beds and joints in *opus quadratum*; and during the republican and early imperial period each block was carefully fastened to the adjacent ones with dowels or clamps. As Vitruvius (ii. 8. 4) says — *cum his ansis ferreis et plumbo frontes vinctae sunt.*

The iron clamps were usually very massive; they were turned down at each end, and then fixed with melted lead.[1] Other dowels of a dovetail shape were very commonly used; these appear to have been of wood. Vitruvius (i. 5. 3) says they should be of olive-wood, charred, *taleae oleagineae ustulatae.*

The Romans called them "swallow-tail" clamps, from their spreading ends.

Travertine. Travertine was probably not much used before the first century B.C., and then chiefly for ornamental purposes, and for giving extra strength at certain points (see vol. ii. p. 94). When used for walls it was not cut into regular courses, as the *tufa* and *peperino* blocks usually were, but was worked up so as to involve as little labour as possible, and the least amount of waste, being both much harder and more valuable than the *tufa*, or even the *peperino*.[2]

Pseud-isodomon. This masonry with unequal courses is the *pseudisodomon* of Vitruvius (ii. 8. 6); and when walls were built of *tufa* or *peperino*, mixed with *travertine*, the former are cut in unequal courses so as to range with the latter. The finest example of a solid travertine wall in Rome is perhaps what remains of the

---

[1] In the interesting Greek inscription found at Lebadea in Boeotia the iron clamps are specified to be either ἐπιμεμολυβδοχοημένοι or περιμεμολυβδοχοημένοι; see Choisy, *Devis de Livadie*, Paris, 1884, pp. 180, 181.

[2] The primitive walls of Tibur (Tivoli) are built of *tufa*, which had to be brought some distance, though there is an abundant supply of travertine on the spot. The tufa was so much easier to work that it was worth while to carry it a long distance to avoid the necessity of using the hard travertine.

wall round the *podium* of the *Temple of Vespasian*; here the *Travertine masonry.*
massive and perfectly jointed blocks of travertine were simply
used for the sake of strength, as they were completely cased
with marble. The great iron clamps which unite all the blocks

Fig. 1.
Arch of mixed travertine and peperino opening into the Forum Pacis, built by Vespasian.

are really quite superfluous—as there was no lateral pressure, and the immense weight of each stone was amply sufficient to keep it in position.

In some cases, as is mentioned above, thick walls were made *Ashlar facing.*

Outer facing.

with a facing of *opus quadratum* on both sides, the internal part being filled in with rubble or concrete. Vitruvius points out the danger of this method if loose rubble is used, owing to unequal settlement; see Vitr. ii. 8. 2, and 3. With the solid concrete of the Romans no such failure could occur, the inner mass of concrete being quite as strong as the stone masonry. It was only by degrees that the Romans found out how strong their concrete was, and under the early Empire we find it occasionally used with needless timidity and caution.

Mixed materials.

In most cases *travertine* was used for archways, and other points of extra strain. In the *Forum Julii* it is used only for the keystones and springers of the tufa flat arches (see vol. ii. on p. 5), and in the *Forum of Augustus* travertine is used for the cornice and the *voussoirs* of the large skew arch, now called *l' arco de' pantani*; see fig. 2. The smaller arches are built, like the rest of the wall, of *peperino*.[1]

Similarly, in the existing wall of the *Forum Pacis* the *voussoirs* and jambs of the archway are of *travertine*, while the rest is of mixed *tufa* and *peperino*; see fig. 1.

The way in which *travertine* is mixed with *tufa* in some of the lofty inner walls of the Colosseum, in order to give additional strength, is shown in vol. ii. p. 94. Some of the travertine blocks used in the arcades of the Colosseum are as much as 15 feet long by 8 wide.

Depth of courses.

It should be noticed, as a valuable guide in some cases to the date of a Roman building, that when a wall is partly built of travertine the adjoining blocks of tufa or peperino are no longer worked to the regular 2-foot courses, but range with the travertine blocks, which are never cut to regular sizes, probably to avoid waste both of labour and material in cutting up the harder and more costly stone. Fig. 61, vol. ii. p. 94, shows a very instructive example of the use of travertine piers, built in flush at intervals to increase the strength of a tufa

---

[1] A similar arch with travertine *voussoirs* in a wall of peperino is used for the door of the *Tabularium*; see fig. 48, vol. i. p. 376.

wall. This is done in all the radiating cross walls of the Colosseum.

In this case the irregular tufa courses are arranged to work in with the varying sizes of the travertine blocks; one of the

Mixed materials.

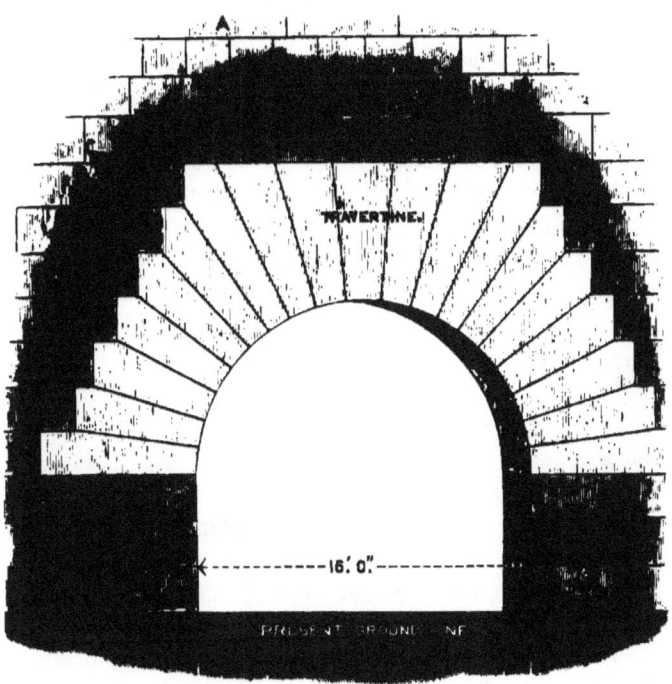

Fig. 2.

Skew arch opening into the Forum of Augustus, now called *l' arco dei pantani*. The *voussoirs* are of travertine, and the rest of the masonry is of peperino.

facts which show that the travertine piers are not later insertions, as Mr. J. H. Parker asserted in his work on the Colosseum, but were inserted owing to the builders' want of confidence in the strength of the tufa walls.

Concrete. Concrete, *structura caementitia.* The most striking feature in the construction of the buildings of ancient Rome is the extensive use of concrete for the most varied purposes.[1]

The reason why this material was so largely and so successfully used in Rome was chiefly because immense beds of pozzolana exist over a great part of the area of the Campagna. This substance when mixed with lime has the peculiar property of forming a sort of natural hydraulic cement of the very highest excellence in strength, hardness, and durability; while its hydraulic properties, or power of setting hard, even under water, are very remarkable.

This mixture of pozzolana and lime was employed for a great variety of purposes, according as they were used alone or mixed with other materials, such as broken bricks or stone; it was equally valuable for stucco to cover walls, and for the rough concrete of foundations.

Pozzolana. It is to this remarkable natural product that the great durability of the majority of the buildings of Imperial Rome is due.

A very interesting chapter in Vitruvius' work (ii. 6) is devoted to this *pulvis puteolanus* or pozzolana, which is a volcanic product, as is mentioned above, at p. 8, and lies in thick strata below and around Rome, just as it was showered down from the now extinct craters in the Alban Hills.

The best kind is a dull chocolate red in colour, and resembles a sandy earth mixed with larger lumps about the size of coarse gravel. To make wall-stucco or fine mortar it requires to be passed through a sieve.

Early use of concrete. The use of concrete dates from a very early period; it is laid in thick beds for the floors of the prehistoric houses of

---

[1] Vitruvius (vi. 8. 9) mentions the three chief methods of building which might be selected by a Roman who wished to build himself a house, "in domini est potestate utrum *lateritio* an *caementitio* an *saxo quadrato* velit aedificare," that is, he might use crude brick, concrete, or "ashlar" (smooth squared blocks of stone).

Tiryns and Mycenae, and we also find it used as a backing to the massive "wall of Servius" on the Aventine.

As a foundation it occurs under the Tabularium wall, as shown in fig. 48, vol. i. p. 376.

From the first century B.C. onwards concrete was the chief material used for the walls of buildings in Rome.

The materials of which it is made are often a useful indication of the date of a structure. Till the time of Julius Caesar it is usually made with broken lumps of tufa, though in some cases, under the later Republic, pieces of peperino were also used. Under the Empire, though concrete was still largely made of tufa and peperino, we find broken bricks or travertine frequently employed. In all cases the other ingredients are pozzolana, and lime usually made by burning travertine (*lapis Tiburtinus*). *Materials of concrete.*

In the restored walls of the Flavian Palace on the Palatine great quantities of fragments of fire-stained marbles of all kinds can be seen mixed with the broken brick and other materials of the concrete. Evidently the builders used up in this way all the costly marble columns and facing slabs that were too much damaged by the fire to be otherwise utilised. *Broken marble.*

During the mediaeval period concrete for building was often made of broken marble taken from the ruins of ancient Rome. The remains of the massive walls of the *Turris Chartularia*, built in the twelfth century, consist of concrete made only with marble; see vol. i. p. 229.

Where foundations of great strength were required below weighty structures the concrete was made with lumps of lava, the *silex* of Vitruvius and Pliny, taken from the great stream of lava which, issuing from the Alban Hills during the post-tertiary period, flowed in a great stream towards the future site of Rome. *Foundations.*

Another sort of concrete, made not for strength but for lightness, was mixed with lumps of pumice stone; this was used for arched vaults in order to diminish the weight. An *Vaults.*

example of this is shown in fig. 78, vol. ii. p. 168. Lastly, in late times concrete was sometimes made with a large admixture of marble or porphyry. This usually marks the destruction of some older building.

Timid use of concrete.   It appears to have been some time before the Roman builders realised how great was the strength of their concrete; and it was at first used very cautiously, simply to fill up the space under the floors in temples which had solid masonry below their walls and columns.

The Temple of Castor in the Forum is a striking example of this; see fig. 36, vol. i. p. 278.

Massive podium.   Here the lofty stylobate is formed of a sort of box made of massive peperino walls; concrete was poured into this up to the level of the cella floor. A projecting spur of solid masonry was built outside the "box" to form a foundation for each column of the peristyle, and the whole of this substructure of peperino and concrete was finally concealed by the marble casing of the stylobate. Thus the only weight the concrete had to carry was that of the marble steps and mosaic paving.

A similar system of construction is to be seen in the remains of the temples of Saturn, Concord, and Vespasian, at the opposite end of the Forum Romanum.

Concrete walls.   The next stage was to use concrete for independent walls; and the various methods in which it was employed may be classified thus:

I.—*Concrete unfaced.*

II.—*Concrete faced*:

(A.) With *opus incertum*; second and first centuries B.C.;

(B.) With *opus reticulatum*; first century B.C. to second century A.D.;

(C.) With *opus testaceum* or brick; first century B.C. to end of Western Empire;

(D.) With so-called *opus mixtum*; third century A.D. to end of Western Empire.

The last four sub-classes are arranged in the chronological order of their introduction into use; the unfaced concrete was employed throughout all the periods for special purposes, usually for the walls of foundations and substructures below the more important stories of a building.

The manner in which walls of unfaced concrete were formed was this; see fig. 3.

Upright posts 10 to 15 feet high were stuck in the ground along the line of both faces of the future wall at intervals of about 3 feet, and against these posts wooden boards 10 or 11 inches wide were nailed horizontally, overlapping each other; thus a sort of long wooden box was formed, into which the concrete was poured. The wall was in fact *cast*, and on its faces clear imprints were left both of the upright posts and the horizontal boards. It should, however, be noticed that though the main bulk of the concrete was a semi-fluid mass, yet from the regularity with which the larger pieces of stone appear (like the raisins in a plum-cake), it seems that these larger stones were thrown in separately by hand, not poured in at random as was the rest of the mixture.

Cast concrete.

The work appears to have been done by an alternation of processes. First a semi-fluid mixture of lime, pozzolana, and small stones or brickbats was poured in; then a layer of larger stones, from 3 to 6 inches across, was laid by hand, then a second layer of the fluid cement was poured in, and so on. At regular intervals the top of the wall was levelled to receive the course of tiles mentioned below.

Method of work.

The word *concrete* rather than *rubble* should be used to describe the walls thus constructed, as the result was a perfectly coherent mass like a solid block of stone, particularly unlike what is now usually known as rubble-work.

The same method of forming the wall within wooden boarding seems to have been applied both to the walls of unfaced concrete and to some of those which were faced with the triangular bricks.

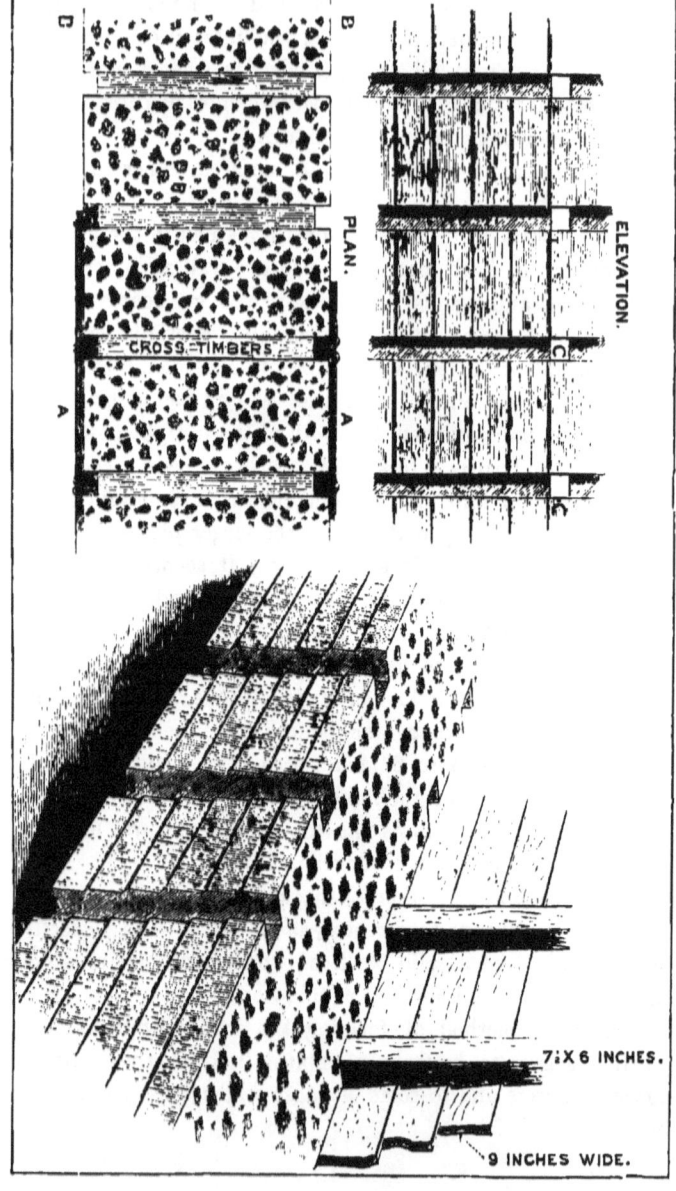

Fig. 3.

Method used in Rome of casting concrete walls inside wooden boarding.

In many cases the first 10 or 15 feet of a wall, forming the foundation and the basement of a building, are composed of *unfaced concrete* with sharp prints on its face of the boarding in which it was cast. *Marks of boarding.*

Then suddenly, at the level of the principal floor, the *brick facing* begins, and yet there is no visible change in the character of the concrete mass of the wall; see for example fig. 78, vol. ii. p. 168.

Moreover, in some cases, as in the remains of the *Golden House* of Nero under the *Thermae* of Titus, distinct marks of the wooden boarding are visible on the surface of the brick facing, showing that the concrete needed lateral support while it was in a semi-fluid, unset state, even if it had the facing of triangular bricks.

These marks on the brick facing can, however, only be traced when a wall has been newly exposed by excavation. They soon vanish under exposure to the weather. The other method of forming brick facing with grooves exactly like those in the unfaced concrete is mentioned below, in vol. i. p. 58.

The hydraulic pressure against the wooden boarding must have been heavy, and in some cases we find a regular series of holes going through the concrete wall, showing where cross-timbers were fixed as ties to keep the boarding in its place till the concrete had set. *Cross ties.*

When the first tier had got sufficiently hard the wooden framework was stripped off it, and refixed as before at the top, and then a second quantity of concrete was thrown in; the whole process being repeated till the wall was formed to the required height.

In most cases the holes through the wall are absent, and the boarding must then have been supported from the outside by a series of raking shores or props. *Raking shores.*

The upright grooves on the face of the concrete wall caused by the print of the posts were often filled up, after the woodwork was removed, by the insertion of small square bricks thickly set in mortar,[1] as in the case of the grooves in brick facing.

In foundations and walls of cellars the grooves were usually left open and visible.

Examples of concrete. The finest specimens in Rome of lofty and massive walls of unfaced concrete were those in the Gardens of Sallust, part of the great imperial villa which originally belonged to the historian. These noble examples of Roman construction were wholly destroyed in 1884-85 to make room for rows of "jerry-built" houses, which now disfigure what was once one of the most beautiful and interesting parts of Rome. At the same time a long piece of the Servian wall was pulled down, and its massive tufa blocks broken up to make cheap rubble-work in the new speculative houses.

Strength of concrete. This horrible process of destruction was instructive, as showing how much stronger and more durable a well-made concrete wall is even than the most massive structure of masonry. The great blocks of the Servian wall were easily removed one by one, but the concrete building formed one perfectly coherent mass of great strength, and could only be destroyed in a very laborious way—like that of quarrying stone from its native bed.

This method of using concrete without any facing seems in every way so successful that one cannot help wondering why it was as a rule only used for substructures: the fact, however, remains that in almost all cases the concrete walls of *Faced concrete.* the main part of each building were laboriously faced in one of the methods mentioned in the list above. As the wall-facing, whether of brick or stone, appears almost invariably to have been covered with stucco or marble slabs, the facing cannot have been added for the sake of appearance.

In one respect, and a very important one, the smooth

[1] It need hardly be said that the Romans did not leave the wooden framing to rot in the grooves of the concrete, as has sometimes been stated.

facing was a positive disadvantage : the rough concrete forms
the best possible key for the coating of stucco over it, while
the smooth *opus reticulatum*, or brick, afforded but little hold
to the stucco, and so the whole surface had to be roughened
to give the necessary key to the stucco. This was done in a *Key for stucco.*
very laborious and costly way by driving large iron nails all
over the wall-surface, or else by inserting plugs of marble,
each about 1 inch square by 2 inches long, into holes drilled
in the joints of the brick facing. Very often both methods
were used together—an iron nail and a marble plug being
wedged into the same hole.

In some cases, as in parts of the Flavian Palace on the
Palatine, a bronze wedge is used to fix each marble plug into
its hole.

In this case, and in many others, this system of plugs is *Key for cement.*
used not to form a key for ornamental painted stucco, but
simply to afford a hold for the cement backing behind the
marble slabs with which the walls were lined.

In one exceptional case, in the lower part of Hadrian's
exedra in the Palatine Stadium, rooms decorated with painted
stucco are built of the unfaced concrete, and here the stucco
still adheres to its place far better than it ever did to any
brick-faced walls, in spite of their marble and metal plugs.

We will now consider the different kinds of facing used *Three kinds of facing.*
for concrete walls.

(A.) *Opus incertum.*

This is the oldest kind of concrete facing. Vitruvius *Opus incertum.*
(ii. 8) speaks of it and the following class thus: ". . . *reticulatum quo nunc* (*i.e.* in the reign of Augustus) *omnes
utuntur, et antiquum, quod incertum dicitur.*" In forming
opus incertum the face of the concrete wall was studded with
irregular-shaped pieces of tufa, 3 or 4 inches across, each
having its outer face worked smooth and the inner part
roughly pointed. A on fig. 4 shows its usual appearance

Opus incertum. on the face, and also (at C) the manner in which it tails into the concrete. Examples of this, dating probably from the second century B.C., exist in the thick concrete wall at the foot of the "Scalae Caci" on the Palatine, in the Emporium, a series of store-chambers on the banks of the Tiber near the Aventine, and in some houses built against the Servian wall, near the railway station, now doomed to destruction.

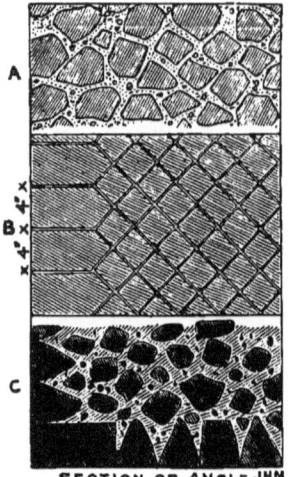

Fig. 4.

A. Opus incertum, in *elevation.*

B. Opus reticulatum with rectangular quoins at an angle, in *elevation.*

C. Horizontal *section*, which is the same in both.

(B.) *Opus reticulatum.*

Opus reticulatum. So called from its resemblance to the meshes of a net (*reticulum*); see B on fig. 4.

This is similar to *opus incertum*, except that the stones are carefully cut, so as to present a square or lozenge-shaped end, and are fitted very closely one to another. These little blocks of about 3 inches square are arranged so as to run in diagonal lines; the angles of the wall have neatly worked quoins, with the inner end pointed, so as to work in with the small lozenges; see fig. 4, B. The arches over doors and windows in walls of this class have accurately worked rectangular *voussoirs*, generally about 9 inches long by 3 or 4 inches wide. The effect of this sort of facing is very neat and pretty to look at, but its beauty appears—usually outside a building, and invariably inside—to have been concealed by stucco. The most notable examples in Rome of

Opus reticulatum.

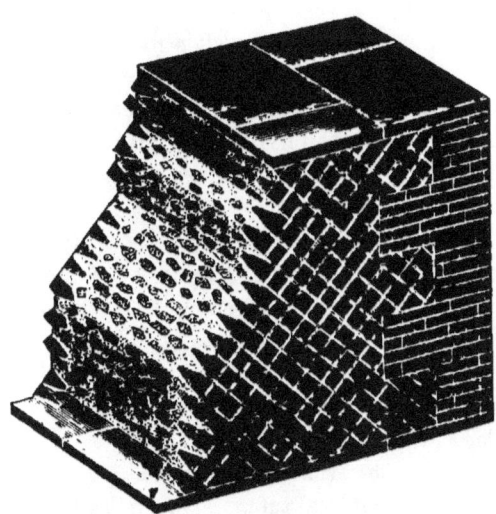

Fig. 5.

A concrete wall faced with *opus reticulatum*, except at the angle where it is faced with brick, forming regular quoins.

As in fig. 8 there are occasional courses of *tegulae*, extending through the whole thickness of the wall.

fine *opus reticulatum*, used without any admixture of brick facing, are the "muro torto" built into the wall of Aurelian under the Pincian Hill, the so-called "house of Maecenas" on the Esquiline, and the "house of Livia" (or "Germanicus" as it is also called) on the Palatine Hill ; see fig. 10.[1] All these examples probably date from the time of Augustus.

[1] See vol. i. p. 64.

Mixture of brick.

Early in the first century A.D. *opus reticulatum* ceased to be used as a facing alone: the arches and angles then began to be faced with brick instead of the neat little tufa voussoirs and quoins, and surface bands of brick, about a foot deep, at intervals of 2 or 3 feet, were introduced, as for example in part of Caligula's Palace on the Palatine, facing on to the Nova Via; see fig. 6.

In some cases the *opus reticulatum* was only used as a sort of large panel in the middle of a brick-faced wall: *e.g.* in the substructures of the Thermae of Titus, over the Golden House of Nero. Hadrian's villa near Tivoli supplies one of the latest examples of this mixed use of *opus reticulatum* and brick facing.

Hadrian's villa.

It was, however, but rarely used as late as Hadrian's time; even towards the close of the first century A.D. the use of *opus reticulatum* had mainly been given up in favour of complete brick facing. It does not appear to have been used in Rome after the reign of Tiberius without an admixture of brick, the proportion of the *opus reticulatum* in each wall growing smaller and smaller as time went on.

It should be observed that in Rome *opus reticulatum* is always made with the local tufa. A few miles from Rome, in tombs on the Via Appia, peperino and lava are both used, but only at places where these materials were close at hand.

In all cases, however, the use of *opus reticulatum* alone—that is, unmixed with bands or quoins of brick—appears to be an indication that the structure is not later than the first half-century or so of the Empire.

(C.) *Concrete faced with brick (testae).*

Brick facing.

Till the first century B.C. only unburnt bricks (*lateres*) appear to have been used in Rome, and no example of brick earlier than the time of Julius Caesar is now to be seen. The remarks of Vitruvius on the subject of bricks for walls do not apply to any which now exist in Rome, as he only mentions rectangular bricks, while those used in existing walls

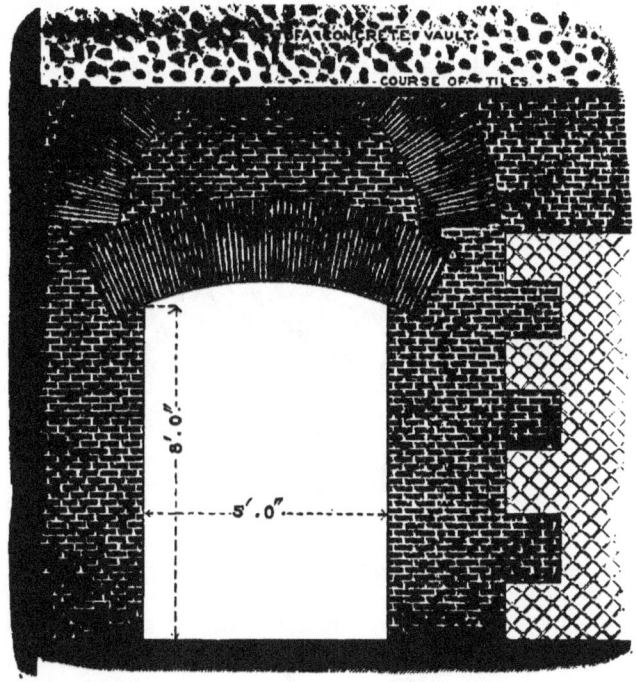

Fig. 6.

A doorway in Caligula's Palace, facing on to the Nova Via, with the combined use of facings of *opus reticulatum* and brick, as shown in fig. 5.

This sketch indicates clearly the useless nature of the superficial "relieving arches," the upper part of the arch being omitted where the concrete vault of the room abuts against it. This curious method of building only parts of "arches" occurs very frequently among the remains of ancient Rome. Another example in the Baths of Caracalla is illustrated in vol. ii. p. 168.

are invariably triangular in shape; see Vitr. ii. 3. The reason of this is explained above at p. 10.

Crude bricks.

It is evident that he is referring to *lateres* (*crudi*), sun-baked bricks, of which no example in Rome now remains, though they must once have been very common.

These unfired bricks lasted perfectly well as long as they were covered with stucco to protect them from the rain, but when once the roof was gone, and the stucco began to fall off, the process of decay would be very rapid and complete. Recent discoveries have shown that this system of building with sun-baked bricks (like the modern Mexican *adobes*) was very common among the Greeks for many centuries: for

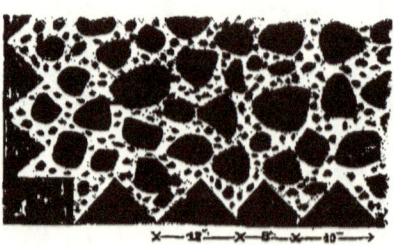

Fig. 7.
Concrete wall faced with triangular bricks.

example, the great wall round Athens, which was destroyed by Sulla, appears to have chiefly consisted of unbaked bricks, the lower part only being of stone. The same is the case in the prehistoric houses of Hissarlik, Mycenae, and Tiryns.

Fired bricks.

The most important point to notice about the use of burnt bricks in Rome is that (in walls) they are only used as a thin facing for concrete, and in no case is a wall formed of solid brickwork.[1] The shape of these bricks is always triangular (see fig. 8), probably for the sake of getting a good bond into the concrete behind. So universal is this rule as to walls in Rome not being solidly built of brick, that even thin party-

[1] The tops of old walls in Rome are now often protected by a covering of square bricks made to look like old ones, and this gives the wall a delusive appearance of being formed of solid brickwork.

walls of small rooms, sometimes only 7 inches thick, are not built solid, but have an inner core of concrete faced by small brick triangles; see fig. 9.

This elaborate construction for so thin a wall must have caused an extraordinary waste of labour.

It is difficult at first to realise while looking at the immense surfaces of fine brickwork among the remains of ancient Rome that all these walls are really formed of concrete, and

Skin of brickwork.

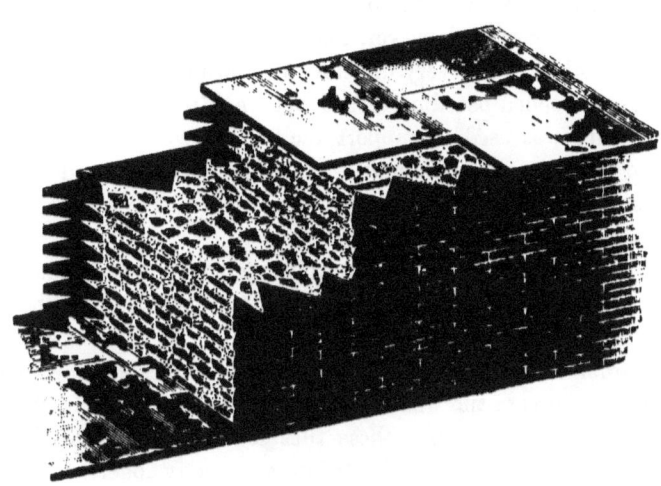

Fig. 8.

Sketch showing a concrete wall faced with triangular bricks and having, at intervals, single courses of *tegulae bipedales*.

that the brick is but a thin facing tailing into the wall an average depth of 4 or 5 inches only; yet such really is the case.

It is evident that during the formation of these walls the brick facing, which was so insignificant a part of the whole thickness of the wall, could not have supported the hydraulic pressure of the soft concrete.

Wood supports.

It was, therefore, necessary to support the outside brick skin

Wood framing. with a system of wooden framing like that used for the unfaced concrete. In most cases the brick facing has prevented any imprint of the framing from being left, but in some cases, as *e.g.* in the Golden House of Nero, under the Thermae of Titus, the channels caused by the upright posts are clearly visible. These upright grooves on the face of the wall are about 6 inches wide by 4 inches deep, and they were afterwards filled up by the insertion of little rectangular bricks so as to make a smooth, unbroken surface for the plastering.

In many cases, however, the surface of the brick facing is so smooth that it is very difficult to believe that it was formed against wooden boarding. And yet since, in many walls, the boarding was used to support the brick-faced concrete till it had set, one can hardly understand why it was not used in all cases, especially as the general character of the concrete is always much the same.

Tile courses. In addition to the facing of triangular bricks, we find in most cases single courses of large tiles (*tegulae bipedales*) about 1 foot 11 inches square, introduced at regular intervals of from 3 feet to 5 feet in the height of the building, and passing through the whole thickness of the wall; see fig. 9.

As bonding courses these tiles seem to be quite useless, because the concrete itself sets into a perfectly coherent, rock-like mass.

In reality they were points of weakness, and in fallen walls one always finds that a breakage has occurred far more readily along a course of tiles than in the mass of the concrete itself. It is, however, possible that they were useful as bonding courses for a short time after the wall was formed, as long as the concrete remained unset.

Sham arches. In the same way the arches which occur in the brick facing are only skin-deep, and can be of no real constructional use. That the Roman builders did not regard them as being constructionally important is shown by the fact that they often omitted the upper portion of a "relieving" arch; as, for

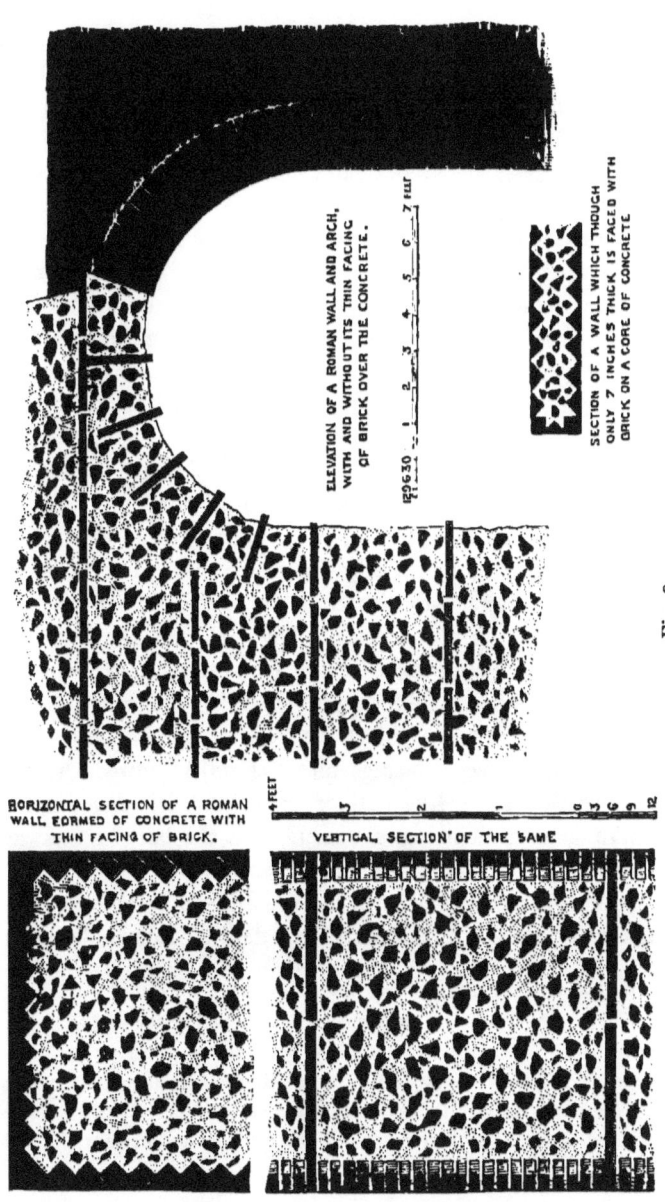

Fig. 9.

Shows the use of triangular bricks as a facing for concrete walls, and also an arch faced with rectangular slips of tile, with a whole tile inserted at rare intervals.

60   THE PANTHEON   CHAP.

Sham arches. example, at D in fig. 78,[1] the brick surface-arch is omitted where the marble frieze came in front of it, though the lower part of the arch, which was equally hidden by a marble lining, was put in.[2]

In these facing-arches most of the bricks used are only narrow slips, tailing into the concrete about 4 inches, but at intervals whole square tiles occur; see fig. 9, p. 59.

Pantheon. A conspicuous example of the insertion of these apparently useless arches in brick facing occurs in the walls of the Pantheon, built in 27 B.C. All round the building tiers of these arches appear, and judging from their external appearance they concentrate the weight of the walls on to certain points.

But the real fact is, that while the whole mass of the wall is of concrete nearly 20 feet thick, the brick facing, including the arches, only tails into the walls to an average depth of 5 or 6 inches, so that in reality these apparent relieving arches are of little more use (as regards the pressure) than if they were painted on the surface. The fact that the Pantheon *Skin of brickwork.* brickwork is a mere skin on the massive concrete wall was clearly shown in 1882 during the removal of the modern houses which had been built against the back of the Pantheon. At many points deep cuttings into the walls showed the real construction to be like that of the other brick and concrete buildings in ancient Rome, namely, that the bulk of the wall, like that of the dome, was solid concrete.

Dates of brickwork. With regard to the brick facing it should be observed that the most valuable indication of the date of Roman buildings

[1] See vol. ii. p. 168, and fig. 6, vol. i. p. 55.

[2] That the brickwork in Roman walls, including the arches, is only skin-deep, can be readily seen in a great many places owing to the frequent mediaeval custom of pecking off the brick facing in order to use the fragments of brick for the concrete of new buildings. In all cases the removal of three or four inches of the wall-surface exposes the solid concrete which forms the bulk of the structure.

is given by the size and quality of the triangular facing bricks and the thickness of the mortar joints.

And here it may be noted that Mr. J. H. Parker's rule, that "the more courses of brick there are to a vertical foot the earlier the date of the brickwork," is wholly fallacious.

Number of courses.

The fact is that as time went on while the bricks got thinner the joints got thicker; so a wall of the time of Severus may have the same number of courses to a foot as one of two centuries earlier.

The following table gives some typical examples of different dates, beginning with what appear to be the earliest existing specimens of brickwork in Rome:—

Table of sizes of bricks.

	Date.	Average Thickness of Bricks.	Average Thickness of Joints.
Rostra of J. Caesar	44 B.C.	1½ inch.	¼ inch.
Pantheon of Agrippa	27 B.C.	1½ ,,	⅜–½ ,,
Praetorian Camp of Tiberius	23 A.D.	1¼–1¾ ,,	¼–½ ,,
Aqueduct of Nero (Aqua Claudia)	c. 62 A.D.	1–1¼ ,,	⅜–½ ,,
Baths of Titus	80 A.D.	1½ ,,	½ ,,
Palace of Domitian	c. 90 A.D.		
Temple of Venus and Rome	c. 125 A.D.	1½ ,,	1 ,,
Palace of Severus	c. 200 A.D.	1 ,,	¾ ,,
Aurelian's Walls of Rome	c. 271 A.D.	1¼–1¾ ,,	1¼–1½ ,,

It will thus be seen that the thickness of the mortar joints must be noted as carefully as the thickness of the bricks, in order to arrive at any safe conclusion as to date.

Thickness of joints.

These examples are selected from the common kinds of brick facing, but it should be observed that in those rare cases where the brickwork was not covered by stucco or marble thinner bricks and finer joints were used.[1]

---

[1] As for example in Nero's Aqueduct for the Aqua Claudia, in the Praetorian Camp of Tiberius (see vol. ii. p. 234), and in the great hemicycle of shops in Trajan's Forum.

As a rule the brickwork under each emperor was very uniform in appearance; but at least in one case, namely, in part of the Golden House of Nero, extraordinary varieties of brickwork occur in the same building.

One and a half inches is the usual limit of thickness of a brick in Rome, but in one part of Nero's palace some bricks occur as much as 2½ inches thick, mixed up with those of the common size.

Length of bricks. The length of bricks as they appear in a wall-face is little or no guide to date, owing to the fact that many of the sharp points of the triangles were broken off before the bricks were used—a thing very easily done in the process of loading and unloading. Thus in all Roman brickwork the visible lengths vary very much, according as more or less of the points was broken off; see above, fig. 7, in vol. i. p. 56.

(D.) *Facing of opus mixtum.*

Opus mixtum. This is a modern term used for a variety of concrete facing, which did not come into use till the close of the third century A.D.; the usual facing of triangular bricks, in this sort of work, is varied by bands at regular intervals of small rectangular blocks of tufa, about 10 inches long by 4 deep, and tailing 3 to 5 inches into the concrete backing.

The earliest existing example is to be seen in the outer wall of the Circus of Maxentius, built about 310 A.D. by the emperor in memory of his deified infant son Romulus.

It also occurs in the latest alterations of the Flavian Palace, and in the Stadium on the Palatine, both probably executed c. 510 A.D. in the time of Theodoric, after whose reign, during some centuries, the destruction of existing buildings, rather than the erection of new ones, occupied the degenerate inhabitants of ancient Rome.

Support for all concrete. In all the above-mentioned varieties of walling, whether the facing was of opus reticulatum, brick, or opus mixtum, the main concrete mass appears to have been temporarily supported by wooden framing, arranged in the way described for the unfaced concrete walls.[1] This was necessary to prevent the thin facing from being pushed out by the semi-fluid concrete.

With regard to the statement that in Rome the bricks used in walls are always *triangular* in shape and were employed only for *facing*, it should be noted that modern rectangular bricks, very like the old ones in appearance, have been largely used within recent years to repair many ancient walls and to protect their top surfaces from the rain. This is very liable to mislead the observer. The fact really is that wherever rectangular bricks occur in an ancient wall in Rome they may safely be taken for modern additions.[2]

Triangular bricks.

The result of the Roman system of concrete building was a far superior permanence and durability of structure than could ever have been gained by true brickwork or masonry.

Great strength of concrete.

In some cases a wall remains hanging (as it were) in the air when its lower part has been cut away.

A very striking example of this is to be seen in the Thermae of Caracalla, at a place where a brick-faced concrete wall originally rested on a marble entablature supported by two granite columns. In the sixteenth century the columns and the marble architrave over them were removed for use in other buildings, and yet the wall above them remains hanging like a curtain from the concrete vault overhead.

Hanging wall.

Another remarkable instance exists in the Basilica of Constantine, where the column which was under the springing of part of the vault of the great hall has been removed,[3] and yet

---

[1] See above, fig. 3, p. 48.

[2] Adamy, *Architektonik des Alterthums*, 1883, vol. ii. p. 100, gives a good drawing showing the construction of a Roman concrete vault, but that at p. 96 is quite imaginary; it shows a wall of solid brickwork faced with triangular bricks such as was never built in Rome.

[3] This column now stands in the piazza at the east end of S. Maria Maggiore, forming the pedestal of a very poor statue of the Virgin.

an enormous mass of concrete vault remains, with no support under it, simply adhering laterally to the top of the wall.

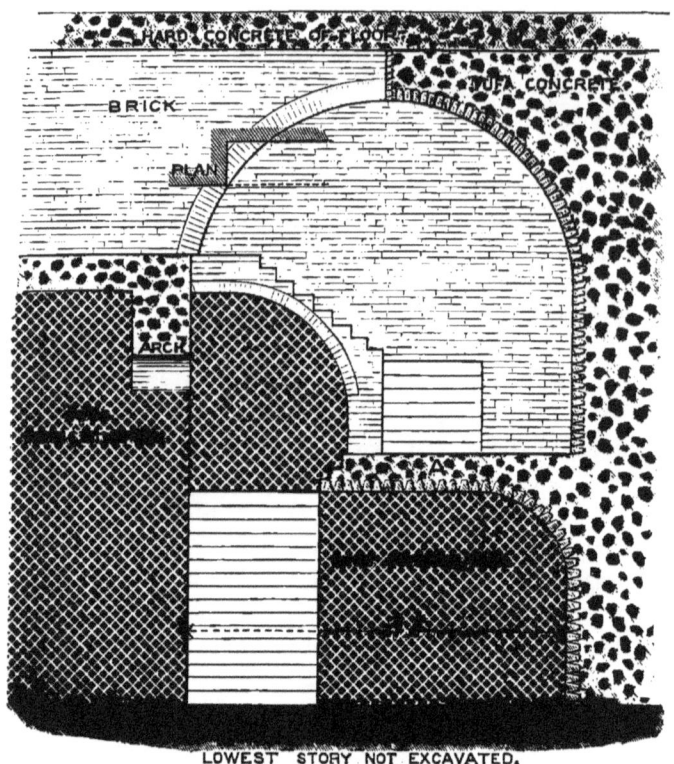

Fig. 10.

Illustrates the wonderful strength of the Roman concrete, which in this staircase is treated exactly as if it were one solid block of stone. The landing A projects from the wall, having no support at one edge. The lower part is faced with opus reticulatum, the upper part with brick.

Concrete stairs.   In other cases stairs of concrete exist with none but a lateral support, as, for example, on the Palatine Hill near the

south-west angle of the "Wall of Romulus"; see fig. 10. *Concrete stairs.*
Countless other examples can be seen which show the extraordinary advantages of this method of construction.[1]

One remarkable proof of the exceptional strength of the Roman methods of building is the fact that little or no signs of settlement are to be seen in any of the chief existing structures, even when they are built on alluvial soil.

One reason for this is the extreme care that was taken to make a solid foundation of masonry and concrete, as, for example, in the case of the Temple of Castor; see vol. i. p. 278. *Foundations.*

Here, and in other Roman temples, the whole *podium* is practically one solid mass of enormous strength and power of resistance to crushing strains. In buildings of a different kind, such as the great *Thermae*, the whole area is usually covered with a massive series of substructions resting on a thick bed of concrete which binds the whole together and distributes the upper weight over the whole area of the building. Again, the concrete used for the Roman walls and vaults was so hard and well set that each building behaved very much as if it had been cut out of one mass of stone, and if any settlement did take place the whole structure went down together. In such a building as the Pantheon, with concrete walls nearly 20 feet thick, a considerable amount of settlement, even of an unequal kind, might take place without rending the solid mass of concrete wall, bound together by its concrete vault. Lastly, in most cases the Roman builders were careful to carry their concrete foundations deep below the ground level if the upper layer of earth were at all yielding. *Solidity of concrete.* *Foundations.*
It was not uncommon for buildings in Rome to have founda-

[1] These facts are a sufficient reason for not giving the name *rubble* to the concrete construction of the Romans. No rubble wall would hold together if its lower part were removed. Moreover, a rubble wall would not be *cast* in a wooden mould, as is shown above at p. 48.

VOL. I   5

tions under each wall reaching as much as 15 to 20 feet below the ground.

If, however, the whole area of the building was covered by a solid mass like that shown in fig. 36,[1] it was not usual to carry the foundation deep below the ground as in those cases where the concrete foundations were only under the walls.[2]

Concrete vaults.

Concrete Vaults. The Roman use of concrete for vaults was even more striking and more daring than their use of it for walls, and had a very important effect upon the general forms adopted by the Roman architects under the Empire.

Absence of thrust.

As the use of buttresses had not been systematised, it would have been impossible for the Romans to build and vault their enormous spans if they had used vaulting of brick or masonry, such as were built in mediaeval times. The Roman concrete vault was quite devoid of any lateral thrust, and covered its space with the rigidity of a metal lid. Such vaults as those over the chief halls of the great Thermae would at once have pushed out their supporting walls if a true arched construction had been used. But by using the form without the principle of the arch these apparently daring structures stood with perfect safety. It is true that in many cases, such as the Basilica of Constantine, and the Thermae of

Superficial arches.

Caracalla and Diocletian, brick arches are embedded in the concrete vaults at various points, especially at the intersection of two vaults, but, just as in the brick facing of the walls these arches are merely superficial, and only tail a few inches into the mass of concrete vault, which very frequently is as much as 6 feet thick.

The elaborate drawings published by Fergusson and Violet-le-duc in their treatises on Roman construction are wholly

[1] The Temple of Castor ; see vol. i. p. 278.

[2] The method of building, during the Imperial period, with thin marble facing slabs made it especially important to have secure foundations. Any settlement in a wall would have made its marble lining fly off in all directions.

misleading from their not recognising the superficial character of these brick arches in the concrete vaults.[1]

Most serious catastrophes would have occurred if the Romans had really built in the way suggested by these writers. *Absence of thrust.*

An example of this on a smaller scale is shown in vol. ii. p. 168, where the vault C, over the peristyle walk of Caracalla's Thermae, has no cross-tie at its springing, although one side simply rests on a row of marble columns, which would at once have been pushed outward if the vault above them had been a true arch.

As mentioned above, the concrete for these vaults is frequently made of the very light pumice stone; but when an upper floor rested on the vault, a bed of concrete made with hard stone, about a foot or more thick, was laid on the top of the pumice concrete to form a level surface for the cement *nucleus* of the mosaic or marble floor; see C in fig. 78. *Upper floors.*

Centering. Wooden centering of immense size and strength must have been required to receive the mass of concrete required for the vaults of the large halls; and great mechanical skill and ingenuity were, no doubt, displayed in the construction of these enormous timber framings. Prints left on the surface of existing vaults show various methods of covering the extrados of the centering, so that the semi-fluid concrete should not fall through. In the ambulatories of the Colosseum we see the print of wooden boards about 10 inches wide. In the sub-vaults of Constantine's basilica the impress of a sort of thatch of reeds is left. *Wood centering.*

In parts of the Thermae of Caracalla, and elsewhere, small square tiles were laid flat over the top of the centering; when

---

[1] In M. Choisy's beautiful work, *L'art de bâtir chez les Romains*, more importance is given to the constructional use of brick than it really possesses in Rome itself. Outside of Italy the case is different, mainly owing to the absence of *pozzolana*, which made the Roman builders trust far less to the strength and coherence of their concrete.

the centering was removed these tiles remained firmly attached to the soffit of the concrete vault, and were finally covered by a coat of ornamental stucco.

Centering for concrete. Fig. 11 shows a not uncommon late Roman method of arranging the centering of wide arches so that it was not

Fig. 11.
Method of forming concrete and brick arches on centering which rests on the impost of the arch at A.
When the centering was removed the ledge was filled up by the addition of the bit of brickwork at B, thus giving the opening the form of a segmental arch, not a complete semicircle.

necessary to support it all the way up from the ground. The springing or impost of the arch was formed with an offset (A on fig. 11), and then, when the arch was finished and the centering removed, the angle B was filled in with concrete and brick to match the rest of the wall. This explains why so many Roman arches of the third and fourth centuries A.D. appear not to be complete semicircles, as, for example, is the case in the existing arches of the *Basilica of Constantine*.

In building arches with solid stone *voussoirs* another method *Centering for stone.*

Fig. 12.

Centering for stone arches supported on corbels, so as to enable the arch to be built with the small amount of centering shown in this drawing.

was often adopted to diminish the amount of centering which was required; see fig. 12. Up to the points AA the springing of the arch was built without centering, each *voussoir* tailing into the wall so as to have sufficient support without the aid of centering.[1] Then, at the level AA, projecting cor-

[1] This principle was adopted by Brunelleschi when he performed the wonderful feat of building the great dome of the Florentine Cathedral

Stone corbels.

bels were built in, worked out of the same blocks as the adjacent *voussoirs* CE; on these corbels the small amount of centering required for the remainder of the arch was constructed.

In other cases complete centering was used, resting on similar corbels at the springing of the arch. These corbels were allowed to remain in case of repairs or rebuilding of the arch being needed. Examples of these are mentioned in vol. ii. p. 367.

Barrel vaults.

The great concrete "barrel vaults" (*camerae*) in the buildings of the Imperial period were very commonly decorated with deeply sunk panels or "coffers" (*lacunaria*), which were copied from the marble *lacunaria* over the peristyles of Greek temples. One of the best existing examples in Rome of these richly decorated vaults is in the Palatine Palace of Hadrian, described in vol. i. p. 213. Fig. 13 shows a section and elevation of one of the panels. The mass of the vault is of pure concrete, and all the visible surface is lined with fine *caementum marmoreum*. The angle of each offset of the coffer is decorated with an enriched moulding in similar marble-dust stucco, and the whole was covered with brilliant colour and gilding. Pliny (*Hist. Nat.* xxxiii. 57) speaks of gilding being used even for the *laquearia* and *camerae* of private houses.[1]

Concrete floors.

In the second and third century A.D. the Roman builders, having learnt by experience how very strong a substance their concrete was, used it in some cases in the most strikingly daring way. For example, in the upper part of the palace of

without using any kind of centering. To do this Brunelleschi had the bricks, of which the dome is constructed, moulded into a form like that of the stone *voussoirs* at E in fig. 12.

[1] *Laquearia* are flat panelled ceilings of wood: *camerae* being curved vaults; *lacunaria* are the sunk panels in ceilings of marble, stone, or concrete. The dome of the Pantheon is decorated in this way; see fig. 69, vol. ii. p. 131.

Severus on the Palatine, we find hollow hypocaust floors of

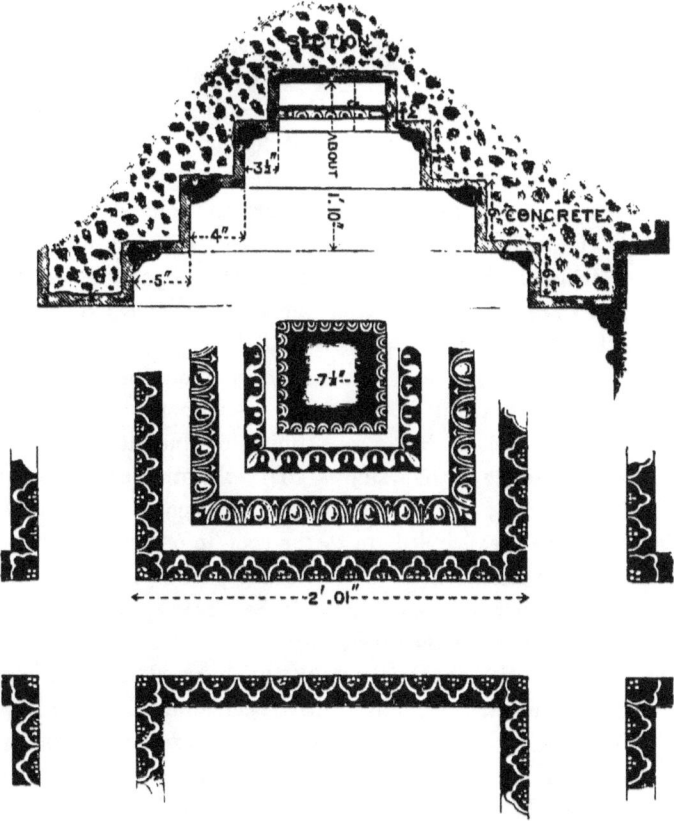

Fig. 13.

Section of one of the deeply sunk panels (*lacunaria*) in the concrete vault of a room in Hadrian's Palace, on the Palatine Hill.

The coffer is decorated with enriched mouldings in fine *caementum marmoreum*.

concrete unsupported by any of the usual *pilae* or short brick pillars. These floors consist simply of a large flat slab of concrete, about 14 inches thick, which has no support except from the adherence of its edges to the walls of the room. Even in upper floors this was done, as, for example, in the house of the Vestals (see *Archaeologia*, vol. xlix. p. 402), where a room in the first floor, over the ground-floor bath-room, had its floor formed by a flat slab of concrete, with a bearing of more than 20 feet, only supported by a row of small stone corbels along its edges. In these cases the whole concrete floor is treated exactly as if it were one solid slab of stone.[1]

Modes of heating. Fig. 65 [2] shows hypocausts in the Thermae of Caracalla, in which both methods of forming the *suspensurae* on hollow floors are shown—one after the older fashion with *pilae*, the other quite unsupported except at the edge.

This section also shows two methods of heating: one, employed for the hottest rooms, has not only the hot air under the floor, but also a lining of flue-tiles covering the whole surface of the wall (see DD); the other system was used for *tepidaria*; in this the hot air and smoke from under the hypocaust are carried up to the roof in one circular flue-pipe deeply bedded in the concrete wall; thus the walls of the chamber would be cool, the only heat being supplied from the warmth of the hollow floor.

Concrete in Italy. It should be noticed that these very daring methods of using concrete seem only to have been adopted by the Romans in Italy, where they could get the pozzolana on which the immense coherence of the concrete depended.

In other places, such as Gaul and Britain, they had to use the weaker local materials, and here we never find the hypocausts unsupported by *pilae*, or upper floors formed only of flat slabs of concrete; see Middleton in *Archaeologia*, vol. lii. p. 651 *seq.*, on "Roman Villas in Britain."

[1] The position of this room is shown on fig. 42, vol. i. p. 308.
[2] See vol. ii. p. 121.

OPUS ALBARIUM AND OTHER CEMENTS.

Cements and Stucco. The very fine kind of stucco (*tectorium*) *Wall stucco.* which Vitruvius calls *Opus albarium* or *Caementum marmoreum* [1] was among the Greeks, as it was in Rome, one of the most important of all materials used in buildings, both for practical and decorative purposes. It was made, as its name indicates, of lime mixed with powdered white marble, and tempered with water mixed with some albuminous or glutinous substance, such as white of egg, size made by boiling down parchment or the gum or sap of some tree, such as the fig tree. The lime was of the purest, whitest kind, made by burning white marble.

Pliny (*Hist. Nat.* xxxvi. 177) mentions that the walls of *Greek* the *Temple of Athene* at Elis were covered with stucco to *stucco.* receive the paintings by Panaenus, the brother of Pheidias, and that the stucco was tempered with milk mixed with saffron, the last-named substance being probably intended to tone down the white of the marble and give a creamy tint to the stucco; see also *Hist. Nat.* xxxv. 194.

Much additional strength was given to the ancient stucco by this use of milk, or other glutinous substance, instead of simple water.

Great care was taken to crush and mix the various ingredients by pounding in a wooden mortar; see Pliny, *Hist. Nat.* xxxvi. 177, and Vitr. vii. 3. 10.

Another important point was that the lime should be old, *Old lime.* and should be thoroughly well slaked by being macerated with water for some months before use; see Vitr. vii. 2. A very interesting account of the methods of preparing and laying the different kinds of stucco (*tectorium*) is given by Vitruvius, who devotes chapters 2 to 6 of his seventh book to this important subject. The result of all this care was that the marble-dust cement, *opus albarium*, had, when it was set, the *Opus albarium.*

[1] Pliny's remarks on this subject (*Hist. Nat.* xxxvi. 171 to 177), like the rest of his information on constructional matters, are nearly all taken from Vitruvius.

Opus albarium. colour and texture of real white marble, and was but little inferior to it in durability.[1] In point of hardness some ancient examples of stucco, especially from Greek buildings, even surpass real marble, and thus a coating of this substance enabled buildings of inferior stone, and even those of sun-dried bricks, to resist the weather as well as if solid marble had been used in their construction.

Both in Greece and in Rome during the Republican period all the temples that were built of stone appear to have been coated with this *caementum marmoreum*. This was the case with the Greek temples at Paestum, with those throughout Sicily, and in fact wherever stone not marble was the building material used.

When complete and decorated with the painting which was at least in part applied to all Greek and early Roman buildings, it must have been impossible, except by close examination, to distinguish one of these cemented buildings from one constructed of real marble.[2]

Crude brick. It has only been realised within quite recent years how very largely crude brick was used for the buildings of Greece and of Republican Rome. In both places for private houses crude bricks were almost universally used, and at an early period even temples of great importance were commonly constructed of the same perishable substance.[3]

[1] The same care was taken by the Italian fresco painters of the fourteenth and fifteenth centuries.

[2] It should be observed that the modern words "cement," "stucco," and "plaster" give a very wrong notion when applied to so beautiful and noble a substance as the *caementum marmoreum* of the Greeks and Romans.

[3] The Temple of Hera at Olympia was an example of this which lasted as late as the time of Pausanias. Its *cella* walls were of crude brick, and its columns were of timber, the latter being gradually replaced by stone as the wood decayed. This interesting fact has been successfully established by Dr. Dörpfeld, to whom we owe so many important discoveries.

It was solely to their coating of *caementum marmoreum* that all these countless buildings of crude brick owed their power of resisting the weather, and it must therefore be classed among the most important of the building materials of Greece and of ancient Rome.

Again, as a decorative material, especially to receive wall paintings, this cement was of no less importance. It formed the best possible substance for the painter to work on, being impervious or nearly so to damp, and just sufficiently absorbent to hold the pigments. Its surface could be worked to the highest possible smoothness, and, when required, could receive a perfect mechanical polish just as real marble does: as Vitruvius remarks (vii. 3. 9), well polished stucco would reflect like a mirror. *Painted stucco.*

The Roman *caementum*, fine as it was compared to the stuff we now call cement, was not quite equal either in beauty or hardness to the best wall-stucco of the Greeks.

Vitruvius (vii. 3. 10) speaks of slabs of old Greek cement being cut off walls to be used as marble tops for tables (*abaci*).

Another proof of the strength of this material is given by the fact that we read of Greek paintings on stucco being removed from their walls and brought safely to Rome; Pliny, *Hist. Nat.* xxxv. 154 and 173, and Vitr. ii. 8. 9. *Removal of mural paintings.*

As a rule, in Greek buildings the coating of stucco is quite thin, frequently laid on in one coat only, and of a substance not much thicker than stout cardboard.

In Rome, on the contrary, it was usually applied in many coats, and was commonly more than an inch in thickness, sometimes as much as 3 inches.

In some of the stone temples of the Republican period the mouldings and enrichments were all worked in the *caementum marmoreum*, the stone cornices and other features being only blocked out roughly in the stone and buried, as it were, in the thick mass of the cement which formed all the projecting mouldings. Examples of this can be seen among the fragments *Stucco mouldings.*

of early buildings on the Palatine Hill; and in the *Temple of Fortuna*, so called, in the *Forum Boarium*, the stone frieze of the main order was worked quite plain, and all the reliefs were modelled in the applied stucco; see vol. i. p. 161, and vol. ii. p. 190. Vitruvius (vii. 3. 3) describes the methods of forming both plain and enriched mouldings in cement, *coronae purae et caelatae*. In the following paragraph he gives directions for applying stucco to walls. In order to form a good ground for painting on, he directs that no less than six coats (*coria*) of stucco are to be applied; the first three coats (*trullissatio*) are to be of coarser "rendering" in cement made of lime and sand. The last three coats are to be of *caementum marmoreum*, each coat being composed of more finely pounded marble as it approaches the finished surface;[1] see also Vitr. vii. 6, where directions are given for pounding the marble in an iron mortar till it is not only *contusum* but *molitum*, finely powdered.

Vitruvius on stucco.

Many coats.

Each of the six coats (*coria*) of cement was carefully worked over, levelled and allowed to dry before applying the next layer.[2]

Use of gypsum.

For internal work, especially for stucco decorations in relief, it was usual to mix a certain proportion of *gypsum* (plaster of Paris) with the marble dust; see Vitr. vii. 3. 3, and Pliny, *Hist. Nat.* xxxvi. 183.

Examples of this beautiful kind of decoration are described at p. 182, and vol. ii. p. 250.

The coarser kinds of cement, used in Rome as undercoats or as backing to marble wall linings, are made of lime mixed with *pozzolana* or else with *testae tunsae*, pounded pottery; see vol. i. p. 85.

[1] See p. 93 for a further account of the preparation of stucco to receive painting.

[2] A painting in a house at Pompeii represents plasterers at work; they are using wooden "floats," exactly like those still in use; see *Ann. Inst.* vol. for 1881.

CEMENT FLOORS

The latter had the advantage of resisting damp in a very remarkable way.

In some cases a fine hard marble cement was used as paving for houses or temples. Vitruvius (vii. 4. 5) describes the process of making a floor of black cement, after the Greek fashion. First a thick bed of concrete is laid down, and then on it a layer of black cement made of lime, sand, ashes, and charcoal. When this has set it becomes hard as stone, and is then polished by rubbing down with pumice and whet-stones. Vitruvius recommends this kind of floor for use in dining-rooms, as it is, he says, easily kept clean and is not cold to the naked feet of the slaves.

Cement floors.

An interesting receipt for making fine *caementum marmoreum* after the ancient manner is given in the Bodleian MS. of Pirro Ligorio, written about 1565 A.D.[1]

"Take three parts of pounded Parian marble, easily got from among the ruins of Rome, from broken statues; add one part of lime, which is to be perfectly slaked by letting it lie in a heap, covered with *pozzolana*, and exposed to sun and rain for at least a year.

Ligorio on marble cement.

"The lime must be made from pure white marble, not from travertine or any yellowish limestone. Mix a day before it is used on a clean tile floor. The first coat is to be made with coarsely powdered marble allowed to dry thoroughly before applying the subsequent coats made with lime and finely powdered marble."

---

[1] See Middleton, *Archaeologia*, vol. li., 1889. Ligorio was one of the chief architects and antiquaries of the second half of the sixteenth century. He has left an immense mass of interesting notes on the buildings of ancient Rome; most of his MSS. are in the public library in Turin and in the Vatican library. A third collection of Ligorio's notes is in the Bodleian library, *Canonici MSS. No.* 138. It should, however, be observed that Ligorio's information must always be used with caution, especially when he quotes inscriptions, of which he appears to have invented a great number.

This receipt shows that Ligorio had both studied Vitruvius and had carefully examined ancient examples of *opus albarium*.

Inscriptions. The following inscription, which was found in 1886 by the start of the *Pons Aemilius*, records that a certain Roman covered with smooth stucco the walls and vaults of the Guild-house of the staircase-makers (*scalarii*) :—

MELLAX · VEIDIANUS · DECUR · ITER · PARIETES · ET · CAMERAS SCALARIORUM · OPERE · TECTORIO · EXPOLITUM · D · S · P · D · D (*de sua pecunia dono dedit*) C · CAESARE · L · PAVLLO · COS · (See *Bull. Com. Arch.* 1886, p. 368.)

Another inscription (*C. I. L.* vi. 10377) records a similar act of munificence :—

LUCRIO · VEDIAN · DECUR · DEDIC · SCALARIA · PRIMA · OPERE TECTORIO · EXPOLIENDA · ET · PAVIMENTUM · EODEM · LOCO · D S · F · (*de sua pecunia fecit*).

Stucco on stone. This coating of fine white marble cement appears to have been invariably applied to buildings of stone which were of an ornamental character, such as temples and the like, and, as among the Greeks,[1] even white marble was in some cases coated with a thin skin of *opus albarium*; the object of this was to afford a more absorbent ground for painted decorations than that of the marble itself; see vol. i. p. 92.

Marble linings. Even when walls of Roman buildings were to be lined with marble they were first covered with a thick coat of the coarser cement, in order to give a firm bed to hold the marble slabs. The brick wall-facings were, however, so smooth that they afforded very little hold or "key" either for the painted stucco or for the cement backing of the marble.

The modern practice of forming an uneven surface by raking out the joints of the brickwork, was not employed by

[1] The beautiful pure white Pentelic marble of the interior of the so-called "Temple of Theseus" in Athens was coated with a thin skin of similar *caementum marmoreum* to that which was used in Rome, and was then covered with pictures.

the Romans, who adopted instead a much more expensive and laborious method. This was to drive large iron nails at intervals into the joints of the brickwork, all over the surface of the wall, as is described above at p. 51 ; these projecting nails gave the stucco or cement a sufficient hold, and were concealed from view by the finishing coats. Very frequently small plugs of marble were driven into the wall, either alone or in conjunction with the iron nails.[1] When driven in by the side of the nails their object appears to have been to give the iron something harder than brick to bite upon. *Nails to roughen the wall.*

In fine stucco nothing but pounded white marble (*marmor minutum*) was used with the lime, but for the commoner work on the exteriors of buildings lime and sand were used (just as in modern mortar), and then washed over with limewhite, that is, a mixture of pure unslaked lime and water. A very interesting inscription, found at Puteoli, gives the combined contract and specification for building a porch with folding doors in the year 105 B.C. ; see *Cor. In. Lat.* i. p. 163. The wall (*paries*) is to be stuccoed *calce harenato*, with lime and sand, and then whitened with a wash of lime and water, *calce uda*[2] *dealbata*. *Coarser stucco.*

A specially hard kind of cement, called *opus signinum* (Vitr. viii. 6), or else *opus e testis tunsis*, was made of lime and *pozzolana* mixed with pounded brick or pottery.[3] It was *Opus signinum.*

[1] It is very easy to overlook these iron nails, as their projecting part has usually rusted away, but a close examination will reveal their stumps, or the stains left by them, in almost all cases when brick-faced walls in Rome were either covered with stucco or cement backing behind marble slabs. The marble plugs are more visible, and can be seen in a very large number of the buildings of ancient Rome. In *opus reticulatum* the nails were not always used ; but instead of this the surface of the tufa squares was slightly pecked over in order to roughen it and so hold the stucco.

[2] Calx is made both masculine and feminine in this inscription. The Roman phrase meaning "to play fast and loose" is *duos parietes dealbare* ; Cic. *ad Fam.* vii. 29.

[3] Enormous quantities of this were used, and *Monte Testaceio* was

Opus signinum. specially used to line the channels (*specus*) of aqueducts, cisterns, and for other hydraulic purposes, and very commonly as one of the cement layers under mosaic pavements and under-floors of *hypocausts*. It was of very great strength, and had the double advantage of perfectly resisting both water and fire, hence its use alike for aqueducts, water-tanks, furnaces, *hypocausts*, and other similar purposes.

Mosaic paving. Vitruvius (vii. 1) describes the various kinds of concrete and cement used to form a bed for marble pavings and mosaics. First, a good foundation was to be secured, in the case of ground-floor pavements, by excavating over the whole area down to firm ground and carefully levelling the surface. *Statumen.* On that the *statumen* was to be laid—a layer of broken stones each not less than what would fill a man's hand. *Rudus.* The next layer, called *rudus*, consisted of smaller stones mixed in the proportion of three to one of lime about 9 inches thick carefully rammed with wooden "beetles" to an even surface.

Nucleus. On this bed of concrete the *nucleus* was laid—a layer of cement on which the marble slabs or *tesserae* of the pavement were bedded. This *nucleus* was, like the *opus signinum*, made of pounded pottery or burnt brick (*testae*) in the proportion of three to one of lime.

Marble floor. When the marble slabs or mosaic (*sectilia seu tesserae*) had been carefully and evenly laid on this bed (*nucleus*) a fine fluid cement made with pounded marble was to be poured over the whole area of the floor (modern "grouting"), so as to fill up all the interstices between the pieces of marble; Vitr. vii. 1. 4. Finally, when the whole was set and hard the whole surface of the pavement was to be rubbed down and polished to a perfectly true level by

probably a storeheap of broken pots for use in making *opus signinum*. This wonderful mound consists chiefly of broken *amphorae* and other coarse pottery in which provisions had been imported for storage in the neighbouring vast range of *emporia* and *horrea*.

friction with sand and water and by using various kinds of rubbers.[1]

The whole process is described with great detail by Vitruvius, *loc. cit.* His description agrees accurately with existing examples of Roman mosaics; but in many cases the fine marble cement is used to bed as well as to grout the *tesserae*.

Most of the rest of this interesting chapter (vii. 1) is devoted to a description of how mosaic pavements are to be laid on the wooden floors of upper stories (*contignationes*). No ancient examples of this now exist, though mediaeval and modern floors of this kind are common throughout Italy. In the main the process was the same in both cases, except that the lower bed of rough concrete was omitted. A double layer of oak boards, crossways, was to be nailed on the floor joists, and over the boards a bed of straw or dried fern to protect the wood from contact with the lime in the cement *rudus*. Pliny's remarks on this subject (*Hist. Nat.* xxxvi. 186) are copied from Vitruvius. *Upper floors.*

Pavements made with a surface of hard white or black cement, made of coarsely pounded marble, or with lime and sand mixed with charcoal, have been described above. For an example in the *House of the Pontifex* see vol. i. p. 303.

For common floors the square *tegulae bipedales* were very frequently used, and also small bricks, about 4 inches long by 1 wide, set on edge herring-bone fashion; this was called *opus spicatum*, from *spica*, an ear of bearded wheat; see Vitr. vii. 1. 4. *Brick floors.*

Mosaics; opus musivum. Among the various methods of decoration used by the Romans none were of greater importance than the many kinds of mosaic (*opus musivum*) which *Mosaic floors.*

[1] One of these rubbers for finishing mosaic floors has been found at Silchester and is now in the little museum there. It consists of a smooth slab of white marble about 9 by 5 inches with an iron handle fixed with lead at the back.

82   GREEK MOSAIC   CHAP.

were employed for every part of a room, floors, walls, and ceilings or vaults.

Pebble mosaic. Like most architectural forms of decoration used in Rome, the art of mosaic-working was derived from the Greeks, among whom simple forms of mosaic were in use at a very early period. In its earliest form Greek mosaic (λιθόστρωτα) consists simply of river-worn pebbles stuck in the upper surface of concrete and cement floors, as, for example, in the prehistoric palaces at Mycenae and Tiryns.

Mosaic patterns. The next stage was to select pebbles of different colours and arrange them in their concrete bed so as to form patterns, as we see in the pronaos of the Temple of Zeus at Olympia, built in the fifth century B.C.[1] A further development was to use roughly squared bits of stone (*tesserae*) instead of the river-worn pebbles, and this later form is the one which was mainly adopted by the Romans.

Mosaics in Rome. Much interesting information about the early use of mosaic in Rome is given by Pliny (*Hist. Nat.* xxxvi. 184 to 189), but his remarks about the practical method of forming mosaic floors are copied from Vitruvius, vii. 1 and 4. According to Pliny the use of mosaic was introduced into Italy by Sulla, c. 85 B.C. The various kinds of Roman mosaic-work may be classified under these heads—

Chief varieties. I.—*Opus tesselatum* or *vermiculatum* made of squared *tesserae*, *calculi*, or *abaci* of stone, marble, or glass, arranged so as to form patterns or even pictures.[2]

II.—*Opus sectile*, made of thin pieces of marble or porphyry cut into shapes to suit the pattern; see vol. i. p. 202. A very rich variety of this, much used under the later Empire, was known as *opus Alexandrinum*, so

---

[1] In the temple of the Pythian Apollo at Delphi a mosaic representation of two eagles was worked (ἀπὸ συνθέσεως λίθων) in the pavement where the sacred *Omphalos* stood; see Scholiast on Lucian, Περὶ ὀρχήσεως, 38, quoted by the present writer in *Jour. Hell. Stud.* ix. p. 295.

[2] See Lucilius quoted by Cicero, *Orator*. 149.

called, according to one story, from its having been introduced into Rome by the Emperor Severus Alexander, but it was used in Rome some years earlier than his reign. Another name for this shaped mosaic was *opus scutulatum*; Pliny, *Hist. Nat.* xxxvi. 185.

III.—*Opus spicatum*, not a true mosaic, but merely a sort of paving made with small bricks laid on their edges in herring-bone fashion.

The most magnificent sort of mosaic, used in Rome in the most profuse way during the Imperial period, was made with brilliantly coloured glass *tesserae*, looking like false jewels, ruby, emerald, turquoise, and the like.

The glass mosaics were mostly used to decorate walls and vaults, not floors. An example of this in the *crypto-porticus* leading to the Flavian Palace on the Palatine Hill is mentioned in vol. i. p. 197.

The earliest recorded example of the use of glass mosaic in Rome was on the *scena* of the *Theatre of Scaurus*; see Pliny, *Hist. Nat.* xxxvi. 114 and 189.

Its use for vaults (*camerae*), Pliny thinks, came in later, or else if it had been known Agrippa would certainly have used it to decorate the ceilings of his magnificent *Thermae*; see Pliny, *loc. cit.*

The glass mosaics on Roman walls were frequently large and elaborate pictures with many figures executed with great skill and minuteness. Among the most remarkable examples is the mosaic with three doves sitting on the rim of a gold bowl, found in Hadrian's Villa near Tibur, and now in the Capitoline Museum. This mosaic, apart from its exceptionally skilful workmanship, is interesting from the fact that it is evidently a Roman copy of a Greek mosaic at Pergamus which is described by Pliny, *Hist. Nat.* xxxvi. 184.

Among the many fine glass mosaics found at Pompeii one with a theatrical scene is noticeable from its having the signature of its Greek artist, ΔΙΟΣΚΟΥΡΙΔΗΣ ΣΑΜΙΟΣ ΕΠΟΙΗΣΕ.

Defeat of Darius. Another large mosaic from Pompeii is of exceptional importance as representing a historical scene, *The Defeat of Darius by Alexander* at the battle of Issus, in 333 B.C., and also because it probably preserves for us the general design and composition of an important picture by some famous Greek painter. It may possibly be a copy of the defeat of Darius painted by Philoxenus of Eretria which is mentioned by Pliny, *Hist. Nat.* xxxv. 110.

Sectile mosaic. Glass *sectile* mosaic of the most elaborate kind was also used to decorate the walls of Roman buildings, each bit of coloured glass being accurately shaped to fit its position in the picture. The whole effect was of the most gorgeous and jewel-like kind. As late as the sixteenth century a building existed in Rome with large areas of wall entirely decorated in this magnificent way with figures of deities, men, and animals, all executed in *opus sectile*. A drawing of this made in the sixteenth century before its destruction has fortunately preserved a record of this wonderful mosaic. A facsimile of it, together with a valuable article on the whole subject of Roman sectile mosaic, is published in *Archaeologia*, vol. xlv. 1879.

Most of the glass used for mosaics both of *opus tesselatum* and *sectile* is not transparent, but has been made into an opaque enamel by the addition of a small proportion of oxide of tin to the other metallic oxides, mostly copper or iron, which give the brilliant colours to the glass.

Painted walls. Vitruvius gives many interesting details about the manner of painting on stucco walls (vii. 5 and 6): this was done to a certain extent on the last coat while it was wet, like the mediaeval *fresco buono*, but the minute details and finishing touches were usually applied *a secco*; Vitr. vii. 3; see vol. i. p. 94. The lime used was thoroughly slaked and soaked for a long time, that it might not injure the pigments, and with it were mixed both gypsum (plaster of Paris) and powdered marble. This is described more at length at vol. i. p. 93.

In damp places Vitruvius (vii. 4) recommends the walls to be built hollow, as is done in the *Triclinium* of the "House of Livia"; see vol. i. p. 180. .In cap. 5 he describes the various styles of painted decoration; and reprobates the modern custom of representing monsters instead of real objects, and sham architectural subjects with slender reeds and candelabra holding up impossible heavy entablatures—a method of mural decoration which is very common in the houses of Pompeii, and is certainly in the worst possible taste. *Hollow walls.*

Marble linings were usually fixed with great care, and were tied to the wall with long hook-like clamps, the ends of which were fixed with melted lead if the wall was of stone, or if of brick they were wedged into joints. These clamps were usually of iron, but in the more careful work bronze was used. Fig. 15 gives an example of the manner of fixing marble linings, dating from the reign of Augustus; see also fig. 14, on p. 86. The slabs were cut into thin pieces with saws and sand and water, emery being used for the harder stones;[1] see Pliny, *Hist. Nat.* xxxvi. 51 to 54. In cap. 48 Pliny states that sawn slabs of marble were first used in the time of J. Caesar, in Mamurra's house on the Caelian; see vol. i. p. 14. *Marble linings.*

As a rule a considerable thickness of cement backing was laid between the marble slabs and the brick facing which, in most cases, exists behind the marble. Sometimes this bedding *Cement backing.*

---

[1] The drills which were used in working the hard granites and porphyries were both solid and tubular—some as much as 3½ inches in diameter. The circular markings on the sides of drilled holes show by the rapidity of their spirals that the drill must have sunk into the hard granites with wonderful speed. Diamond drills were used by the Egyptians at a very early period, and their use was probably introduced into Rome from Egypt along with the porphyries and granites; see Flinders Petrie, "Mechanical Processes of Ancient Egypt," in the *Jour. Anthrop. Inst.*, August 1883.

Fig. 14.

This drawing shows a common Roman way of arranging the marble wall-linings in panels.

It is taken from a room in the *excubitorium* of the seventh cohort of *Vigiles*; see vol. ii. p. 258. What is defective in the *excubitorium* is supplied from a similar marble-lined wall in the *Atrium Vestae*. Both date from about the middle of the second century A.D.

A shows the marble lining (D in the section), each panel being framed by a thin projecting "bead" or rounded slip of white marble about an inch wide; see C in the section. B shows the cement backing (F in the section) with its surface studded with fragments of marble, slate or tile, E in the section. HH shows the brickwork in section behind the cement and the marble slabs. See also vol. i. p. 14.

of cement made of lime and pozzolana is as much as from 3 to 4 inches thick; see figs. 14 and 15.

It is impossible fully to realise the amount of rich marbles which ancient Rome contained. For more than three centuries marbles, alabasters, and porphyries in endless variety were

Foreign marbles.

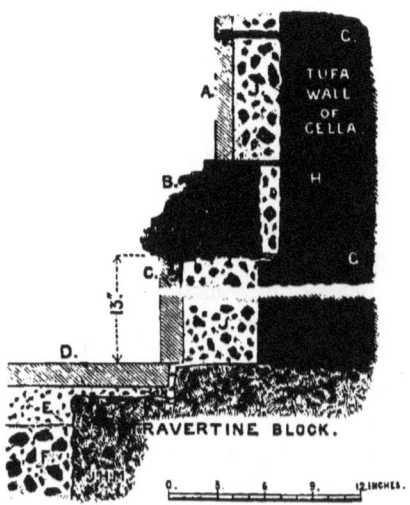

Fig. 15.

Example of marble lining, from the Cella of the Temple of Concord.

    A. Slabs of Phrygian marble.
    B. Plinth moulding of Numidian "Giallo."
    C. Slab of Cipollino (Carystian marble).
    D. Paving of Porta Santa.
    E and F. "Nucleus" and "rudus" of concrete bedding.
    GG. Iron clamps run with lead to fix marble lining.
    H. Bronze clamp.
    JJ. Cement backing.

being dug out in countless Oriental quarries by whole armies of workmen, and were constantly being poured into Rome. Scarcely a church or a palace in Rome is without columns and wall-linings all taken from ancient buildings. The great

88   BUILDING ACTS   CHAP.

Christian Basilicas, and especially the more magnificent private chapels, such as those of the *Corsini*, *Borghese*, and *Cibo* families, owe their splendour entirely to these stolen marbles. Even the immense quantity which still exists gives no notion whatever of what Rome once possessed; by far the greater quantity perished in the limekilns of the Early Middle Ages.

Raphael's report.   As Raphael said in his report to Leo X. on the best methods of preserving the ruins of classical Rome, almost every house in the whole city was built with lime made of the beautiful marbles which were once the glory of Rome.[1]

During the Republican period it is probable that by far the majority of the private houses were built to a great extent of perishable and combustible materials.

Building Acts.   In the reign of Augustus a "Metropolitan Building Act" was drawn up, which did something to improve the stability of Roman houses. Some of the provisions of this Act are mentioned by Vitruvius (ii. 8. 17). Houses in streets, if several stories in height, were to be built "*pilis lapideis, structuris testaceis, parietibus caementitiis*," that is, "on stone piers, or with walls of burnt brick and concrete," instead of the older method of building walls of *lateres*, crude bricks, or of woodwork filled in with "wattle and dab," *cratitii*; see Vitr. ii. 8. 20. In some respects the Roman houses of the Republican period, and under the early Empire, must have resembled those of mediaeval times, especially in the frequent use of upper stories, formed of wood framing (*contignationes*), which projected forwards into the street beyond the line of the wall below. Examples of these projecting upper stories have been found at Pompeii.

Limit of thickness.   In order, therefore, to put an end to the custom of building thick, weak walls of crude, unfired brick, a law was introduced limiting the external thickness of street walls to 2 feet, a thickness which was not sufficient to support upper

[1] Visconti has published this interesting letter: see *Una lettera di Raffaello a Leone X.*, Rome, 1834.

stories if unbaked bricks were used. The practical result of this enactment, which seems a strange one, was thus indirectly to force on the people the use of the stronger materials. Houses shored up with wood and ready to fall are mentioned by Juvenal (*Sat.* iii. 193), and a great part of Rome for a long period consisted of very flimsy and even dangerous structures.

It was, however, not till the reign of Nero that a complete reform was effected in the construction of Roman houses. Nero had a new and elaborate building Act drawn up requiring fireproof materials, such as *peperino*, to be used for external walls of houses; and it appears very probable that he wilfully caused the great fire which destroyed a large part of Rome, in order that he might with effect bring his new Act into operation, and also be able to re-plan the streets on wider and straighter lines; see Suet. *Nero*, 38, and Tac. *Ann.* xv. 38.[1]

Nero's Act.

The Comm. Lanciani has pointed out (*Anc. Rome*, p. 122) the care with which Nero's preparations were made for the wholesale rebuilding of Rome. He employed two architects, named Severus and Celer, to draw out a plan for new streets, public squares, and great *cloacae*, arranged in as regular a form as the uneven level of the site of Rome would allow. All the details of construction and material were thoughtfully provided for. No houses were to be higher than double the width of the street. Unburnt brick and wood were to be replaced by stronger and more fireproof materials.[2]

Scheme for a new Rome.

[1] For the rules of the various building trades see Mommsen, *De Collegiis Rom.* 1843; Heineccius, *De Collegiis Opificum*, in *Sylloge Opusc. var.*; and Roth, *De re municipali Rom.*, Stuttgart, 1801. A new Act was drawn up in Trajan's reign, limiting the height of street houses to 60 feet (see Aur. Victor. *Epit.* 13). An interesting collection of the provisions of various Roman Building Acts is published in the *Mus. Class. Ant.*, 1851, vol. i. pp. 305 to 352; a translation of an article by H. E. Dirksen, Berlin, 1844.

[2] The constant destruction of the houses in Rome, both from fire and

90   GREAT FIRES   CHAP.

Great fire.   We are also told by Tacitus that Nero secretly provided great quantities of tents and booths, ready to shelter the houseless people after the fire which he had determined to cause, and he also arranged for the arrival at Ostia of a number of corn-ships to feed the homeless citizens. When all was ready, Rome was set on fire at many different places, and three out of the fourteen *regiones* were completely destroyed, thus clearing a great space in which the new building scheme could be carried out. The great *Gardens of Nero*, probably those by the Vatican Hill, were devoted, Tacitus tells us, to the temporary housing of the occupants of the burnt dwellings; see Tac. *Ann.* xv. 38 to 43.

Altar on the Quirinal.   After the terrible fire in Nero's reign a number of altars were dedicated in various parts of Rome as an appeal for divine protection against fire. In 1889 one of these altars was discovered while digging the foundations of a new house, near the Church of S. Andrea on the Quirinal. The altar is built of large blocks of travertine, and was covered with slabs of marble. It measures about 21 feet long by 10 feet wide. It stands in the middle of an open area paved with large slabs of travertine, approached by steps from the ancient road *Alta Semita*, under the modern Via del Quirinale; see *Bull. Com. Arch.* 1890, pp. 331 and 379, and Tav. x. In 1640 an interesting inscription was discovered which records the erection of an altar by Domitian in fulfilment of a vow made *quando urbs per novem dies arsit Neronianis temporibus.* It is published by Lanciani, *Bull. Com. Arch.* 1889, pp. 331 to 339.

Causes of fires.   It seems somewhat strange that a city like Rome should have suffered so much from repeated conflagrations, in which not only houses but even temples and other buildings of the same kind were burnt—structures which seem, when we now look at their remains, to consist wholly of non-combustible

from their falling down through weakness of construction, is mentioned by Plutarch, *Crass.* 2; see also Juv. iii. 193.

substances. We must, however, take into account the fact that Roman buildings of all kinds were roofed with timber, and remember that the burning of a wooden roof is quite sufficient to destroy, or at least very greatly to injure, a building in which no other part is of a combustible nature. The destruction of the nave of the grand old Basilica of S. Paolo fuori le mura in 1823 was a sad example of this. *Wooden roofs.*

Probably the only building in Rome of any importance which was wholly constructed without wood was the *Pantheon*; and it certainly is inexplicable (as Comm. Lanciani has pointed out) how such a building can have been injured by fire, as is said to have been the case in the reign of Titus and again in Trajan's time.

Repeated injury done to the *Colosseum* and the *Circus Maximus* is explained by the presence of extensive upper galleries of wooden framing, which, when they caught fire, would burn with enormous heat and rapidity; the blazing beams would fall down the slope of the *cavea*, and would quickly turn the marble columns and wall-linings into lime. *Wooden galleries.*

TECHNICAL METHODS EMPLOYED IN THE MURAL PAINTINGS OF ROME.[1]

Wall-paintings were executed either on a thick coat of stucco, or on stone or marble thinly coated with stucco, or less commonly on slabs of terra-cotta. In the latter case the colours were probably such as would stand fire, and so could be fixed on the surface of the clay by a second baking. This method was probably derived from the Etruscans, whose tombs were frequently ornamented with large slabs of painted earthenware, of which fine specimens are preserved in the Louvre and *Paintings on clay.*

[1] On Roman paintings see Helbig and Donner, *Die Campanische Wandmalerei*, 1873. A large and very fine collection of Roman wall-paintings, discovered during recent building operations, is preserved in the great cloister of the Museo delle Terme.

Paintings on clay. in the British Museum. Some of these slabs are nearly 6 feet long, and must have required great skill to fire them without their being warped out of shape. It is probably to this kind of painting that Pliny (*Hist. Nat.* xxxvi. 189) alludes in describing the manner in which Agrippa decorated his *Thermae—figulinum opus encausto pinxit in calidis, reliqua albario adornavit*; that is to say, that in the hot rooms encaustic pictures on baked clay were used, while in the other rooms the paintings were on white stucco. The more durable paintings on clay were no doubt used for the hot rooms in order that they might not be injured by the condensed steam and the heat of the furnace beneath.

Priming on marble. Even when the surface to be decorated was of white marble it was not uncommon to cover the surface with a thin coat or priming of stucco made of lime and powdered marble, in order to supply to the painter a more absorbent surface than that of the hard marble; this was called *opus albarium*, and stone or marble so treated was called *dealbatum*; see vol. i. p. 282.

This was also the practice of the Greeks; the Cella of the so-called *Theseion* in Athens has still remains on the massive Pentelic blocks of its interior of a thin stucco priming (λεύκωμα), on which a series of mural paintings were executed. Similar priming is used on the white marble Sarcophagus from Corneto in the Florentine Museum, which is decorated with a fine series of paintings of a fight between the Greeks and the Amazons. Though this Sarcophagus was found in an Etruscan tomb its paintings are mainly Hellenic, both in design and in execution; see *Jour. Hell. Stud.* vol. iv. p. 354, and Pl. xxxvi.-xxxviii.

Stucco for painting. *Preparation of stucco for mural painting.* In the case of private houses in Rome the wall-paintings were usually executed on stucco applied in three to five coats, and prepared in the most careful way. If the wall was thought likely to be damp it was often covered with flanged tiles fixed with iron T clamps, or built with an air-cavity extending over its whole area, as is recommended by Vitruvius, vii. 4. 1 and 2; this is the case in the Palatine house; see vol. i. p. 180.

A very minute account is given by Vitruvius (vii. 3) of the manner of preparing and laying the stucco to receive wall-paintings. It is needless to quote Pliny's remarks on this subject, and that of pigments and vehicles (*Hist. Nat.* xxxiii. 122), as they are simply copied from Vitruvius (vii. caps. 3 to 14), in some cases word for word.[1]

Various coats.

The first coat (*corium*) of stucco was of lime and coarse *pozzolana*, exactly the same as the mortar used in the joints of brick facings. Over this rough coat another layer was spread, often made with lime, sand, and finely crushed pottery, *testae tunsae*. The third coat was of coarsely pounded white marble, lime, and sand, the next of marble more finely crushed without sand, and the finishing coat of pure white lime mixed with almost impalpable marble dust, which set very hard and received a polish as brilliant as that of real marble. The lime itself, to insure absolute purity of colour, or rather absence of colour, was made by burning white marble.

Six-coat stucco.

To make the best sort of *tectorium* Vitruvius recommends six coats to be applied, the first three of the coarser kinds of stucco, and the last three of the stucco made with pounded marble; *ita cum tribus coriis arenae, et item marmoris solidati parietes fuerint.* The first coats are called *trullisatio*, modern "rendering coat." The instructions given by Vitruvius (vii. 3. 6) are illustrated by most of the existing specimens of wall-stucco in Rome. Many of these show five or six successive coats, such as are described above, but in the commoner houses or inferior rooms less care was taken, and in these there are frequently only three coats of stucco. A great part of the brilliance of the Roman coloured grounds on stucco depends on a mechanical polish, the stucco being so hard that it could be polished exactly as if it had been a slab of real marble;

Polished stucco.

[1] Pliny usually quotes his authority, but in the case of his frequent borrowings from Vitruvius he has not done so.

see Vitr. vii. 3. 9, and ii. 8. 10, where he speaks of stucco being polished till it reflects like a mirror. See also vii. 6. 1, on the pounding and grinding of the marble dust.

The whole mass of stucco, including all the coats, was called (*opus*) *tectorium*; the layer made of pounded pottery was *opus e testis tunsis*; and the white finishing coats were called *opus albarium* or *caementum marmoreum*.[1]

Stucco mouldings. The mouldings and other reliefs were made of mixed powdered marble and gypsum—plaster of Paris, but this mixture could only be used for internal work, as it would not stand the weather; Vitr. vii. 3. 3. Vitruvius distinguishes plain mouldings, *coronae purae*, from enriched mouldings, *coronae caelatae*, the former being, he says, more suited for winter *triclinia*, as they are more easily kept clean from the smoke and dust produced by braziers.

The paintings on the prepared stucco were executed in many different ways, and with a great variety of vehicles.

These methods may be divided into four kinds :—

I. *Fresco*; II. *Tempera*; III. *Varnish paintings*, resembling modern painting in oil; IV. *Encaustic*.

True fresco. I. *Udo tectorio.* The first of these methods, true *fresco*, or *fresco buono* as it is called in Italy, is mentioned by Vitruvius, vii. 3. 7,—*colores autem udo tectorio cum diligenter sunt inducti, ideo non remittunt*, " but when the colours are carefully laid on moist stucco, then they do not fade."

This true *fresco* appears, judging from existing examples, to have been chiefly used for the plain colouring of large surfaces, or for the grounds of figure subjects.

The colour applied to the wet surface of a freshly applied patch of *opus albarium* sank slightly into the stucco, and stained a thin skin extending below the surface, so that it could receive a mechanical polish without the colour being rubbed off, as would have been the case if it had merely rested on the surface. This sinking of the pigment below the sur-

[1] For a further description of marble-dust stucco see above, vol. i. p. 76.

face can be traced in many existing examples of Roman painting.

Only earth or mineral pigments could be used for this work on wet stucco, owing to the corrosive properties of wet lime, hence the colours were limited in number, and had not brilliance enough of tint to please the Romans, who delighted in gaudy hues; on this account it was not very much used, except for plain grounds. *Wet lime.*

Pigments, colores, χρώματα. The chief pigments applicable to true *fresco* which were used in ancient times were brown, yellow and red ochre, ultramarine blue (κύανος, *coeruleum*), made from *lapis lazuli*, and the artificial *coeruleum* made by colouring a vitreous frit with carbonate of copper, and then grinding the fused mass; Vitr. vii. 11. Some other varieties of natural coloured earths are mentioned by Vitruvius (vii. 7) in his chapter *de nativis coloribus*, which includes nearly all the pigments which could be used on fresh stucco.[1] *Fresco pigments.*

The more brilliant pigments used in *encaustic* or *tempera* (*fresco secco*) are described by Vitruvius, vii. 8 to 14. *Tempera pigments.*

The most important were *red lead* and *vermilion* (sulph. of mercury), to both of which the same name *minium* (μίλτος) was sometimes applied. *Ostrum*, a fine purple made from the *murex* shell-fish; *verdigris* green, and white lead.

II. *Tempera* or *distemper* paintings were executed on dry stucco, with a medium of gum, size, or the glutinous sap of the fig tree, which closely resembles the cream-like sap of the India-rubber tree. Any pigments could be used for this, but the work was perishable, and could not stand weather or damp. *Tempera painting.*

III. Another method was to use resin, bitumen, or mastic for a medium, probably dissolved in a natural mineral oil, as the Romans do not seem to have practised the distillation of *Spirit media.*

[1] The simpler earth colours used for fresco painting were called *colores austeri*; the more brilliant but less durable pigments were called *colores floridi*; see Pliny, *Hist. Nat.* xxxv. 30.

essential oils.¹ This method had the advantage of being able to resist external wet, and any pigments might be used.

Egyptian painting. In Egypt pigments were commonly used with a varnish medium; and varnishes made of some gum or amber dissolved in naphtha were used to protect the paintings with which wooden coffins are usually covered. In preparing for the painting the wood was first carefully covered with linen closely glued all over it, and then an absorbent coat of fine stucco (priming) was applied over the linen to receive the painting. Finally, one or more coats of varnish were applied.²

Wax encaustic. IV. The *Encaustic* method seems to have been that which was chiefly used by the Romans both for panel pictures and for paintings on stucco.

This process (ἔγκαυσις) was, like most Roman artistic methods, adopted from the Greeks. Many allusions occur both in Greek and Latin authors to the combined use of wax and fire, which was the essential part of encaustic painting.

Greek epigrams. This is the case with two epigrams in the *Anthologia* on the famous picture of Medea meditating the slaughter of her children, of which copies (probably) exist among the mural paintings of Pompeii—

Ἔρρε καὶ ἐν κηρῷ, παιδόκτονε· σῶν γὰρ ἀμέτρων
Ζήλων εἰς ἃ θέλεις καὶ γραφὶς αἰσθάνεται.

And again—
φεῦγε πανώλη
Μητέρα κἂν κηρῷ τεκνοφονοῦσαν ἔτι.

So Statius, *Silv.* I. i. 100, writing in praise of the Emperor's beauty, speaks of the *cerae*, the wax pigments of Apelles, as wishing to depict Domitian's form—

Apelleae cuperent te scribere cerae.

---

¹ An interesting account of the natural springs of naphtha in the districts of Babylon and Ecbatana is given by Plutarch, *Alexan.* 35.

² This is exactly the same method as that employed by the mediaeval painters in the preparation of their wood panels.

THE ENCAUSTIC OF VITRUVIUS

The point of the following epigram depends on the use of fire to fix the wax pigments, as is described below—

*Encaustus Phaethon tabula tibi pictus in hac est.
Quid tibi vis, dipyrum qui Phaethonta facis?*
Martial, *Ep.* iv. 47.

Even for colouring the letters of inscriptions cut on marble, wax encaustic was used, as is mentioned in the inscription from Lebadea recording work done to the Temple of Zeus; see Choisy, *Inscrip. Grecques*, p. 176.

In the case of Roman wall-paintings the method employed appears to have been as follows :— *Roman encaustic.*

The pigments, not restricted to the earth colours necessary for fresco work, were finely ground dry, first in a mortar, and lastly on a smooth marble or basalt slab with a rubber of the same material. The *medium* used was melted white wax (*cera Punica*) mixed with oil to make it more fluid. Resin was also used to mix with the wax medium. The pot containing the wax was kept over a brazier while the painter was at work, in order to keep the melted wax from solidifying. The stucco itself was prepared by a coating of hot wax applied with a brush, and it was polished by being rubbed with a wax candle, and finally with a clean linen cloth. After the picture was painted the wax colours were fixed, partly melted into the stucco and blended with the wax of the ground by the help of a charcoal brazier, which was held close to the surface of the painting, and gradually moved over its whole extent, thus melting down the uneven lumpy surface of the wax pigment and driving it into the pores of the smooth stucco. *Method of painting.*

The evidence of existing paintings is made much clearer by a very interesting passage in which Vitruvius (vii. 9. 3) gives directions for the painting of a flat vermilion ground : *At si quis subtilior fuerit, et voluerit expolitionem miniaceam suum colorem retinere, cum paries expolitus et aridus fuerit, tum ceram Punicam igni liquefactam paulo oleo temperatam saeta inducat;* *Vitruvius' account.*

Vitruvius on encaustic. *deinde postea carbonibus in ferreo vase compositis eam ceram apprime cum pariete calefaciundo sudare cogat, fiatque ut peraequetur: deinde tunc candela linteisque puris subigat, uti signa marmorea nuda curantur;* "But if the painter would be more skilful, and would have his polished vermilion ground retain its colour, let him, when the wall-stucco is polished and dry, *Cf. Pliny, Hist. Nat. xxxi. 83, 84.* lay on with a brush a coat of melted Punic wax tempered with oil. Then, with the help of a brazier of hot charcoal he should heat all the waxed surface, forcing the wax to melt (and sink into the stucco) in an even way over the whole surface. Finally, he should rub the wall with a wax candle, and then polish it with a clean linen cloth, just in the way that nude marble statues are treated."

Pliny on encaustic. Pliny (*Hist. Nat.* xxxv. 122) describes the process as "painting with wax pigments and then burning the picture in," *ceris pingere ac picturam inurere.* This process was called *encaustic* (ἔγκαυστος) or "burnt in," from the way in which the brazier was used to fix the colours on the walls. Greek painters, according to Pliny (*loc. cit.*), frequently signed their works ἐνέκαεν, "*burnt in*," instead of "painted."

Pliny's remarks on encaustic painting (*Hist. Nat.* xxxv. 149) are unintelligible, and the reading appears to be corrupt, or else Pliny's notes are hopelessly mixed and blundered—a not uncommon thing in the *Historia Naturalis*. His meaning is quite plain at xxxiii. 122, but here he is simply copying from Vitruvius, vii. 9. 3.

Circumlitio. The colouring of statues (*circumlitio*, ἀγαλμάτων ἔγκαυσις), mentioned by Vitruvius (vii. 9. 3) was done, not usually by the sculptor, but by a much honoured class of artists called ἀγαλμάτων ἐγκαυσταί; see Pliny, *Hist. Nat.* xxxv. 133, and Plutarch, *De glor. Athen.* vi. In this passage Plutarch names three classes of decorators of sculpture: ἀγαλμάτων ἐγκαυσταί, καὶ χρυσωταὶ καὶ βαφεῖς, i.e. *painters in wax-encaustic, gilders, and painters in tempera.* Examples of these three methods can clearly be distinguished on much of the

Greek sculpture that has recently been found in Athens and elsewhere. All three methods were often used for one statue, the *wax* for the flesh, the *tempera* for the draperies, and *gold* for the hair. See also Plato, *Repub.* iv. 420 C, who speaks of οἱ ἀνδριάντας γράφοντες, *painters of statues*.[1] The word γάνωσις was also applied to one kind of colouring used for statues. Plutarch, *Quaes. Rom.* 98, tells us that the γάνωσις of the terra-cotta sculpture in the Temple of Capitoline Jupiter was one of the chief annual duties of the Censors: cf. Cic. *De Divin.* i. 10, 16.

Treatment of statues.

In Pliny's time (*Hist. Nat.* xxxv. 118) distinguished artists devoted themselves to easel pictures (*tabulae*), and the decoration of walls was apparently left to a less talented class of painters. Thus we find that a large proportion of the existing examples in Pompeii and Rome are the work of very inferior artisans, who, however, in many cases have evidently copied the composition of some famous painter.

Mural pictures.

In the same way in Greece *mural painting* was the earliest branch of the art, but about the time of Alexander the chief artists, such as Apelles, mainly devoted themselves to the production of easel pictures on panel (πίνακες). The wax encaustic process was as applicable to paintings on wood as to those on stucco.

Numerous examples of this have recently been discovered in the tombs of Egypt of the third century A.D., in the form of very realistic portraits fastened over the faces of mummies. These portraits are skilfully painted with pigments of rich colour on very thin slices of cedar wood, about $\frac{1}{10}$ to $\frac{1}{16}$ inch thick. The rather lumpy surface or *impasto* which comes from the use of a wax medium is very obvious on these pictures. The melted wax rapidly hardened when the brush touched the cold surface of the panel, and so prevented the pigment from

Egyptian encaustic.

[1] In an inscription on the base of a statue a sculptor from Aphrodisias signs himself ἀγαλματοποιὸς ἐγκαυστής; see Loewy, *Inscr. Gr. Bildh.* No. 551.

being laid in a smooth, even manner. The wood was not, like stucco, sufficiently absorbent for the subsequent application of heat to get rid of the lumpy surface by driving the superfluous wax below the surface.[1]

Framed picture.

One of these Egypto-Roman portraits was discovered by Mr. Flinders Petrie, not fixed over the face of a mummy, but framed and glazed for hanging on the wall of a tomb; a most valuable example of the ancient method of treating easel paintings. The frame, which is now in the British Museum, is simple in design, very like what is now called an "Oxford frame" with long projecting tenons which cross at each angle. The glass was slid in from the top, fitting into grooves at the sides. The picture was hung to a nail by a piece of stout cord; and the whole arrangement is very like that of a modern picture frame.

Triptyches.

It was not uncommon for Roman pictures to have double doors, like a mediaeval triptych; examples of this are represented in "the House of Livia"; see vol. i. p. 176. The use of wax encaustic painting on wood is mentioned by Vitruvius (iv. 2. 2) as being applied to the *triglyphs* of wooden entablatures, which were coloured blue.

Paintings on panel representing Roman victories or captives were sometimes carried in triumphal processions. For example, Livy (xxv. 20) relates that M. Marcellus carried in triumph a *tabula cum simulacro captarum Syracusarum.*

Painters' boxes.

Some very interesting sets of painters' pigments and tools have been found at different times in Egyptian tombs both of the Ptolemaic and Roman periods, and in Pompeii, and at other places. Among them the following objects occur: bronze boxes divided into compartments, with closely-fitting lids, to hold pigments, brushes, and other implements; what Varro (iii. 17, 4) calls *loculatas magnas arculas.* Small pestles and mortars, and flat slabs with rubbers for grinding the

[1] The National Gallery in London possesses some very fine examples of these mummy portraits.

colours, made of marble, basalt, granite, and alabaster. Large flat palettes made of similar materials; palette knives and *spatulae* of bronze, flat iron knives for taking up the mixture of wax and colour. Spoons of various materials, including rock crystal. *Stili* of bronze and ivory for drawing outlines; brushes (*saetae*) with bone or wood handles; glass cups, used probably to hold a natural spirit-medium, such as mineral naphtha. Glass bottles, little clay pots, ivory boxes, and other receptacles for the dry pigments, in great numbers.

Painters' tools.

As many as eighty glass bottles of pigments were found in the grave of one lady artist, which was discovered in 1849 at S. Médard-de-Près in the Vendée; see Fillon, *Tombeau d'une artiste Gallo-Romaine*, Fontenay, 1849. Among the mediums (φάρμακα) found in such collections have been wax, resin, and various other varieties of gums, together with little charcoal braziers for melting them together.

Pigments and media.

The pigments which occur most frequently are red and white lead, cinnabar (vermilion), ochres of many colours, red, yellow, and brown; and blue of the most brilliant tint (*cyanus*). Green of verdigris and *terra vert*; black made, like Chinese ink, of finely divided carbon, usually in the form of lampblack. Purple and other more delicate colours made by staining a white earth with highly concentrated animal and vegetable dyes, such as *murex* and indigo; together with many other kinds of pigments.

These discoveries show that the varieties of pigments and methods of using them were very large and varied among the painters of late classical times.[1]

In the Republican period things were different; mural paintings (as in Greece of the fifth century B.C.) appear then to have taken the first rank, and were executed by the most celebrated painters, some of whom belonged to wealthy Roman

Early Roman painting.

[1] Long lists of colours are given by Pliny, *Hist. Nat.* xxxiii. 89 to 91, 111 to 122, and xxxv. 29 to 50; and by Vitruvius, vii. 7 to 14; on the use of gums as "vehicles" see Pliny, *Hist. Nat.* xiii. 67, and xxviii. 236.

families; as, for example, Fabius the historian, surnamed *Pictor*[1] from his skill as an artist, who decorated the walls of the *Temple of Salus*, which was built about 304 B.C., and was burnt in the reign of Claudius; see Pliny, *Hist. Nat.* xxxv. 19. Paintings were executed on the walls of the *Temple of Hercules* in the *Forum Boarium* about 180 B.C., by the tragic dramatist Pacuvius, the nephew of the poet Ennius.

Esquiline tombs. In one of the Esquiline tombs, built of tufa blocks of *opus quadratum*, which were discovered in 1875-76, there was on the wall a very curious series of early mural paintings, with battle scenes arranged in four bands or zones like those in some Etruscan tombs.

In one picture two of the figures have their names painted by them, Q·I'ABIO and M·I'AN, for *Quintus Fabius* and *Marcus Fannius*.

In an interesting article by Visconti (*Bull. Com. Arch.* 1890, p. 340, and Tav. xi. xii.) the suggestion is made that these pictures are reduced copies of the historical series painted on *Fabius Pictor.* the walls of the *Temple of Salus* by Fabius Pictor in 304 B.C. Visconti thinks that the subject represented is an incident in the Samnite war, the capture of Luceria by Q. Fabius Maximus Rullianus. The style of these paintings is vigorous, but coarse and clumsy in design; see Dion. Hal. xvi. 6, for an account of the style of Fabius Pictor's paintings.

Etruscan style. It is interesting to notice that the style of these early Roman paintings shows distinctly an Etruscan influence. Both in technique and in design they resemble the wall-paintings found in the tombs of the chief cities of central Etruria. This shows that painting in Rome followed the same course of development as did the Roman architecture and sculpture.

In all three arts the influence of the Etruscans was paramount in early times, and lasted till it was succeeded by a new wave of overpowering force from the far more artistic inhabitants of Greece and her colonies.

[1] See Livy, i. 44 and 52; ii. 40; viii. 30; and x. 37.

HISTORICAL SUBJECTS

Though the tomb itself has been destroyed, the paintings were cut off the walls and are now preserved in the Capitoline Museum. In the inscription the form I¹ for F is noticeable; cf. the use of II for E which lasted till the first century A.D.

Pliny in his account of the history of painting in Rome (*Hist. Nat.* xxxv. 19 to 26) says that the art gained dignity through the growth of historical painting executed to commemorate Roman victories. *Historical painting.*

He speaks of M. Valerius Messala exhibiting in the *Curia Hostilia* panel pictures of his own victories. So also L. Scipio Asiaticus dedicated a painting representing scenes from his conquests in Asia in the Capitoline Temple of Jupiter. A picture of the capture of Carthage was exhibited publicly by the conqueror L. Hostilius Mancinus—a thing which, Pliny says, won him many votes at the next election of Consuls, especially as he amused the people by acting as showman and explaining the incidents represented in the painting.

The conquests of L. Mummius, who sacked Corinth in 146 B.C., did much to arouse an interest in art of all kinds among the inartistic Romans. Not only immense numbers of statues, but even pictures were brought to Rome from various parts of the Hellenic world. At *Hist. Nat.* xxxv. 25, Pliny tells an amusing story about a Greek picture which was hung in the Forum *sub veteribus*, along the old line of shops. *Greek spoils.*

Many other pictures, Pliny tells us (*ib.* 24), were placed in the Forum itself, in addition to the immense number dedicated in the various buildings grouped round the Forum.

Overbeck, *Die antiken Schriftquellen*, Leipzig, 1868, pp. 429 to 466, gives an interesting collection of passages from classical authors which relate to the works of art and the artists of ancient Rome.

CHAPTER III

PREHISTORIC PERIOD AND TIME OF THE KINGS.

VERY little that is of real historical value with regard to the early settlers on the banks of the Tiber can be gleaned from the mythical traditions of the Romans themselves; but many discoveries that have been made within the last few years combine to show that the site of Rome was populous at a very remote and quite prehistoric period. Flint implements and other remains of the early Bronze Age have been found on the Aventine and in other places; and, especially on the Esquiline, tombs have been brought to light of the most primitive construction, dating probably from a much more remote period than the time traditionally given, 753 B.C., as that of the founding of Rome.[1]

Prehistoric remains.

Esquiline tombs.

In February 1883, between the Piazza Vitt. Emmanuele and the Via di Napoleone III., on the Esquiline, a number of very primitive cist tombs were found, formed in the most simple way of three slabs of stone, two set on edge for the walls, and a third stone laid upon them for the lid; see *Notizie degli scavi*, February 1883.

In 1874 the very important discovery was made of a large Necropolis also on the Esquiline, near the arch of Gallienus, the tombs of which were Etruscan in character and contained

[1] Some of the tombs found on the Aventine were Etruscan in style, of that primitive subterranean sort to which access is given by a descending shaft like that of a well, with holes cut at intervals for foothold (see Bartoli, *Sepolcri Antichi*, Tav. 1. 695).

many objects, fictile vases and the like,[1] of that combined *Foreign imports.* Hellenic and Oriental character which is peculiar to a large class of objects, archaic in style, which have been discovered at many widely distant places on the shores of the Mediterranean, and were evidently introduced by some far-reaching and active commercial system, probably carried on by the adventurous traders of the Phoenician coast.[2]

Among the vases discovered in the Esquiline Necropolis *Island pottery.* were *aryballoi*, of that rare early kind which combines Hellenic modelling with the enamelled decoration of Egypt or Assyria. These were in the shape of a well-formed human head of the Silenus type, bearded and clothed in a lion's skin, the whole being coated with a true vitreous enamel made white and opaque by oxide of tin, and coloured with pigments made from metallic oxides. Other pieces of pottery were found decorated with brilliant blue and green plumbo-vitreous glazes, coloured with oxides of copper. These methods of decoration are not Hellenic,[3] but were practised very largely in Egypt and *Oriental influence.* Assyria; and also, to a certain extent, in some of the Greek islands where Phoenician colonisation or trade had created schools of handicraft in which Hellenic design was combined

[1] The objects found in these tombs are now placed in the new *Magazzino archeologico Municipale*, in the garden below the Church of SS. Giovanni e Paolo, on the Caelian Hill.

[2] A very unexpected proof of a hitherto almost unknown commercial connection between Egypt and various ports of the Greek shores and islands, as early as from fifteen to twelve centuries B.C., has recently been established by the discovery in tombs of Upper Egypt of pottery of the common Mycenae and Tiryns type. Most probably these vases were imported into Egypt in Phoenician ships; see Flinders Petrie in *Jour. Hell. Stud.* vol. xii. p. 199 *seq.*

[3] Some exceptions to this rule exist; the principal one is a *rhyton* in the British Museum, in the form of Cupid riding upon a goose. This is covered with a stanniferous enamel, and was probably produced in Rhodes, which was one of the chief places where the *technique* of Egypt was practised in conjunction with the designs of Greece.

with Egyptian technique. Examples of this class of objects, exactly resembling those found in Rome, have also been discovered in the Island of Aegina, and at Cameiros in the Island of Rhodes.

In other tombs on the Esquiline Hill scarabs with Egyptian hieroglyphs were found, some of them made of glass like those discovered in the wells of Ialysos and Cameiros.

Pre-Roman settlement. The discovery of this large Necropolis makes it probable that a city of some size and importance existed even before the legendary regal period, on one of the largest hills of the *Septimontium*, and is strong evidence against the theory of a purely Latin supremacy having been established on previously uninhabited sites among the hills of the future Rome.

In other places in Rome pottery incised with letters and inscriptions of very archaic type has been found; examples of these are figured and described in *Ann. Inst.* for 1880.[1]

Early myths. Some dim traditions of these earlier inhabitants existed among the Romans down to the literary period, as, for example, in the story of the Arcadian Evander, the son of Mercury and the nymph Carmenta, who settled on the site of Rome about sixty years before the Trojan war. Then came a line of Latin kingly deities; Saturn, who gave his name to the *Mons Saturnius*, afterwards the *Capitolium*; Janus, who named the *Janiculan Hill*; and Picus and Faunus, other demigods who ruled as kings on the banks of the Tiber. Next came Hercules with a group of companions, of whom a record was supposed to exist in the altar and subsequently in the Temple of Saturn in the *Forum Romanum*; see vol. i. p. 265. Then, according to the story, Aeneas and the scanty remnant from Troy arrived, and, landing at the Tiber mouth, lived in

[1] A good account of part of the Esquiline Necropolis is given in *Ann. Inst.* 1879, p. 253; 1880, p. 265; and 1882, p. 5 *seq.*; *Mon. Inst.* xi. Tav. 37; and De Rossi in *Bull. Inst.* 1885, p. 72. See also *Not. d. Scavi*, 1887, p. 534; and 1888, pp. 59 and 132.

alliance with the aboriginal King Latinus at Lavinium, about fifteen miles from the coast.[1]

Even to a late period Lavinium was regarded as the cradle of the Roman nation; some of its ancient temples were treated as shrines of special sanctity, and were solemnly visited by Consuls and other chief officials of Rome before commencing a term of office. *Lavinium.*

Some of the dim traditions with regard to these primitive dwellers on the site of Rome existed in very strange forms. A curious instance of this occurs in the following fragment from Dion Cassius, who, to account for the existence of a town on the Palatine Hill earlier than the traditional *Roma Quadrata*[2] of Romulus, invents an earlier Romulus and "Romus" to be its founders:— *Dion Cassius.*

πρὸ δὲ τῆς μεγάλης ταύτης 'Ρώμης ἦν ἔκτισε 'Ρώμυλος, περὶ τὴν Φαυστύλου οἰκίαν ἐν ὄρει Παλατίῳ ἑτέρα τετράγωνος ἐκτίσθη 'Ρώμη παρὰ 'Ρώμου καὶ 'Ρωμύλου παλαιοτέρων τούτων; Dion Cass. iii. 5, Leipsic Ed. of 1829. In a fragment of lib. v., an earlier settlement called Οἰνωτρία is mentioned; see Becker, *Handbuch der Röm. Alterth.*, Leipsic, 1843, vol. i. pp. 105, 106.

Another ancient name for the city of Evander was said to be *Valentia, strength*, meaning the same as 'Ρώμη; see Solinus, cap. i. *De Consecr. urbis*.

The Pomoerium. The most important existing relics of the time when Roman history begins, though dimly, to take a *Pomoerium.*

---

[1] The modern *Civita Lavinia* is not the ancient *Lavinium*, but stands partly on the site of the ancient *Lanuvium*. Excavations made in 1884 by Sir Savile Lumley and Mr. R. P. Pullan exposed remains of a fine temple, probably that of Juno Sospita, and many fragments of sculpture, including parts of a fine quadriga of Greek marble (now in the British Museum), apparently an ancient copy of some Greek group belonging to a good period of art.

[2] The name *Roma Quadrata* was derived from its rectangular shape; see also vol. i. p. 189.

definite shape, are the so-called "Walls of Romulus" round the circuit of the famous *Roma Quadrata* of the Palatine.

Pomoerium. Unfortunately the accounts given by Tacitus and others of the extent of the *Pomoerium* give but little help towards defining its circuit. The word *pomerium* is derived from *pone* or *post moerium*, "beyond the wall"; its precise nature is now impossible to discover. Even in the first century B.C. it was a matter of only archaeological interest, and the notions existing as to its primitive form were very vague and contradictory; see Varro, *Lin. Lat.* v. 143; Liv. i. 44; and Dionys. i. 88. What is fairly certain about it is, that the *pomoerium* was an encircling band of ground which followed the line of the city wall, and was traced in some way by a furrow turned by a plough drawn by a cow and a bull.[1] This ceremony, performed before founding a new town, was of Etruscan origin, like the greater part of the religious rites of the Romans; see Bunsen, *Besch. d. Stadt Rom.* i. p. 138, and Mommsen, *Hist. Rom.* vol. i.; and cf. Plutarch's *Life of Romulus*, 11; see also Aul. Gell. xiii. 14. Tacitus (*Ann.* xii. 24) describes the line of the *Pomoerium* thus:—

Sulcus primigenius.

Tacitus on the pomoerium. Sed initium condendi et quod pomoerium Romulus posuerit noscere haud absurdum reor. Igitur a foro Boario ubi aereum tauri simulacrum adspicimus, quia id genus animalium aratro subditur, sulcus designandi oppidi coeptus, ut magnam Herculis aram amplecteretur. Inde certis spatiis interjecti lapides per ima montis Palatini ad aram Consi, mox ad Curias Veteres, tum ad Sacellum Larum, Forumque Romanum; et Capitolium non a Romulo sed a Tito Tatio additum urbi credidere.

In this passage Tacitus gives a series of points in the sacred circuit round the walls of *Roma Quadrata* on the Palatine. Unfortunately, the known points in this list are

---

[1] On Roman coins, both of the Republican and the Imperial periods, the regular type used to record the founding of a colony is a man driving a plough drawn by two oxen (or rather by the orthodox cow and bull) in the act of tracing the *pomoerium* furrow.

precisely those which mark the line of wall about which there could be no doubt, both from the contour of the ground and the existing remains; that is to say, the line of wall on the side towards the valley of the *Velabrum*, with its angles by the *Circus Maximus* at the west and the *Forum Romanum* at the north.

Known points.

It should be observed that the *Pomoerium* line, as described by Tacitus, was considerably outside that of the wall itself. According to the ancient Etruscan custom a strip of ground was left all round the city, between the furrow of the *Pomoerium* and the actual wall; this was considered sacred, and no houses could be built on it. The "Wall of Romulus," described below, stood on an artificially formed shelf of rock, rather more than half-way up the slopes or cliff of the hill, while the various points mentioned as being on the *Pomoerium* line were *ad ima montis*, at the very foot of the hill, in the valleys which surround it.

Earliest wall.

The starting-point in Tacitus' list is at the bronze statue of a bull[1] in the *Forum Boarium*; this point marked, probably, the western corner. Thence the sacred furrow (*sulcus primigenius*) was drawn along the *Vallis Murciae*, probably near the line afterwards occupied by the *spina* of the *Circus Maximus*. It first passed the *Ara Maxima*, a prehistoric altar sacred to Hercules (see *Mon. and Ann. Inst.* for 1854, p. 28); this apparently stood at the north-west end of the valley, near the *carceres* or starting-point of the circus; Dionys. i. 40.

Circuit of pomoerium.

The next point was the *Altar of Consus*, an equestrian Neptune,[2] in the place where Romulus held the *Consualia*, a sacred Festival, celebrated with games and athletic contests, during which, on one occasion, the celebrated capture of the

Altar of Consus.

---

[1] The work of the celebrated Greek sculptor Myron, a contemporary of Pheidias, but rather older than he. Pliny (*Hist. Nat.* xxxiv. 10) mentions it as an example of a statue made of Aeginetan bronze.

[2] Compare the Greek *Poseidon Hippios*; in earlier times Consus appears to have been a god of the crops.

Ara Consi. Sabine women took place. In later times the *Altar of Consus* existed in or below part of the *spina*, near the *prima meta*, which most probably was not the one near the starting-place, but the first *meta* round which the chariots turned, that is, the one farthest from the *carceres*. The *Ara Consi* is said to have been usually hidden, but during the celebration of the *Ludi Circenses* it was uncovered and exposed to view; see vol. ii. p. 51; Tertull. *De Spec.* v. 8; Plut. *Rom.* 14; and Varro, *L. L.* vi. 20.[1]

Curiae Veteres. Of the position of the next-mentioned stages in the circuit little is known; these were the *Curiae Veteres* and the *Sacellum Larum*. The former is mentioned by Varro as the place where "things divine" were discussed, as "things human" were by the Senate in the *Curia Hostilia* by the *Forum Magnum*. The *Sacellum Larum* is probably the "*aedes Larum in Summa Sacra Via*" mentioned in the Ancyrean inscription as being rebuilt by Augustus; see vol. i. p. 385.

The last point mentioned by Tacitus is the *Forum Romanum*, marking the northern angle of the circuit;[2] this brings the *End of circuit.* line to the valley of the *Velabrum*, which bounded the whole north-west side of the Palatine, and so to the starting-point in the *Forum Boarium*.

It will be seen that this description of the circuit of *Roma Quadrata* leaves uncertain the whole boundary of the south-east side, that opposite the *Velabrum*. To determine this we can only have recourse to a few other passages in classical authors which mention the circuit, and, secondly, to the existing remains of the ancient wall.

The circuit of *Roma Quadrata* as described by Solinus

---

[1] Sacrifice was specially offered to *Consus* by the drivers of chariots in the Circus races, to gain his protection from the serious risk of upset at the sharp turn round the *metae*.

[2] According to one method of punctuation, the words "*Forum Romanum*" are coupled with "*Capitolium*," as being parts outside the city of Romulus, which were added by the Sabine king Tatius; but it is more probable that the passage ought to run as given above.

(cap. i.) is unintelligible, and was written at a time when tradition on this point had become very vague:—*Dictaque est primum Roma Quadrata quod ad aequilibrium foret posita. Ea incipit a sylva quae est in area Apollinis et ad supercilium scalarum Caci habet terminum, ubi tugurium fuit Faustuli; ibi Romulus mansitavit.* This is possibly a vague tradition of a primitive city, which only occupied the western half of the Palatine Hill. *[Solinus on the pomoerium.]*

The Palatine Hill, before its surface was levelled during the construction of many of the extensive palaces which, under the Empire, occupied its whole summit, was divided into two parts by a natural valley, which ran from near the *Arch of Titus* and the *Porta Mugonia* the whole way across it, to the side of the *Circus Maximus*.[1] *[Palatine Hill.]*

The point which has been most disputed is, whether the primitive *Roma Quadrata* occupied the whole summit of the Palatine, or whether it was confined to the half of the hill on the *Velabrum* side? The latter theory was adopted by Comm. Rosa; see *Ann. Inst.* 1865, p. 346. There is, however, very strong evidence to show that the former supposition is the true one, and that *Roma Quadrata* was really co-extensive with the whole hill. *[Roma Quadrata.]*

Cicero (*De Rep.* ii. 6) says, *Murum Romuli . . . definitum ex omni parte arduis praeruptisque montibus*; and Aulus Gellius (xiii. 14) also says, *Antiquissimum Pomoerium . . . Palatini montis radicibus terminabatur.* This language would certainly not apply to a city which occupied one-half of the Palatine only.

Excavations during the last fifteen years have, moreover, exposed remains of the primitive wall at several points along the southern half of the hill—both a little to the east of the supposed site of the *Porta Mugonia*, and also near the so-called "*Domus Gelotiana*," on the slope towards the *Circus Maximus*. *[Existing remains.]*

[1] For an account of the buildings which filled and covered this valley see vol. i. pp. 166 and 200.

Projecting spur. A projecting spur of the wall still exists issuing at right angles to the main line, and looks very much as if it crossed the hill at this point; but further excavations showed that it again turned to the south-east, and continued along the cliff in the direction of the Palace of Severus (see fig. 22), making it almost certain that the so-called "Wall of Romulus," part of which still exists, really included the whole circuit of the Palatine. This theory by no means excludes the notion that an earlier settlement only occupied part of the Palatine Hill.

EXISTING REMAINS OF "THE WALL OF ROMULUS."[1]

Earliest wall. The very primitive date of this once massive circuit-wall is shown both by the character of its masonry and by the manner in which it is set with reference to the natural line of the cliff; in both respects exactly resembling the fortifications of many very ancient Etruscan cities. The natural strength and adaptability for defence of the Palatine Hill were skilfully and with great labour much increased in the following manner :—

The base of the circuit wall was set neither at the foot of the cliff nor at its summit, but on an artificially cut shelf, at an average distance of about 40 feet from the top. The tufa cliff above this shelf all round the circuit, where the natural contour of the rock was at all abrupt, was cut into an almost perpendicular precipice, slightly battering or sloping back towards the hill (see fig. 16). On this long rock-cut shelf the wall was *Scarped cliff.* built against the face of the artificially scarped cliff, rising to the summit of the hill, and probably a little above it, sufficiently high to protect the garrison from missiles thrown from below.

The accompanying figure shows the section of the wall and cliff at the point where it is still most perfect. The wall is

---

[1] This name is a convenient one to use in spite of the purely mythical character of the early traditions about the founding of Rome.

THE WALL OF ROMULUS

10 feet thick at the base, and grew rather thicker as it went up, owing to the cliff behind leaning away from it. The wall was in fact a sort of "retaining wall," except that it was not built to hold up the ground behind it, but in order to insure a more even and perpendicular surface than that of the cliff

Section of wall.

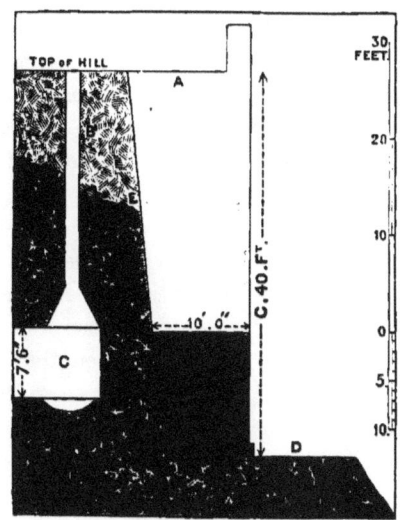

Fig. 16.
Section of primitive wall of Roma Quadrata.
A. Original height of wall.
B. Upper part of cliff, now crumbled away.
C. Cistern cut in the tufa rock.
D. Levelled platform to receive base of wall.
EE. Cliff made steeper by cutting.

itself; the many fissures in which would easily have supplied foothold to external assailants. In other parts of the hill, where the natural rock was not so steep, the circuit wall may have been arranged differently; but no example of this now remains on the Palatine.[1]

[1] The almost equally primitive wall of the *Capitolium*, of which

Materials of early wall. *Construction of the " Wall of Romulus."* The stone used in the "Wall of Romulus" was probably quarried on the Palatine itself; it is that friable sort of warm brown tufa which is thickly studded with pieces of pumice stone and masses of charred wood; see vol. i. p. 3. These lumps, varying usually from the size of a walnut to that of a man's two fists, are very visible in all the blocks of the existing remains of this wall; see fig. 17, in which these embedded lumps are indicated. As is mentioned in the chapter on Roman methods of construction, the blocks of which this wall is built were cut with metal tools, probably of bronze. Tools of at least two kinds were used, namely, sharp-pointed picks, and chisels varying in width from $\frac{1}{4}$ to $\frac{1}{2}$ inch.

Style of masonry. The blocks are cut in courses which measure roughly two Roman feet in thickness, varying (that is) from 22 to 24 inches; their width across the ends varies from 18 to 22 inches (average about 21 inches); the lengths are extremely irregular, ranging from 3 feet 3 inches to 4 feet 10 inches. The blocks are roughly "hammer-dressed" on the exposed face; but in all cases the beds or horizontal joints are worked very truly, while the vertical joints are in some instances left with a considerable space between the blocks. In most cases, however, they are fitted fairly accurately. In many instances the blocks are worked with hollow joints —cut, that is, so as to fit accurately at the exposed edge only.

Absence of mortar. No mortar or any kind of clamps are used—a sign of very early work; in certain places in the later wall of the Kings a thin bed of mortar is used. In most cases, though not always, the blocks are set in *emplecton* work, first, that is,

remains exist on the (popularly called) *rupes Tarpeia*, was set at the edge of the cliff at its summit, the rock below being cut into a perpendicular precipice. The Capitoline tufa is harder and more regular in texture than that of the Palatine, so that no artificial wall could improve on it when it was quarried into a smooth surface.

THE WALL OF ROMULUS

a course of *stretchers* (blocks set lengthways), and then a course of *headers* (blocks set endways).

The chief remains of this wall exist at the western angle of the hill (near the modern entrance to the Palatine); and in places where the wall itself is gone, imprints of its blocks remain visible on later concrete walls which have been built against it. All along the north-west side (toward the *Velabrum*) pieces of the "Wall of Romulus" exist, embedded in the walls

Existing remains.

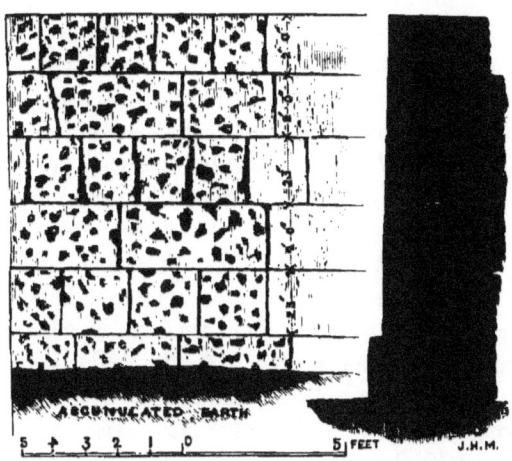

Fig. 17.
Existing piece of the "Wall of Romulus."

of houses of the late Republican and early Imperial periods, which were built in a long row extending along the shelf at the foot of the wall. When these houses were constructed the greater part of the then useless fortification wall was pulled down, and its blocks were probably used in the walls of the later houses; see No. 2, 2, 2 on fig. 22, p. 156.

Where, however, the blocks of the ancient wall came into the right place for the walls of the later houses they were left in their place and incorporated into the row of dwellings.

Existing remains. Pieces of the primitive wall exist at nearly regular intervals of about 12 feet, embedded in the later walls of concrete faced with *opus reticulatum*,[1] for a considerable distance opposite the round Church of S. Teodoro, near the present entrance to the Palatine. And other pieces exist in the many-storied building near the west angle, especially by and under the long flight of brick and concrete stairs leading up to the summit of the hill; see No. 6 on fig. 22.

S.W. side. Another long piece of this primitive wall also exists incorporated into part of the so-called *Domus Gelotiana*, about halfway along the side overlooking the *Circus Maximus*.[2] This piece is rather difficult to understand, as it appears to project a long way from the main line of the circuit, running in a diagonal direction down the slope towards the Circus.

Other portions of the wall were discovered a few years ago near the supposed site of the *Porta Mugonia*, and immediately below the lofty *Podium* of the Flavian Palace. Exposure to rain and frost has unfortunately destroyed nearly the whole of these interesting remains, which have now crumbled away into a shapeless heap of volcanic earth.[3]

Cistern. *Rock-cut Chambers.* A very interesting reservoir for rain and spring water, of very early date, exists at one point towards the *Velabrum*, behind the "Wall of Romulus."[4] It is shown in section on fig. 16, and its position is indicated by No. 8 on fig. 22. The "Wall of Romulus" in front of it is now mostly gone, and an entrance which did not originally exist has been broken into this rock-cut cistern through the face of

[1] The regular occurrence of these pieces of ancient masonry looks as if there had been at this part a row of buttresses projecting from the face of the "Wall of Romulus."

[2] No. 49 on fig. 22 shows the "Domus Gelotiana," and No. 2 near it indicates this fragment of the primitive wall.

[3] No. 41 on fig. 22 shows the position of this piece of wall.

[4] An almost exactly similar rock-cut cistern and well-shaft, also of very great antiquity, exists near the site of the ancient Alba Longa.

the cliff; but as it was originally formed it had no access except from the top of the hill down two circular well-shafts. Under one of these a round basin is cut in the rock into which buckets let down from above would fall.

Rock-cut cistern.

This extensive rock-cut cistern was probably intended specially for use during siege, so that the inhabitants of *Roma Quadrata* might not be starved out from want of water. Other quarry cisterns with well-shafts of a later date are mentioned below; see vol. i. pp. 162 and 164.

A long passage with a semicircular roof, leading from this circular cistern, runs inwards under the hill for a considerable distance, but it has not been completely cleared of rubbish.

Rock-cut passages.

At another point in the cliff, nearer to S. Teodoro (No. 9 on fig. 22), another long passage, about 2 feet 6 inches wide and 7 feet high, is excavated in the tufa hill for a long distance, winding about in a very curious way. It is still partly choked with earth, and its use is not apparent.

In this long passage the nature of the tufa which composes the core of the Palatine can be well examined. Here the rock is of a light yellowish colour, very soft and homogeneous, quite free from fissures, and unmixed with any pumice stone or charcoal. It probably belongs to an earlier formation than that of which the "Wall of Romulus" at the western angle is built.

Tufa rock.

GATES IN ROMA QUADRATA.

According to the ancient Etruscan custom every walled city had at least three gates, dedicated to the three chief deities of the Rasena—*Tinia, Thalna,* and *Menrva,* whom the Romans called Jupiter, Juno, and Minerva; see Servius, *Ad Aen.* i. 422.

Early gates of Rome.

Varro (*Lin. Lat.* v. 34) describes three gates in the Romulean wall thus:—

Praeterea intra muros video portas dici—in Palatio "Mugionis" a mugitu, quod ea pecus in bucita circum antiquom oppidum exige-

bant. *Alteram " Romanulam," quae est dicta ab Roma, quae habet gradus in Nova Via ad Volupiae sacellum. Tertia est " Janualis," dicta ab Jano: et ideo ibi positum Jani signum*; see also Plut. *Rom.* 9; Dionys. ii. 65; Livy, i. 7 and 9.

Porta Mugonia. The *Porta Mugonia* is mentioned by Solinus (i. 24) as being above the *Summa Nova Via*. Near it was the house of Tarquinius Priscus, whose house is elsewhere recorded to have been near the Temple of Jupiter Stator. Remains of what was supposed to be the *Porta Mugionis* or *Mugonia* were discovered during excavations made by Rosa for Napoleon III., together with a lava-paved road leading up to the Palatine from the *Summa Sacra Via*, and this attribution was confirmed in 1883-4 by the discovery of the *Summa Nova Via* where it joins the Palatine road close by the Arch of Titus (see fig. 22).[1] This gate is probably the *veterem Portam Palatii* of Livy, i. 12, through which the Romans fled when repulsed by the Sabines of the Capitol. Varro's derivation of the name *mugionis*, from the lowing of oxen, is very improbable, as is also that given by Festus (ed. Müller, p. 144).

Porta Romana. The *Porta Romana.* The derivation of the name of the second gate, *Romanula* or *Romana*, is explained thus by Festus, p. 262—*Sed Porta Romana instituta est a Romulo infimo clivo Victoriae, qui locus gradibus in quadram formatus est; appellata autem Romana a Sabinis praecipue, quod ea proximus aditus erat Romam.* These indications enable the site of this gate also to be identified, with some probability, as having been at the lowest point of the road where it passes from under the lofty substructions of Caligula's Palace.

Clivus Victoriae. That this road was the *Clivus Victoriae* is very probable, from the discovery near it of the Temple of Victory (see vol. i.

---

[1] See p. 168 for a description of the remains, which have been supposed to belong to the *Temple of Jupiter Stator*, close by the *Porta Mugonia*. The soft tufa blocks, of which the supposed remains of this gate were built, have now wholly crumbled away, though they were sharp and well preserved when they were exposed about the year 1868.

p. 189).¹ It is at the corner nearest the Capitol, in accordance with the indication of Festus, and almost its exact position on the *clivus* is given by continuing the line of the cliff and the remains of the "Wall of Romulus" on the north-west side of the hill. The original approach to this gate apparently was from a road sloping up the lower extra-mural part of the hill from the direction of the *Velabrum*. In later times a more direct ascent was made to it from the *Forum Romanum* by a flight of steps, of which remains still exist, and which are shown on the *marble plan*; see vol. i. p. 222, fig. 22, and *Forum Plan*.

Scalae anulariae.

The *Porta Romanula* was probably destroyed long before Caligula built his palace over the *Clivus Victoriae*.

The Porta Janualis. Of the position of the third gate, called *Janualis* by Varro, nothing is known, and indeed it appears doubtful whether the *Porta Janualis* was on the Palatine at all. Macrobius (*Saturn.* i. 9) speaks of it as being on the slopes of the Viminal Hill.²

Porta Janualis.

Other Gates of Roma Quadrata. It is very probable that *Roma Quadrata* possessed at least one entrance on its southern half, and judging from the contour of the ground it appears likely that this gate was at some point under the existing substructures of Severus' Palace, probably where the road descends from the end of the great Stadium, passing under the palace to the valley between the Palatine and the Caelian Hills.

Scalae Caci. One entrance through the primitive wall of *Roma Quadrata* still exists on the side of the *Circus Maximus*.

Stairs of Cacus.

---

¹ What appears to be part of this road is represented on a fragment of the marble plan with the inscription CLIVVS VICTORIAE, but the buildings shown near it cannot be identified with any of the existing remains.

² For an account of the walls and gates of *Roma Quadrata* see Becker, *De muris et portis Romae*, Leipsic, 1842; *Ann. Inst.* 1857, p. 62, and *Ann. Inst.* 1871, p. 40; and *La fondazione di Roma* in *Bull. Comm. Arch. Rom.* 1881, vol. ix.

Scalae Caci. This is not a chariot road but a long flight of steps which would not rank as one of the three chief entrances to the city. These stairs are probably the *Scalae Caci*[1] of Solinus, i. 18; see also Plutar. *Rom.* 20.[2]

It is a broad flight of steps cut in the tufa rock, and lined at the sides with a wall of roughly cut blocks of soft tufa like the rest of the "Wall of Romulus." On one side of these stairs are a number of early tufa buildings, described below (see vol. i. p. 158). The wall on the opposite side is a restoration in concrete of Imperial date, probably of the time of Caligula, who is recorded to have restored these stairs. In later times the ancient rock-cut steps appear to have been covered with a pavement of polygonal blocks of lava, a few of which still remain near the top. The name of the gate which once existed at the foot of these stairs is not known.

Lupercal. The *Lupercal.* Probably not far from the *Stairs of Cacus*, near the western angle of the hill, was the *Lupercal*, a large cave in the rock, shaded with trees, traditionally dedicated by the Arcadians under Evander, as a shrine to *Lupercus*, probably a native Latin deity, who was afterwards identified with the Greek Pan.[3] According to the story, this was the den of the she-wolf that suckled Romulus and Remus. See Dionysius (i. 32, 79) who quotes the early Roman historian Q. Fabius Pictor. Lupercus was a god specially worshipped by shepherds as the protector of their flocks against wolves.

In later times the *Lupercal* was transformed into some sort

---

[1] The name of these stairs was said to be derived from a certain Cacius who lived by them; not from the fabulous robber, Cacus, who lived in a cave in the Aventine, and was killed by Hercules after his crafty theft of the oxen. See Servius, *Ad Aen.* viii. 90, and Propertius, IV. i. 9.

[2] In this passage Plutarch states that Romulus lived near the *Scalae Caci*, which led from the top of the Palatine Hill down to the Circus Maximus; see p. 160.

[3] The exact position of the *Lupercal* is unknown; what Mr. Parker mistook for it was the *castellum* or *piscina* of an aqueduct.

of building; possibly its entrance was adorned with columns and an entablature supporting sculpture, like the *Choragic monument of Thrasyllos* at Athens, of 320 B.C., which forms the entrance to a cavern excavated in the rock of the Acropolis.[1] The Ancyrean inscription records its rebuilding by Augustus; see vol. i. p. 385.

The Ficus ruminalis. Near the *Lupercal* was the fig tree under which the twins were stranded by the retiring waters of the Tiber. This fig tree, called *ficus ruminalis*, from *rumes*, the teats of the she-wolf (Festus, ed. Müller, p. 400),[2] was miraculously transported to the *Comitium* by the Augur Attus Navius, and a tree which passed for the original one existed till the times of the Empire. Near it the Aediles Cnaeus and Quintus Ogulnius, in 296 B.C., dedicated a bronze statue of the wolf suckling the twins (Liv. x. 23); this is very probably the statue, of Etruscan style, which is now in the Capitoline Museum.[3]

Sacred fig tree.

The Hut of Romulus. Also near the western angle of the Palatine, on the side towards the Circus Maximus, stood the *casa Romuli*, or hut of Romulus; see Dionys. i. 79; Plut. *Rom.* 20. Dion Cassius records that it twice caught fire during the reign of Augustus (xlviii. 43 and liv. 29), so even then some primitive thatched wooden hut was probably preserved as a sacred relic of the founder of Rome. It appears probable that at some time this hut was moved to the Capitoline Hill, as Vitruvius (ii. 1. 5), Seneca (*Contr.* i. 6), Macrobius (*Saturn.* i.

Hut of Romulus.

---

[1] The *Cave of Pan*, which exists in the cliff of the Athenian Acropolis, near the Propylaea, is probably somewhat similar in position to the Roman *Lupercal*.

[2] A goddess called *Rumia* presided over the suckling of children.

[3] A representation of this or a similar group occurs very frequently on the reverses of early Roman *denarii*, and on an enormous number of small brass coins of the fourth century A.D. The Capitoline wolf is one of the most perfect existing examples of early Roman or Etruscan workmanship. The two infants are a modern restoration.

Hut of Romulus.

15), and the Greek historian Conon, quoted by Photius (*Bibl.* 186), all distinctly mention it as being on the *Capitolium*, while it seems clear that there was not more than one hut of Romulus; see Ovid, *Fast.* iii. 183; Val. Max. iv. 4; and Livy, v. 53.[1] In this last passage this famous hut, with its sacred memories—*casa illa conditoris nostri*—is mentioned in the eloquent speech made to the Senate by the dictator M. Furius in 390 B.C., after the Gaulish invasion, when the proposal was being discussed as to whether the people should desert the ruined city of Rome and migrate in a body to Veii. In this impassioned speech the dictator appealed to the Senate not to desert this and other sacred spots in their ancient and holy city.

Hut of Faustulus.

The Hut of Faustulus. Another relic of the primitive city was preserved at this part of the Palatine under the name of the hut (*tugurium*) of Faustulus, the shepherd who found and adopted Romulus and Remus. It is, however, possible that this is only another name for the *casa Romuli.*

In addition to the stone wall built round *Roma Quadrata*, Romulus is also said to have surrounded the Capitoline and Aventine Hills with an *agger* and *vallum* (Dionys. ii. 37); but this method of fortification appears quite unsuited to places such as these, with precipitous sides,[2] and no traces of such a structure now exist. It is very doubtful whether Dionysius is right on this point.

---

[1] The regionary catalogues mention it among the contents of *Regio X.* or *Palatina*, but many objects are catalogued in these lists which had long ceased to exist in the places named.

[2] This method of fortification was specially used on level ground, where the garrison had no natural advantages of position; a deep trench (*fossa*) was dug, and the earth from it was heaped up into a bank (*agger*) on the inner side, on the top of which a wooden palisading (*vallum*) was fixed. The *agger* of the later kings was supported by a massive retaining wall, which rose above it, instead of the wooden fence; see vol. i. p. 136.

The Regal Period.

According to the traditional early history of Rome, the period of the seven kings lasted from 753 to 509 B.C. The remains of various structures, which were said to have been the work of the later kings of Rome during the sixth century B.C., may mostly be regarded as coming within the beginning of a real historic period, founded on something more than dim mythological traditions.[1] The most important of the existing remains of this early period is the great circuit wall, by which a number of isolated towns or village forts, on separate hills, originally occupied by independent communities, were linked together and formed into one large city by the fusion of several different races and tribes into a united people, under one president, who was elected, not for a term of years, but for life, and was dignified with the name of king.[2]

The kings of Rome.

Circuit wall.

This great wall, many pieces of which still exist, is the large circuit of fortification said to have been begun by Tarquinius Priscus, and mostly built by Servius Tullius; see Livy, i. 36 and 38; and Dionys. iii. 37. It enclosed seven of the hills of Rome, embracing all those which had already been included in the city, namely, the Palatine, the Capitoline, the Aventine, the Quirinal, and the Caelian; and

Seven hills enclosed.

---

[1] It need hardly be said that this can only be called a historical period in a very modified sense. It is, for example, impossible that only seven kings, some of whom were elected late in life, when they were elderly men, can have reigned so long as 244 years.

[2] The principal races thus fused into one people appear to have been Etruscans, Latins, Sabines, and Greek colonists; it was, of course, a long time before the individuality and race jealousy of each lost itself in the compact unity and solidarity of the *Populus Romanus*. It is a notable fact that only two of the kings are said to have been of Latin race—Romulus and Tullus Hostilius, a fact which throws doubt on the traditional supremacy of the Latins among the allied tribes.

it also included two others—the Esquiline and the Viminal;
see Varro, *Lin. Lat.* iv. 41 and vi. 24. Virgil (*Georg.* ii. 535)
mentions this great work of fortification—

Septemque una sibi muro circumdedit arces.

Separate forts. It is probable that certain parts, such as some of the existing wall on the *Capitolium*, may belong to the earlier fortifications, those, that is, which enclosed each separate hill, but the main part of the existing remains of this great work certainly belong to the comprehensive circuit which was said to have been planned by the Greek Tarquinius Priscus.

Janiculan fort. In addition to the fortified group of seven hills known as the *Septimontium*,[1] there was also, on the other side of the Tiber, a separate fort on the Janiculan Hill, remains of which still exist near the Church of *S. Pietro in Montorio*. Access to this was given by the wooden *Pons Sublicius*, with which it was connected by long walls, probably resembling on a small scale the celebrated *long walls* which united Athens to its harbours of *Piraeus* and *Phalerum*. This is said to have been the work of Ancus Martius; see Livy, i. 33.

Regions of Servius. *Regiones of Servius.* The space included in the enlarged circuit was divided by Servius Tullius, for religious, military, and political purposes, into four *regiones* (Varro, *Lin. Lat.* iv. 46 to 54), each of which contained six *vici* or parishes, and each parish a shrine known, for what reason is doubtful, as an *Argive* or *Argean Chapel* (*Argeorum Sacraria*). These *sacraria*, however, existed before the formation of the *regiones* of Servius, and are said by Varro to have been founded by Numa, to whom the Romans attributed most pieces of sacred and secular organisation, the origin of which had been forgotten.

The following were the *regiones* of Servius :—

[1] The word *Septimontium* originally had a different meaning ; see Plut. *Quaes. Rom.* 69 ; and Burn, *Rome and the Campagna*, p. 37.

I. SUBURANA, which included the Caelian[1] Hill, the *Suburana.*
Carinae, the Sacra Via, the Subura, with the slope of the
Esquiline immediately above it, and probably most of the
valleys adjoining the Caelian. Varro, quoting Junius, derives
Suburana from *sub urbe*.[2]

II. ESQUILINA, including the Esquiline Hill, with its spurs *Esquilina.*
the Oppius and the Cispius. Varro suggests that Esquiline is
derived "*ab excubiis regis.*" It really means the dwellers
"outside," *es-quil-iae*. The same root occurs in *in-quil-inus*,
"dwellers within."

III. COLLINA, including the Viminal and Quirinal Hills, *Collina.*
which were called *colles* in contradistinction to the other five
hills, which were called *montes*.

IV. PALATINA, the Palatine Hill, and its outlying parts *Palatina.*
the Germalus or Cermalus, and the Velia; see vol. i. p. 219.
One of Varro's derivations of the *Palatium* or Palatine Hill is
from the Greek hero Pallas, who came to Italy with his father
Evander.

It will be observed that these four *regiones* do not include
the Aventine, the Capitoline, and some of their adjacent
valleys, an omission for which it is difficult to account, as
they were included in the Servian circuit. Becker suggests
that the Capitoline Hill was excluded on account of its sacred
character, while the Aventine was not yet thickly populated,
and the Janiculan was only occupied by a fortress; see

---

[1] So called, Varro says, from the Etruscan chief Caelius Vipenna,
Romulus' ally against the Sabine Tatius, who with his followers settled
on this hill, and remained there till they were moved by the jealousy of
the Romans to the valley near the *Velabrum*, on the road which was
afterwards called from them the *Vicus Tuscus*, or Etruscan Street.

[2] The *Subura* was the valley from whence the "*Cloaca Maxima*"
started, and was close under that part of the Esquiline which was called
the Carinae, probably the ridge where the Church of S. Pietro in Vincoli
now stands; a flight of steps now leads down to the valley of the
Subura, from the piazza in front of the church.

Handbuch, i. p. 386, and *Ann. Inst.* 1861, p. 61. It should be remembered that the four *regiones* were specially formed for political purposes.

THE SERVIAN WALL.

Circuit of the wall.   The Line of the Servian Wall and its Gates (see *Map of Ancient Rome*). Excavations made during the last fifteen years have done much to determine the circuit of this massive wall. Great portions of it have been discovered and then destroyed during the extensive works of levelling and digging foundations for the new quarters which have been laid out on the Quirinal, Viminal, and Esquiline Hills.[1]

River quay.   At one point, for a short distance, the Tiber formed the defence of the city, and here there was no wall, but a massive stone embankment or quay, the καλὴ ἀκτὴ of Plutarch (*Rom.* 20), formed of great blocks of tufa in the usual two foot courses. In this the arched exits of the "*Cloaca Maxima*" and other smaller drains are still well preserved, and can be seen from the *Ponte rotto* or *Pons Cestius*.[2] Near this bridge the wall started from the river bank and ran inland to the *Capitolium*, between the *Forum Olitorium* on the outside, and the *Forum Boarium* inside the city. In this short length, where it crossed the plain between the river and the Capitol, there were three gates.

River gate.   (i.) *The Porta Flumentana* (*river gate*). This was close to the bank of the Tiber, near the back of the so-called "House of Rienzi"; see Cic. *ad Att.* vii. 3, and Livy, xxxv. 19 and 21.

[1] Unhappily, in very few instances have these priceless remains of the early history of Rome been saved from utter destruction.

[2] Since this was written all that remained of the Pons Cestius, with the exception of one arch, has been destroyed, and a very hideous iron bridge has been erected by it.

The exit of the Cloaca Maxima now appears behind a modern arch in the new river embankment, which has concealed all that remained of the old quay wall.

(ii.) *The Porta Triumphalis*, the exact site of which is *Triumphal gate.* unknown; it is usually only mentioned in connection with triumphal processions; see Cic. *in Pis.* 23, and Josephus, *Bell. Jud.* vii. 5. 4. It probably was not used except on those occasions when processions in honour of victorious generals passed from their starting point in the *Campus Martius* to the *Sacra Via*, and so up to the Capitoline Hill.

(iii.) *The Porta Carmentalis*, in the wall at the foot of the *Porta Carmentalis.* *Capitolium*; see Solinus, i. 13; Livy, ii. 49, xxiv. 47, xxv. 7; and Ascon. ad Cic. *In toga*, Orell. p. 90.[1] This gate was named from an altar to the nymph Carmenta, the mother of Evander; see Virg. *Aen.* viii. 337. According to the note of Servius on this passage, its name was afterwards changed to the *Porta Scelerata*, because from it the ill-fated Fabii set out to fight the people of Veii on the banks of the river Cremera, in 478 B.C.; see Livy, ii. 49.

The Capitoline fortress. The whole Capitoline Hill, in- *Capitoline Hill.* cluding the *Capitolium*, the *Arx*, and the intermediate depression called the *Asylum*, was already, before the formation of the Servian circuit, surrounded with a complete wall of its own, and was incorporated as a link in the chain of forts which were united by the wall of Servius. Several parts of this primitive fortress-wall still exist, and are now exposed to *Remains of wall.* sight.[2] One of these is at the top of what is popularly called the Tarpeian rock, and can be seen from the foot of the cliff at the end of the *Vicolo della rupe Tarpeia*. A short piece about six courses high remains, set at the edge of the perpendicularly scarped rock.[3] Remains of a part of the wall where it skirted

---

[1] Plutarch, *Camill.* 25, mentions the *Porta Carmentalis* as being below the steepest part of the Capitoline Hill; see also Ovid, *Fasti*, ii. 201.

[2] Dionysius, ix. 68, speaks of these early fortifications being set—ἐπὶ λόφοις . . . καὶ πέτραις ἀποτόμοις.

[3] It should be remembered that till as late as the fourteenth century there was no access to the Capitoline Hill on this side. Both the great flights of steps which now lead up, one to the central *asylum*, and the

the *Asylum* were exposed during the recent formation of a winding carriage road up from the *Campus Martius*. At this point the wall is set, like that of *Roma Quadrata*, not at the highest point, but on a shelf cut about half-way down the slope.

Capitoline fort. A third piece of wall, five courses high, has been exposed on the rock above the Mamertine prison, opposite the north-east end of the *Tabularium* and separated from it by the steep road which leads past it from the *Temple of Concord*, up towards the *Asylum* and the Church of *Ara Coeli*. This is built of soft reddish tufa, and possibly belongs to the original fortification of the *Arx*, when it was an isolated fortress. In character of masonry this very primitive piece of wall resembles the so-called "Wall of Romulus" on the Palatine Hill. Some parts of the wall, built of a harder kind of tufa, have similar masons' marks to those figured at p. 138, and are evidently of about the same date as other existing pieces of the Servian wall.

Porta Ratumena. The *Porta Ratumena* was close to the cliff of the *Arx*, where the Servian wall starts from the Capitoline Hill. It was called Ratumena (so the legend says) from a chariot-driver whose horses ran away during races at Veii, and did not stop till they came to Rome, and here upset the car and killed him; see Pliny, *Hist. Nat.* viii. 161; and Plut. *Publ.* 13. At this gate, the *Via Lata*, modern Via di Marforio, issued from the city, and in it, close without the gate, are remains of the tomb of Bibulus, and other tombs, built into the modern houses.[1] Remains of the wall and the *Porta Ratumena* have

other to *Ara Coeli* (the *Arx*), are of mediaeval date. The 124 white marble steps which lead up to the Church of Ara Coeli were constructed in 1348 A.D., out of marble taken from the so-called *Temple of the Sun* on the Quirinal Hill. The three entrances mentioned by Livy (iii. 7, v. 26. and 28; and Tac. *Hist.* iii. 71, 72) were all from the interior of the city, on the side towards the *Forum Romanum*.

[1] In later times the ascent from the Forum to this gate was called the *Clivus Argentarius*. A number of the tombs which lined the *Via Lata*

been discovered under the house in the *Via di Marforio*, numbered 81 C and 81 E.

From the Capitoline *Arx* the wall of Servius passed to the *Rocky spur.* Quirinal along a spur of elevated ground which once linked together these two hills. This rocky spur, together with a large portion of the slope of the Quirinal, was completely cut away by Trajan to form a level site for his great Forum and Basilica (see vol. ii. p. 24), so that here no traces exist of the ancient wall.

After passing Trajan's Forum the next existing piece of the wall is on the slope of the Quirinal, in the gardens of the Colonna Palace, under the Baths of Constantine; and near here, towards the foot of the Quirinal, was the *Porta Fontinalis*; see Livy, xxxv. 10.

The Porta Fontinalis. In the middle of the new Via *Porta Fontinalis.* Nazionale a small piece of the wall has been preserved, and close by it, in the Palazzo Antonelli, are further remains, with a massive stone archway, which has been supposed to be the *Porta Fontinalis.* It seems, however, small for one of the principal gates, being only 6 feet 6 inches wide, and 5 feet 2 inches to the springing of the arch. The courses of the wall here vary from 19 to 23 inches in depth; the arch is in one stone ring, 1 foot 11 inches deep; it stands on concrete foundations. In late times, under the Empire, another ring of brick and concrete has been added over the stone arch.

Near the *Porta Fontinalis* a number of fluted columns made *Long porticus.* of tufa were discovered in 1885. It is possible that these belonged to the *porticus* which led from this gate to the Temple of Mars in the *Campus Martius*. According to Livy, xxxv. 10 and xl. 45, this *porticus* was built in 193 B.C. by the Aediles Aemilius Lepidus and L. Aemilius Paullus.

With these columns was found the fine bronze statue of an

near the tomb of Bibulus have recently been destroyed to make room for the monument to Victor Emmanuel, which will soon disfigure the Capitoline Arx.

Bronze athlete.

athlete 6 feet 10 inches high, which seems to be of the school of Lysippus, and according to Dr. Helbig is possibly a portrait of Philip V. of Macedon.

The pose of this statue somewhat resembles that of the so-called Meleager of the Vatican Belvedere: its eyes are hollowed to receive coloured enamels, and below the breast are these letters or numerals incised, L · VIS · L · XXIIX (56½, 78 ?) Their meaning has not yet been interpreted.

Bronze gladiator.

Not far from the same place another large bronze statue was found, of very different and inferior style, representing a bearded gladiator, seated, of rather brutal type, with swollen ears and malevolent expression, a characteristic example of purely Roman art.

Bronze Bacchus.

A third bronze statue, discovered about the same time in the bed of the Tiber, is of a more beautiful type, a Graeco-Roman figure of the youthful Bacchus, 5 feet 6 inches high, the lips inlaid with copper, and his ivy wreath decorated with silver inlay of very delicate workmanship.[1]

Porta Sanqualis.

The Porta Sanqualis. The next gate was also on the Quirinal; Festus (ed. Müller, p. 345) calls it *proxima aedi Sanci*; from this temple its name was derived; see also Livy, viii. 20. In 1866 the position of this gate was determined on the slope between the Trevi fountain and the Quirinal Palace by the discovery of some roadside tombs, which were immediately outside the line of the wall, thus showing the course of the street which issued from the gate.

The next part of the wall passed under the modern palace, and through the gardens of the Quirinal. No further remains are known till the garden of the Barberini Palace is reached, where a small piece of wall exists at a point where there was once an abrupt cliff, now cut away.

Porta Salutaris.

The *Porta Salutaris* was a little beyond this, near the

[1] These statues are now in the Museum which has been formed in the monastery of S. Maria degli Angeli, on the site of part of the Thermae of Diocletian, now called the Museo delle Terme.

Quattro Fontane; this was named from a *Temple of Salus*, built in 306 B.C. by the Censor C. Junius Bubulcus, on the site of one of the primitive *Argean Chapels*; see Livy, ix. 43; and Festus, ed. Müller, p. 327.[1]

Extensive remains of the wall have been recently discovered and destroyed in and near the Villa Barberini, where the wall skirted the *Horti Sallustiani*, on the north side of the street now called *Via del Venti Settembre*. At this point there was a rocky cliff, at the foot of and against which was built the magnificent house thought to be the Imperial Villa which originally belonged to the historian Sallust.[2] The Servian wall skirted the edge of this cliff, and then turned southwards at a right angle, passing under the new *Ministero delle Finanze*. *Gardens of Sallust.*

The Porta Collina. During the excavations made for the foundations of the last-named building the *Porta Collina* was discovered; not on the line of the present road to the *Porta Pia*, but a little to the south of it. *Porta Collina.*

The *Porta Collina* was one of the chief gates of Rome, and from it issued the main road to the country of the Sabines;[3] see Dionys. ix. 68; Strabo, v. 3; and Livy, ii. 11. Thus far in its course from the Tiber the Servian wall mostly skirted the edges of hills, once much more precipitous than they are now, but from the angle by the *Horti Sallustiani* for a long distance southwards the wall had to cross a level plain. On this account the *Porta Collina* was the gate which was most

---

[1] The names of this and others of the Servian gates are much later than the supposed time of Servius; what their original names were is not known.

[2] This deep valley, which separated the Quirinal from the eastern part of the *Collis Hortorum*, or Pincian Hill, is now being filled in with rubbish, to make a level building site for new boulevards, under the scheme called the *Piano regolatore*, the carrying out of which has already caused the destruction of a great quantity of valuable ancient remains; see vol. ii. p. 242.

[3] The *Porta Collina* was also called *Agonalis* or *Quirinalis*.

Weak point. frequently attacked by foreign enemies: as, for example, by the Gauls in 360 B.C., by Sulla in 88 B.C., and by the Democrats and Samnites in 82 B.C., when it was the scene of one of the bloodiest battles that occurred in the history of the Republic.

Hannibal, too, encamped outside this gate when he was preparing to make an attack on Rome, which might possibly have been successful if his courage had not failed, causing him to retreat after throwing one javelin at the city; see Mommsen, *Hist. of Rome*, iii. pp. 264, 318, and 340.

Beginning of the Agger. On account of the circuit of the city for a long distance, from the angle near the Colline Gate to the most southern part of the Esquiline Hill, having to pass over a level plain, where the inhabitants of the city had no natural advantage of position, a different and more elaborate method of fortification was adopted, in order to gain by artificial means the strength which elsewhere was given by the contour of the ground.[1]

Vitruvius in his interesting chapter on fortification walls (i. 5) describes at sec. 6 the necessity for constructing an *agger* and *fossa* wherever a city wall is on level ground.

Agger of Servius. Along this plain was constructed the great fortification line of combined *Agger* and *fossa*, which was considered one of the chief wonders of Rome. It is described with some minuteness by Dionysius, ix. 68; and the accuracy of his account of it has been proved by recent discoveries. It is also mentioned by Strabo, v. 3, who gives its length as 6 stadia, not 7, as Dionysius does. Its position at the junction of the Quirinal, Viminal, and Esquiline Hills is accurately described by Livy, ii. 44.[2]

---

[1] Close outside the *Colline Gate* was the *Campus Sceleratus*, in which erring Vestals were buried alive; see vol. i. p. 294. The north-east angle of the modern Palazzo delle Finanze is, according to the Comm. Lanciani, close by the *Campus Sceleratus*.

[2] The existing remains of the Agger of Servius are described below.

The Porta Viminalis. Besides the *Colline Gate*, the *Agger* had two others, first, the *Porta Viminalis*, out of which issued the road which passed through the existing closed gate (*Porta Chiusa*) in the wall of Aurelianus. Its exact position was discovered in 1872, while digging the foundations of the new Public Offices, by the exposure of the lava-paved road which passed through it, very nearly in the middle of the *Agger*—ὑπὸ μέσῳ τῷ χώματι, as Strabo says. *Viminal gate.*

The *Porta Esquilina*, which was the other gate in the *Agger*, was discovered in 1876; its foundations are in contact with the existing *Arch of Gallienus*, which was built against it on the outside. The adjoining Church of S. Vito is very largely built of blocks taken from the retaining wall of the *Agger*. *Esquiline gate.*

Near it, on the outside, was the *Campus Esquilinus*, once a squalid cemetery for slaves and the poorest classes, which was laid out as gardens by the wealthy Maecenas, who built himself a magnificent villa at this place. The improvement of this quarter near the *Agger* is mentioned by Horace, *Sat.* i. 8. 14—

*Nunc licet Esquiliis habitare salubribus, atque
Aggere in aprico spatiari.*[1]

The further course of the wall from the southern end of the *Agger* across the Esquiline and the valley of the Colosseum is the least known part of the circuit. It appears probable from the contour of the ground that it first skirted the *Mons Oppius*, one of the spurs of the Esquiline, along the modern Via Merulana. *S. end of the Agger.*

Probably in the valley was the *Porta Querquetulana*, and a

[1] Remains of what has been called the "Villa of Maecenas" have been exposed, built close against the ancient wall of Servius; see vol. ii. p. 239. A large apsidal-ended room, with recesses and stages for flowers, built with neat *opus reticulatum* facing, is the best preserved part; it stands close to the road between the Basilica of S. Maria Maggiore and the Lateran; *Bull. Comm. Arch.* ii. p. 137.

134 THE SERVIAN WALL CHAP.

little beyond it, on the Caelian Hill, the *Porta Caelimontana*.
After crossing the Caelian, the wall turned westwards along
its southern cliff, and then crossed the valley which was partly
Porta occupied by the *Circus Maximus*. In this valley was the *Porta*
Capena. *Capena*, foundations of which were discovered by Mr. Parker
not far from the Church of S. Gregorio, together with remains
of the Marcian Aqueduct which passed over it. On account
of the leaking of this aqueduct it was called *madida*, "the
damp gate," by Juvenal, iii. 11; and Martial, iii. 47.

From the *Porta Capena* issued the *Via Appia*, the oldest
of the Roman paved roads, and a little way outside the gate
the *Via Latina* branched off to the left. Several large temples
Temples of stood near this gate, two dedicated to Mars, and one to *Honos*
Mars.
Temple of *et Virtus* (Honour and Valour) founded by Marcellus after his
Honos. capture of Syracuse with its rich spoils of Greek art, in 212
B.C.; Livy, xxv. 40. It was dedicated in 208 B.C., after some
difficulties had been raised by the *Pontifices*, on the ground
that a single *Cella* should not be consecrated to two deities,
because if it were struck by lightning, or if any prodigy
occurred in it, it would be difficult to know to which of the
two gods the sign should be attributed. On this account a
separate chamber for *Virtus* was added; see Livy, xxvii. 25.

Long Like the *Porta Fontinalis* and the *Porta Trigemina* (Livy,
Porticus.
xxxv. 10), the *Porta Capena* had a long porticus outside it,
reaching to the *Temple of Mars*, in which the Senate met on
several occasions; see Ov. *Fast.* vi. 191.[1]

After crossing the valley of the *Via Appia*, the wall
reaches the Aventine Hill, and forms a loop, encircling all
except the northern part of the hill.

Several fine remains of the wall exist on the Aventine,
especially a piece of 11 courses high, near the Church of S.
Balbina. Another very noble length of wall, 25 courses high,

[1] Probably from this temple were taken the fine blocks of white marble
used by Honorius in building the lower part of the *Porta Appia*, in the
Aurelian wall.

containing a fine arch, exists in the Vigna Torlonia, not far from the Baths of Caracalla (see below, fig. 20, p. 140); a third piece exists near the Church of S. Sabina.

Under the Aventine the wall appears to have touched the *Pons Probi*. river near the foundations of a bridge, which are still visible, especially when the water is low; this has been taken for the site of the Sublician Bridge, the first built in Rome, made to connect the main city with the Janiculan fortress (Livy, i. 33), but there is no doubt that the *Pons Sublicius* really stood higher up the river; see voL ii. p. 362.

At this point, close by the river, was the *Porta Trigemina*; *Porta Trigemina.* see Livy, xxxv. 10; Plaut. *Capt.* 90; Solinus, i. 8; and *Ann. Inst.* vol. xxix. p. 64.

In 1887 a fine arch of large tufa blocks, with a span of about 12 feet, was discovered at the foot of the Aventine, not far from the Church of S. Maria in Cosmedin and near some remains which appeared to be part of the Servian wall. This archway has been thought to be the *Porta Trigemina*. It spanned a road of some importance, paved with lava polygons; see *Not. d. Scavi*, 1887.

Thence to the *Porta Flumentana*, the Tiber, with its massive *Tiber quay.* stone embankment or quay, formed the bulwark of the city; and this completes the circuit to our starting-point near the *Pons Cestius*.

A fragmentary passage of Varro mentions two other gates, *Uncertain gates.* one called *Naevia*, named after a certain Naevius who farmed the land near it, and the other called *Rauduscula*, i.e. the bronze gate, *aes "raudus" dictum*. The sites of these are not known. Varro appears, according to some editions, to mention a third gate called *Porta Lavernalis*, but here the word *porta* is an insertion, and the phrase "*hinc lavernalis*" may perhaps merely mean that the word is etymologically similar.

Many other gates existed, not in the outer circuit of the wall, but opening from the separate forts into the inside of the city; such as, for example, the *Porta Pandana*, which led from the *Forum Romanum* to the enclosure of the Capitoline Hill.[1]

REMAINS OF THE AGGER AND WALL OF SERVIUS.

Agger of Servius. The construction of the railway station and other new buildings has first exposed and then destroyed a great part of

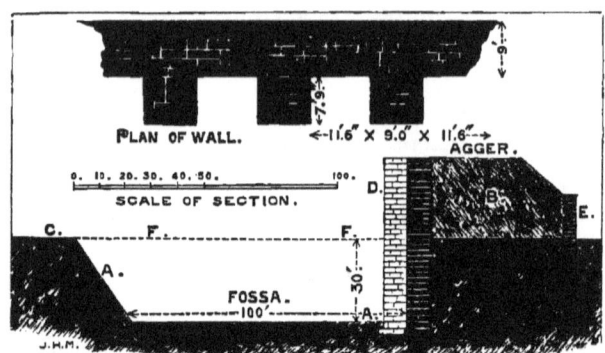

Fig. 18.
Section of Wall and Agger of Servius.

AA. Undisturbed earth of fossa.
B. Earth excavated from the fossa, and heaped up to form the Agger.
C. Road at brink of fossa.
D. Wall and buttress.
E. Back retaining-wall of Agger.
F. Level to which the fossa was filled up and built upon under the Empire.

The plan is given to double scale.

Existing wall. this. One great length of wall is, however, still standing, though the actual *Agger* or bank behind it has been removed, and the rough face of the wall, which was not intended to be exposed, is now visible.[2] Fig. 18 shows the section as actually

[1] See a valuable article on the Servian walls by Comm. Lanciani, *Ann. Inst.* 1871, p. 40 *seq*.
[2] This noble piece of wall has now been fenced off from the rest of the precincts of the railway station.

discovered, agreeing very well with the description of Dionysius, ix. 68, who says that the *fossa* or ditch was 30 feet deep and 100 feet wide at the lowest part. A road ran along the top edge of the *fossa*, at C on fig. 18, and another at the bottom at A. The earth taken out of this enormous ditch was heaped up to form the *Agger* or bank, and was kept up by a massive stone retaining-wall in front, and another lower and thinner wall behind it, E on fig 18. The strata of clay, sand, and other kinds of soil, as they appeared on the sloping side of the ditch, were traceable in the *Agger*, but of course reversed by the process of digging out and heaping up; the top layer of the ditch being the lowest of the *Agger*. *Fossa.*

The wall is built of great blocks of stone, the ἀμάξιοι λίθοι of Dionysius. Tufa of several kinds and peperino (*lapis Albanus*) are used, but the former predominates: no mortar or iron clamps are used, and though the beds are worked very truly the upright joints in some places are rather wide. The blocks average two Roman feet in depth, varying mostly from 22 to 24 inches, and in width from 19 to 25 inches; the lengths are not at all regular, ranging from 3 feet 6 inches to nearly 8 feet. *Massive masonry.*

In some cases the courses do not run evenly, and some of the blocks are set on edge, not on their natural bed, and consequently have split. As a rule the courses are alternately *headers* and *stretchers*. The main wall is 9 feet thick; a long piece of it, as much as 30 feet high, still exists. In certain parts massive buttresses closely set project on the outside; see fig. 18. A large variety of tools have been used in working the blocks; some were chisels as much as 1¼ inch wide, others were picks with a sharp point. *Careless work.* *Masons' tools.*

The back of the wall, now exposed by the removal of the *Agger*, is quite rough; but the front is fairly regular, each block being worked to a sort of bossy surface, in some cases with a smooth band or draught round the joints.

Several varieties of workmanship occur in the wall of the

Agger, and it is certainly not all of one date. According to Dionysius it was partly the work of Tarquinius Superbus, having been left incomplete by Servius Tullius.

The *Agger* or bank behind the wall is not of the same thickness everywhere; the dimension given by Dionysius, namely, 50 feet including the wall, is probably about the average. He estimates the length at 7 stadia, about 1400 yards, and this corresponds with the actual discoveries.

Water channels. In some places the *specus* or channels of Aqueducts have been in later times carried through the *Agger*, or in the ground under it. At one point where the *Agger* was exposed, and

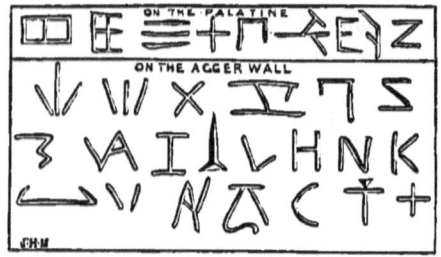

Fig. 19.
Masons' marks on walls of the Regal period. They vary from 10 to 14 inches in height.

then destroyed by the laying out of the modern Via del Principe Umberto, the *specus* of three Aqueducts—the *Aqua Julia*, *Marcia*, and *Tepula*—passed along it close together.

Masons' marks. A large number of masons' marks (see fig. 19) exist on the ends of many of the blocks at the back of the lofty piece of wall near the railway station. They are very deeply cut in the soft tufa, and frequently occur in groups, as if a whole batch of stones sent at once had all had the same mark; the marks average 10 to 14 inches in height. None appear on the face of the wall, so that when the *Agger* of earth existed they were all hidden.

Some of these marks are single letters, others are monograms, some are numbers, and one is the sign ψ, which may be the Etruscan CH or the early Roman numeral 50. Many of the characters resemble Etruscan letters, and some are distinctly Greek; the digamma F, Γ, and the early form of the aspirate ⊟ with closed top occur. Other similar marks exist on the blocks of the very primitive tufa buildings by the *Stairs of Cacus* on the Palatine.[1]

Later houses built against the Agger. Under the Empire the great ditch appears to have been filled up, and a row of houses built over it, against the outside of the Servian wall. This filling up was probably done in the time of Augustus; a large part of the Servian circuit wall had at that time been destroyed and built over, so that even then it was not easy to trace its whole line; Dionysius (iv. 13) says . . . τῷ τείχει τῷ δυσευρέτῳ μὲν ὄντι διὰ τὰς περιλαμβανούσας αὐτὸ πολλαχόθεν οἰκήσεις.

Later houses.

The remains of these houses against the *Agger* wall are built of concrete faced with brick and the latest sort of *opus reticulatum*, very rudely executed. They appear to have been rows of vaulted rooms two stories high, and are covered with painted stucco, which also covers parts of the Servian wall where it forms the ends of the various rooms. Brick stamps show these buildings to be of the time of Hadrian.

Another row of houses was built facing on to the ancient road which skirted the upper edge of the ditch; so the two rows formed a long street occupying the whole width of the filled-in *fossa*. At one point in this street, near the existing lofty piece of wall, there is a very curious circular structure dating probably about the time of Augustus, which has evidently been connected with one of the aqueducts.[2] It is a small round tower, built of massive blocks of tufa, with a roof

Inspection shaft.

[1] See Bruzza in *Ann. Inst.* 1876, p. 72; and Jordan, *Topographic der Stadt Rom*, i. p. 259.

[2] See Lanciani's valuable work on Frontinus and the Roman water supply, *Comment. di Front.* pl. vi.

and intermediate band of travertine: it is about 6 feet in diameter inside. Its lower part is still buried, but it stands about 12 feet high above the present ground level. It is probably a shaft to give access to a subterranean aqueduct; see vol. ii. p. 337.

Existing remains.

Other remains of the Servian wall. On the southern slopes of the Aventine, in what is now called the Vigna Torlonia, are some extensive remains of the Servian wall, part of

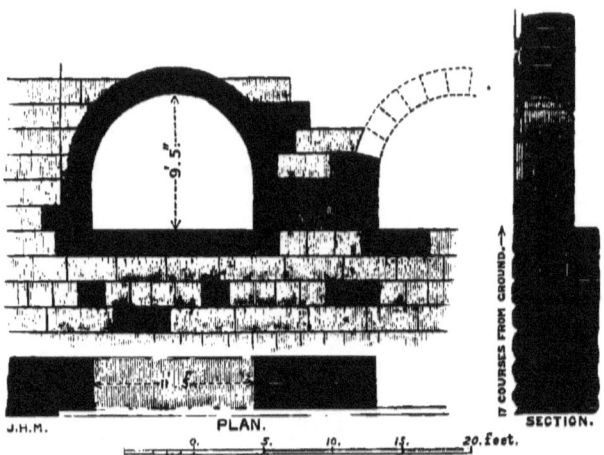

Fig. 20.
Part of the Servian wall on the Aventine.

which is still 50 feet high, and 10 feet 6 inches thick. In the upper part of the wall there were semicircular open arches 11 feet 6 inches wide, of which one is perfect and the start of the next exists; their sill is 34 feet above the foot of the wall; see fig. 20. The arches are built of a hard red tufa, while most of the plain wall is a very soft and friable yellow tufa. The blocks, which are of the usual two feet courses, are arranged regularly in *emplecton*, of alternate courses of *headers* and *stretchers*. The workmanship is much more careful

Style of masonry.

than in the *agger* wall, the jointing is very neat and accurate, and a thin stratum of pure lime mortar is laid on the joints and beds.[1] Each block is cut with a bossy surface, draughted neatly round the joints. There is no reason for supposing the arches to be later additions, they have every sign of being contemporary with the rest of the wall. The use of these arches is unknown; it has been suggested they are openings in which *balistae* or catapults were set, possibly to defend an adjacent gateway.

Draughted joints.

In later times, under the early Empire, the wall at this point has been cut through and partly removed to make room for a house with thick concrete walls, faced with *opus reticulatum*. A part still exists of the large *cloaca* which drained this house. The top of the drain is formed of two tiles (*tegulae bipedales*) set leaning together.

Behind the part of the Servian wall which has the open arches a great mass of concrete backing has been poured in to give additional solidity. This appears to be contemporary with the stone masonry,[2] and if so it is one of the earliest known examples of concrete in Rome.[3]

Concrete backing.

[1] The *Tullianum* is a still earlier instance of the use of thin beds of lime mortar; see vol. i. p. 152.

[2] Concrete was certainly used in Rome as early as the Regal period. Most writers have placed the date of the first use both of mortar and concrete in Rome very much too late. The concrete foundations under the arch in the Palazzo Antonelli (mentioned above at p. 129) must of course be as old as the arch itself.

[3] For further accounts of the Servian wall see Nibby and Gell, *Le Mura di Roma*, 1820; Becker, *De Romae Muris*, Leipsic, 1842; Lanciani, *Ann. Inst.* 1871, p. 40 *seq.*; and *Mon. Inst.* ix. Tav. 27. See also *Ann. Inst.* 1857, p. 62; and *Mon. Inst.* vi. Tav. 4. A little book by Quarenghi, *Le Mura di Roma*, 1880, is mainly an abstract of Lanciani's papers on the subject: compare Vitruvius, i. 5, on walls of fortification.

THE CLOACAE OF ROME.

Cloacae. The early *cloacae* of Rome are said by Dionysius (iii. 68) to have been the work of the Greek Tarquinius Priscus. He correctly describes them as draining every street of Rome, and as being works of most marvellous magnitude. It was the construction of these and later *cloacae* that made many valleys in Rome, originally mere marshes interspersed with pools of water, such as were the *Forum Romanum*, the *Velabrum*, and most of the great Campus Martius, into dry and habitable ground, and thus contributed very largely to the growth and prosperity of the city. These great drains must have been constantly flushed and kept clear by the fact that they carried away, not only the sewerage of the city, but also the water of a number of natural springs and an enormous flood of pure water constantly poured into Rome by the great aqueducts.

Pliny on the sewers. An interesting description of the *cloacae*, as being among the principal marvels of Rome, is given by Pliny (*Hist. Nat.* xxxvi. 104 to 109), who, like Dionysius, attributes them to Tarquinius Priscus. He speaks of the largest one as being big enough for a loaded hay-cart to drive up—"*Amplitudinem cavis eam fecisse proditur ut vehem faeni large onustam transmitteret.*" And he records that M. Agrippa, the friend and minister of Augustus, during his aedileship in 33 B.C. inspected some of the *cloacae* by penetrating a long way up them in a boat; a striking instance of his zeal as minister of public works.

"Cloaca Maxima." One of the largest of the sewers,[1] now commonly called the "*Cloaca Maxima*" in allusion to Pliny's phrase, forms a conduit for a considerable body of water, issuing from the valley of the *Subura*. Numbers of fish, attracted by the offal in the

[1] The great sewer which has its exit near the circular temple in the *Forum Boarium* is usually known as the "*Cloaca Maxima*," in spite of its not being actually the largest of the existing sewers of Rome.

THE CLOACA MAXIMA

drain, appear to have penetrated up it a long distance from the Tiber exit, and to have been caught and eaten by the poorer classes of Rome.[1]

This great *cloaca* has its exit in the quay wall which lines the river bank by the *Forum Boarium*. At this point its arch, which is nearly 11 feet wide and more than 12 feet high, is formed of three rings of peperino *voussoirs*. The wall of the quay is of tufa, and tufa is also used for the barrel vault of the *cloaca* everywhere except at the exit. This vault is in one ring only of *voussoirs* 2 feet 2 inches deep. The "*Cloaca Maxima*" starts in the valley of the Subura, at the foot of the *Carinae*, the elevated spur of the Esquiline, on which now stand the Churches of S. Pietro in Vincoli and S. Francesco di Paolo. It then crosses the *Forum Romanum* at its lowest part (see *Forum Plan*), passing under the south end of the *Basilica Julia*, where a break in the vault allows the *cloaca* to be seen. Thence it runs under the *vicus Tuscus* and the valley of the *Velabrum*, till it reaches the Tiber near the round temple in the *Forum Boarium*.

River exit.

Line of the cloaca.

In 1890 a long piece (about 230 yards) of the "*Cloaca Maxima*" was cleared out, and can now be visited without difficulty. This was the part of the *cloaca* between the *Forum of Augustus* and the verge of the *Forum Romanum* where it passes at right angles under the modern Via della Salaria Vecchia and Via Alessandrina, and then to the *Forum Romanum*, between the site of the *Basilica Aemilia* and the *Curia*.

Visible part of the cloaca.

The *cloaca* here is built of massive blocks of peperino (*lapis Gabinus*); it is 10 feet 6 inches wide, and about 14 feet high to the crown of the vault. Its floor is paved with polygonal blocks of lava, like a Roman street.

Along part of its course the stone vault has been replaced in Imperial times with one of concrete.

[1] The unhappy parasites mentioned by Juvenal in his fifth Satire were given these sewer-fish to eat—"*Solitus mediae cryptam penetrare Suburae,*" *Sat.* v. 106.

Smaller sewers. Many smaller sewers branch into it on both sides; and at intervals there are manholes to give access to the *cloaca* from the ground level above.

This very interesting relic of early Rome has been well described and illustrated by the Comm. Lanciani, *Bull. Com. Arch.* 1890, p. 95, and Tav. vii. and viii.

The masonry of this *cloaca*, both walls and vault, and especially its peperino arch at the mouth, are very neat and well jointed. The latter resembles the arch in the Servian wall *Other cloacae.* on the Aventine. The exits of other similar *cloacae* with stone barrel vaults could, till recently, be seen in the great quay wall near the "*Cloaca Maxima*"; and a whole network of these primitive drains exists under various parts of the city.

One of the many large sewers which drains the wide area of the Campus Martius is even larger than the one usually known as the "*Cloaca Maxima.*" As Pliny rightly suggests, nothing in Rome is really more remarkable than the very complete way in which the great area of the whole ancient city (within the Aurelian walls) is drained with a perfect system of massive stone sewers as main arteries, and countless branches of various shapes and dimensions, according to the work they had to do. So complete is the network extending under the whole of Rome that Pliny (*H. N.* xxxvi. 104) may be said to have been speaking literally when he calls Rome an *urbs pensilis*, or "hanging city."[1]

Various forms of sewers. The construction of the Roman drains varies according to their date and size.

Next to the great tunnels, as they might be called, with stone barrel vaults, come a number of other large and primitive sewers built of similar blocks of stone, but roofed

[1] In Imperial times, when monolithic columns and other blocks of marble or granite of immense weight were being brought through the streets of Rome, the building contractors were frequently required to give security to the Aediles against injury being done to the vaults of the sewers over which the heavy blocks were transported.

over with triangular tops formed of courses of stone on level beds, each course projecting over the one below. The same archaic method of construction is used in the *Tullianum* and in the "beehive" tombs of prehistoric Greece, such as the great "Tomb of Atreus" at Mycenae.[1] *Triangular sewers.*

In later times, under the Empire, great sewers were formed of concrete faced with brickwork and covered with semicircular vaults.

Smaller drains, from about 3 feet wide and below that, were commonly roofed with large tiles (*tegulae bipedales*) set leaning together in a triangular form. One of these, draining the *Nova Via*, is shown in the section of the *Atrium Vestae*, fig. 42, vol. i. p. 308.

There is some reason for believing that the notion of building the great arched *cloacae* was derived, like most of the early Roman architecture, from the partly Hellenised Etruscans. At the Etruscan city of Graviscae, by the sea near Tarquinii, there is an exactly similar stone *cloaca*, 14 feet wide, which also has its exit in a massive quay wall about 20 feet high, built both as a barrier against the water and also to form a landing-place for ships. Other Etruscan examples are known. *Etruscan cloacae.*

RIVER EMBANKMENT.

Comparatively little now remains of the Roman quay wall which Plutarch (*Rom.* 20) calls the καλὴ ἀκτή; the name *pulchrum littus* is a modern translation of this phrase, which does not occur in classical writings. In the last century a *Tiber quay.*

---

[1] This method of construction, in which frequently the form of the arch without the arch principle is used, was much employed by Moslem builders in India during the Middle Ages to avoid the lateral thrust exerted by all true arches. This constant pressure on the haunches is expressed by the Oriental saying that "an arch never sleeps." In later times lateral thrust was avoided by the use of concrete for arches and vaults; see vol. i. p. 66.

*Embank-
ment wall.* magnificent piece of this noble wall still existed, about 100 yards long, and is shown by Piranesi in one of his etched plates.

In later times this quay was extended on both sides of the river, apparently along the whole extent of the city; pieces of it remained till recently at various points along the *Campus Martius* and elsewhere, but all is rapidly being destroyed by the widening of the river and the new embankment which is now being constructed.

River works of Augustus. The reconstruction of the river wall and the deepening of the Tiber bed were among the countless improvements carried out by Augustus. Suetonius (*Aug.* 30) writes: *Ad coercendas inundationes, alveum Tiberis laxavit ac repurgavit, completum olim ruderibus et aedificiorum prolapsionibus coarctatum.*

Ligorio, in his MS. notes now in the Bodleian,[1] gives several inscriptions, which were found in the sixteenth century, cut on marble *cippi* to record the restoration of the river wall and of the arched exits in it of the great *cloacae*.

One of them, dated 121 A.D., runs thus—

Cippus. EX·AVCTORITATE·IMP·CAESARIS·DIVI·TRAIANI·PARTHICI·F
DIVI·NERVAE·NEPOTIS·TRAIANI·HADRIANI·AVG·PONTIF·MAX
TRIB·POTEST·V̄·IMP·IIII·COS·III·L·MAESSIVS·RVSTICVS
CVRATOR·ALVEI·ET·RIPARVM·TIBERIS·ET·CLOACARVM·VRBIS·R
R·(*recto rigore, along the course of the river*) RESTITVIT·SEC-
VNDVM·PRAECEDENTEM·TERMINATIONEM·PROXIM·CIPPI·PED
CXVS (115½ feet).

Ligorio quotes other similar inscriptions of various dates recording the repairs done to certain specified lengths of the quay wall.

Curators of the Tiber. These inscriptions were set up by special *curatores alvei et riparum Tiberis*, whose duty it was to keep the river bed free by dredging, and also to repair, when needed, the embankment wall and the mouths of the sewers. These *curatores*

[1] See note, vol. i. p. 77.

were organised by Tiberius in 15 A.D. Many examples of their inscribed *cippi* have been recently discovered along the banks of the Tiber, and are now preserved in the central part of the cloister of the Museo delle Terme.[1]

The following is specially full and interesting :—

[AELIVS · HADR]IANVS · ANT[ONINVS] · AVG · PIVS · PONTIFEX
MAXIM · TRIB · POT · XXIIII · IMP · II · COS · IIII · P · P · A · PLATORIO
NEPOTE · CALPVRNIANO · CVRAT · ALVEI · TIBERIS · ET · RIPAR · ET
CLOACAR · VRBIS · TERMINOS · VETVST · DILAPSOS · EXALTAVIT
ET · RESTIT · RECT · RIGORE · PROXIMO · CIPPO · P · POSITOS · EX
AVTORITATE · IMP · CAES · DIVI · NERVAE · FIL · NERVAE · TRAIANI
AVG · GERM · PONT · MAX · TRIB · POTEST · V · COS · IIII · P · P · CVRATORE
ALVEI · TIBERIS · ET · RIPAR · ET · CLOACAR · IVLIO · FEROCE.

Cippus.

This records that in the year 161 A.D. Platorius Nepos Calpurnianus the curator under Antoninus Pius set up along the river (*recto rigore*) the fallen *cippi* which had been originally placed there in 101 A.D. by Julius Ferox; see *Bull. Com. Arch.* 1890, p. 327.

The *cippus* mentioned below (vol. ii. p. 368) as recording the existence of a *Pons Agrippae* is of interest from its mention of the four senators who formed the *Collegium* of the *Curatores alvei.* The members of this commission held office only for one year, after which four new curators were appointed; see *Not. d. Scavi*, 1887, pp. 322 *seq.* Among the many *cippi* of this class which have been found during the construction of the new Tiber embankment there are ten of the original *cippi* of Augustus, set up in the year 7 B.C. The holes and metal pins in the sides of these river-bank *cippi* show that they formed part of a low open balustrade or parapet to prevent people falling into the river.

River parapet.

The spaces between the marble uprights were filled in with iron or bronze railings.

[1] On the *Curatores alvei Tiberis* see an interesting paper by Prof. Gatti in *Bull. Com. Arch. Rom.*, 1887, p. 306 *seq.*

River stairs. At intervals, all along its course, flights of steps led down to the river,[1] and rows of very magnificent houses were built along the quay. Several of these steps appear on fragments of the marble plan, which show the river and its stone embankment at a point beyond the Aventine, near the *Marmoratum* or wharf where imported marbles were landed. On the opposite side of the Tiber the plan shows a small harbour and a porticus or covered colonnade; see Jordan, *Forma Urbis Romae*, Nos. 51 and 169.

Carved corbels. At one place, not far below the mouth of the "*Cloaca Maxima*," a piece of the original wall exists, with long projecting corbels, the fronts of which are carved into the form of lions' heads, sculptured in the bold and effective Etruscan style.[2] These corbels are pierced with holes for the ropes of moored ships. At the *Marmoratum* there are also a number of enormous travertine unsculptured corbels, 8 feet long by 3 deep, each *Holes for ropes.* pierced with a hole one foot in diameter to receive the hawsers of ships fastened here while discharging their cargoes of marble blocks. They project from the long quay wall at regular intervals of about 50 feet. Five of these still exist, though most of the wall itself has disappeared. The wall of this great wharf was chiefly built of hard tufa in massive blocks, some over 8 feet in length; in parts the wall is built of travertine, in others peperino is used, and there are later restorations in brick-faced concrete.[3]

---

[1] In 1879 a travertine block was dredged up from the Tiber on which was an inscription of the first century B.C., recording the restoration of one of these river stairs—

P · BARRONIVS · BARBA · AED · CVR
GRADOS · REFECIT

[2] These were first noticed by Mr. Parker; they are usually hidden by brushwood. They will shortly be destroyed in the course of the modern improvements.

[3] Immense quantities of rough blocks of marble were found on this marble wharf some years ago, and on them were many interesting quarry

In 1890, during the excavations made for the construction of the new Tiber embankment, two very interesting inscribed pedestals of travertine were found, the inscriptions on which are unusually early examples of Latin epigraphy.

Archaic inscriptions.

One of them, which probably dates from near the year 500 B.C., reads as follows :—

M·C·ΠOMΠLIO·NO·DEDRON·F·HERCOLE

Marcus et Caius Pompilius Norii filii dederunt Herculi. The form *dedron* is new, and may be added to the other early epigraphic examples of the same verb, *dedrot* and *dedro.*

The other inscription, of rather later date, has a hitherto unknown form of the name Aesculapius,

AISCOLAΠIO

Both have the early Attic forms of the P and L ; see *Not. d. Scavi,* 1890, pp. 10 and 33.

The enormous *Horrea* or storehouses, which were built along the verge of this chief landing-quay of Rome, to receive cargoes of food and other merchandise, are described below, at vol. ii. p. 260.

Horrea.

Marble Wharf by the Campus Martius.

Some very interesting remains of another great pier for landing marble were discovered in 1891 during the demolition of the *Teatro Tor di Nona,* about 175 yards above the bridge of S. Angelo (*Pons Aelius*) on the bank of the *Campus.*[1]

Marble wharf.

This wharf was probably constructed in the reign of Augustus, when the *Campus* was being rapidly made into the

marks, which are described in a very able article by Bruzza, *Ann. Inst.* 1870, p. 106 *seq.*

[1] The position of this marble wharf can be seen on the *Map of Modern Rome,* close by the syllable "Tor" in the name of the street " *Tor di Nona.*"

Marble wharf.

most magnificent quarter of Rome by the erection of an enormous number of public buildings, all richly decorated with a variety of foreign marbles, granites, and porphyry. It would have been very inconvenient to land this immense quantity of marble, much of which was in the form of heavy monolithic columns, at the older *marmoratum*, at the foot of the Aventine Hill, as the great blocks would have had a long and troublesome journey through the streets before reaching their destination. For this reason a new marble wharf was constructed higher up the river; and from it a wide well-paved road led to the *Statio Rationis marmorum*, the central depôt and administrative offices of the State marble quarries.

Statio marmorum.

In 1737, during the reconstruction of the Church of S. Apollinare, the site of this *Statio* was discovered, together with a number of inscriptions which explained its use. Round it, and on each side of the road leading to the wharf, there were numerous workshops of sculptors and marble-masons.

The newly-discovered marble wharf is of exceptional interest from its form and elaborate construction.

Remains of wharf.

The main portion consists of a great pier, built of blocks of tufa, faced with travertine; it projects diagonally into the Tiber, being about 85 feet long, 16 feet high, and 46 feet wide. On each side of it there is a wide lower landing-place, but little raised above the ordinary level of the river.

The heavy monoliths were probably first pushed on rollers from the ships on to the low landing and then raised to the top of the higher part of the wharf by great cranes.

In order to prevent injury to the wharf from the ships bumping against it while discharging their cargoes, the landing was sheathed in a very solid and elaborate way by a series of closely-driven piles, which formed a complete wooden casing all round its water edge. Each of these piles was a squared baulk of oak, about 20 inches by 22 inches in section, and 24 feet to 26 feet long, shod at the foot by an iron spike. Each pile had a dovetail projection on one side, which fitted into a

Wood casing.

corresponding dovetailed mortice in the edge of the adjacent pile. Over the whole surface of the wooden casing of piles sheets of lead $\frac{3}{16}$ inch thick were nailed. *Lead casing.*
Very great care and skill must have been required to drive these piles so that the dovetail projection slid with accurate smoothness down the groove in the adjoining pile.

An interesting description of this wharf is given by Marchetti, *Bull. Com. Arch. Rom.* 1891, pp. 45 to 60 and Tav. iii. and iv. When remains of this wharf were previously discovered, during the building of the theatre which has just been destroyed, they were thought to belong to a bridge.

THE MAMERTINE PRISON.[1]

There can be no doubt as to this being the prison mentioned by Livy, i. 33, as the *carcer . . . media urbe imminens foro*, and that alluded to by Juvenal, iii. 312, as being the only one which was required for Rome in the happy bygone period of the Kings— *Tullianum.*

> . . . . . *felicia dicas*
> *Saecula quae quondam sub regibus atque tribunis*
> *Viderunt uno contentam carcere Romam.*

Dion Cassius, lviii. 11, speaks of the *carcer* as being near Temple of Concord, and at lviii. 5 as being at the foot of the steps leading up to the Capitol.

It consists of two parts; the lower of these, a circular chamber called the *Tullianum*, is partly excavated in the rock and partly built of tufa blocks (see fig. 21), each course projecting a little over the one below so as to form a cone. The *Lower chamber.*

---

[1] In the early mediaeval period the name *Mamertine* was given to this prison from a statue of Mamertinus or Mars which stood near it on the *Clivus Argentarius*. Hence also the modern name of the street *Via del Marforio*.

blocks are very neatly worked with close joints, and all are

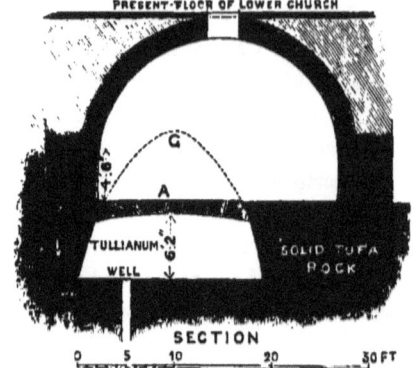

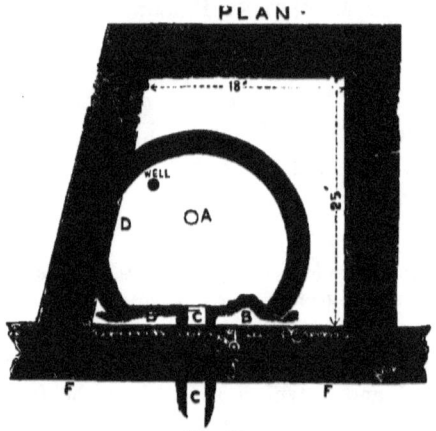

Fig. 21.
Plan and Section of the Mamertine Prison.
A. Opening in floor over the Tullianum; the only access.
BB. Solid tufa rock.
CC. Branch of Cloaca.
DE. Position of modern stairs and door.
FF. Front wall of prison with inscription of 22 A.D.
G. Probable original top of Tullianum.

bedded on a thin skin of lime mortar, probably an earlier instance of the use of mortar than even the Servian wall on the Aventine.[1] The upper part of the cone or domical covering of this chamber was probably cut off when the room over it was formed.

In the floor of the Tullianum is a well containing a spring of clear water, and the whole chamber was apparently built originally as a cistern. Its name is derived from an archaic word *tullius*, meaning a jet of water. Varro (*Lin. Lat.* v. 151) wrongly derives it from Servius Tullius—*Tullianum ideo quod additum a Tullio rege*, evidently a double mistake, as the *lower* chamber could certainly not have been added after the *upper* one. The *Tullianum* is described by Livy, xxxiv. 44, as *inferiorem carcerem*; and at xxix. 22 he mentions a criminal being thrown into it. *Early cistern.*

That its original use as a cistern was abandoned is shown by the *cloaca* which leads from it to a branch of the "*Cloaca Maxima*," along which any water in the *Tullianum* would have escaped. The present stairs are modern, and there was no access to this horrible dungeon except by a hole in the stone floor above it. This floor is made of large blocks of tufa jointed so as to form a flat arch; see A in fig. 21.

The room over it is larger and much loftier: it also is of very early date, but later than the *Tullianum*. It is built of tufa, and has a stone barrel vault, not quite semicircular, but segmental. A projecting string-course on the outside records a restoration in the reign of Tiberius by the *Consules Suffecti* for the year 22 A.D. C · VIBIVS · C · F · RVFINVS · M COCCEIV[S · NERVA] COS · EX · S · C · (*Senatus Consulto*). *Upper chamber.*

The two chambers of the prison are described thus by Sallust, *Cat.* 55, *Est locus in carcere, quod Tullianum appellatur, ubi paullulum ascenderis ad laevam, circiter XII pedes humi depressus. Eum muniunt undique parietes, atque insuper camera lapideis fornicibus juncta; sed inculta tenebris, odore foeda, atque* *Sallust on the prison.*

[1] This skin of mortar is easily overlooked, but by means of a careful examination it can be traced in all the joints throughout the whole structure.

terribilis ejus facies est. The entrance to the upper prison was on the left hand side of the ascent from the Forum to the *Clivus Argentarius*, leading to the *Porta Ratumena*; this is apparently what Sallust means by *ubi paullulum ascenderis ad laevam.*

Plutarch. The lower chamber or *Tullianum* is called τὸ βάραθρον (the abyss) by Plutarch, *Marius*, 12. Into it the unhappy Numidian king Jugurtha was flung, and there starved to death or strangled. It was the scene of countless butcheries and slow cruelty, such as the Romans delighted in. During a Triumph, in his course up to the Capitol, each victorious general paused for a while near the Carcer, till word was brought him that some of his principal captives had been killed. It was here that Lentulus, Cethegus, and the Catiline conspirators were executed. Their death was announced by Cicero to the expectant crowd in the Forum by the single word *vixerunt*, "they have lived"; Plutar. *Cic.* 22.

Scalae Gemoniae. *Scalae Gemoniae.* The flight of steps which led from the door of the upper prison down to the Forum was called the *Scalae Gemoniae*: or, according to Pliny (*Hist. Nat.* viii. 145), *Gradus Gemitorii*, "the stairs of sighs"; see also Tac. *Hist.* iii. 74 and 85.[1] On it the body of Sabinus, and a few days afterwards that of the murdered Vitellius, were thrown (Suet. *Vit.* 17); and in the reign of Tiberius the bodies of Aelius Sejanus, his family and friends, after they were cruelly murdered by the Emperor's orders, were exposed on these *Scalae* to the number of twenty in one day; see Suet. *Tib.* 61.[2]

It appears to have been the custom to expose on the *Scalae Gemoniae* the bodies of all who were killed in the adjoining

[1] These stairs, of which some remains may still exist, are buried under the modern road, and will probably be discovered when the excavations are continued in that direction.

[2] Pliny (*Hist. Nat.* viii. 145) tells a story about a faithful dog which watched day and night by his master's body, and brought food to it while it was lying on the *Scalae Gemoniae*; see note in vol. i. p. 333.

prison. The endurance by the Romans of such hideous sights and their savage want of respect for the dead are strong examples of that innate coarseness which underlay their thin varnish of Hellenic refinement. The rare occasions when the Romans showed any mercy to a fallen enemy appear to have resulted from their vanity rather than from any germ of chivalrous feeling.

According to Varro (*Lin. Lat.* v. 151) the district immediately round the prison was called the *Latomiae* or *Lautumiae*, stone quarries (λᾶας-τομή); he suggests that the name was taken from the Syracusan quarries, which were used as prisons.[1] But it appears probable that the tufa rock of the hill here was once quarried for building material, and that may have been the origin of the primitive cistern or *Tullianum*, it being a very frequent custom to use the cavities formed by quarrying rock as water reservoirs; see vol. i. p. 164.

Stone quarries.

Other remains of the Regal period exist in Rome, especially in the foundations of some of the temples,[2] but none of these are of much importance. The numerous fires and the wholesale rebuilding of temples and other public buildings under the Empire, on a grander scale and of richer materials, caused the destruction of nearly all the primitive structures of Rome, both sacred and secular. To these causes must be added the fact that soft varieties of tufa were largely used; a friable stone which lasted well as long as it was covered with a coating of stucco and sheltered by a roof, but which perishes rapidly when deprived of such protection.

Causes of decay.

[1] Thucydides (vii. 86, 87) gives a terrible account of the sufferings and death of nearly seven thousand Athenian prisoners, taken after the unsuccessful siege of Syracuse during the Peloponnesian War, and imprisoned in the extensive quarries of *Neapolis*, the main suburb of Syracuse. See also Cicero, *In Verrem*, Act. II. v. 55.

[2] For an example in the *Temple of Vesta* and part of the *House of the Pontifex*, see vol. i. pp. 298 and 301.

Fig. 22.

PLAN OF THE PALATINE HILL.

REFERENCES TO FIGURES.

VOL. I.

		PAGE
	1. Present entrance.	171
2,	2. Remains of wall of Roma Quadrata	112
	3. Aqueduct	162
	4. Early buildings of opus reticulatum	172
	5. Scalae Caci.	119
	6. Buildings of mixed brick and opus reticulatum	172
	7. Altar to the unknown God.	174
	8. Reservoir cut in the tufa rock	116
	9. Passage cut in the rock	117
	10. So-called Temple of Cybele.	165
	11. Very early structures of tufa	159
	12. Tufa arcade and paved road	160
	13. Building with travertine piers of the later Republican period	166
	14. So-called Temple of Jupiter Victor	162
	15. Well communicating with subterranean rock-cut reservoirs.	162
16,	16. Small chambers and paved road, part of Tiberius' building.	183
	17. Piscina, or water tank	182
	18. House of Germanicus or of Livia (so called)	175
19,	19. Crypto-porticus.	197
20,	20. Early building of tufa buried and covered by Domitian's building	166
	21. So-called academy and library, part of Domitian's Palace	206
	22. Triclinium of Domitian's Palace.	202
	23. Nymphaeum and piscina	202
	24. Peristyle; the number 24 also marks the position of the buried villa of early Imperial date.	200
	25. Small rooms at side of peristyle.	203
	26. Stairs down to the crypto-porticus	205
	27. Throne-room of the Flavian Palace	203
	28. Lararium (so called)	204

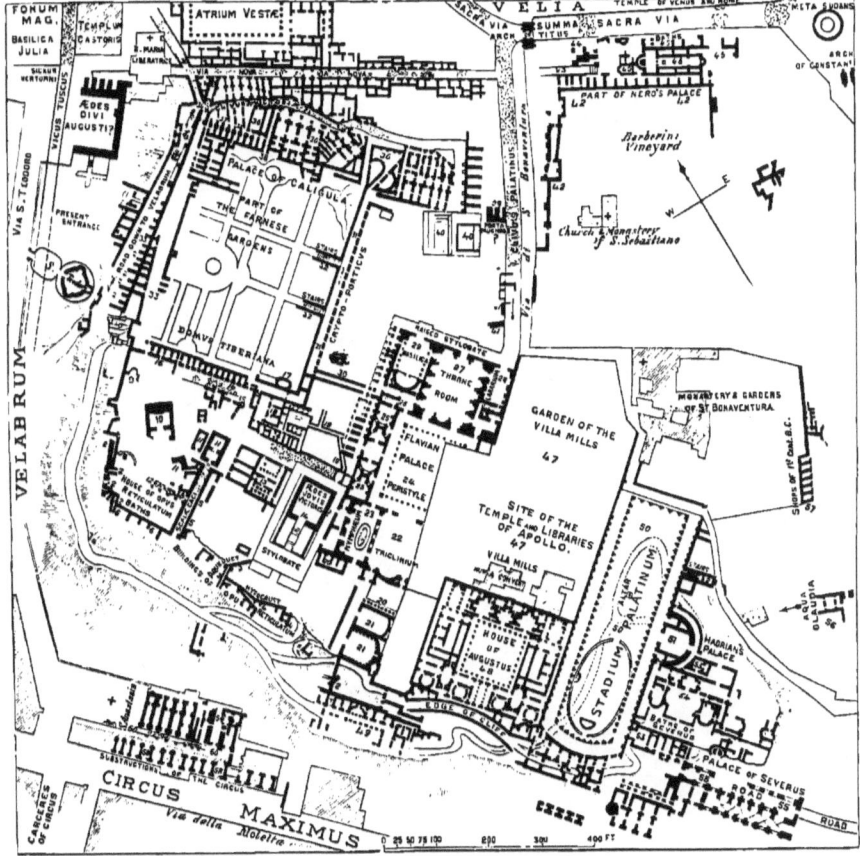

Fig. 22. Plan of the Palatine Hill.

		PAGE
	29. Basilica	204
	30. Branch of crypto-porticus leading to Domitian's Palace	197
	31. Crypto-porticus of Caligula.	198
32,	32. Stairs from crypto-porticus to higher level	197
33,	33. Early buildings of opus reticulatum	171
34,	34. Stairs from Forum to Porta Romanula	196
35 and 38.	Stairs to upper rooms of Caligula's Palace	191
36,	36. Substructures of Caligula's Palace	195
	37. Caligula's bridge (so called)	194
	39. Porta Mugionis	167
	40. Temple of Jupiter Stator (so called)	167
	41. Remains of wall of Roma Quadrata, now lost	118
42,	42. Remains of Nero's Palace	228
	43. Great concrete platform	228
	44. Remains of the mediaeval Turris Cartularia	229
45,	45. Series of small bath-rooms of the fourth century A.D.	226
	46. So-called basilica of the fifth century	226
	47. Site of the Temple and libraries of Apollo	184
	48. Palace of Augustus (now destroyed)	184
	49. "Domus Gelotiana"	208
	50. Stadium, with oval hall of Theodoric	211
	51. Exedra of Hadrian	211
	52. Stairs from Stadium to higher level of hill	214
53,	53. Remains of Hadrian's Palace, partly covered by the later Palace of Severus	212
	54. Baths of Severus' Palace	215
55,	55. Lofty substructures of Severus' Palace	216
	56. Aqua Claudia brought on Nero's Aqueduct	218
	57. Shops built of opus incertum.	

VOL. II.

	58. Substructures of the Circus Maximus	54
	59. Remains of early tufa building and brick-faced structures of Imperial times	55
60,	60. Paved road skirting the outside of the Circus Maximus	55

CHAPTER IV

THE PALATINE HILL [1]

Buildings of Prehistoric and Republican Date. Within the walls of *Roma Quadrata* there are a number of very early buildings, some probably dating from prehistoric times; these are mostly grouped in the western angle of the Palatine, by the north-west side of the *Scalae Caci*; see fig. 22, Nos. 2, 6,

Earliest structures. 11, 10. Some of these very interesting remains are built of the softest tufa; and of these, in a few years, nothing will remain. Since they were uncovered and exposed to the weather they have been rapidly crumbling into mere heaps of earth, although, when found, the edges of the blocks were perfectly sharp and well preserved. It appears strange that these primitive buildings, which must have stood exposure to

Rapid decay. air and rain for a thousand years, should fall into such rapid decay on being again uncovered, but it must be remembered that originally these walls were protected with roofs, and (more important still) were completely covered with a thick coat of hard stucco, which afforded an effective protection against wet and frost; see vol. i. p. 73.

Various names, such as the *hut of Faustulus* and the *Auguratorium*, have been given to some of these early structures, but only as a matter of guess-work; any real identification of their names or uses is impossible, and only a vague notion of their

[1] An excellent plan of the buildings on the Palatine Hill as they exist, together with a conjecturally restored plan, is given in the *Gazette Archéol.* for 1888.

dates can be arrived at. That they are of considerable antiquity is certain, not only from their simple form and the primitive character of much of their masonry, but also from the fact that some of the walls are built on a stratum which contains frag- *Early pottery.* ments of pottery, clearly of early date—probably before the fifth century B.C. Other fragments of pottery are covered with the very fine black enamel which was made in Magna Graecia during the fifth to the third centuries B.C., but was not known to the Roman potters.

Whatever these buildings were, it is clear that they were respected and preserved even under the later Empire, when almost the whole summit of the Palatine had become one immense continuous range of Imperial palaces and marble temples.[1] These modest tufa structures were probably regarded as sacred relics of the early history of Rome, and were valued both for religious and archaeological reasons.

Opposite the summit of the *Stairs of Cacus* is a simple *cella* *Early cella.* (fig. 22, No. 11) built, without mortar, of large blocks of soft tufa, some of which have deeply-incised masons' marks, similar in character, though not in actual form, to those on the Servian wall; see fig. 19, vol. i. p. 138.

This simple rectangular chamber, 8 or 9 feet wide, is probably the most primitive form of Roman temple; earlier even than the building with wooden architrave and widely-spaced columns, which the Romans adopted from the more artistic Etruscans.

Near this, on the right hand of the *Scalae Caci* (looking down it), are remains of other buildings in hard tufa, which appear to have been erected over still earlier ones of soft tufa, set at a different angle. A curiously-arranged flight of steps *Flight of steps.* in hard tufa descends here from the higher level, and turns round at right angles, leading down to an open tufa gutter for rain water, which skirts the two existing sides of a chamber of

[1] Hence *Palatium*, the Latin name for the *Palatine Hill*, came to mean any *palace*.

fine well-jointed tufa masonry, probably of early Republican date. These steps appear to have led up to a large paved area, part of which, with its well-jointed pavement of tufa blocks, still exists. This stone platform may possibly be the *Auguratorium*; see vol. i. p. 369.

Stone cistern. *Early Cistern.* A little lower down the slope, and set partly on and against the primitive soft tufa wall which once flanked

Fig. 23.
Remains of an early Cistern by the Scalae Caci.

AA. Line of stone barrel vault.
B. Hole for water-jet.
C. Sinking for water-pipe.
D. Blocks of soft tufa belonging to some older structure.

the *Scalae Caci*, is a very curious little structure of well-wrought blocks of hard tufa, once covered with a barrel-shaped stone vault; see fig. 23. This little chamber, barely 8 feet wide inside, appears to have been a fountain or cistern. In the end wall, which is well preserved, is a large central hole for the water-jet, and a groove is cut for the pipe to supply it. This fountain is apparently of early Republican date; it stands on a single course of much older masonry, resembling that of the "*Wall of Romulus*."

Branch road. At this point a branch basalt-paved road (fig. 22, No. 12) runs into the *Scalae Caci* at right angles; it was drained with a curious square drain cut out of blocks of tufa, with a tufa slab as a lid, closely fitted on to it. Facing on to this cross road are remains of a very interesting arcade of Republican date, with a series of semicircular peperino arches in a concrete wall faced with early *opus reticulatum*. *Early arcade.*

Group of Houses. Between this arcade and the line of the circuit-wall, overlooking the west angle of the cliff, are extensive remains of private houses, part of which are built of *opus reticulatum*, with many handsome marble baths, probably of the time of Augustus; see fig. 22, between Nos. 2, 2 and 12. *Later houses. Bath rooms.*

The greater part, however, of this group of houses, with all its complicated heating arrangements — hypocausts and walls lined with square flue-tiles,—is of concrete faced with brickwork, not earlier than the beginning of the second century A.D., while a considerable part is of the third century. Some of the lead water-pipes are still *in situ*, embedded in the late brick and concrete walls. The whole of this angle of the hill is rich in these well-preserved remains of domestic buildings, and merits careful examination: the various forms of heating apparatus are specially noticeable.

Early Temple of stuccoed stone. Returning to the higher level at the top of the *Scalae Caci*, there are other remains of early buildings, and especially a number of fragments of a temple built of peperino, covered with fine hard white stucco made of pounded marble. These fragments, which are very valuable specimens of early Roman architecture, include drums of fluted columns about 3 feet 6 inches in diameter, Corinthian capitals, and many pieces of the cornice, together with the apex stone of the pediment. The design of this cornice is a very primitive Romanised form of the Greek Corinthian, the *consoles* being plain without leaves or volutes, and the mouldings unenriched with surface ornament. *Early temple.*

On the top of the cornice is a channel 11 inches wide to *Rain-water gutter.*

Eaves gutter. catch the rain; it is lined with *opus signinum*, a very hard waterproof cement made of broken earthenware, the same as that used for channels of aqueducts. This channel acted as an eaves gutter, and the water from it was discharged through pierced lions' heads set at intervals in the *cymatium*. The *Fine stucco.* stucco is very thickly applied, completely smothering the carving and details cut in the peperino, so that the whole had to be modelled afresh, almost as if the stucco had been applied to a rough shapeless stone. This stucco is a beautiful hard composition of lime and pounded white marble, the *caementum marmoreum* or *opus albarium* of Vitruvius, capable of taking a polish like real marble, and nearly as durable. Other massive fragments lie near here of a large architrave worked in travertine, also coated with stucco, belonging to some building of rather later date.

Well-shaft. **Early Well.** A well-shaft close by (fig. 22, No. 15), neatly lined with blocks of peperino, communicates with a very extensive series of subterranean rock-cut chambers, originally formed by quarrying the tufa for building purposes, and afterwards used to store rain or spring water; in later times these rock-cut cisterns were supplied by an aqueduct, remains of which exist against the cliff opposite the so-called *Temple of Jupiter Victor*; fig. 22, No. 14. A piece of the *specus* of this aqueduct can be traced passing on the top of the ground, in a slanting direction, toward the subterranean cisterns under the " *Temple of Jupiter* "; fig. 22, No. 3, 3.

Temple of Jupiter Victor. **Temple of Jupiter Victor** (so called). This temple, the real dedication of which is doubtful, stands on a lofty platform of tufa rock, artificially levelled. It occupies a very commanding position, overlooking the *Vallis Murcia* and the *Circus Maximus*. Little except the concrete core of the *podium* still remains; but, at one point on the south, part exists of the massive stone wall of early date which once enclosed the whole of the concrete foundation; a method of construction similar to that of the Temple of Castor; see vol. i. p. 278.

This *podium* wall is of mixed tufa and peperino, set with very thin beds of lime-mortar, an interesting example of the early use of mortar in Rome; the blocks are the usual 2 Roman feet in thickness, and the stone wall appears once to have been 15 feet thick. The whole empty space, now bridged over in wood, between the *podium* itself and the foundations of its great flight of steps in front, was once filled by this very massive tufa wall, all the stones of which have been removed for building material. In many of the existing remains of buildings in Rome the position and thickness of the missing masonry are clearly indicated by the voids in the concrete mass of the *podium* and by the prints of the blocks on the face of the concrete backing. This is specially the case in the *Temple of Divus Julius* in the Forum; see vol. i. p. 285. Small chambers are formed in the concrete mass of the foundations of this temple, as appears to have been always the case with Roman temples if they were built on a high *podium*. *Voids in concrete.*

A whole network of passages and chambers is excavated in the tufa rock on which this temple is built: access to these is given by a subterranean flight of steps on the south-east side, leading down from the floor of a long *Crypto-porticus*, one end of which starts from a distant point in the so-called "House of Livia," while the other end of this long subterranean passage issues near the "Temple of Jupiter Victor" into remains of an early Republican house, built of tufa, at a level much below that of the rock on which the temple stands.[1] *Underground chambers.*

These underground stairs and the end of the *Crypto-porticus*

[1] In its original state the top of this half of the Palatine was very far from being the level surface to which it was gradually reduced under the Emperors. More than one valley or natural depression has been filled up, and in many places rocky peaks have evidently been cut away. Under Domitian especially the most gigantic substructures were built, in order to form an enormous platform, on which his great series of state rooms was erected.

can be reached by descending through that part of the early house (No. 20 on fig. 22) which abuts against the end of the *Nymphaeum* of the Flavian Palace. Another part of the same or a similar house of the Republican period is deep underground outside the apsidal end of the Flavian *Triclinium*; also marked 20 on fig. 22.

Rock-cut cisterns.   The full extent of the subterranean quarry-chambers under the "*Temple of Jupiter Victor*" is not known, but they certainly extend a long way beyond the temple, and formed very extensive cisterns for storing water. In some places they consist of narrow winding passages, which occasionally expand into more spacious chambers.

A few architectural fragments, which belong to this temple, were found near it, and have been set on the top of the *podium*; these are a number of tufa drums of fluted columns, about 3 feet 3 inches in diameter, once thickly coated with stucco, and decorated with painting.[1]

Inscribed base.   A very interesting inscription is now set on the steps of the temple (Fig. 22, No. 14), though it was found at some distance from it. It is cut on the lower part of a circular column-like pedestal of white marble, 3 feet 1 inch in diameter, the upper part of which has been sawn off, and a fluted basin formed in its top surface. This pedestal and the statue which probably once stood on it were erected out of spoils won by Gn. Domitius Calvinus, one of J. Caesar's generals, who commanded the centre of Caesar's army at Pharsalia: he was Consul in 53 B.C. and again in 40 B.C. The inscription is—

[1] This temple, as well as many others on the Palatine and in the Forum, have suffered much injury from the fanciful restorations of Comm. Rosa, who conjecturally gave it the name of *Jupiter Victor*, on the strength of the following entry in the *Notitia*, under *Regio* X. "*Arca Palatina et aedem Jovis Victoris*"; other entries in this list—*casa Romuli, Auguratorium*, and *tugurium Faustuli*—suggested the names which have been arbitrarily given to the very early remains by the *Scalae Caci*.

CN · DOMITIVS · M · F · CALVINVS
PONTIFEX
COS · ITER · IMPER
DE · MANIBIEIS [1]

In 36 B.C. Domitius Calvinus rebuilt the *Regia* at the east of the *Forum Romanum* out of his Spanish spoils; see below, vol. i. p. 305.

At the back of the "*Temple of Jupiter Victor*" are some fine marble fragments of some very handsome Corinthian building, with large fluted columns and entablature. A very curious mason's mark, resembling the common monogram of Christ's name, occurs on the bed of one of the marble drums. *Marble fragments.*

Porticus of early date. On the north-east side of the temple are remains of a curiously-planned building, a sort of *Porticus*, of late Republican date, with tufa walls, and rows of travertine columns; its name and use are quite unknown; fig. 22, No. 13. *Early porticus.*

In the area of this building is another well-shaft, lined with *opus reticulatum*, which, like the previously-mentioned well, communicated with the subterranean rock-cut cisterns under the temple.

The so-called Temple of Cybele. Farther to the north-west, between the primitive tufa structures and the edge of the cliff overlooking the *Velabrum*, are enormously thick concrete walls of a large cella, completely stripped of all its architectural decorations, and much concealed by ilex-trees; see fig. 22, No. 10. The concrete is formed of alternate layers of soft tufa and hard peperino, and in parts is faced with *opus incertum*. It appears to be a work of late Republican or early Imperial times, and was once faced with blocks of stone or marble. *"Temple of Cybele."*

By it is a fine colossal female figure in Greek marble, of the first century A.D., which is supposed to be a statue of Cybele, and hence this temple is conjecturally called after *Statue of Cybele.*

---

[1] The archaic *ei* for long *i* is used.

her.[1] It is a noble figure seated in a throne, wearing the *stola* bound by a girdle, and over it the *pallium*; the hair falls in front over the shoulders. The arms and head, which were worked in separate blocks of marble, are missing, but the rest of the statue is very well preserved.

Early houses. *Houses of Republican date.* The very interesting remains of an extensive house of Republican date, near this point (fig. 22, No. 20, 20), are only partly visible, as the house was buried under the great artificial platform on which Domitian built his palace. Some rooms of this house are now accessible below the later level of the hill, at the end of the *Cryptoporticus*, which leads to the "House of Livia," just below the *loggia* of the sixteenth-century *Casino*, which is still left standing among the ruins. Other rooms of a similar house can be seen deeply sunk below the so-called *Bibliotheca* of Domitian; *Former valley.* showing how deep a valley was filled in and covered by the Flavian Palace. It is difficult to realise that the floor of these lofty rooms, about 30 feet below that of the Flavian buildings, was once at the ground level of the Palatine at this point. The walls are built of hard tufa blocks, very neatly jointed, with simple arched doorways — a very valuable example of the domestic architecture of Republican Rome, but not yet fully exposed.

The rooms under the "*Bibliotheca*" are not accessible, though they are visible at the bottom of a well-like excavation, but those at the end of the *Crypto-porticus*, which passes underground near the foundations of the so-called *Temple of Jupiter Victor*, can be easily examined. These rooms appear to have continued in use during late Imperial times, and show several late alterations and additions, namely, brick-faced concrete

---

[1] An *aedes Matris deum* occurs in the list of the *Notitia* for the Palatine, *Regio* X.; and in the *Ancyrean Inscription* Augustus records AEDEM MATRIS · MAGNAE · IN · PALATIO · FECI; but this building more probably formed part of the great group of temples built by Augustus in the Area of Apollo; see vol. i. p. 183.

walls, and a coarse mosaic floor decorated with large fishes, probably not earlier than the time of Caracalla. The other rooms appear to have been buried and abandoned, like the house under the great *Peristyle* of Domitian. *Late mosaics.*

We pass now to another part of the Palatine, to the north of the Flavian Palace.

The *Temple of Jupiter Stator* was traditionally one of the earliest buildings of Rome,[1] being built by Romulus in fulfilment of a vow made during the repulse of the Romans by the Sabine inhabitants of the Capitoline Hill; Liv. i. 12. *Temple of Jupiter Stator.*

During this battle the Romans were driven back within the walls of *Roma Quadrata*, retreating through the *Porta Mugonia*, and it was near that gate that the temple of *Jupiter Stator* is said to have been built, 'Ρωμύλος μὲν ἱδρύσατο ἱερὸν 'Ορθωσίῳ Διὶ παρὰ ταῖς καλουμέναις Μυκωνίσι πύλαις, αἳ φέρουσιν εἰς τὸ Παλατίον ἐκ τῆς ἱερᾶς ὁδοῦ; Dionys. ii. 50. Its position is also described by Ovid (*Fast.* vi. 793) thus— *Porta Mugonia.*

> *Tempus idem Stator aedis habet, quam Romulus olim*
> *Ante Palatini condidit ora iugi.*

See also *Trist.* iii. 1. 31—

> *Inde petens dextram, Porta est, ait, ista Palati;*
> *Hic Stator; hic primum condita Roma fuit.*

And Plutarch (*Cic.* 16) speaks of it as being "built at the start of the Sacra Via"; see also Plutar. *Rom.* 18.

This temple was also close by the house of Tarquinius Priscus; see Livy, i. 41; and Solinus (*Polyhistor*, i. 24) mentions that Tarquin lived by the *Porta Mugonia*,[2] the site of which, *House of Tarquin I.*

---

[1] The temple of *Jupiter Feretrius*, on the *Capitolium*, is the only other temple which is recorded as being earlier than this.

[2] "*Tarquinius Priscus (habitavit) ad Mugoniam Portam, supra Summam Novam Viam.*" The Summa Nova and the Summa Sacra Via almost meet a little way outside the *Porta Mugonia*; see fig. 22. Pliny

on the road leading from the *Summa Sacra Via* (by the Arch of Titus) up to the Palatine, has been with some probability identified; fig. 22, No. 39.

Temple of Jupiter Stator. According to Vitruvius (iii. 2. 5) the *Temple of Jupiter Stator*, which was designed by Hermodius, was *hexastyle, peripteral*, with eleven columns on the sides. It was burnt during the great fire of Nero's reign. On several occasions it was used as a meeting-place for the Senate, being selected for its strength and the safety of its position; Cicero's first Oration against Catiline was delivered before the Senate in this building; see Cic. *In Cat.* i. 1. Plutarch, *Cic.* 16, says—'Ο Κικέρων ἐκάλει τὴν συγκλητὸν (the Senate) εἰς τὸ τοῦ Στησίου Διὸς ἱερὸν, ὃν Στάτωρα 'Ρωμαῖοι καλοῦσιν, ἱδρυμένον ἐν ἀρχῇ τῆς ἱερᾶς ὁδοῦ πρὸς τὸ Παλατίον ἀνιόντων.

Existing remains. Just within the supposed site of the *Porta Mugonia* are extensive remains of a concrete *podium*, the surrounding masonry of which has been wholly removed; see 40, on fig. 22. From the size of these remains it was suggested by Comm. Rosa that they are part of the *Temple of Jupiter Stator*; but if so, the whole temple down to its lowest foundations must have been rebuilt under the Empire, a very improbable thing, *Late concrete.* as the concrete is made not of tufa or peperino only, as was the case with the concrete of early times, but contains, even in its lowest layers, travertine, brick, and even marble; a sure sign of work later than the end of the Republic. It seems, however, much more probable that the real site of the Temple of Jupiter Stator was lower down the hill, nearer to the *Sacra Via*, and the place where the *Arch of Titus* now stands.[1]

(*Hist. Nat.* xxxiv. 29) mentions a statue which stood in the porch of the house of Tarquinius Superbus, and was opposite the *Temple of Jupiter Stator*.

[1] Mr. F. M. Nichols is inclined to place the Temple of Jupiter Stator still farther away "close to the Forum, at the bottom of the Sacred Way"; see Nichols, *Roman Forum*, 1877, pp. 310 to 318.

It should be observed that the *Temple of Jupiter Stator* is not in-

At one side of this ruined *podium* an excavation has been made, which shows the mouth of a large brick drain; and leading down to it from the surface of the ground, close by the temple, are remains of a shaft or vertical drain built of blocks of tufa, on two of which are inscribed the names of two Greeks, possibly stonemasons, *Diocles* and *Philocrates*, in characters of the third or second century B.C.

Sewer.

Inscribed block.

```
FILOCR A E
DIOC[E
```

These inscribed blocks have been wrongly supposed to be part of the foundations of the temple, but their size, shape, and position show that they belong to a separate structure, and were simply part of a down-shaft, possibly to carry surface rain water into the sewer below.

The road mentioned by Plutarch (*Cic.* 16), as going up to the Palatine starts from a point where the *Summa Nova Via* runs into the *Clivus* near the Arch of Titus: this junction of the three roads was exposed to view in 1884; some of the basalt paving is formed of exceptionally massive blocks, and is earlier in date than most of the roads in the Forum.

Clivus Palatinus.

Private Houses. In the first century B.C. that part of the Palatine Hill which faces towards the *Sacra Via*, the *Forum Romanum*, and the Capitoline Hill, appears to have been the favourite quarter for the houses of rich and influential Roman citizens; see Pliny, *Hist. Nat.* xxxvi. 109 to 112. Here was the house of the orator Lucius Crassus, valued at six million sesterces (£60,000),[1] which had in its Atrium six small columns of Hymettian marble, which were thought an extravagance, unsuited to the modesty of a Roman citizen (Pliny, *Hist. Nat.* xxxvi. 114), and gained him the nickname of the Palatine

Palatine houses.

House of Crassus.

cluded among the buildings of the Palatine Hill in the Regionary Catalogue, but is catalogued in *Regio* IV. along with the *Temple of Romulus* and the adjacent *Templum urbis Romae*; see vol. ii. p. 17.

[1] A million sesterces, roughly speaking, was equal to about £10,000.

House of Crassus. Venus, given him by M. Brutus, Caesar's murderer (see Pliny, *Hist. Nat.* xxxvi. 8); this house apparently became the property of M. Aemilius Scaurus, a man of enormous wealth, who in 58 B.C. built the temporary theatre, which the stern Pliny (*Hist. Nat.* xxxvi. 114) also highly reprobates for its luxurious splendour; see vol. ii. p. 62. This house, enlarged and made more magnificent by Scaurus, was bought by Clodius for nearly fifteen million sesterces, about £150,000; see Ascon. ad Cic. *Pro Scauro*; and Pliny, *Hist. Nat.* xvii. 6.

Cicero's house. Cicero's house was on the lower slopes of the Palatine towards the *Domus Publica* of the Pontifex Maximus, where Julius Caesar lived while he held that office.[1] Cicero's house was originally built by M. Livius Drusus, and then passed to a namesake and relative of the orator Crassus, from whom it was bought by Cicero; see Cic. *Pro Domo*, 37, and *De Harus.* 8, 33. That it was immediately below the house of Clodius is shown by Cicero's threat to add new stories to his house in order to block out from Clodius the sight of the city he had sought to destroy (*De Harus.* 15). The house Cicero refers to was one previously possessed by Clodius, not the house which had belonged to Scaurus, as Clodius only bought the latter very shortly before his death.

House of Catulus. A large house in this northern angle of the Palatine was possessed by Q. Lutatius Catulus, the builder of the *Tabularium*; see vol. i. p. 372. Its Porticus was built out of the spoils won by him and Marius from the Cimbri in 102 B.C.; see Cic. *Pro Domo*, 43, and Val. Max. vi. 3. 1. Catiline, and Q. Hortensius, Cicero's rival, also had houses in this quarter; as well as several other wealthy Romans.

The commanding view, and the vicinity of this site to the *Forum Romanum*, no doubt were among the chief reasons for its popularity, and hence the feelings of indignation aroused when Caligula absorbed nearly the whole of the ground

---

[1] Cicero called himself "Caesar's neighbour"; *Ad Fam.* v. 6, and *Ad Att.* xii. 45.

occupied by these, the finest among the private houses of Rome, in order to build his gigantic palace, which has obliterated all traces of these memorable buildings.

The present entrance to the Palatine Hill from the line of the *Vicus Tuscus* leads first to the remains of a row of buildings of Imperial date, which have been constructed on the slope of the Palatine, outside the old line of wall, where the hill rises out of the low ground of the *Velabrum*. Remains of these houses and of some stairs have recently been excavated. The stairs, which are formed of blocks of travertine, form a communication between the different levels of the hillside and the valley of the *Velabrum*. *Remains by the entrance.*

Nearly opposite the present entrance to the Palatine, set high up against its steep and artificially-scarped side above the *Velabrum*, there are still existing extensive remains of a row of buildings in *opus reticulatum*, apparently of the first century B.C.; fig. 22, No. 2, 2, 2. These appear to be portions of a long series of private houses, built against the cliff along the line of the primitive circuit-wall of *Roma Quadrata*,[1] and rising, when they were complete, above the level of the summit of the hill. They are partly concealed by brick-faced walls of the early Imperial period; but remains of a fine building, in the neatest sort of *opus reticulatum*, can be seen just opposite the Church of S. Teodoro, high up, through arched openings in the later concrete and brick wall. *Houses facing the Velabrum.*

Passing now to the south-west of the Palatine, the side towards the *Circus Maximus*, there are, on the outside of *Roma Quadrata*, very extensive remains of buildings, in a long line from the west angle of the hill towards and beyond the *Scalae Caci*; fig. 22, Nos. 6, 3, 4. *S.W. side.*

[1] The present entrance to the Palatine brings the visitor opposite this line of buildings, immediately on passing through the turnstile, near the circular Church of S. Teodoro.

These rows of chambers have been supposed to be part of the *Domus Tiberiana*, or Palace of Tiberius; see Suet. *Tib.* 5; Tac. *Hist.* i. 27, and iii. 71. This supposition is supported by the construction of the existing remains; the beautiful *opus reticulatum*, with which the older concrete walls of these buildings are faced, may from its style be attributed to a period not later than the first part of Tiberius' reign.[1]

Fine remains.

This long line of buildings is set, like the "Wall of Romulus," on a sort of shelf cut in the tufa rock. They are built against the cliff, partly in place of and partly covering the primitive wall, in such a way that the third or fourth story is level with the top of the hill; stories higher still rose above the summit of the Palatine, so that these once very lofty buildings were entered at two different levels, one from the lower platform about half-way down the slope, and the other from the top of the cliff. There are many other Roman examples of this method of building houses against the face of a scarped cliff. Another interesting example of this, in the *Horti Sallustiani*, is described at vol. ii. p. 242.

Lofty houses.

What the precise use of these long rows of vaulted chambers may have been is difficult to guess, but they were probably for slaves or soldiers on guard. The rooms are mostly small, and some are mere cells; the larger and handsomer rooms were probably in the higher stories which no longer exist.

These small vaulted chambers are all remarkable for the beauty of their construction; tufa only is used both for the concrete and also for the facing, except that some of the semicircular vaults are made of concrete formed of pumice stone mixed with the lime and *pozzolana*, instead of tufa, for the sake of its superior lightness. Those parts where brick

Neat construction.

---

[1] Some parts, especially at the extreme west angle, are faced with the mixed *opus reticulatum* and brick; exactly resembling that of the lower part of Caligula's Palace, described at vol. i. p. 53. But those buildings which have facing of *opus reticulatum* unmixed with any brick, even at the angles, are probably earlier in date than Caligula's time.

facing occurs are all later additions. At many points remains of stairs exist, leading from the lower level to the summit of the hill. These buildings, except at one point, are not yet excavated to their lowest story, and it is evident that they were once much more extensive. They were in fact great substructions by which the level top of the Palatine was once extended over series of vaulted chambers, piled one above the other, in the direction of the great Circus below, in the same way as the Palace of Caligula extends over the slopes of the Palatine towards the Forum. *Great substructures.*

At one place, near the top of the present winding path, opposite the *Temple of Jupiter Victor* (so called), there are remains of a large *hypocaust*, the under floor of which, formed of hard *opus signinum* or *testaceum*, and covered with the stumps of the square *pilae* on which the upper concrete floor rested, still exists at a level flush with the top of the hill. This *hypocaust* once extended far beyond the edge of the cliff, over the top of some of these many-storied substructures; fig. 22, No. 4, 4. *Hypocaust.*

Traces of painted stucco remain on the walls of these interesting early buildings, and some of them have well-preserved mosaic floors, with simple patterns of small neatly-fitted *tesserae* in white marble and brown lava.

Altar to the Unknown God. In front of this line of buildings, on the level midway between the Velabrum and the top of the hill, a very interesting altar, dedicated by C. Sestius Calvinus to an *unknown god* or *goddess*, was discovered in 1820, and is still *in situ*; fig. 22, No. 7. The form of this altar is a very primitive one, and this example, though not earlier than about 100 B.C., is certainly a copy of a much older altar, such as that in the Cortile of the Palazzo dei Conservatori on the Capitol, which is cut in tufa. *Early altar.*

The Palatine altar is of coarse travertine, once covered with fine white stucco (*opus albarium*); on it is inscribed in archaistic form—

SEI · DEO · SEI · DEIVAE · SAC(rum)
C · SEXTIVS · C · F · CALVINVS · PR(aetor)
DE · SENATI · SENTENTIA · RESTITVIT [1]

Mommsen (*Cor. In. Lat.* i. 632) attributes the restoration of this altar to the younger C. Sestius Calvinus, the son of the

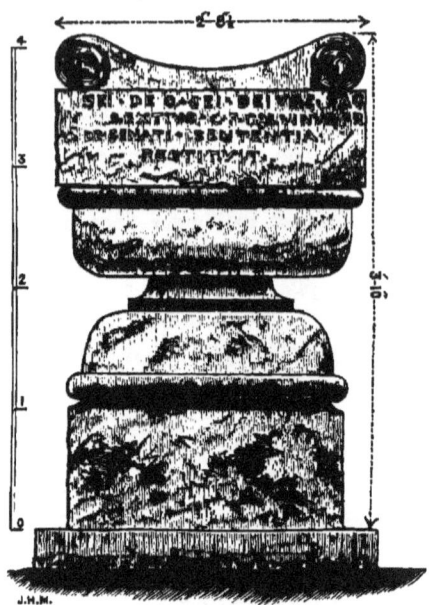

Fig. 24.
Altar to the Unknown God.

Consul of that name, who is mentioned by Cicero as being a candidate for the Praetorship against C. Servilius Glaucia in 100 B.C.; see Cic. *De Orat.* ii. 61. 249.

Altar of Aius loquens. The vague dedication of this altar [2] recalls that one which

[1] The ei for i, in *sei* and *deivae*, and the genitive *senati*, are early forms.

[2] Compare *Acts of the Apostles*, xvii. 23; Aul. Gell. ii. 28; Plutar. *Camil.* 30; and Cato, *De re rus.* 139.

Varro (*ap.* Aul. Gell. xvi. 17) mentions as being consecrated to *Aius loquens*[1] (the speaking voice) in the *Lucus Vestae, in infima nova Via*, in commemoration of a ghostly voice heard in the night as a warning of the approach of the Gauls. This latter altar must have been moved when Caligula built his great palace over the sacred grove of Vesta; and Mommsen suggests that the existing one is that which once stood in the *Lucus Vestae*. The absence, however, of any mention of *Aius loquens* on the inscription makes this seem improbable. Moreover, this is not the only instance of a Roman dedication to an unknown deity.[2]

Aius loquens.

"HOUSE OF LIVIA," OR "HOUSE OF GERMANICUS" (No. 18 on fig. 22).

The so-called "*House of Livia*" is a very well preserved and complete specimen of a Roman house of the time of Augustus. Like the "*Domus Tiberiana*," it is constructed of tufa concrete, with very neat *opus reticulatum* facing, and with quoins and arches of small rectangular tufa blocks, a very fine example of the earliest sort of *opus reticulatum*, without any of that admixture of brick courses or quoins, such as appear to have been used soon after the reign of Augustus; see fig. 4.

Augustan house.

Like other buildings on this part of the Palatine, this house shows that once the level was much more uneven and broken into hollows and ridges than it was under the later Empire. The lower story of the house, with its more public rooms, is set in a sort of hole against the side of a low rocky ridge, in such a way that the upper story behind is level with the road which runs along the higher ridge.

[1] The Romans appear to have been fond of a strange reduplication of names for a deity; besides *Aius loquens* or *locutius*, they had a *Fors Fortuna*, and other similar phrases.

[2] Cf. the invocation on an inscription of the *Fratres Arvales*, "*Sive deo sive deae in cujus tutela hic lucus locusque est.*" Marini, *Atti dei frat. Arval.* pl. xxxii. and p. 370.

A flight of travertine stairs, with vaulted roof (fig. 25, B), leads down to the open *Atrium* at the lower level, and into this, on two sides, various public rooms open; the bedrooms and private apartments are all behind, at the higher level of the hill (fig. 25, EEE).

Mural paintings. The paintings on the walls of the rooms opening on to the *Atrium* are fine and well-preserved examples of Roman wall-painting, earlier in date than most at Pompeii, and equal in execution to the best of them; see *Mon. Inst. Arch. Rom.* xi. Tav. 22, 23; and Renier, *Les peintures du Palatin*, Paris, 1870.

In the centre, opposite the entrance, is the *Tablinum*, a sort of parlour; in the middle of the wall on the left is a fine painting of Io watched by Argus, while Hermes approaches stealthily round a large rock, preparing to kill Argus and so liberate Io. This picture is well composed, and painted with *Greek names.* some delicacy; it appears to be the work of a Greek artist, as the names of the figures represented were painted under each in Greek letters. ΕΡΜΗC is the only one now legible, as this and all the paintings in this house have suffered much since they were exposed to light in 1869 to 1870.

Street scene. On the same wall is a curious street scene at night, with fanciful architecture; lofty houses, from the windows and porticoes of which figures are looking out; others are walking bearing lanterns and torches.

Easel pictures. Near this, and on the end wall also, are small gracefully-designed paintings, which represent easel pictures hung on the walls, and are of special interest, as showing the form of the movable pictures of the Romans. They are represented as panel-paintings, each with folding doors, like a mediaeval *triptych*; the doors are shown open, in perspective. The subjects of these sham easel pictures appear to be sacrificial or domestic scenes; they have gracefully-draped female figures, partly Hellenic in style, and recalling the style of figures on certain late Greek vases.

On the end wall is a large painting, now much damaged,

of the Cyclops Polyphemus, with Cupid on his shoulder watch-

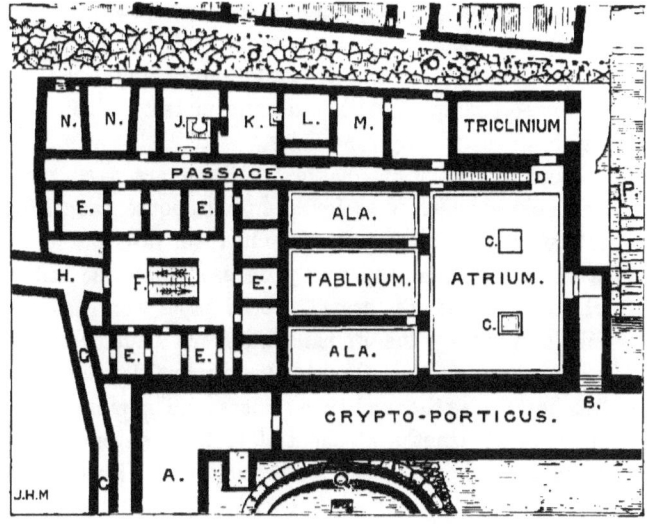

Fig. 25.
Plan of the so-called "House of Livia."[1]

A. Crypto-porticus leading to Caligula's Palace.
B. Stairs down to the Atrium.
CC. Pedestals for statues in the Atrium.
D. Narrow stairs from the Atrium to the upper floor.
EE. Bedrooms.
F. Stairs to highest story, now destroyed.
G. Narrow Crypto-porticus, not fully excavated.
H. Crypto-porticus leading to the Flavian Palace, and branching off to the cisterns under the so-called "Temple of Jupiter Victor."
JKLM. Series of bath-rooms.
NN. Shops opening into the public street, OO.
P. Remains of an early tufa building.
Q. Piscina.

ing the nymph Galatea, who is riding on a sea monster among the waves.

[1] This plan is by mistake placed upside down with reference to the general plan on fig. 22.

178   LEAD PIPES   CHAP.

Debased style. The lower part of the walls has a plain dado; and in the upper part, between the pictures, are series of slender columns, entablatures, and other sham architectural details, painted in violent perspective, and in imitation of relief with strong shadows—examples of that decline in taste which Vitruvius (vii. 5. 3) so strongly reprobates.

Lead pipes. Against the walls of the *Tablinum* are fixed some lead water-pipes, which were found in this house, though later in date than the building itself. On them inscriptions are cast in relief, repeated apparently on each plate of lead out of which the pipes are formed. Lead pipes were not cast into tubular form by the Romans, but were made of cast plates, rolled round, and joined with a longitudinal lap or seam, which was beaten together and then soldered. The pipes were joined endways, in lengths of about 10 feet, by an enlarged socket being formed in one end by beating it over a wooden conical core, while the other was contracted by hammering so as to slip into the enlarged part, and then the two ends were soldered together. The plates out of which these pipes are rolled were about 16 inches wide, 10 feet long, and $\frac{1}{4}$ to $\frac{1}{3}$ inch

Inscribed pipes. thick.[1] Their inscriptions are (1) IVLIAE · AVG · —probably the Julia who was the daughter of Titus; (2) F · PESCEN-NIVS · EROS · CAESARVM—an imperial freedman; and (3) IMP DOMITIANI · CAESAR · AVG · SVB · CVRA · EVTYCHI · L · PROC FEC · HYMNVS · CAESAR · N · SER ·, that is: "*In the reign of the emperor Domitianus Caesar Augustus; under the care of the procurator [aquarum], the freedman Eutychius. Hymnus, a slave of our Caesar, made it.*" The oval water-tank (fig. 25, Q), on the other side of the *Crypto-porticus*, appears to have been constructed at some later time to supply the house of Livia.

Mural paintings. On each side of the *Tablinum* is a side-room (*ala*); that on the left has sham architectural paintings of columns and entablature on a plinth or dado. At the end are graceful

[1] Further information about Roman water-pipes of lead and other materials is given in vol. ii. chap. x.

winged female figures and hanging foliage, designed with great spirit, and very delicately executed. The dado is painted so as to imitate marble and red porphyry, a tasteless method of decoration which the Romans used very largely; gaudiness and much show at little cost being characteristics of the art of Rome under the Empire. Vitruvius (vii. 5. 1) speaks of the painting of sham marbles on walls as being an early method of decoration, used before the introduction of real marble into Rome. *Sham marbles.*

The *ala* on the right of the *Tablinum* also has painted columns, from which hang large wreaths of fruit and foliage, richly designed, and painted with much effective realism. There is also a curious intermediate frieze, painted in a monochromatic way with various shades of yellow; it is divided into long panels, representing fanciful landscape scenes, with rivers, bridges, temples, men, and animals, among which are some camels; it is all very minute in scale, and has very little decorative effect. *Landscapes.*

The *Triclinium*, also, has a painted series of columns on a plinth; the panels are mostly vermilion, and above is a frieze of rudely-painted sham marble; and above that, small panels containing glass vessels full of fruit. The fruit seen through the transparent glass is cleverly rendered. Below are large panels of rudely-painted trees, birds, and animals, evidently the work of a very inferior artist to the Greek who painted the pictures in the *Tablinum*. *Dining-room paintings.*

In technique these paintings resemble those found at Pompeii, and appear to be executed by more than one process.[1] The plain-coloured grounds, over which the pictures are painted, were probably done by the *encaustic* process, that is, the pigments were applied with a hot wax medium; fresh wax was then rubbed over the surface, and melted into the stucco by the application of a brazier of charcoal, and the whole surface then brought to a high mechanical polish by *Encaustic method.*

[1] On Roman wall-paintings, see vol. i. p. 94 *seq.*

rubbing with linen. Over this polished surface the pictures were painted, and then fixed by a further application of wax and the hot brazier; the process is described by Vitruvius (vii. 9. 3); see vol. i. p. 97.

Styles of painting. The styles of painting used in this house are described by Vitruvius (vii. 5) at some length. He objects to the fanciful architectural designs, and to such weak and incongruous things as candelabra being made to support entablatures; and also to the human figures growing out of foliage. The "House of Livia" was certainly built and decorated about the time that Vitruvius was writing, and it is interesting to find how closely its paintings illustrate his remarks.

Tile linings. In those walls of the *Triclinium* which are on the outside of the house, and therefore exposed to damp, special precautions have been taken to protect the paintings from wet soaking through; the whole walls are lined on the inside by flange-tiles, so fixed as to leave an air-cavity between the wall and the thick coating of stucco, which is afterwards laid over the tiles.

These "flange-tiles" have a projecting rim along two sides, thus ⌐   ⌐, and are set with the rims touching the wall, so that there is an air-space, equal in thickness to the projection of the rims, between the face of the wall and the flat surface of the tile on which the painted stucco is laid.

A very minute description is given by Vitruvius (vii. 4. 2) of two methods to prevent wall-paintings from being injured by damp. One system is to cover the whole inner surface of the wall with a layer of tiles with an air-space between them and the wall—very like the method adopted in *Hollow walls.* this house. The other system is to build the wall hollow, the method still in use for houses in damp or exposed situations. In both cases Vitruvius is careful to provide for the ventilation of the air-cavities, and also for a system of drainage, by which any water which got into the cavity might harmlessly drain away at the foot of the wall. Another form of tiles used for wall-linings was the *tegula mammata* (Vitruvius, vii. 4. 2), with *Tegulae mammatae.* four small projecting bosses which rested against the wall and so made an air-cavity between it and the main surface of the *tegula*. Examples of these have been found in Rome, at Pompeii, and other places in Italy.[1]

The flange-tiles, with projecting rims along two sides, were called *tegulae cum marginibus*; see Vitr. v. 10. 3. They were commonly used for roofing, as well as for wall-linings.

The floors of these rooms have simple mosaic patterns of *Mosaics.* hexagons and triangles in grey lava and white limestone, with small *tesserae* like those of the *Domus Publica* (see vol. i. p. 303).

The *Triclinium* is paved with white mosaic, studded with irregularly-shaped bits of coloured Oriental marbles and alabaster, then much rarer in Rome than they afterwards became; they appear very brilliant from contrast with the white ground.

Next to the *Triclinium* is a dark room, vaulted in tufa concrete, as are the rooms above mentioned; this is possibly a kitchen, and by it a narrow stair (fig. 25, D) ascends to the upper story, part of which could also be entered from the road at the higher level.

Upper Floor. The numerous upper rooms (fig. 25, EEE) *Upper floor.* are very small, some are barely 6 feet square. Remains of a staircase (fig. 25, F) exists which once led to a higher story still, now destroyed. At this part of the house there are foundation walls of some later building, cast in rough concrete, and easily distinguishable from the neat *opus reticulatum* of the original structure.

A door opposite this staircase leads into the long *Crypto-* *Crypto-* *porticus* (fig. 25, H) which branched in three directions; see 19, *porticus.*

[1] Good examples of *tegulae mammatae* are preserved in the Opera del Duomo at Orvieto. Each tile was fixed by four large iron nails which passed through holes in the centres of the projecting bosses. Others, found in Rome, are in the Museo delle Terme.

Crypto-porticus.

19 on the Palatine Plan, fig. 22. One branch leads into the ancient Republican house described above, and from it stairs descend to the rock-cut chambers under the Temple (so called) of Jupiter Victor; another branch (fig. 25, G) turns off at a sharp angle to the left, and a third continues in a straight line towards the *Flavian Palace*; the two latter are not yet cleared out, but the main passage is accessible and well worth exploring. It is easily entered at the point mentioned, close by the stairs in the upper story of the "House of Livia," and will lead the visitor out to the daylight again in one of the rooms of the massively-built house of the Republican period.[1]

Shops.

In addition to the private rooms in the "House of Livia," the part of the house which faces on to the road at the higher level contains two small shops which open on to the road, but have no doors leading into the house itself; fig. 25, NN.

Crypto-porticus.

Another *Crypto-porticus* starts from near the top of the stairs leading down to the Atrium, and communicates with the long *Crypto-porticus* (fig. 22, No. 31), which runs into the Palace of Caligula, and afterwards was connected with the Flavian Palace. In the part of this passage (fig. 25, A) which connects this so-called "*House of Livia*" with Caligula's *Crypto-porticus*,

Stucco reliefs.

the vault is decorated with very beautiful and spirited reliefs, modelled in wet stucco, representing cupids, birds, animals, and graceful foliage, designed with great taste, and moulded with wonderful skill; each figure or group is enclosed in a moulded panel, with egg and dart enrichments round it. Near the angle where the *Crypto-porticus* turns towards the "House of Livia" is a large oval *piscina* or water-tank, lined with the hard *opus signinum*—hydraulic cement made of lime and pounded pottery; see Q on fig. 25.

The manner in which the house is connected by a side passage with the *Crypto-porticus* of Caligula makes it very probable that this so-called "*House of Livia*" is the house of Caligula's father Germanicus, into which the murderers of

[1] This house is described above at p. 175.

Caligula escaped after stabbing him in the passage, while he was returning to his palace from some theatrical shows in the *Area Palatina*, which was probably the site now occupied by the Flavian Palace; this is described by Josephus, *Ant. Jud.* xix. 1. 14, and by Suet. *Cal.* 58. In any case, this house is certainly earlier than the time of Germanicus, and was probably built during the reign of Augustus.

Death of Caligula.

Near the "House of Livia" there is a row of small vaulted chambers opening on to a paved road (fig. 22, No. 16, 16), which leads towards the cliff overhanging the *Velabrum*; these look like shops, and have travertine thresholds grooved for wooden shop-fronts; they are supposed to belong to the *Domus Tiberiana*, but are probably later than the reign of Tiberius.

Shops.

Between these shops and the "House of Livia" is the interesting well already mentioned (fig. 22, No. 15), with a deep round shaft lined with blocks of *peperino*, and above ground a plain stone *puteal* or well-mouth which shows the wear of the ropes which drew up the buckets.

THE DOMUS AUGUSTANA AND THE AREA OF APOLLO.[1]

Nothing of this marvellous group of buildings is now visible (fig. 22, Nos. 47, 47 and 48), but a portion of the Area of Apollo was excavated in the sixteenth century. That part of the Palatine, on the south-west of the *Area Apollinis*, which contained the *Palace of Augustus* was excavated in 1775, when its plan was published by Guattani, *Monumenti antichi inediti di Roma*, 1785; and from the drawings made then the plan given, at No. 48 on fig. 22, is taken. At present a nunnery (the Villa Mills) stands over the ruins of Augustus' Palace; and the foundations of this modern building have probably destroyed much that was seen by Guattani.

Palace of Augustus.

[1] See an excellent paper on this subject by the Comm. Lanciani, in *Bull. Com. Arch. Rom.* fasc. iv. 1883.

The *Palace of Augustus* (fig. 22, No. 48), though a very handsome building, rich with Greek and Oriental marbles, was but small compared to the enormous palaces of the succeeding emperors. It stood in a noble position, near the edge of the cliff towards the *Vallis Murcia* and the *Circus Maximus*, with a fine view of the Aventine Hill opposite. The Villa Mills now covers most of its site, and no part of it is visible above ground.

Site of palace.

The palace consisted of a large *Peristyle*, surrounded with rooms on all sides, two stories high; the *Peristyle* itself was in two stories, having a second tier of columns over the first. None of the surrounding rooms are large, but they appear to have been very graceful in proportion, with rich marble panelling and pilasters on the walls. The ceilings were domed or formed with barrel vaults, and the walls contained many niches for statues. The floors had simple mosaics or coloured marbles in patterns, like that of the Flavian (so called) *Library*; and the whole house appears to have been designed with great taste and elegance, very unlike the gigantic and somewhat coarse splendours of the later palaces. A good set of drawings, plans, sections, and details are given by Guattani in the above-mentioned work, now doubly valuable, as no other record exists of what this most interesting of imperial residences once was like.

Modest size.

The *Temple* and *Area of Apollo*, which occupied a large part of the centre of the Palatine (No. 47, on fig. 22), was approached from a road leading out of the *Summa Sacra Via*, near the line of the modern Via di S. Bonaventura. The entrance, through lofty marble *Propylaea*, probably the "*Arcus*" of Pliny (*Hist. Nat.* xxxvi. 36), led into a very large open *Peristyle*, surrounded with at least fifty-two Corinthian columns of the rich Numidian *giallo antico*; the rest of the building was of white marble from Luna and Athens.

Area of Apollo.

In a sort of shrine or *aedicula* on the summit of the great entrance archway Augustus placed a celebrated group of

Quadriga.

Apollo and Artemis in a quadriga by the Greek sculptor Lysias; see Pliny, *Hist. Nat.* xxxvi. 36. Pliny says that the group was cut out of one block of marble, but he was probably mistaken, as he was when he made the same statement about the Laocoön group.

In the middle of this great *Peristyle* or *Porticus* stood the large *octastyle peripteral Temple of Apollo Palatinus*, so called to distinguish it from another Temple of Apollo, outside the *Porta Carmentalis*, which from its cedar-wood statue, the gift of C. Sosius, was called the *Temple of Apollo Sosianus*; see vol. ii. p. 70. [margin: *Temple of Apollo.*]

The *Palatine Temple of Apollo* was begun by Augustus in 36 B.C., after his Sicilian victory over Sextus Pompeius (Dion Cass. xlix. 15, and Vell. Pat. II. lxxxi.), and it was dedicated in 28 B.C. The Ancyrean inscription records — TEMPLVM APOLLINIS · IN · SOLO · MAGNAM · PARTEM · EMPTO · FECI. See also Dion Cass. liii. 1; and *Cor. In. Lat.* i. p. 403. Propertius, who was present at its consecration, gives a glowing account of its splendours (*El.* iv. (v.) 6 to 11), which must have surpassed anything that existed even in magnificent Rome, not only from the beauty of its materials and architecture, but also from the countless works of art it contained in gold, silver, ivory, gilt bronze, and marble, many of which were the work of the great Greek sculptors of bygone days, and others by the scarcely inferior Greek artists who thronged Rome in the Augustan Age. [margin: *Works of art.*]

Inside the *Cella* of the temple were statues of Apollo by Scopas, Latona by Cephisodotus the son of Praxiteles, and Diana by Timotheus (Pliny, *Hist. Nat.* xxxvi. 24, 25, and 32); round the walls were statues of the nine Muses; see Juv. vii. 37.

In the *aetos* of the Pediment there were bronze statues by Bupalos and Athenis, the sons of Archermos[1] (Pliny, *Hist.*

---

[1] Archermos was a famous sculptor in the sixth century B.C., a native of Chios. His sons were no less celebrated; see Pliny, *Hist. Nat.* xxxvi. 11 to 13.

Nat. xxxvi. 13), and on its apex stood a magnificent colossal group of Apollo in a quadriga made of gilt bronze. The folding doors were covered with ivory reliefs, representing the fate of Niobe's children, and the discomfiture of the Gaulish pillagers at Delphi by the apparition of Apollo holding the aegis.

Silver statues.
No less than eighty silver statues of Augustus had been dedicated in his honour by various donors; and in the Ancyrean inscription Augustus records that he sold these statues of himself, and with the proceeds presented "golden gifts," in the form of tripods, to the Temple of Apollo, dedicating them jointly in his own name, and in that of the original donors of the silver statues; see also Suet. *Aug.* 52.

Treasures.
Within the *Cella*, in addition to the gold tripods, there was a large collection of statues, lamps, vases, and other works of art in gold and silver (Suet. *Aug.* 52), as well as a very valuable collection of engraved gems, dedicated by the young Marcellus, whose premature death was so grievous a blow to his uncle Augustus; see Pliny, *Hist. Nat.* xxxvii. 11.

Sibyl's books.
Under the statue of Apollo inside its pedestal was a secret chamber, in which the Sibylline books were preserved in gilt caskets (Suet. *Aug.* 31), and they continued in safety during more than one fire which did much injury to the Temple; the books even survived the great fire of 363 A.D., which utterly ruined the whole of this group of buildings; Ammian. xxiii. 3.

Libraries.
Libraries of Apollo. The sides of the great *Peristyle* were flanked by two large halls used as libraries, one for Greek, the other for Latin books; see Suet. *Aug.* 29. According to the Scholiast on Juv. *Sat.* i. 128, this library was a *Bibliotheca juris civilis et liberalium studiorum*, a somewhat wide classification, but not including, it appears, works on history.[1]

---

[1] Librarians of various grades were appointed to each of these libraries, under a general director called *Procurator Bibliothecarum Augusti*; see *Cor. In. Lat.* vi. 2, 2132, 4233, 5188, 5189, 5190, etc.

A third side of the Peristyle was occupied by another still larger hall, in which Augustus, when old and failing in health, used occasionally to convene the Senate; Tac. *Ann.* ii. 37. In this hall stood a very beautiful gilt bronze colossal statue of Apollo, of Etruscan workmanship, 50 feet high (Pliny, *Hist. Nat.* xxxiv. 43); and on its walls were portrait reliefs of celebrated writers, in the form of medallions (*clipei*) of gilt bronze;[1] see Tac. *Ann.* ii. 37 and ii. 83; and cf. Pliny, *Hist. Nat.* xxxv. 9 to 11, on the custom of decorating libraries with portraits. *Great hall.*

Works of art.

Pliny also mentions (*Hist. Nat.* vii. 58) examples of ancient Greek inscriptions cut on bronze *tabulae*, which were preserved in the Palatine library. One of them, he says, had the following dedicatory inscription—Ναυσικράτης Τισαμένου 'Αθηναίος ἀνέθηκεν.

Between the Numidian columns of the *Peristyle* stood fifty statues of the daughters of Danaus, and opposite each Danaid, in the open area of the court, there was an equestrian statue of her murdered bridegroom,[2] one of the sons of Aegyptus; see Schol. ad Pers. ii. 56; and Ovid, *Trist.* III. i. 61. *Statues of Danaids.*

Many fragments of these statues, and some pieces of the fifty-two fluted columns of Numidian *giallo*, were found in the time of Pope Alexander VII., and again in 1869. Among them was a statue of Heracles, the pedestal of which was inscribed with the name of Lysippus, ΛΥΣΙΠΠΟΥ ΕΡΓΟΝ. This statue was taken to Florence by Duke Cosimo de' Medici, where it still exists; see Vacca, *Memorie*, pp. 32 and 77, vol. iv. of Nardini, *Roma Ant.*, ed. Nibby, 1820.

In the middle of the open area, in front of the steps of the Temple, was an altar, surrounded by the celebrated statues of four oxen in bronze by the Greek sculptor Myron— *Oxen by Myron.*

[1] It appears to have been usual for the Romans to decorate their libraries with portraits of famous authors, in bronze, marble, modelled in stucco, or painted. For an example of the latter see Pliny, *Epis.* iv. 28.

[2] Murdered, all except one; see Hor. *Od.* iii. 9. 21-52.

188   TEMPLE OF VESTA   CHAP.

*Atque aram circum steterant armenta Myronis,
Quatuor, artificis vivida signa, boves.*
Prop. *El.* II. (III.) 23-27.

A great many fine pieces of sculpture have been found at different times among the remains of these buildings; one of the most beautiful is the ancient marble copy of the Apollo Sauroctonos of Praxiteles, now in the Vatican.

Temple of Vesta.   *Palatine Temple of Vesta.* Behind this great *Peristyle*, between it and the Palace of Augustus, a small round *Temple of Vesta*, a copy probably of the ancient one by the *Forum Romanum*, was built by Augustus when he was elected *Pontifex Maximus* in 12 B.C. The dedication of the Altar and Temple of Vesta is thus recorded in an inscription (*C. I. L.* I. p. 392) [AEDICVL]A · ET · [ARA] · VESTAE · IN · DOMV · IMP · CAESARIS AVGV[STI·PO]NTIF·MA[XIMI]·DEDICATAST · QVIRINIO·ET·VALGIO
House of Pontifex.   COSS. On that occasion Augustus gave the official residence of the Pontiff to the Vestal Virgins; and having built himself a palace adjoining the *Area of Apollo Palatinus*, he built near it a new temple to Vesta, in order that he, in his quality of chief Pontiff, might live (as the *Pontifex Maximus* always had lived) with a temple to Vesta close to his door. Ovid (*Fast.* iv. 949), with the flattery of a Court poet, speaks of this part of the Palatine as being shared by three deities, Apollo, Vesta, and Augustus—

*Phoebus habet partem, Vestae pars altera cessit;
Quod superest illis tertius ipse tenet.
State Palatinae laurus, praetextaque quercu
Stet domus; aeternos tres habet una deos.*

Cf. Ovid, *Metam.* xv. 864.

Round temple.   The circular temple discovered in the sixteenth century on this part of the Palatine was probably Augustus' *Temple of Vesta*; a sketch of it is given in a MS. by Ligorio, *Cod. Ursin. Vat.* 3439, fol. 25; and is reproduced by Lanciani, *Bull. Com. Arch. Rom.* 1883, Tav. 17. It was built of blocks of tufa, possibly for religious reasons, tufa being the most primitive building material in Rome.

"*Roma Quadrata.*" Within the *Area of Apollo* was also a mysterious object (some kind of βαιτυλός), which appears to have symbolised the ancient *Roma Quadrata*. This sacred object, which was probably a cubical block of stone used as an altar, was called *Roma Quadrata*, and was surrounded by a circular trench, the *Mundus*, a symbol of the mystic plough-turned furrow, the *sulcus primigenius*, by which the *pomoerium* or sacred circuit-line was marked, in accordance with the primitive religious ceremonies performed while founding a new city.

Cubical altar.

The *Temple of Victory*, which gave its name to the *Clivus Victoriae*, was originally built on the site of a prehistoric altar to Victory; Dionys. i. 32. In 294 B.C. it was rebuilt by the Consul L. Postumius Megellus, out of money collected in the form of fines by the Curule Aediles; Livy, x. 33. In the Temple of Victory, in 204 B.C., was placed a sacred *Baetylus* or meteoric stone, which was supposed to be the symbol of the Phrygian goddess *Mater Idaea*; Livy, xxix. 14. A few years later a special Temple of the *Magna Deum Mater* was built to enshrine it.

Temple of Victory.

The temple was rebuilt by Augustus, and restored by later emperors; it is shown on a rare bronze medallion of Gordianus III., with a domed cella and projecting portico, on the pediment of which is inscribed ΝΕΙΚΗ · ΟΠΛΟΦΟΡΟΣ or "*Armed Victory*"; see Grueber, *Roman Medallions*, London, 1874, pl. xlii.

Medallion type.

In 1725-28, excavations on the slope of the Palatine, towards the Church of S. Maria Liberatrice, brought to light considerable remains of this *Temple of Victory*, and fragments of its frieze inscribed, [IMP · C]AESAR · DIVI · F · [AEDEM VI]CTORIA[E · REFEC], recording, as the Comm. Lanciani suggests, the rebuilding by Augustus. Its columns were of Numidian *giallo*, and the rest of white Parian marble; see Bianchini, *Pal. dei Cesari*, 1738, p. 236.

Small shrine.   In 193 B.C. M. Porcius Cato built near it another small *aedicula* to Victory; Livy, xxxv. 9.

The smaller Temple of Victory appears to have been circular in plan, with a ring of Corinthian columns, like the Temple of Vesta.

Inscribed bricks.   The Comm. Lanciani, in the valuable paper on the *Area of Apollo* above mentioned, tells us that an excavation made in 1869-70 in the garden of the nunnery exposed part of some walls which he believes to have belonged to the buildings of Augustus. Some of the bricks then found had the following *bolli* or stamps :—

EX · FIG · DOM · L · VALER · SEVERI } and { CN · DOM · AMANDI
L · ALLI ·   MAXIMI   VALEAT · QVI · FEC.

Others have

OPVS · DOL · EX · PR · FAVS · AVG · EX · FIG · PONT · LAN · FESTVS ;
FORTVNAT · DOMITIORVM · LVCANI · ET · TVLLL.[1]

These bricks are considerably later than the time of Augustus, and must have belonged to some restoration of the original building during the Flavian period or even later.

THE PALACE OF CALIGULA.

Palace of Gaius.   The *Palace of Caligula* (fig. 22, Nos. 36, 37, 38) occupies a very large area of the northern angle of the Palatine, the original contour of which was very much cut away and altered to form a site for this gigantic building,[2] which spread not only over a large space on the top of the hill, but also over the sacred *Grove of Vesta*, and the ground once occupied by the houses of Clodius, Cicero, and other wealthy Romans; see vol. i. p. 169.

[1] For an explanation of these and similar inscriptions see above, p. 13.

[2] The extravagant size of Caligula's Palace, like that of Nero's *Golden House*, is commented on by Pliny (*Hist. Nat.* xxxvi. 111), who remarks, *bis vidimus Urbem totam cingi domibus principum Gai et Neronis, hujus quidem, ne quid deesset, aurea.*

With the *Lucus Vestae* the *Sacellum Volupiae* and the altar of *Aius loquens* must have been destroyed or moved.

Caligula's palace extends across the ancient *Clivus Victoriae*, which, however, was respected by Caligula to the extent that he did not block it up, but raised his palace above it on a series of immensely lofty arches. The lower part of the palace faced on to the Nova Via, which separated it from the *Atrium Vestae*, and extended along this road nearly as far as the point where it joins the *Clivus Palatinus* near the Arch of Titus. What now exists is little more than the massive and lofty substructures by which Caligula raised, as it were, the lower slopes of the Palatine to a level with its summit, and it was mainly from this highest level that the grand rooms of the palace appear to have been entered. The whole building must have reached the astonishing height of over 120 feet, and possibly a good deal more, as it is now impossible to tell how high the palace once reached above the top of the Palatine Hill.

Clivus Victoriae.

Immense substructures.

The rooms of the existing substructures were entered from various levels, the lowest from the *Nova Via*, the next from the foot of the *Clivus Victoriae*, near the site of the ancient *Porta Romanula*, other rooms from the top of the *Clivus*, where the modern Casino now stands, and lastly the rooms (now mostly destroyed) which were entered from the highest part of the Palatine at its northern angle.

Various levels.

These various levels are connected by numerous staircases, some wide and easy of ascent, like the one on the left immediately on entering the palace at the foot of the *Clivus Victoriae*, others very steep and narrow. Some stairs which start from the right of the *Clivus* are only 1 foot 9 inches wide. The steps of these narrow stairs, probably only used by slaves, are made of large square tiles of earthenware; those leading up from the *Nova Via* are of *travertine*; and the more important stairs to the state rooms were of marble on a concrete foundation.

Stairs.

Dark substructures.

It is impossible to make out the precise uses of a great many of the rooms in the substructions of the palace; many are lighted only by small square openings in the vault, or by borrowed light, while some had no natural light at all, and look as if they could only have been store-rooms. They are probably partly rooms of slaves and soldiers on guard, whose comfort was but little regarded by the Romans.

Rows of shops.

On both the *Nova Via* and the *Clivus Victoriae* rows of vaulted chambers open, which appear to have been shops, as they have wide openings with long *travertine* thresholds, grooved to hold a movable wooden front and counter, very similar to those in the bazaars of modern Oriental cities. Pivot-holes and quadrant-shaped marks on the *travertine* sills show where small side doors in the wooden fronts opened inwards.[1] In many of these chambers simple mosaic floors remain, and traces of painted stucco on the walls.

Shop-front restored.

Fig. 26 shows one of these shop-fronts; the woodwork is restored from existing evidence of many kinds, namely, the grooves and holes for fixing the wood in the existing stone and brickwork, and also from casts that have skilfully been made at Pompeii, by pouring plaster into the voids in the ashes left by the burning of the wooden shop-fronts and doors. The arrangement was very simple; part of the front was hinged, so that it could be let down to form a projecting counter, and at night pulled up to form a closed shutter.

Type of shops.

Every Roman shop, whether in Italy or in distant colonies, seems to have been arranged in this way. Moreover, all Roman shops appear to have been quite small, exactly as is

---

[1] All Roman shops appear to have been arranged with these wooden fronts and small side doors; these can be clearly traced in the row of shops in the curved side of Trajan's Forum against the Quirinal Hill (see vol. ii. p. 33), and in many other places. The large sill, with its long groove and flat sinking at one side for the door, always bears witness to the existence of a shop. These are very common among the existing remains of ancient Rome.

still the case in the East. A rich dealer may have a large warehouse, but his actual shop is no larger than those of his poorer fellow-tradesmen.

In mediaeval times the same arrangement of shop-fronts

Fig. 26.

Typical example of a Roman shop-front, restored from existing evidence in Rome and at Pompeii.

On the right hand side of the sketch the counter is shown pulled up so as to form a shutter completely closing in the shop-front.

was almost universal throughout Europe, and still survives in a few remote places.[1]

In some cases a variety of the arrangement shown in fig. 26 was used. In addition to the flap which formed the

[1] Jost Amman's interesting series of cuts representing various trades and handicrafts, printed at Frankfort, 1568, shows several shop-fronts of precisely the Roman design.

counter, the upper part of the front was hinged so as to pull upwards, and form a projecting shelter over the counter.

Upper gallery. Looking up to the right, on ascending the *Clivus Victoriae*, well-preserved remains can be seen of the start of what has been supposed to be the bridge by which Caligula connected the Palatine and the *Capitolium*; see p. 273. This is a gallery or passage partly supported on large stone corbels carrying a series of low concrete and brick arches; the soffit of these and the side of the bridge are richly decorated with delicate reliefs, modelled in stucco, of figures and foliage, in a network of panelling with enriched mouldings, all once covered with gold and coloured decoration, and designed with great skill and beauty of effect. The floor of the bridge has simple *Marble balustrade.* mosaic, and at one point its marble balustrade still remains *in situ*, formed of light openwork in white marble, imitating wooden tresselling, with round bosses to emphasise the intersection of the cross pieces. This special design for balustrading appears to have been universally used in Rome; other existing *cancelli* or screens, such as those in the *Flavian Basilica* and the fragments in the Forum from the *Rostra* and the *Basilica Julia*, resemble this one even in the details of the moulded plinth and capping.[1]

Stucco reliefs. Several small rooms or ante-chambers, through which the emperor must have passed on his way to "the bridge," are richly decorated with a combination of coloured stucco reliefs and painting on the flat, very gorgeous in effect, but almost invisible from want of light, except that of lamps, especially when the whole of the upper vaulting was perfect.

Summit of the hill. On the right of the higher part of the *Clivus Victoriae*, extending over the summit of the hill, are a number of larger rooms, once richly decorated with numerous statues, marble

[1] Such screens were commonly used to fill up the lower part of the intercolumniations of open colonnades, such as those round the peristyles of large houses, and between the piers or columns of the great public *Basilicae*.

columns, mosaics, and wall-linings of various coloured marbles.¹ These handsome rooms were probably part of the emperor's state apartments. At the back of this part of the palace a large number of extensive dark substructures reach to the end of Caligula's *Crypto-porticus* (fig. 22, 31, 31), and it was above these that the emperor's chief state rooms appear to have been, but are now almost completely gone. The modern *Casino* is built upon part of these massive under-chambers, some of which were evidently used for grinding corn, baking bread, and other domestic purposes. {*Great substructures.*}

Methods of Construction. The methods of construction employed in Caligula's Palace are worthy of attention. {*Construction.*}

The lower part, that between the *Clivus Victoriae* and the *Nova Via*, is of concrete faced with mixed brickwork and *opus reticulatum*; all quoins and inner angles, and all the facing arches, have the brick lining, but the central space of each concrete wall is faced with the tufa *opus reticulatum*, alternating with bands of brick facing, one foot deep. In this sort of work, which is a transition from the old *opus reticulatum* to complete facing of brick, the use of cut tufa voussoirs for arches, or rectangular blocks for angles, is avoided.² {*Mixed facing.*}

In the upper part of the palace none but brick facing to the concrete is used; it is very sound, solid work, but not quite so neat as other rather later examples. The bricks are of the usual triangular form, about 12 inches long by $1\frac{1}{4}$ to $1\frac{1}{2}$ thick, with joints $\frac{3}{8}$ to $\frac{1}{2}$ inch. At intervals of about 2 feet 6 inches one bond-course of tiles, 2 Roman feet square, is built {*Brick facing.*}

---

[1] Pliny (*Hist. Nat.* xxxvi. 38) mentions a number of statues by famous Greek sculptors which were placed *in Palatinas domos Caesarum*.

[2] An example of this is illustrated above, fig. 5, vol. i. p. 53. The finest example in Rome of this mixed use of brick and *opus reticulatum* facing is to be seen in the lower walls of the *Thermae of Titus*, where they cut through the remains of Nero's *Golden House*; see vol. ii. p. 149. On the date of the *opus reticulatum* facing, both with and without an admixture of brick, see vol. i. p. 54.

into the concrete of the wall and passes through its whole thickness; these tiles are about 2 inches thick.

The concrete core of the walls is either of broken bits of brick or tufa, or both mixed; in some places a few bits of white marble are mixed with the other materials of the concrete; and occasionally broken travertine replaces the tufa or brick fragments.[1]

Clay pipes. Earthenware socketed pipes, about a foot in diameter, are built into the concrete wall at intervals all over the building, reaching from the lowest to the highest points of the walls; some of these are smoke flues, others are rain-water down-pipes.

Concrete vaults. The vaulting and arches of the whole building are cast by pouring fluid concrete on to wooden centering; in some places numbers of *amphorae* are imbedded in the vaults to diminish the weight on its haunches. None of the fine brick facing was originally left visible; the whole of it was either covered with painted stucco or with marble linings. A thick coat of cement backing was laid between the marble slabs and the smooth brick facing, the whole surface of which was studded with large iron nails or marble plugs, to form a key or hold for the cement backing or stucco facing. The *Cast concrete.* foundation walls, in some places to a considerable height above the ground, are of *lava* concrete, cast in wooden framing; the impress of the wooden uprights is visible at regular intervals, as is shown in fig. 3 in vol. i. p. 48.

Stairs to Forum. *Scalae Anulariae* (?); Suet. *Aug.* 72. From near the entrance to Caligula's Palace at the *Porta Romanula* a wide flight of steps (fig. 22, No. 34) descends to the *Nova Via*,[2] and thence probably continues down to the Forum under the modern

---

[1] This variety of material comes from the fact that all the broken bits of marble, stone, or brick, which otherwise would have been wasted, were utilised for making the concrete for the walls.

[2] See vol. i. p. 222 for an account of the *Nova Via*, and classical references to these stairs. They are also shown at No. 54 on the *Forum Plan*.

Church of S. Maria Liberatrice. The lower stage of these steps (not yet excavated) is partly shown on a recently discovered fragment of the *Marble Plan* (see *Plan of Forum*), passing in a sloping direction towards the *Temple of Castor*. These steps are partly cut in the tufa rock of the hill : they were once lined with marble, and appear from the character of the brick facing on the side walls to be contemporary with Caligula's Palace. It is probable that an earlier flight of steps existed here in the reign of Augustus.

The *Crypto-porticus* (No. 31 on fig. 22), probably that in which Caligula was murdered, starts from the substructions of his palace, near the so-called " *Temple of Jupiter Stator*," and runs for about 130 yards in a straight line, till it reaches the short richly-decorated part which leads into the house supposed to be that of Germanicus ; see vol. i. p. 182. *Cryptoporticus.*

Near the north-eastern end some interesting pieces of sculpture are preserved, among them a fine marble sarcophagus, with a series of reliefs illustrating the story of Jason's inconstancy and Medea's double vengeance. *Fine reliefs.*

This long semi-subterranean passage was covered with a barrel vault, ornamented in parts by painting, and in other parts by very magnificent mosaics of mixed marble and glass *tesserae*. It was lighted by a series of windows on one side, formed in the springing of the vaulted roof : the floor was of simple mosaics, and the walls were covered with slabs of polished marble of many colours, fixed by clamps of iron and bronze, many of which still remain. On the north-west side two staircases lead up to the higher level of the hill overlooking the *Vicus Tuscus*; fig. 22, No. 32, 32. *Mosaic vaults.*

Marble linings.

The socket-jointed clay pipes for carrying the rain-water from the roof of the *Crypto-porticus* into the drain under its floor can be seen embedded in the concrete walls at regular intervals.

At the farther end of this passage, a short branch, at right angles (fig. 22, No. 30), leads under the ground to the *Flavian* *Private passage.*

Palace; and a staircase at its termination communicates with an ante-room behind the apse of the *Flavian Basilica* (fig. 22, No. 29). This is evidently so arranged that the emperor could pass to and from his seat in the Tribune of the *Basilica* by a quite private way, unseen and uninterrupted by the crowd of suitors or lawyers who thronged the emperor's Hall of Justice. This branch passage is not earlier than the *Flavian Palace*, and part of it has been rebuilt in the reign of Severus, about 195 A.D.

Other restorations of the time of Severus, very carelessly executed, are visible in the short passage leading to the "House of Germanicus or Livia." These later walls have cut through and destroyed a great deal of the beautiful stucco reliefs on the vaulting, as is mentioned above at p. 182.

CHAPTER V

THE PALATINE HILL (*continued*).

THE *Flavian Palace*, mostly built by Domitian, was the next great addition to the buildings by which the Roman emperors gradually covered the whole of the Palatine Hill; see fig. 22, Nos. 21 to 29. *Flavian buildings.*

The enormous theft of land from the Roman people which Nero had accomplished in order to build his Golden House was atoned for by the politic Vespasian and Titus who destroyed the sumptuous Palace of Nero, and devoted a great part of its site to the pleasures of the people, by building the *Colosseum* and the great *Thermae of Titus* on the Esquiline.

It appears probable that, after he had destroyed the *Golden House* of Nero, the Emperor Titus began to build this Palace on the Palatine Hill, though the building cannot have been far advanced at the time of his premature death. Pliny (*Hist. Nat.* xxxiv. 55) mentions a bronze group of two boys playing with knuckle-bones (*astragalizontes*) by the famous Polycleitus of Sicyon as having been placed *in Titi imperatoris atrio*. *House of Titus.*

It is, however, possible that Pliny refers to the *Thermae of Titus* on the Esquiline, as he speaks of the Laocoon group, which was found in the *Thermae*, as being *in domo Titi*; see *Hist. Nat.* xxxvi. 37, and below, vol. ii. p. 157.

Partly, no doubt, to make up for this great loss of Imperial state rooms, Titus began and Domitian completed, on the central part of the Palatine Hill, a very large and magnificent series of public rooms, the south-west part of which flanked the *Palace of Domitian.*

State rooms. house of Augustus, while on the other side they were connected with the Palace of Caligula by the *Crypto-porticus* mentioned above. This great building of Domitian contained no private rooms or domestic offices; it was merely a vast series of state apartments,[1] and was an adjunct to the earlier palaces, which the emperors continued to use for all private purposes.

Lofty platform. The construction of this great palace caused very important changes to be made in the contour of the hill at this part. It is raised on a very large and lofty platform, forming a great level area extending over a natural valley, so that part of the floor of the Flavian Palace is high above the natural surface of the ground. The manner in which this platform has covered an ancient house is described in vol. i. p. 166, and in a similar way another house, of the early part of the first century A.D., is buried under the floor of Domitian's great *Peristyle*; near No. 24 on fig. 22.

Early house. *Buried House.* This house was built in a valley which appears once to have divided the Palatine Hill into two portions; this depression was filled and obliterated by the Flavian Palace being built over it at a level even higher than that of the rising ground on each side. Steps have now been formed down to the buried house under the central area of the *Peristyle*, so that part of it is now visible, together with the great concrete foundation walls of the palace above, which cut through and have partially destroyed this once richly decorated little house.

Rich decoration. Parts of its walls and vaults, decorated with moulded panels of stucco and painted ornaments, are still in good preservation; as is also part of its very beautiful floor, covered

[1] To impress on the Roman people the public character of this palace, the Emperor Nerva (according to the younger Pliny) inscribed outside it the words AEDES · PVBLICAE.

Part of the Flavian Palace, with its columns still in their place, is shown by Bianchini, *Palazzo dei Cesari*, Verona, 1738; but his plans are very fanciful.

with polished Oriental marbles of unusual brilliance and richness.

The concrete foundations which cut through this house show clearly the Roman method of casting concrete walls with a framework of upright timbers and planking forming a sort of long box, into which the semi-fluid concrete was poured. The imprint of the upright stakes, which left deep grooves 7½ inches wide by 6 inches deep, are as fresh as if the concrete had only just set; and so are the marks of the horizontal boards 8 inches wide, nailed against the upright posts, which were set at intervals of 3 feet.

Cast concrete.

When these chambers were first cleared out even the grain of the wood boards was quite visible in some places printed on the cement face of these concrete walls. This is one of the best places in Rome for examining the method of casting concrete walls in the boarded framework shown in fig. 3 in vol. i. p. 48.

The Palace of Domitian, with all its splendour of wall-linings and columns of rich marbles, and the countless statues which adorned it, are enthusiastically described by the courtier-poet Statius (*Silv.* iv. 11. 18), who gives an account of a banquet given by Domitian, at which he was present, in terms of the most exaggerated adulation.

Statius on the Flavian Palace.

This palace consists of a large open *Peristyle* or *Porticus*,[1] as the Romans called it (fig. 22, No. 24), and round it are grouped the various public state-rooms of which the palace consists. The *Peristyle* was a sort of cloister, open in the middle, and surrounded with a Corinthian colonnade originally two stories high. The shafts of the columns and the fluted pilasters against the walls were of the rich purple-marked *pavonazetto* from Phrygia, with capitals, bases, and entablatures of white Luna marble.

Peristyle.

The walls were lined with coloured Oriental marbles, highly polished, and divided into panels with moulded framing. A

Rich marbles.

[1] The Roman *porticus* was taken from the *stoa* of the Greeks.

Marble linings.   good deal of the moulded plinth of this wall-lining is still *in situ*; the lower part is of the golden yellow (*giallo*) of Numidia; the upper part was arranged to give highly-decorative effects by varying the panels and framing with different combinations of all the various coloured marbles used in Rome, with an admixture of the even more gorgeous red and green porphyries and Oriental alabaster. In parts grey and red granite from Egypt was used and many large monolithic columns were of these granites; others were of the deep red porphyry of Upper Egypt, from the quarries mentioned in vol. i. p. 24. The pavement was of similar Oriental marbles and porphyries in large slabs. There was probably a statue of colossal size between each pair of columns.

Triclinium.   The *Triclinium*, or state banqueting-room (fig. 22, No. 22), opens out of the south-west side of the *Peristyle*. It was decorated in an even more gorgeous way, with marble and porphyry columns, statues, and wall-linings. The emperor's seat at table was in a slightly curved recess, like an apse, opposite the
Opus sectile. entrance from the *Peristyle*. The pavement of this, part of which is still well preserved, is the most beautiful ancient example that yet exists in Rome. The patterns are simple—circles within squares, leaf-like curved figures, and the like, but the rich colours of the materials used, and the skill with which they are arranged, so as each to enhance the brilliance of the pieces next to it, give the whole an effect of much splendour. Red and green porphyry and many different-coloured marbles are used in this *opus sectile* pavement.

Nymphaeum.   *Nymphaeum.* The room on the south-east of the *Triclinium* has not been excavated, as the ground is still in the possession of the nuns who inhabit the Villa Mills; but the room opposite is fairly well preserved; fig. 22, No. 23. This is a *Nymphaeum*, a room completely lined with various kinds of marble, native and foreign, with niches for statues; in the centre is an elaborate oval fountain, with a large water-basin, into which jets poured from the central raised part, containing statues of nymphs and water-gods, which were arranged in a series of small semicircular recesses. Aquatic plants and flowers in pots were probably set among the statues. Some large windows open from the *Triclinium* into the *Nymphaeum*, so that the banqueters would be cooled and refreshed by the splash of the falling water and the scent of the flowers. The floor was of the rich Oriental alabaster, from Arabia or Egypt.

Green-house.

Adjoining the *Nymphaeum*, on the north-west side of the *Peristyle* (fig. 22, No. 25, 25) is a row of small rooms all once richly decorated with coloured marbles and statues; a similar series of rooms, probably, occupies the corresponding position, as yet unexcavated, on the opposite side.

Throne-room.—The north-east side of the *Peristyle* is mainly occupied by the grand *throne-room* (fig. 22, No. 27), where the emperor gave receptions on state occasions. This was, architecturally, the most magnificent hall of all; it was surrounded by colossal statues cut in red and green porphyry,[1] set in

Throne-room.

[1] There is no stronger symptom of the decadence in taste which was growing in Rome at the end of the first century A.D. than the liking which was then beginning for statues carved in these enormously hard substances, the brilliant colour and markings of which render them quite unfit for sculpture, their chief attraction being their very great cost, and the immense labour that must have been wasted on each. No tool, except some form of the diamond drill, will work these materials, and the process of grinding and drilling them into shape must have been extremely slow; moreover, to bring out the rich colours it was necessary to polish them— a process of great difficulty with the varied contours of a statue. It was from Egypt that the Romans derived their taste for statuary in refractory materials, and probably from the same country they got the special tools required to work them; see vol. i. p. 85. Pliny (*Hist. Nat.* xxxvi. 57) mentions as a great curiosity a statue made of porphyry, which was brought from Egypt as a present to the Emperor Claudius; Pliny's good taste did not approve of it—"Non admodum probata novitate. Nemo certe postea imitatus est"—showing that at least till the middle of the first century A.D. no porphyry statue had been made in Rome. A very fine

seven large niches, alternating with seven richly-ornamented doorways, between which were set Corinthian columns of *pavonazetto* and *giallo*, 24 feet high, each a perfect monolith. The entablatures, thresholds, and other parts were of white Pentelic and Luna marble, and the various coloured Oriental marbles lined the walls, the niches, and the floor.

Costly marbles.

In 1720 to 1726 excavations made here by the Farnese Duke of Parma brought to light an immense quantity of colossal basalt and porphyry statues, both whole and fragmentary, now scattered in various places, and also much of the rich architectural marble work, including sixteen Corinthian columns of *pavonazetto* and *giallo*, and an enormous door-sill of Pentelic marble, now used as the *mensa* of the high altar in the Pantheon.[1]

Porphyry statues.

This Farnese Duke owned a great part of the Palatine, which was called after his family the Orti Farnesiani; they were connected with the Neapolitan royal family.[2] The discoveries then made are published by Bianchini, *Palazzo dei Cesari*, Verona, 1738, and some of the statues are described by Guattani, *Notizie di Antichità*, 1798.

On the south-east side of the *throne-room* is a room containing an altar (fig. 22, No. 28), which, without much reason, has been called the *Lararium* or private chapel of the emperor, and next to it are remains of the grand staircase which led to the upper story, now entirely destroyed. All this part had similar wall-linings of rich marbles.

'Lararium.'

The *Basilica*, or Imperial Court of Justice (fig. 22, No. 29), on the opposite side of the Palace, is of special interest.

Basilica.

basalt bust of Drusus the younger in the British Museum is Egyptian both in material and workmanship.

[1] Among the statues discovered in 1724 are two colossal figures of Hercules and Bacchus cut in green porphyry from Mt. Taygetus. They are now in the museum at Parma.

[2] Hence many of the statues discovered here are now in the Museum of Naples.

Though its upper gallery over the aisles is gone, yet it is not impossible to make a fairly complete restoration of the whole hall, which is by far the best-preserved example of that special form of the classical *Basilica* which afterwards became the model, almost unaltered, for the Christian church. *Upper gallery.*

As shown on the plan, it is a rectangular hall, consisting of a central nave with an aisle on each side, and a semicircular apse at the end opposite the public entrance. The aisles had each six bays, with slender Corinthian columns, unfluted, but once decorated with metal ornaments, probably of gilt bronze; the pins for fixing these still remain in the existing perfect column. Over these were a marble entablature and an upper gallery, exactly similar in arrangement to the early Christian *gynaecaeum* or women's gallery, as existing in the Roman churches of the *Quattro Santi Incoronati* and *S. Agnese fuori le mura.* Stairs to this gallery start from the colonnade outside, on the north-west, and other stairs wind up behind the apse. *Apse. Aisles. Gallery.*

At the apsidal end was the Tribune, in which was the emperor's seat of judgment; and the whole apse was screened off from the nave or body of the hall by open marble *cancelli*, with pilasters at the end, designed with the trestle pattern, mentioned above as existing along "Caligula's bridge." *Tribune.*

This screened-off tribune in the Christian church became the *presbytery* or sanctuary, afterwards called the *chancel*, from the *cancelli*;[1] and the celebrant occupied the central throne. *Chancel.*

Part of the colonnade which once extended outside on the front towards the *Nova Via* formed a porch to the public entrance to the *Basilica*, corresponding to the *narthex* of the early Christian church.

On each side of the apse is a private door leading to the rest of the palace, and also (more immediately) to the stairs which descend to the *Crypto-porticus*, which formed a private *Private entrance.*

[1] The chief secretary of the court sat within the railing, and was hence called the *cancellarius*, the origin of our word *chancellor*.

approach from the Flavian Palace to the older Palace of Caligula; see above, p. 198.

Paving. The marble decorations of the *Basilica* were similar to those of the rest of the palace. The floor had a fine pavement of Oriental marbles, apparently a restoration of the time of Severus. The marble slabs were bedded on an under-paving of large earthenware tiles, which bear the maker's stamp, and a common augury of good luck — CN · DOMITI · AMANDI — VALEAT · QVI · FECIT — "May the maker thrive."

Outer columns. The outside of this palace had a handsome colonnade, once two stories high, with unfluted columns of *cipollino* at the end, and *travertine* at the side.

The whole stands on a lofty *podium*, and the end towards the *Porta Mugonia* and the *Sacra Via* occupies a very commanding position, rising high above the slope of the hill.

S.W. end. At the other end of the palace, towards the Circus Maximus, is an outlying block of handsome buildings, which have been with some probability called a *library* and *lecture-hall* (*bibliotheca* and *academia*), though nothing is really known of their names or use; fig. 22, Nos. 20, 21, 21.

Of the former but little remains except some fine paving of Oriental marbles, with simple patterns of squares set diagonally within other squares, a frequently repeated pattern in Roman pavements. A row of *cipollino* columns, with Corinthian capitals and bases of white marble, has been set along the side of this room by Comm. Rosa, but it is doubtful whether they stood so originally. Below the floor at this part remains are visible of the fine Republican house mentioned in vol. i. p. 166. The next room, supposed to be the *academia*, has one end curved, and seats rise against the walls in tiers, with rows of niches above them. The whole was richly decorated with marble linings.

Modes of construction. Construction. The concrete foundations of the whole building are made of fragments of the hard *lava* (*silex*) which was commonly used for the paving of roads. Above that the walls are of concrete, mostly made of broken brick, or in part bits of travertine, with a little marble. Among the late restorations of the third century, some walls occur made wholly of marble concrete, mixed with a few bits of porphyry.[1]

The brick facing which covers the concrete walls is of the characteristic Flavian type, with rather thick triangular bricks, very regular in appearance, set in the most excellent cement. They average rather over $1\frac{1}{2}$ inches in thickness, by 12 inches long; the joints vary from $\frac{1}{2}$ to $\frac{5}{8}$ inch. The whole surface of this brick facing is studded with the usual iron nails and marble plugs, but in some cases bronze is used instead of iron. The clamps which held the marble linings in their place were mostly of bronze. At intervals, of from 4 to 5 feet, bond tiles, 2 Roman feet square, are built in through the whole thickness of the concrete walls. *Brick facing.*

The vaults were partly of brick concrete and partly of *tufa*, or pumice-stone concrete. *Vaults.*

In the outer walls, at regular intervals, channels running upwards are formed in the face of the wall, about 12 by 10 inches, to hold the socketed smoke flue or rain-water pipes.

The travertine colonnade on the outside of the palace was covered with the usual marble dust stucco, and decorated with painting.

In many places signs of extensive rebuilding and restorations are evident, especially those carried out by Severus, after a fire in 191 A.D., which devastated a great part of the Palatine buildings. Much of the existing marble decorations of the palace appears to be of the time of Severus. *Restoration.*

Even in the fourth century alterations were being made, and by the *Nymphaeum* there is a wall, faced with "*opus mirtum*," of small tufa blocks and brick courses set alternately, which is always a sign of late work.[2]

[1] After damage by a fire all the injured marble columns and wall-linings seem to have been broken up to make concrete for the new walls.

[2] The great Circus of Maxentius on the Via Appia, built soon after

The "Domus Gelotiana."

S.W. side of the hill.
On the south-west slope of the Palatine, outside the walls of Roma Quadrata, about the middle of the slope towards the *Circus Maximus*, are extensive remains of a house (fig. 22, No. 49), which, on insufficient evidence, has been supposed to be the *Domus Gelotiana*, from which Caligula is recorded to have watched the races in the *Circus* below; see Suet. *Cal.* 18. But little, however, which still exists of this building appears to be as early in date as the time of Caligula.

This once extensive house is built against the remains of the "*Wall of Romulus*," and over a spur-wall, belonging to the same primitive fortifications, which runs at an angle from the main line of the circuit down the slope; see fig. 22, No. 2, near No. 49.

Rooms and porticus.
The house consists of a series of small vaulted rooms, once several stories high, with a *Porticus* or colonnade of Corinthian columns in front, at its lower level. This *Porticus*, which is now largely restored, appears to be of the time of Severus. The rooms were partly lined with marble, and partly covered with painted stucco; in one part, by the staircase, a second painted coat of stucco has been laid over an earlier decorated layer.

Graffiti.
Incised Inscriptions. One of the most interesting things about this building is the large number of *graffiti*, or incised inscriptions, which are deeply cut into the plaster. One of these, now in the Museo Kircheriano, is the rude drawing of a crucified man with the head of an ass or jackal, and a standing figure, apparently in act of adoration, with the rudely scratched inscription, ΑΛΕΞΑΜΕΝΟC CEBETE ΘEON, Ἀλεξάμενος σέβεται Θεόν; *i.e.* "Alexamenos worships God." This is usually taken to be a caricature of the crucified Christ,

300 A.D., is probably one of the earliest instances in or near Rome of the use of this method of wall-facing.

but is more probably a scene of *Gnostic* worship, representing the Egyptian god Anubis. A similar device occurs on certain late Gnostic gems of Egyptian origin. *Gnostic device.*

Many of the inscriptions have now crumbled away, and others are rapidly following. One, now wholly gone, had a sketch of an ass turning a corn-mill, with the superscription LABORA · ASELLE · QVOMODO · EGO · LABORAVI · ET · PRODERIT TIBI. "Work, O Ass, as I have worked, and it will profit thee."

Other *graffiti* seem to show that this building was used at one time as a school (*paedagogium*) for imperial slaves, *e.g.* *Boys' names.*

| CORINTHVS · EXIT DE · PEDAGOGIO. | and | MARIANVS AFER · EXIT DE · PEDAGOGIV. |

"Corinthus (or Marianus Afer) goes out of school."

A number of names appear to have been scratched by soldiers: some which still exist are HILARVS · MI · V · D · N, i.e. "*Hilarus Miles Veteranus Domini Nostri*" (the Emperor): ЄΠΙΤΥΝΧΑΝΟC · V · D · N; a mixture of Greek and Roman letters: "*Epitynchanos Veteranus Domini Nostri.*" Other names which occur are C · EMELEVS · AFER; DORYPHORVS; ASIATICVS; ΑΚΙΝΘΟC; and ROGATVS; with many varieties of blundered spelling. The same name sometimes occurs ·written both with Greek and Latin characters, *e.g.* ΦΗΛΙΚΙ · · · ; FELICIS. *Soldiers' names.*

It has been supposed from these soldiers' names that the building was in part a guard-house, for guards on duty about the Imperial palaces. After one pair of names is inscribed PEREG, implying that they belong to the Corps called *Peregrini*, or "*Foreign regiment*," whose Camp was on the Caelian Hill; see *Notitia, Reg.* ii. *Guard-house.*

THE PALATINE STADIUM.

Stadium.
On the southern side of that elevated plateau which was occupied by the *Area of Apollo* and the *House of Augustus* there appears to have been a sudden fall of the level, down to a long valley, which lent itself readily to the formation of a *Stadium* or racecourse. Its plan is shown on fig. 22, No. 50; it occupies a very large area, having the exposed end very slightly curved,[1] and a sort of aisle or colonnade, once two stories high, running all round it.

This enormous building, of which little or no record exists in any classical writings, appears to have been begun by Domitian, mostly built by Hadrian, and either finished, or in parts rebuilt, by Severus. The earliest part is the whole outer wall, with the curved projection or *exedra* on one side (fig. 22, No. 51) and a few of the piers of the colonnade near the excavated end.

Brick facing.
The brick facings of the time of Domitian and of Hadrian are so similar in character that it is often difficult to distinguish between them. Some brick stamps, however, in the facing of the outer wall are of the Flavian period, and seem to show that the *Stadium* was at least begun by Domitian. One of the marks is FLAVI · AVG · L · CLONI, that is, "*of Clonius a freedman of the Flavian Augustus.*" In the curved recess, however, and other parts of the outer wall, brick stamps of Hadrian's time appear. The brick facing of Severus is easily distinguishable, being very different in appearance from that of Hadrian; see vol. i. p. 61.

Marble lining.
Like other buildings on the Palatine, this was wholly covered with slabs of fine marbles. The engaged columns of the ambulatóry all round the *Stadium* are of concrete neatly faced with moulded bricks, and then covered with marble casing; many of the moulded Corinthian bases of these

[1] This is the starting end, the other is not yet excavated.

columns still remain *in situ.* The capitals and their entablature were of solid Greek marble. In spite of the Corinthian moulding of the bases, the capitals, a few of which exist, are of the Tuscan order. The intervals between the piers with their half-columns were filled in by *cancelli* or low marble screens, with a richly-moulded plinth, which was simply a continuation of the base-moulding of the engaged columns. One pier near the recess has still *in situ* the return of this moulding, and its start along the plinth of the screen. Behind each pier there is a corresponding pilaster on the face of the outer wall, against which once stood a marble column. *Screens.*

Strange to say, all these wall pilasters, and all the piers with half-columns, except a few at the curved end, are of the time of Severus, showing either that the *Stadium* was left by Hadrian in a very unfinished state, or else that it had suffered so much from fire or earthquake as to need a very extensive rebuilding by Severus.

The lower part of the great apse or *exedra* of Hadrian (fig. 22, No. 51) is divided into several rooms, the barrel vaults of which supported an upper floor, which was probably a sort of enormous state box, from whence the Imperial party watched the games below. The upper gallery over the colonnade all round must also have held a large number of spectators. *Exedra.*

The semicircular *piscinae* or fountains at the end and one side are late additions; and in the fourth and fifth centuries A.D. the building appears to have been clumsily altered, and cut up into separate rooms for some purpose, quite different from that of a racecourse. *Late additions.*

These later additions, consisting especially of a great oval chamber, are in some places built over the rich marble linings in the most ruthless and brutal way, and the level of the floor appears then to have been raised about 2 feet above the old paving. Some of these walls are faced with the ugly brickwork of the fourth century, while others have the so-called "*opus mixtum,*" brick and tufa alternating. The complete decay into which this once magnificent building had even then fallen is clearly shown by the materials of which the concrete of these latest walls is made; namely, broken pieces of rich Oriental marbles, with large quantities of the valuable red porphyry and green basalt. It appears probable that these last alterations were the work of the Gothic King Theodoric, in about 500 to 510 A.D.

Theodoric's alterations.

Theodoric's enlightened good taste and respect for antiquity led him to do very much in Rome not only to stop the pillaging of temples and public buildings, but also in actual works of restoration and repair. He spent large sums in this way on the Forum and Basilica of Trajan, the Baths of Caracalla, and other buildings.

PALACE OF HADRIAN.

Along the south side of the great *Stadium* and at its western end were a large number of very handsome and extensive rooms, which once formed a large palace, part of which overlooked the *Circus Maximus*, while another part occupied the higher level of the hill behind the great apsidal recess; fig. 22, Nos. 51, 53, 54.

Palace of Hadrian.

This palace, built by Hadrian, is now mostly destroyed, partly through the fall of its lofty buildings on the slope leading to the *Circus*, and partly because it was destroyed and buried by Sept. Severus, when he built his extensive and enormously lofty palace over the southern angle and slopes of the Palatine. With care, however, much of Hadrian's Palace can still be traced, and some idea formed of its original magnificence.

Outside the curved end of the *Stadium*, parts of its lofty upper vaulting with deep-sunk *lacunaria* are still standing; and further remains, insignificant in height, were exposed in the summer of 1884, extending towards the slope of the hill. The many fragments of rich architectural decorations found

Coffered vaulting.

here show that it was adorned with unusual magnificence and delicacy of detail. Elaborate mouldings, cornices, plinths, and the like were found, cut not only in the usual Oriental marbles, but also in the rarer deep red *rosso antico*, and the refractory red and green porphyries. Oriental alabaster appears to have been used for several of the pavements, and the whole building must have been a glowing mass of rich polished stones in countless variety of tint, while the vaults had their sunk coffers richly decorated with elaborate mouldings in stucco, all brilliantly coloured, and picked out with gilding. *Rich detail.*

One handsomely-vaulted room (fig. 22, No. 53 near the words " BATHS OF SEVERVS "), on the south side of the *Stadium*, near the curved end, is still in a very perfect state, but is partly choked up by rubbish. It has a large window opening into the *Stadium*, and communicates by a staircase with the upper rooms of Hadrian's Palace. The ceiling is formed by four intersecting barrel vaults, decorated very richly with deep *lacunaria*, with elaborate stucco mouldings and central rosettes; see fig. 13 in vol. i. p. 71. *Rich vaulting.*

This room also communicates with a row of small vaulted chambers, opening one into the other, and facing on the road (fig. 22, No. 55) which leads from the end of the *Stadium* downwards to the valley of the Caelian, under the lofty arches of Severus' Palace.[1]

Other rooms of Hadrian's Palace can be traced, half buried and concealed under the complicated and extensive substructures of Severus' Palace. Delicate stucco reliefs still exist in rooms which are cut through by the foundation walls of Severus' building, and are now quite shut off from light. Wooden steps at several places have been fixed, so that the visitor can traverse these interesting and somewhat puzzling remains, passing through them from the road by the *Stadium*, and reaching at last the higher ground at the top of the hill.[2] *Buried rooms.*

[1] This road has not yet been excavated to its old level.
[2] Since this was written the access to this most interesting part of the

Cause of destruction. The reason for the destruction of so large a part of Hadrian's Palace by Severus arose from the fact that in the palace of the latter emperor the whole of the state-rooms and baths were raised to the higher level above the top of the Palatine, and not built, as some of Hadrian's handsome rooms were, on the lower slopes of the hill. It is the gigantic substructures by which Severus raised the chief floor of his palace to an enormous height that have buried and partly obliterated the last-mentioned portions of Hadrian's Palace.

Summit of hill. In addition to these low-lying rooms, other parts of Hadrian's Palace are built on the top of the hill, and considerable remains of these exist at the back of the apsidal *exedra* of the *stadium*. These rooms are very lofty, and have similar vaulted ceilings, with enriched stucco coffers, all once elaborately coloured and gilt. They extend some way southwards from the back of the apse, and join on to the Palace of Severus. The great difference in the brick facing of these two buildings makes it very easy to distinguish one from the other, even when their walls are mixed in a very intricate way. No. 52, fig. 22, shows the stairs to these upper rooms.

Brick facing. The brickwork of both is equally sound and neat, but can easily be distinguished one from the other by noticing the following details. In Hadrian's building the bricks are thicker and the joints thinner, namely—*bricks*, $1\frac{1}{2}$ inch; *joints*, $\frac{1}{2}$ inch: In Severus' work—*bricks*, 1 inch; *joints*, $\frac{3}{4}$ inch.[1] In both

---

Palatine has been cut off, and an iron gate has been placed to prevent visitors from reaching the lower rooms of Hadrian's Palace, including the very handsome room with the coffered vault mentioned above, which is one of the finest and best preserved of all the Palatine buildings.

[1] These are the *average* dimensions. The bricks of Severus are hard well-burnt triangles, 12 to 14 inches long; their stamps show that they were made of clay from imperial brickfields—OP · DOL · EX · PR · DOMINI N · AVG—i.e. *Opus doliare ex praedis Domini nostri Augusti*, "Earthenware from the estates of our lord Augustus." Names of various brickmakers occur; see examples quoted above, at pp. 13 and 190.

cases lumps of tufa and broken bricks are used for the concrete mass of the walls, and usually concrete made of *lava* for the foundations.

PALACE OF SEVERUS.

Though a vast series of substructures is still standing, comparatively little remains of the once lofty and magnificent state apartments which occupied the south corner of the Palatine, and extended over its slopes into the valley by the Caelian Hill.

The chief existing remains on the top of the hill are those of one of the grand marble staircases (near No. 54 on fig. 22) leading to the upper rooms, of which no other portion now remains.[1] Near this there are extensive ruins of baths and *nymphaea*, reaching as far as the *Stadium*, and stretching over the buried remains of Hadrian's lower palace. These baths were all sumptuously decorated in the usual way with marble linings and enrichments of porphyry, alabaster, and brilliant glass mosaics, many of the coloured *tesserae* of which still lie thick among the rubbish.

Palace of Severus.

The methods of heating with *hypocausts* and walls covered with flue-tiles can be well studied here, and remarkable examples exist showing the enormous strength and cohesion of the Roman concrete.

Methods of heating.

Instead of the upper floor or *suspensura* being carried on a number of little pillars (*pilae*), in many of the rooms it had no support whatever except at its edges, so that the whole concrete floor is treated as if it were one immense slab of stone, having in some cases a bearing of 20 feet or more. In some of the rooms there are deep, strangely-formed chambers below the *lower* floor of the *hypocausts*, the use of which is quite inexplicable; probably they are only waste spaces occasioned by

Deep substructures.

---

[1] Scattered around are many large fragments of the concrete vaulting which supported the upper floors, which were paved with coarse mosaics.

the necessity to raise the floor of the baths to a high level on tall foundation-walls.

Great height. It is difficult, from the scanty existing remains of the upper portion of this palace, to realise what its immense extent and height must have once been. It not only towered many stories above the highest summit of the hill, but also reached far beyond the hill, extending over the slope and into the valley below. This outlying part of the palace, built at the lower level, was constructed on immense arches and tiers *Artificial platform.* of vaulted substructions, forming an enormous platform, equal in height to the hill itself, and then on this platform, already of stupendous height, a great part of the actual palace was built, rising high above it, as if this platform had been the natural level of the ground. Or, to put it in another form, the Palatine Hill was materially enlarged at this southern part by an artificial hill of massive concrete walls and vaults.

One portion of this great platform, built of tiers of lofty arches, now reaches out towards the south in a sort of isolated promontory, but originally the great gap between this and the baths on the hill was filled up and bridged over with similar lofty substructions which have now fallen.

Road. Below this a road (fig. 22, No. 55, 55) sloped steeply down to the valley, forming one of the main approaches to the Palatine. This has not yet been excavated to its original level, and the paving of the lower end of the road still remains buried as high as to the lower tier of arches which spanned it like a series of bridges. These arches really are *flying buttresses*, like those which cross the *Nova Via* from the *Palace of Caligula* to the *Atrium Vestae*; see fig. 42 in vol. i. *Concrete.* p. 308. The arches of the lofty platform under which this road passes, like the rest of the palace, are built of the usual hard rock-like concrete, in many respects even more durable than masonry. The whole is faced with the very neat though wide-jointed brickwork which is characteristic of about the years 190 to 250 A.D.

Travertine corbels are built in at the springing of all these arches; these were to support the wooden centering or framework on which the semi-fluid concrete was cast into the required form of arches and vaults, and have the double advantage of doing away with the necessity for lofty wooden scaffolding to support the original centering, and of making future repairs or rebuilding comparatively easy.[1] *Stone corbels.*

The substructions of Severus' Palace, which are built more immediately against the slope of the southern angle of the hill, contain a large series of kitchens and other domestic offices, which are well worthy of attention though they are rather devoid of light.

Part of the arrangements for a plentiful supply of aqueduct water is at one point well preserved, and can be visited through a vaulted room which opens at the lower level, parallel to the foot of the eighteenth-century staircase which now leads from near the descending road up to the top of the hill.[2] On passing through this vaulted chamber towards the inner rooms the end of a sloping water-channel, formed like the *specus* of an aqueduct, is reached. The top of this is now gone, and the *specus* itself forms a convenient passage, leading at a gentle slope into a series of large water-cisterns like small vaulted rooms, two of which are well preserved. Both these cisterns and the channel are lined with the hard waterproof cement (*opus signinum*) which was specially used for hydraulic purposes. *Water supply.*

These cisterns are arranged at different levels, with com- *Cisterns.*

---

[1] Similar corbels for centering at the springing of arches are to be seen in the Roman bridges across the Tiber, in many of the aqueducts, and in other places; see fig. 12, in vol. i. p. 69.

[2] The access to this very interesting part of the building has been recently cut off; this is a serious loss to the student of Roman antiquities, as this part of Severus' buildings was among the most interesting of the existing remains on the Palatine Hill. The modern staircase is not shown on fig. 22.

218 WATER SUPPLY CHAP.

Series of cisterns. municating openings, so as to overflow from one to the other, and are made to supply different parts of the lower rooms of the palace. A narrow and steep flight of stairs descends into the upper cistern, so that it could be reached for repairs or cleaning. The steps are coated with *opus signinum* like the rest of the cisterns, and the whole surface, including that of the *specus*, is covered with a hard deposit of carbonate of lime, in many thin successive layers, such as was usually formed by the rather hard water brought by the aqueducts.[1]

This is perhaps the most interesting and well-preserved example in Rome of the cisterns and water-channels used in the palaces and houses of the emperors and wealthy citizens.

The water-channel leads to rooms which appear to have been kitchens, sculleries, and the like, and through these a communication exists with the upper portions of the palace on the top of the hill.

The water supply of this lofty part of the Palatine was brought in the Claudian aqueduct, some of the arches of which still exist near the foot of the hill on the side towards the Caelian Hill. The position of this fragment of the Aqua Claudia is shown at No. 56 on fig. 22.

Septizonium. The *Septizonium* was an outlying part of Severus' Palace, in the valley at the south angle of the hill, which was once remarkable for its architectural magnificence and its great height. It stood near the point where the continuation of the *Via Appia*, within the *Porta Capena* of the Servian wall, led to the end of the *Circus Maximus*.[2] This was the road by which travellers from Africa and the south generally approached Rome, and the *Septizonium* is said to have been built here by Severus in order that his Numidian fellow-countrymen might

[1] This process of deposit is still rapidly going on in all the cisterns and pipes which supply modern Rome with aqueduct water.

[2] The site of the *Septizonium* does not come within the limits of the plan on fig. 22. It would be a little way outside the lower right hand corner of the plan.

be impressed with his magnificence immediately on entering the walls of Rome ; see Spartian. *Sept. Sev.* 24. Its name was probably derived from its seven stories or *zonae* of colonnades towering one above another. It has been doubted whether the *Septizonium* can really have been as many as seven stories high, but this does not seem impossible or even improbable when the immense height of the main block of the palace is considered.[1]

Origin of name.

The three lower stories of this building, with handsome marble columns and other decorations, existed as late as the reign of Sixtus V. (1585-90), who destroyed it in order to use its columns and marble entablatures in the new Basilica of S. Peter. Drawings of it, as then existing, are given by Du Perac in his *Vestigj di Roma*, 1575, by Palladio, *Archi.* lib. iv., and in other works of the sixteenth century.[2]

Towards the *Circus Maximus* another lofty block is built, projecting farther down the western slope of the hill. This has been supposed to be an Imperial *Pulvinar*, or building from which the emperor could watch the races in the Circus below. It appears mainly to be the work of Heliogabalus and Severus Alexander, who both added to and restored the Palace of Sept. Severus; see Dion Cass. lxxii. 24 ; and *Hist. Aug. Sept. Sev.* 19. 24 ; *Sev. Alex.* 24. 25, and *Heliog.* 3. 8, 24.

Later wing.

VELIA, GERMALUS, AND THE ROADS NEAR THEM.

The *Velia* and the *Germalus* or *Cermalus* were two outlying parts of the Palatine Hill. Varro, *Lin. Lat.* v. 54, mentions them thus, *huic (Palatio) Germalum et Velias conjunxerunt . . . Germalum a germanis Romulo et Remo, quod ad Ficum Ruminalem ibi inventi sunt.*

[1] See a valuable paper by Jordan, *Bull. Inst.*, 1872, p. 145.

[2] Records of the destruction of the *Septizonium*, and of the quantity of columns and other marbles which were obtained by its demolition, are published in *Bull. Com. Arch.*, 1888, pp. 269-298.

Germalus. The position and extent of the *Germalus* are very doubtful, but it probably was some ridge at the western angle of the Palatine, near the corner between the *Velabrum* and the *Circus Maximus*. Owing to the great alterations that have been made in the contour of the hill, both in its lower slopes and higher points, it is now very difficult to define these primitive districts.

Velia. The *Velia* may, however, with much probability, be identified with the ridge between the Palatine and the Esquiline, on which the remains of the *Temple of Venus and Rome* now stand, and which is crossed by the *Summa Sacra Via* under the Arch of Titus. This ridge was evidently once considerably loftier than it is now; part of its native tufa rock is visible where it has been cut away to form a level area for the temple.

Moreover, the extent to which the foundations of Nero's Palace on the edge of the Esquiline, near the temple, are exposed to sight, shows that in Nero's time the ground here was much higher than at present. From 20 to 30 feet high of rough foundation-wall is now laid bare.[1]

Houses on the Velia. Tullus Hostilius is said to have had a house on the *Velia*, where afterwards the *Aedes Penatium* stood; Solinus, *Polyhist.* i., writes thus, *Tullus Hostilius (habitavit) in Velia, ubi postea Deum Penatum aedes facta est.*

That the *Velia* was once a ridge of more commanding height is shown by the story of P. Valerius Publicola, who began to build himself a house on the *Velia*, but, being suspected by his fellow-citizens of entertaining too ambitious views, he rebuilt it on a more humble site, at the foot of the *Velia* instead of on its summit;[2] see Cic. *De Rep.* ii. 31; Livy, ii. 7; and Plutar. *Public.* 10.

Varro (*Lin. Lat.* v. 54) derives the word *Velia* from *vellera*,

---

[1] This part of Nero's Palace is shown in fig. 87, in vol. ii. p. 227.

[2] This act of humility was so highly appreciated that at the death of Publicola the Senate voted him the very unusual honour of a tomb within the city walls near the Forum—σύνεγγυς τῆς ἀγορᾶς, Dionys. v. 48.

the fleeces of the sheep that pastured there; but more probably it is derived from a root Ϝέλος, meaning a marsh, as in *Vel*abrum.

The *aedes Penatium* and the *aedes Larum*, which stood on the *Summa Sacra Via*, were rebuilt by Augustus, as is recorded in the inscription of Ancyra—AEDEM · LARVM · IN · SVMMA SACRA · VIA · AEDEM · DEVM · PENATIVM · IN · VELIA · · · FECI. The *aedes Larum* is probably the same as the *Sacellum Larum*, mentioned by Tacitus (*Ann.* xii. 24) as one of the points in the line of the *Pomoerium* round *Roma Quadrata*; see vol. i. p. 110.

Aedes Larum.

The Velabrum.[1] The site of the *Velabrum* can be identified with greater precision. It is part, if not all, of the long valley which runs from near the river, at the end of the Circus Maximus, past the cliff of the Palatine to the lowest point of the *Forum Romanum*, where the "*Cloaca Maxima*" passes under the *Basilica Julia.* Till the construction of this great sewer the Velabrum appears to have been, even in dry weather, a marsh interspersed with pools of stagnant water. A record of its name still exists in the Church of *S. Giorgio in Velabro*.

Velabrum.

Its position is described by Varro (*Lin. Lat.* vi. 24) *Velabrum extra urbem antiquam* (i.e. *Roma Quadrata*) *fuit, non longe a porta Romanula*; and in another place Varro mentions it as being at the foot of the ascent to the *Infima Nova Via.* It was a district full of shops; see Plaut. *Capt.* III. i. 29, and Hor. *Sat.* II. iii. 229.

The *Vicus Tuscus* passes through the *Velabrum* on its course from the *Forum Romanum* to the *Circus Maximus*; see Dionys.

Vicus Tuscus.

[1] Varro, *Lin. Lat.* v. 43, derives *Velabrum*, "*a vehendo*," from the ferry across its marshy pools; but Dionysius more correctly gives the word *velus*, a marsh, as its origin.

Plutarch's derivation (*Rom.* 5) is from the *vela* or awnings which were sometimes fixed along the whole course of the *Velabrum*, between the Forum and the Circus Maximus.

Velabrum gate. v. 26. The marble gateway erected in honour of Severus and his sons by the silversmiths and other merchants of the quarter formed an entrance from the *Velabrum* into the *Forum Boarium*; cf. Dionys. i. 40; and see vol. ii. p. 304.

Whether the Velabrum extended so far as the *Forum Romanum* or not is doubtful, nor is it possible to identify its subdivisions into *Velabrum minus* and *majus* (see Varro, *Lin. Lat.* v. 43 and 156), except that the former was probably near the Forum, and the latter at the end towards the Aventine. It is indeed possible that these terms refer to pools of water, quite distinct from the district generally called the *Velabrum*.

Nova Via. The *Nova Via*. Among the most interesting excavations of recent years has been that of the *Nova Via*, from close by the Church of S. Maria Liberatrice to its junction with the road which leads up the Palatine to the *Porta Mugonia*, starting close by the *Summa Sacra Via* at the Arch of Titus; see fig. 22.

Lucus Vestae. The *Nova Via* appears originally to have skirted the sacred Grove of Vesta (Livy, v. 32. 50; and Cic. *De Div.* i. 45), but the site of this grove is now occupied by the great Palace of Caligula, remains of which face on to almost the whole side of the course of the *Nova Via*, as far as it has yet been excavated.

On the opposite side a long piece of the frontage of the *Nova Via* is occupied by the *Atrium Vestae*; and a series of arches, spanning the road, act as flying buttresses to support both the palace and the *Atrium*; see fig. 42, p. 308.

Stairs to Forum. Ovid (*Fast.* vi. 395) speaks of a staircase descending from the *Nova Via* to the Forum—*qua Nova Romano nunc Via juncta Foro est*. These steps appear to be shown on the *marble plan* of Rome (see *Forum Plan*), and were a continuation of those leading up from the *Nova Via* to the *Clivus Victoriae*, just outside the *Porta Romanula* and near the end of the *Velabrum* (see above, p. 191).[1] Varro (*Lin. Lat.* v. 3) writes, *Hoc*

[1] It is not improbable that these are the *Scalae Anulariae* by which Augustus once lived; Suet. *Aug.* 72.

sacrificium fit in Velabro, qua in Novam Viam exitur . . . non longe a Porta Romanula.

The upper end of the *Nova Via*, where it joined the road up the Palatine Hill, was known as the *Summa Nova Via* (see Solinus, i. 24); and the lower end, where it sloped down to the *Velabrum*, was the *Infima Nova Via*. This part of its course has not yet been determined, but it appears probable that it continued to skirt the lower slopes of the Palatine, turning at the north angle of the hill round in a south-westerly direction, and slanting down till it reached the valley of the *Velabrum*. *Nova Via. Summa and Infima.*

In spite of its name the *Nova Via* was a very ancient road, even in the time of Varro, first century B.C.[1] An interesting account of this road is given by Lanciani, *Notizie degli Scavi*, 1882, p. 234.

The discovery of a cross road leading up from the *Sacra Via*, and passing behind the *Atrium Vestae* to the *Nova Via*, is mentioned below, vol. i. p. 317; see fig. 41. *Cross road.*

In the summer of 1884 a number of interesting remains of buildings were excavated on both sides of the *Nova Via*, at its highest end. On the Palatine side are a series of vaulted rooms, which appear to be part of Caligula's Palace, though much of the walls belong to a later rebuilding. Among these are remains of a very wide and handsome staircase, which must once have formed the chief approach to Caligula's Palace from its lowest level; the whole of its marble steps and wall-linings have been taken away. *Caligula's Palace.*

On the opposite side of the road are a number of chambers, with stairs which led up to higher stories. The earliest of these appear to be of Caligula's time. Facing on to the road is also a curious public fountain in a much ruined state; two *Fountain.*

[1] This is often the case with buildings that are called *new*. *Newgate* was the oldest of the London gates; *New* College is among the most ancient foundations of Oxford; and *New* Bridge is one of the oldest in Oxfordshire.

or more rectangular shallow tanks or basins, lined with *opus signinum*, are still fairly perfect.

Remains of temple.   At the *Summa Nova Via*, near the Arch of Titus, are a few remains of what was probably a large and very magnificent temple. Among these is a large fluted drum of a Corinthian column, made of the Phrygian *pavonazetto*, and some enormous open rain-water channels, sunk in immense blocks of white Athenian marble, which probably surrounded this sumptuous building. These may possibly belong to the Aedes Penatium, rebuilt by Augustus; but, if so, it must have been a temple of greater importance in point of size than its rare mention in classical writings would lead one to believe. It is perhaps more probable that these splendid pieces of marble belonged to the *Temple of Jupiter Stator* mentioned above, see vol. i. p. 167.

THE SACRA VIA.

That part of the *Sacra Via* which passes through the *Forum Romanum* is described in chap. vi.; but the name *Original Sacra Via.* *Sacra Via* was originally applied to part of the road outside the south-east limits of the Forum.

This road was called *Sacra* from its having been traditionally the scene of the solemn treaty concluded between Romulus and the Sabine King Tatius; Festus, ed. Müller, p. 290; or possibly from its skirting the *Temple of Vesta*, the *Regia*, and other buildings of great sanctity. The name *Sacra Via* was originally confined to the part of the road which is near these *Line of Sacra Via.* sacred buildings. In later times the start of the *Sacra Via* was at the *Sacellum Streniae*, the goddess of new-year gifts (French *Étrennes*), an unknown point on the Esquiline (Varro, *Lin. Lat.* v. 47), which probably was somewhere in the quarter now occupied by the Baths of Titus, a portion of the hill known as *Cerolia*. Thence the *Sacra Via* probably (after 80 A.D.) skirted the Colosseum, and then ascended the ridge to the Arch of Titus, which spans it at the highest point called *Summa Sacra Via*; see Plutar. *Public.* 19.

From the *Arch of Titus* the road turned to the north and then passed westwards in front of the *Basilica of Constantine* and the *Temple of Faustina*, skirting the north side of the *Temple of Divus Julius*.[1] At a little distance in front of this temple the *Sacra Via* turned at right angles to the south, towards the front of the *Temple of Castor*, and then skirted the *Basilica Julia*, passing westwards towards the Clivus Capitolinus.

Sacra Via.

As is mentioned below (see vol. i. p. 250), the ancient line of the *Sacra Via* was probably somewhat different. Its present direction, where it skirts the narrow east end of the central space of the Forum, probably dates from the reign of Augustus when the *Temple of Divus Julius* was built.

Change of line.

It is, moreover, doubtful whether in later times the course of triumphal processions did not pass along the road which borders the north side of the Forum, passing under the *Arch of Severus*, and so up the *Clivus Capitolinus*, instead of passing, as it did originally, along the south-west side of the Forum.

The whole of the existing lava paving is very late in date, with the single exception of the bit in front of the steps of the *Temple of Saturn;* see p. 251, fig. 30. The well-known description of Horace's walk along the *Sacra Via* (*Sat.* I. ix.) makes it appear that in his time it passed along an older line, skirting the *Temple of Vesta* as well as the *Basilica Julia*; see line 35.

Existing paving.

But, as is mentioned below in vol. i. p. 300, recent excavations seem to show that the *Sacra Via* never did pass close by the *Temple of Vesta*, but some distance to the north of it, along the side of the *Regia* which Mr. Nichols identified. Though the whole course of this road, from the Esquiline to the Capitoline Hill, came to be known as the *Sacra Via*, yet the

Older Sacra Via.

[1] Anastasius Bibliothecarius, in his *Life of S. Felix IV.*, speaks of the Church of SS. Cosmas and Damianus (Temple of Divus Romulus) as being in the *Via Sacra*.

Older Sacra Via. term was originally used in a much more limited sense, as meaning merely that part of it which reached from the east end of the Forum to the hill where the Arch of Titus now stands, namely, from near the Regia to the House of the Rex Sacrificulus which stood on the slope of the hill. Festus, ed. Müller, p. 290, defines it thus, *Sacra appellanda est* [*Via*] *a Regia ad domum Regis Sacrificuli.* Varro, *Lin. Lat.* v. 47, describes it thus, *Hujus Sacrae Viae pars haec sola volgo nota est, quae est a Foro eunti primore clivo.*

The *Sacra Via*, in its course between the "*Meta Sudans*" and the Arch of Titus, passes a number of interesting buildings on its left; the whole of this distance on the right is occupied by Hadrian's great *Temple of Venus and Rome.*

Late Baths. *Baths of Heliogabalus.* On the left are extensive remains of baths, the marble linings of which, and the flue-tiles on the walls, are in some places well preserved. The brick facing of the walls is of that neat and regular sort, with very thin bricks and thick joints, which is characteristic of the time of Heliogabalus and Severus Alexander—the bricks being only about 1 inch thick and the joints ¾ to 1 inch, by only 9 inches in length; see fig. 22, Nos. 45, 46.

One small Bath-room, with apsidal end, is specially well preserved, and is a valuable example of Roman methods of *Methods of heating.* heating. It contains two small marble-lined baths, one square and the other semicircular filling in the space included by the little apse; both have marble steps for the bather to descend by. The curved wall of the apse is partly open, and had two small columns supporting the wall above the opening. The floor is over a *hypocaust*, and the whole interior of the room, including the baths, is lined with square flue-tiles held by strong pieces of T iron to the wall.

Christian Church ? *Supposed Christian Basilica.* In the middle of these baths a very remarkable building has been erected, probably in the fifth century A.D., which De Rossi considers to be a Christian Basilica, that of *S. Maria Antiqua*; fig. 22, No. 46. The older brick-faced walls of the baths are used for this building wherever they happen to come in the right place; the rest of the walling, added to form the *Basilica*, is faced with so-called "*opus mixtum*" of brick and tufa, and thus can easily be distinguished from the older part.

The plan of this building is a long nave without aisles, with an apsidal end and two small transepts. The part between the transepts is marked off from the nave by a step and two marble columns, which look as if they defined the beginning of the chancel; and the whole aspect of the building is exactly that of a Christian church. One point, however, throws doubt upon this, and that is, that in the apse, in the place which ought to be occupied by the altar, there stands a most unmistakable fountain or marble-lined cistern, semicircular in form, concentric with the curve of the apse, and leaving a very narrow passage between it and the apse wall.

Apsidal end.

Fountain.

This structure appears certainly not later than the apse itself, and if so, its presence is almost fatal to the theory of this building being a Christian Basilica. Another semicircular cistern or bath at the other end of the "nave" is not inconsistent with the "church" theory, as it might be a font; it is lined with the most magnificent varieties of Oriental alabaster.

Another part of this curious building is almost inexplicable —a very small subterranean chamber, almost below the steps between the two columns of the "chancel." It is approached from the "nave" by a narrow steep stair of sixteen steps; the top of this little chamber appears to have communicated with the floor above by a shaft made of clay pipes, such as were used for flues. If this had been under the site of the altar it might have been taken for the *confessio*, or tomb of some saint, which always existed under the altar of primitive churches, but it is not near the apse.[1]

Curious chamber.

All the marble decorations of this building have evidently

[1] The position of this curious little chamber is marked on fig. 22 by a small square near No. 46.

been stolen from some earlier one; the floor in the "transepts" and other places is paved with bits of Oriental marbles, rudely broken into squares of about 2 inches—a method of paving which was much used in the artistically degraded centuries which immediately followed the transference of the seat of the Empire to Constantinople.

Domus aurea. *Palace of Nero.* The whole cliff of the Palatine which overlooks this part of the *Sacra Via* is hidden by remains of Nero's enormous palace (fig. 22, No. 42, 42), which extended over the *Sacra Via* and the whole of that great valley where the Colosseum now stands, and also covered a large space on the top of the Esquiline; see below, vol. ii. p. 227. The part which is built against this cliff of the Palatine consisted of several stories of small vaulted chambers, the lower of which only remain, though the marks of the vaults of the upper rooms can be seen on the lofty wall which here masks the hill.

Existing remains. This lofty structure is built on an immensely thick and solid stratum of concrete made of broken lava, the most durable building material that was ever used. The lower rooms are paved with simple mosaics or herring-bone brickwork, and the walls are studded in the usual way with iron nails to hold the stucco. The brick lining is very neat in appearance, made of hard well-burnt bricks, red and yellow in colour; the brick facing of the arches is particularly regular and sightly, made of the usual 2 feet square tiles broken into two or three pieces, with (at rare intervals) a whole tile inserted in the arch; none, however, of this beautiful brick facing was left visible, as it was all covered with stucco. The vaults are of concrete made of tufa.

Unknown structure. *Building of unknown use.* In front and partly blocking up some of these under-chambers of Nero's Palace there is an enormous mass of *lava* concrete near the top of the hill or Summa Sacra Via. This is a gigantic platform, about 100 feet long and 12 feet high at its highest point, where it is formed into five great steps (fig. 22, No. 43). On it are remains of some very massive building of unknown use, built of very large blocks of *peperino* and *travertine* mixed ; some of the latter measure 8 feet by 4, by 3 feet thick. This building has been almost wholly destroyed for the sake of its valuable blocks of stone, and no idea can now be formed of its original appearance. It is probably of Flavian date, being later than the adjacent parts of Nero's Palace ; and its immense blocks of stone are such as were largely used in the buildings of Vespasian and Titus.

Turris Cartularia. Upon the ruins of this great building are some very thick walls of concrete, made wholly with broken marble, and rudely faced with other fragments of marble ; near No. 44 on fig. 22. These remains belong to a very strong mediaeval fortress which once stood here, partly built over the Arch of Titus. This was the *Turris Cartularia*, or Record Tower ; it was more than once used as a stronghold or place of refuge by the Popes, especially during the eleventh and twelfth centuries.[1] *Mediaeval tower.*

Porticus of late Date. Along the line of the *Sacra Via*, and skirting the *Atrium Vestae*, there are remains of a long sort of *Porticus* (see fig. 41, in vol. i. p. 302), evidently late in date, the massive foundations of which, made of rudely cast concrete, at several places cut into the remains of the earlier *Domus Publica*; see vol. i. p. 299. The level of the floor of this long building was considerably above that of the more ancient *Domus*. The upper part of this *Porticus* appears to have been of travertine, nearly all of which has been stolen for building materials. It probably dates from the fourth century A.D., and Comm. Lanciani has suggested that it is the *Porticus Margaritaria* mentioned in the *Notitia* Catalogue, Reg. viii. *Late porticus.*

Other late buildings, once faced with marble, stand on this line, nearer to the *Sacra Via* : some appear to have been shops, and others have signs of having been baths. A large apsidal

[1] The *Turris Cartularia* was still in existence in the sixteenth century ; it is shown by Du Perac in his etching of the Arch of Titus.

recess faces the *Sacra Via* near this point (see vol. i. p. 302); it too was once ornamented with rich marbles, but its purpose is doubtful. It may possibly have been merely a sheltered seat, with a curved marble bench, such as were frequently erected by the sides of Roman roads and in other public places.

CHAPTER VI

THE FORUM ROMANUM AND ITS ADJACENT BUILDINGS.[1]

AT that remote period in the legendary history of Rome, when the Palatine and Capitoline Hills were still occupied by separate fortified villages, inhabited by hostile tribes, the intermediate valley which afterwards became the chief centre of Roman life—political, social, and religious—was a marshy morass which, especially during rainy seasons, was interspersed with large pools of stagnant water. At times, however, the ground was sufficiently dry to form a battlefield, and it is said to have been the scene of repeated struggles between the Sabines of the Capitol and the Latins of *Roma Quadrata*. A part of it, which afterwards became the *Comitium*, was the neutral ground where the chiefs of both races formed their alliances, or held councils for united action after the political union of the two settlements under one king.   *Ancient marsh.*

The construction of the great *Cloaca*, attributed to Tarquinius Priscus, which still runs across the Forum at its lowest point, was the first step towards the erection of the magnificent group of buildings which gradually grew up around it. The *Cloaca* prepared the way for the future Forum by draining off the pools of water, and turning the marshy soil into firm dry ground, available for the foundations of temples and basilicas, and for a central paved area which remained dry even during the most rainy seasons.   *Cloacae.*

[1] The plate showing the most recent discoveries in the Forum will be found in the pocket at the end of the volume.

Ancient pools.   Ovid (*Fast.* vi. 401) describes the development of the Forum and *Velabrum* out of marshy ground interspersed with pools—

> Hoc, ubi nunc Fora sunt, udae tenuere paludes,
> Amne redundatis fossa madebat aquis.
> Curtius ille lacus, siccas qui sustinet aras,
> Nunc solida est tellus, sed lacus ante fuit.
> Qua Velabra solent in Circum ducere pompas,
> Nil praeter salices cassaque canna fuit.

The memory of two of the marshy pools of this valley was preserved down to Imperial times; though in what form it is difficult to say—probably as fountains or marble enclosures of the nature of a *puteal.*

Lacus Curtius.   Lacus Curtius. One of these was the *Lacus Curtius* (Livy, i. 13 and vii. 6), the draining of which by the *Cloaca* is mentioned by Varro, *Lin. Lat.* v. 148, 149, and by Livy, i. 38 and 56. According to one tradition, it marked the spot where Curtius closed the portentous chasm which had opened in the Forum by flinging himself into it; Livy, vii. 6, and Dionys. ii. 41. In the time of Augustus it appears to have been an enclosed space containing an altar; Suet. *Aug.* 57; cf. Plutarch, *Rom.* 18.

Lacus Servilius.   The *Lacus Servilius* was another of the Forum pools of water. In late times it was memorable as the place where Sulla exposed the heads of the senators murdered under his proscriptions; see Cic. *Rosc. Am.* 32; and Seneca, *De Prov.* 3.

Altar of Saturn.   Altars of Saturn and Vulcan. Another monument of the Forum which dated from a prehistoric period was the *Altar of Saturn*, where the *Temple of Saturn* now stands; it was set up, according to the legend, by the companions of Hercules; Dionys. i. 34, and vi. 1.

Altar of Vulcan.   There was also an *Altar of Vulcan* on the lower slopes of the Capitoline Hill, behind the Arch of Severus. This gave its name to the *Area Vulcani* or *Hephaesteum*, used, like the *Comitium*, at least during the regal period, as a place of public meeting; see Livy, ix. 46; Dionys. ii. 50, vi. 67; Pliny, *Hist. Nat.* xvi. 236; and Plutarch, *Quaes. Rom.* 47.

The *Temple of Vesta* also dates from a prehistoric period, being traditionally founded by Numa Pompilius; or, according to another legend, by Romulus. Dionysius (ii. 65), however, sensibly remarks that so important a shrine would not have been built outside the walls of *Roma Quadrata*, which included the whole city of Romulus; he attributes it therefore to Numa; see below, vol. i. p. 289. *Temple of Vesta.*

In the reign of Tarquinius Priscus the central open space of the Forum is said first to have taken a definite shape by the construction of shops and houses round it; Livy (i. 35) states that *ab eodem rege (Tarquinio), et circa Forum privatis aedificanda divisa sunt loca, porticus tabernaeque factae.*[1] These shops, with a colonnade in front of them, stood on the south-west, where the *Basilica Julia* was afterwards built, facing on the *Sacra Via*. They were called the *tabernae veteres* (Livy, xliv. 16), those on the opposite side of the Forum being called *tabernae argentariae*, shops of silversmiths and bankers; Livy, xxvi. 27, xxvii. 11, and xl. 51; see vol. i. p. 269. At xxvi. 11, Livy mentions that Hannibal, while encamped outside Rome, put up these rich *tabernae argentariae* to auction, in a somewhat premature way, seeing he never succeeded in entering Rome. When these were rebuilt after a fire they were called *tabernae novae*, and the two long sides of the Forum are frequently referred to by classical writers as *sub veteribus* and *sub novis*. Cicero (*Acad. Pr.* ii. 22) speaks of these as being respectively the shady and sunny sides of the Forum. *Tabernae veteres.* *Tabernae novae.*

Pliny, who is quoting Varro, records that the projecting galleries (*Maeniana*) over the line of shops *sub veteribus* were covered with paintings by a theatrical scene-painter called Serapion; see *Hist. Nat.* xxxv. 113 and 25. To amuse the *Paintings.*

---

[1] According to Plutarch, *Gracch.* 12, a humble class of houses bordered the Forum when Gaius Gracchus moved his dwelling-place thither from the more aristocratic quarter on the Palatine Hill.

people, pictures of gladiatorial combats were sometimes exposed in the Forum; see *Hist. Nat.* xxxv. 52.

Temple of Janus.
The *Temple of Janus* was one of the earliest buildings of Rome, of quite prehistoric time; it was founded, according to Livy (i. 19), by Numa; it contained a prehistoric bronze statue of Janus, described by Pliny, *Hist. Nat.* xxxiv. 33. It stood near the *Curia*, on the north-east side of the Forum, near the end of a street called the *Argiletum*; see vol. i. p. 248.

This short list includes all the buildings in the Forum, the origins of which are traditionally referred to a period earlier than the establishment of the Republic.

The *Temple of Castor*, the next in point of date, is described in the order of its position in the Forum; see vol. i. p. 276.

Growth of the Forum.
Unlike the *Fora* of the Emperors, each of which was surrounded by a lofty wall and was built at one time from one complete design, the architectural form of the *Forum Romanum* was a slow growth.

The marshy battlefield of early times became, under a united rule, the most convenient site for political meetings, commercial transactions, public shows, and the pageants exhibited at the funerals of the rich. It was here that one of
Gladiators' combats.
the first gladiatorial fights was held in 216 B.C.;[1] and the Forum continued to be used for this purpose as late as the reign of Augustus; see Livy, xxiii. 30, xxxi. 50, xli. 28; Suet. *Caes.* 39, *Aug.* 43, and *Tib.* 7; and Pliny, *Hist. Nat.* xv. 78. See also Pliny, *Hist. Nat.* xxxv. 52, who tells us that C. Terentius Lucanus exhibited thirty pairs of gladiatorial duels in the Forum, lasting three days, in honour of his dead grandfather.

[1] The earliest gladiatorial show given in Rome was that at the funeral of D. Junius Brutus' father, in 264 B.C., held in the *Forum Boarium*— the cattle-market and shambles—an appropriate place for the scenes of butchery for which the Romans gradually acquired a love; Livy, *Epit.* xvi.

It should be noticed that the earliest gladiatorial combats appear to have been provided on the occasion of the funerals of wealthy Romans, as a sort of survival of the primitive custom of sacrificing human victims, usually slaves, criminals, or prisoners of war, to appease the ghost of the dead man. Pliny the younger (*Ep.* vi. 34) shows that the connection between funerals and gladiatorial fights existed as late as the second century A.D. *[Funeral rites.]*

During games and gladiatorial shows seats of wood and fences were temporarily erected, and awnings were spread to protect the spectators from the sun.[1] *Maeniana*, or projecting wooden galleries, are said to have been first constructed in the Forum for the use of spectators at the gladiatorial shows. Asconius (*in Cic. Divin. in Caecil.* 16) describes the *maeniana* as follows—(*Maenius*) *exceperat jus sibi unius columnae, super quam tectum projiceret ex provolantibus tabulatis, unde ipse et posteri ejus spectare munus gladiatorium possent, quod etiam tum in Foro dabatur.* *[Wooden seats. Wooden galleries.]*

C. Maenius was Censor in 318 B.C. A further account of *maeniana* is given below, see vol. ii. p. 85.

Gaius Gracchus is said to have gained popularity by pulling down the wooden grand-stands which had been erected in the Forum for the use of those who could afford to pay for their seats; see Plutarch, *Gracch.* 12.

In some cases public banquets were given as a termination to the fights or theatrical representations. This was done after the three days' entertainments at the funeral of the Chief Pontiff P. Licinius Crassus, 183 B.C., in which 120 gladiators were engaged; see also Livy, xxiii. 30. *[Banquets.]*

[1] Pliny (*Hist. Nat.* xix. 23) mentions awnings put over the Forum by Julius Caesar. Dionysius (liii. 31) says they were of silk; and (lix. 23) records that in the reign of Augustus they remained the whole of a hot summer. Plutarch, *Rom.* 5, records that during certain festivals awnings (*vela*) were set up along the valley of the Velabrum, all the way from the Forum to the Circus Maximus.

Central area.   *Central Area.* For these various purposes a central space, though but a small one, was kept clear of buildings; but this was gradually encroached upon by an ever-increasing crowd of statues and other honorary monuments, some of which were occasionally cleared away, by order of the Senate, when they had become inconveniently numerous.

Pavement.   The central area of the Forum was bounded (at least under the Empire) by three roads, forming a level paved space about 375 feet long, by 150 feet wide at the Capitoline end, and 110 feet wide at the other end. The pavement is of thick slabs of travertine, averaging from 3 to 6 feet square. Most of this paving, which is badly fitted together and consists of slabs of uneven shape and size, is obviously late in date, probably of the third or fourth century A.D. Other parts, where the slabs are more uniform and neatly jointed, appear to be considerably earlier.

Incised lines.   On those parts where the earlier paving still exists there is a curious series of incised lines (shown in *blue* on the *Forum Plan*), which seem to have divided the Forum into compartments. The use of these lines is unknown, but they may possibly have had something to do with the marshalling of voters of the *Comitia Tributa*, whose place of assembly was the Forum. One primitive way of keeping each tribe in its right place for orderly advance to the ballot-box was by ropes stretched on rows of wooden posts (*septa*); see Dionys. vii. 59.[1]

Comitium and Curia.   *The Comitium and the Curia.* The *Comitia Tributa* was formed of the *Plebs* or Plebeian class, while the *Populus* or Patricians formed the *Comitia Curiata*, and held assemblies on the *Comitium*, a level area which adjoined the Forum on its north-east side. Plutarch (*Rom.* 19) mentions it as a meeting-place for the chiefs of the Sabines and Latins. According

---

[1] The *Septa Julia* is described below, vol. ii. p. 210. See also vol. i. p. 345, on the sculptured marble screens which may have been intended to guide a throng of voters up to the *Comitium*.

to Cicero (*Rep.* ii. 17) the *Comitium* was first surrounded with a fence or screen by Tullus Hostilius, *fecitque idem, et sepsit de manubiis Comitium et Curiam.*

The positions of the *Comitium* and *Curia* were formerly among the most disputed problems connected with the topography of the Forum, but the discoveries of recent years have quite established the sites of both. From the *Curia* or Senate-house a flight of steps led down to the *Comitium—Statua Atti . . . in comitio, in gradibus ipsis ad laevam Curiae fuit* (Livy, i. 36). On the Comitium stood the ancient *Rostra*, and adjoining it was the *Graecostasis* or platform on which foreign ambassadors stood to hear the speeches from the *Rostra* and *Comitium*. And Pliny (*Hist. Nat.* xxxiii. 19) mentions a bronze *aedicula in Graecostasi, quae tunc supra Comitium erat*; see vol. i. p. 338.

Comitium and Curia.

Graecostasis.

A very valuable passage of Varro (*Lin. Lat.* v. 155) describes the buildings at this end of the Forum :—

Varro on the Forum.

COMITIUM, *ab eo quod coibant eo comitiis curiatis et litium causa.* CURIAE *duorum generum, nam et ubi curarent sacerdotes res divinas, ut* CURIAE VETERES,[1] *et ubi Senatus humanas, ut* CURIA HOSTILIA, *quod primum aedificavit Hostilius Rex. Ante hanc* ROSTRA : *quojus loci id vocabulum, quod ex hostibus capta fixa sunt rostra. Sub dextra hujus a comitio locus substructus, ubi nationum subsisterent legati qui ad Senatum essent missi. Is* GRAECOSTASIS *appellatus, a parte ut multa.* SENACULUM *supra* GRAECOSTASIM *ubi* AEDIS CONCORDIAE *et* BASILICA OPIMIA. SENACULUM *vocatum ubi Senatus, aut ubi Seniores consisterent.*

Again, Livy (xlv. 24) speaks of the *Comitium vestibulum Curiae.*

The Curia. It will thus be seen that the position of the *Curia* gives the key to that of a number of other very important buildings, and the identification of its site will enable us to fix

Curia.

[1] The *Curiae Veteres* was one of the buildings on the slopes of the Palatine, which Tacitus mentions to indicate the line of the walls of *Roma Quadrata* and the *Pomoerium.* Its site is now unknown.

with some degree of certainty the sites of most of the structures mentioned by Varro in the above-quoted passage.[1]

Thirty Curiae. The chief place of meeting of the Roman Senate was called the *Curia* from the thirty tribes or *Curiae* into which Romulus was said to have divided the *Populus*, after an alliance had been made between the Latins and Sabines. Livy (i. 30, and xxii. 55) records that Tullus Hostilius enlarged a temple, and made it into the *Curia*, which from his name was called the

Curia Hostilia. *Curia Hostilia*—a title which lasted throughout the Republican period till the building was burnt during the riot at the funeral of Clodius in 52 B.C. The *Curia* was then rebuilt by Faustus Cornelius Sulla, the son of the dictator, under the name of the

Curia Cornelia. *Curia Cornelia* (Pliny, *Hist. Nat.* xxxiv. 26, and Dion Cass. xl. 50); but, owing to party jealousy, was soon after pulled down and rebuilt by Augustus, 29 B.C., its name being changed to

Curia Julia. *Curia Julia* in honour of Julius Caesar. This is recorded in the inscription of Ancyra — CVRIAM · ET · CONTINENS · EI CHALCIDICVM · · · FECI.

Pliny (*Hist. Nat.* xxxv. 27 and 131) mentions a picture by the Athenian Nicias of the nymph Nemea seated on a lion which was brought from Asia by Silanus, and dedicated in the *Curia* by Augustus.

Chalcidicum and Athenaeum. Little is known about the *Chalcidicum* and another adjoining building called the *Athenaeum*, both of which are mentioned by Dion Cassius (li. 22) in connection with the *Curia Julia*, which he calls τὸ βουλευτήριον τὸ 'Ιουλίειον.

The *Curia* was burnt and rebuilt in the reign of Domitian (Hieron. *An. xcii.* i. p. 443), and, lastly, was again rebuilt after a fire by Diocletian; see *Catal. Imp. Vienn.* printed by Preller, *Regionen der Stadt Rom.* p. 143.

Existing remains. *Existing Remains of the Curia.* Without going through all

---

[1] The *Curia* was an inaugurated building, and therefore a *templum*, but not *sanctum*, as is explained by Varro, *Lin. Lat.* vi. 10. In the same way the *Comitium* and the *Rostra* were both *templa*, though they were not roofed over.

the evidence on the subject, suffice it to say that there are many strong reasons for believing with the Comm. Lanciani that the Church of S. Adriano is the *Curia* of Diocletian,

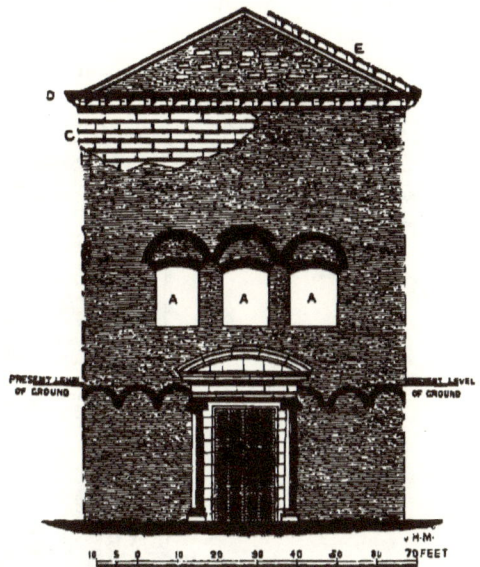

Fig. 27.

The Curia rebuilt by Diocletian, now the Church of S. Adriano; shown as it was in the sixteenth century.

AAA. Original windows now blocked up.
 B. Bronze doors, now in the Lateran; the marble doorway does not now exist, but is shown by Du Perac.
 C. Stucco facing to imitate blocks of marble.
 D. Cornice with marble consoles, and enriched stucco mouldings; both existing.
 E. Raking cornice now gone, but shown by Du Perac and Ligorio.

See *Forum Plan*, Nos. 55, 56.

though greatly altered and partly rebuilt. The end towards the Forum is the best preserved part; see fig. 27. This is of concrete, with the usual brick facing; the whole was once covered with fine hard stucco, divided into lines of false joints,

Existing building. so as to imitate marble blocks. The cornice is of brick covered with enriched mouldings in stucco, and is supported by a series of marble consoles.

A close examination of the brick facing with its sham relieving arches, and the stucco and marble details, show that this is clearly a building of classical times, which closely

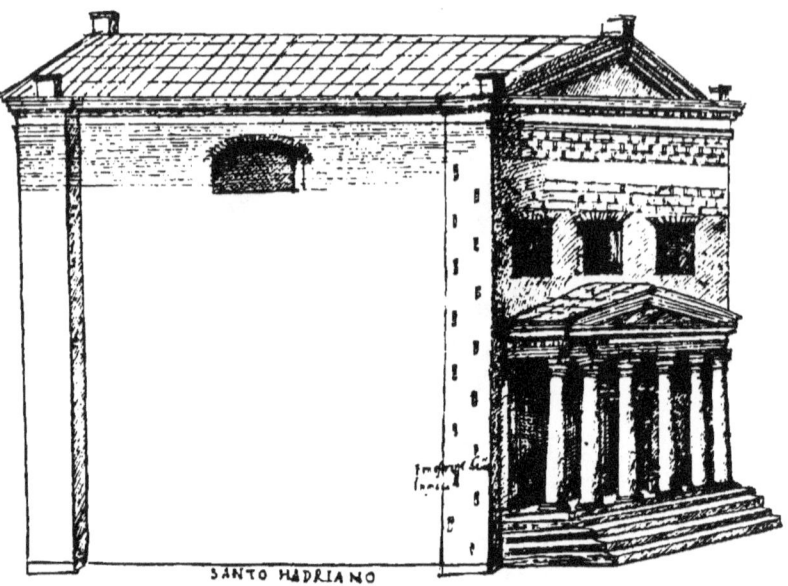

Fig. 28.
Ligorio's sketch of the *Curia* (S. Adriano) showing the winding stairs at the angle and the hexastyle portico.

resembles, even in minute details of the cornice and in the imitation marble blocks, parts of the baths of Diocletian.

Ligorio and Du Perac. Fig. 28 is a facsimile of a sketch in the Bodleian Library made by Pirro Ligorio about 1560, rather earlier than the date of Du Perac's drawing. It does not quite agree with the latter, as it shows a projecting *hexastyle* portico, which, according to Ligorio, had been recently destroyed by Cardinal Bellaio for the sake of its marble columns.

It is possible that the columned architrave of the door shown by Du Perac (fig. 27) existed inside the large portico (fig. 28) and remained for some time after the portico had been pulled down. In that case there would be no contradiction in the two drawings.

The present floor level of the church is nearly 20 feet above that of the Forum; but the old level existed as late as the sixteenth century, and was reached by a flight of steps descending to the large bronze doors, which then formed the entrance to the building. This is shown by Du Perac in his *Vestigj di Roma*, a very valuable set of etchings made about the middle of the sixteenth century. *Old level.*

These ancient bronze doors, certainly considerably earlier than the time of Diocletian, were removed by Alexander VII., and now form the principal entrance at the end of the nave of the Lateran Basilica. At the same time the lower part of the building was filled in with earth, and the level of the floor raised to its present height. *Bronze doors.*

These interesting examples of ancient bronze work are still in perfect preservation. In the seventeenth century, when the Lateran Basilica was remodelled and hideously disfigured, these doors were slightly lengthened by strips of bronze being added at the bottom and top. These additions can, however, easily be distinguished by the stars with which they are ornamented; otherwise the doors are in a perfectly genuine state.

The ancient bronze columns by one of the transept altars in the same Basilica are mentioned below in vol. i. p. 371.

Fig. 27 shows the end of the building; the upper part is taken from measurements of that portion which is now visible, while the lower part is derived from measurements of the existing bronze doors, which give the size of the opening, and show how deeply the original level is buried below the present road. The columns and marble architrave of the door are copied from Du Perac's drawing. *S. Adriano.*

Site of the Comitium. *The Comitium.* This being the *Curia,* we may conclude that the site of the *Comitium* is probably below the present road in front of the door of S. Adriano. It was a paved area, not roofed over, but surrounded with some kind of screen or fence, which probably in Imperial times was of marble decorated with sculpture. Sometimes, while games were being exhibited in the Forum, a temporary roof or awning was placed over the *Comitium.* According to Livy (xxvii. 36) this was done for the first time in 207 B.C.

Level of the Comitium. What the level of the *Comitium* was in relation to the Forum has been a much-controverted point; no clear indication as to this is given by any classical writer,[1] though it has usually been assumed that the Comitium was higher than the Forum.

Recent excavations have, however, exposed the verge of a paved area near the Arch of Severus, which appears to extend towards the supposed *Comitium* under the modern road; see *Forum Plan.* This is about 2 feet *below* the level of the Forum pavement, whence it is approached by three marble steps, which descend to it; see No. 30 on the *Forum Plan.*

Adjoining buildings. In Lanciani's *Ancient Rome,* p. 80, a facsimile is given of a sixteenth-century plan which shows three large halls of ancient date on the north-west side of the *Curia,* extending over the modern Via Bonella and the site of the Church of S. Martina. The façades of these buildings are in the same line as that of the Curia which they adjoin.[2] Probably one of these halls was the ancient *Secretarium Senatus,* which is recorded in an inscription found on the site of S. Martina to have been built by Flavianus in 399 A.D., and restored after a fire by Epifanius, *Praefectus Urbis;* Gruter, *Inscrip.* clxx. 5.

Use of the Comitium. The *Comitium* was not only the meeting-place of the Patrician *Comitia Curiata,* but also the chief legal centre of Rome.

---

[1] A complete account of the existing documentary evidence on this subject is given by Mr. Nichols in his valuable work on the Forum.

[2] This is indicated by a dotted line on the *Forum Plan.*

On it the *Triumviri Capitales* heard criminal cases, and saw punishments, both scourgings and executions, carried out. Foreign envoys were there received by dictators or consuls, and various kinds of important public business were transacted.

The Comitium was the scene of a curious prehistoric piece of ritual called the *Regifugium*. The *Rex Sacrorum* slew a victim and then hastily fled,[1] like the priest who slew the ox on the Acropolis of Athens at the Festival of the *Bouphonia*; Pausan. i. 14. 4. The real but forgotten origin of this curious ceremony was connected with the very primitive rites which took place among many early races when the sacred *totem* animal was offered for sacrifice. Though a necessary piece of ritual, yet the shedding of the blood of the sacred animal was so terrible a thing that various devices and fictions were resorted to, to save any one man from having to bear the burden of the deed. Hence the curious form which was gone through in Athens of trying and condemning for murder the axe which the priest had used, the priest himself being supposed to have escaped by flight. See W. Robertson Smith, *Religion of the Semites*, p. 286, *seq.*; and J. G. Frazer, *Golden Bough*, vol. ii. pp. 38 to 41.

Regifugium.

Early ritual.

The *Comitium* was also at times used for banquets (Livy, xxxix. 46), games, and theatrical shows. For these various purposes wooden seats, desks, platforms, and the like were erected on it; some, being merely temporary, such as spectators' seats for the *ludi scenici*, were removed as soon as the show was over. It was with these wooden fittings that the mob built up a funeral pyre for the body of Clodius, causing the destructive fire, during which the ancient *Curia Hostilia* and other buildings were destroyed.

Fittings on the Comitium.

---

[1] The Romans themselves in later times, having forgotten the true origin of the *Regifugium*, thought that it had been instituted in memory of the flight of Tarquinius; see Ovid, *Fast.* ii. 685, and v. 727; and Plutarch, *Quaest. Rom.* 63.

Original Rostra.

Bronze beaks.

The Rostra. The chief *tribunal* or *suggestus*[1] on the *Comitium*, originally probably a wooden platform, became in time a more permanent structure, and was known as the *Rostra*. This name was given to it after the capture of the Latin fleet at Antium in 338 B.C. by the consuls Camillus and Maenius,[2] in honour of whose victory the bronze beaks (*rostra*) of the conquered ships were fastened on the front of the previously existing platform, which thenceforth was known as the *Rostra* —*Naves Antiatum partim in navalia Romae subductae, partim incensae, rostrisque earum suggestum in Foro exstructum adornari placuit, rostraque id templum*[3] *appellatum*; Livy, viii. 14.[4]

The *Rostra* were the scene of some of the most important political struggles of Rome; from them the Gracchi expounded their laws, and there Cicero delivered his second and third orations against Catiline. On the *Rostra* too were fixed the heads of many of the chief victims of the proscriptions of Marius and Sulla; see Appian, *Bell. Civ.* i. 71. 94; and Cic. *Pro. Sest.* 35. 36.[5]

Statues.

Honorary Statues. The *Comitium* and *Rostra* were the chief early sites for honorary statues. One of the earliest of these was the statue of the Augur Attus Navius, who performed the miracle of cutting the whetstone with his razor; this

[1] The form *suggestum* is also used.

[2] Livy (iv. 17) gives the name *Rostra* to the early platform by anticipation.

[3] The word *templum* had a much wider significance than the modern word *temple*; it was applied to any structure that had been consecrated by the Augurs, whatever its form or use may have been; see Cic. *De Orat.* iii. 3.

[4] The *rostra* of captured ships were commonly carried off by the victors as trophies of naval victories. Livy (x. 2) records that in 302 B.C. the *rostra* taken from the Laconian ships were dedicated *in aede Junonis veteri*; see also Herod. iii. 59. On *rostra* fixed to columns see vol. ii. p. 309.

[5] For an account of the later *Rostra* built on a new site by Julius Caesar, see vol. i. p. 252.

stood, according to Livy (i. 36), by the steps which led up to the *Curia*.[1]

At the corners of the *Comitium* were erected statues of *Statues.* Pythagoras and Alcibiades, selected by the Romans, in obedience to an oracle from Delphi, as being the wisest and bravest among the Greeks; Pliny, *Hist. Nat.* xxxiv. 26. Livy (ii. 10) and Aulus Gellius (iv. 5) mention a statue of Horatius Cocles which was originally placed on the *Comitium*, and was finally moved to the *Area Vulcani*.

Other works of art besides statues were set in this place. *Pictures.* The Aediles Muraena and Varro hung in the *Comitium* a fine painting on stucco which had been cut off a wall in Sparta and brought to Rome fixed in a wooden frame; Pliny, *Hist. Nat.* xxxv. 173.

The *Ficus Ruminalis*, a sacred fig tree, under which Romulus *Sacred* and Remus were found, was near the statue of the Augur; see *fig tree.* Livy, i. 4. This tree was miraculously transported to the *Comitium* from its original place near the Tiber.[2] Under the *Ficus Ruminalis* was placed in 296 B.C. the famous bronze statue of the wolf suckling Romulus and Remus, which is represented on so many Roman coins; see Livy, x. 23. This group was dedicated by the Curule Aediles Cn. and Q. Ogulnius. It is quite possible that this is the bronze wolf which *Bronze* still exists in the Capitoline Museum; the hard archaic *wolf.* modelling of the statue and the conventionally treated hair on the neck of the wolf show that it is a work of early date.

On the *Rostra*, which stood in front of the *Curia*, were fixed the twelve Tables of Law, τοῖς πρὸ τοῦ βουλευτηρίου τότε κειμένοις ἐμβόλοις, Diod. xii. 26.

The ancient *Rostra* were also specially decorated with *Statues on* honorary statues to those Roman ambassadors who had been *the Rostra.*

[1] The scene of Attus Navius cutting the stone in the presence of the King is represented on the *reverse* of a medallion of Antoninus Pius; see Froehner, *Méd. Rom.*, p. 60.

[2] See above, p. 121.

Statues. killed while on foreign service; Livy, iv. 17. Pliny (*Hist. Nat.* xxxiv. 24) mentions as an example of this a statue of Cn. Octavius ordered by the Senate *poni quam oculatissimo loco, eaque est in rostris.* A number of other honorary statues on the *Rostra* are mentioned by Pliny, *ib.* 23. These statues appear to have been removed during Cicero's lifetime (Cic. *Phil.* ix. 2); see also Dion Cass. xliii. 49; and Pliny, *Hist. Nat.* xxxiv. 24.

An interesting remark is made here by Pliny about these very ancient statues. They were, he says, 3 feet high—*tripedaneas iis statuas in foro statutas,* and he adds that this size had specially been used for honorary statues—*mensura honorata tunc erat.*

Removal of the Rostra. The *Rostra* remained in their original position on the *Comitium* till 44 B.C., when they were removed by Julius Caesar to a new site. The new position of the *Rostra* at the extreme end of the Forum is indicated by Seneca, *Dial.* ii. 1-3, when he speaks of the space *a Rostris usque ad Arcum Fabianum per seditiosae factionis manus traditus,* meaning by this the whole of *Limits of the Forum.* the Forum; its north-west limit being marked by Julius Caesar's *Rostra,* as the south-east extremity was by the triumphal *Arch of Fabius.* The removal of the *Rostra* is referred to by Dion Cassius (xliv. 4) in these words, τὸ βῆμα τὸ ἐν μέσῳ που πρότερον τῆς ἀγορᾶς ὂν ἐς τὸν νῦν τόπον ἀνεχωρίσθη. The words ἐν μέσῳ που τῆς ἀγορᾶς must be taken to mean, not "in the middle of the Forum," but "somewhere near the middle of the north-east side," and even then the description is hardly correct. The existing remains of the *Rostra,* as rebuilt by Caesar just before his death, are described below.

Senaculum. The *Senaculum,* mentioned in the passage of Varro quoted above, appears to have been a place of preliminary meeting for the Senate before entering the *Curia;* see Livy, xli. 27, and Val. Max. ii. 2. 6. It probably adjoined the original *Temple of Concord* on the lower slopes of the Capitoline Hill;

and when this was rebuilt on an enlarged scale in the reign of Augustus, it seems not impossible that its large projecting portico became the *Senaculum*; see Dionys. i. 34, and vi. 1. It may possibly have once been identical with the *Area Concordiae* which Livy (xl. 19) mentions in connection with the *Area Vulcani*; cf. Livy, xxxix. 46, and xli. 27.

Basilica Porcia and Aemilia. A great part of the yet unexcavated north-east side of the Forum was occupied by two large *Basilicae*, which were more than once rebuilt under different names. One of these, founded by the elder Cato (M. Porcius Cato Censorius) in 184 B.C., was called after him the *Basilica Porcia* (Livy, xxxix. 44). Plutarch (*Cato Major*, 19) describes its position thus, ὑπὸ τὸ βουλευτήριον τῇ ἀγορᾷ παρέβαλε καὶ Πορκίαν βασιλικὴν προσηγόρευσε. It was burnt with the *Curia* during the riot at Clodius' funeral.

Basilica Porcia.

Adjoining it another *Basilica*, called *Aemilia et Fulvia* (Varro, *Lin. Lat.* vi. 4), was built in 179 B.C. by the Censors M. Fulvius and M. Aemilius Lepidus. According to Livy (xl. 51) it stood "*post argentarias novas*," behind the line of bankers' and silversmiths' shops, which occupied the north-east side of the Forum; see also Livy, xxvi. 27, and xli. 27. At the back of this Basilica was the *Forum Piscatorium* or fish-market (Livy, xl. 51), which was probably absorbed by the later Imperial Fora.

Basilica Aemilia.

Fish-market.

In 50 B.C. the *Basilica Aemilia* was rebuilt by L. Aemilius Paulus (Plut. *Caes.* 29, and Appian, *Bell. Civ.* ii. 26), and was more than once restored by members of the same family, under the name of the *Basilica Pauli.*

Basilica Aemilia rebuilt.

Tacitus (*Ann.* iv. 72) records that M. Lepidus, in the reign of Tiberius, by permission of the Senate, restored and adorned *Basilicam Pauli, Aemilia monumenta.* The Basilica is shown, on a denarius struck by M. Lepidus, as a large building with two stories or tiers of columns and a pedimental roof, with the legend AIMILIA · S · C · REF · M · LEPIDVS.[1] This coin, however,

Aemilian denarius.

[1] In a fuller form this legend would be [*Basilicam*] *Aimiliam* (or *Monumenta Aimilia*) *Senatus Consulto refecit Marcus Lepidus.*

appears to have been struck in the reign of Augustus, and must therefore refer to an earlier restoration than that in the time of Tiberius, probably that which was necessary after the fire in 14 B.C., which also injured the *Temple of Vesta*.

Bronze reliefs.

This Basilica, like other public buildings in Rome, was decorated with circular bronze reliefs (*clipei*) fastened to its walls or to the frieze of its entablature; see Pliny, *Hist. Nat.* xxxv. 13.[1] It is said by Pliny (*Hist. Nat.* xxxvi. 102) to have been remarkable for its magnificent monolithic columns of Phrygian marble (*pavonazetto*).

Marble columns.

According to an early mediaeval tradition the nave columns of the Basilica of S. Paolo fuori le mura are said to have been taken from the ancient *Basilica Pauli*. Most of these noble columns were destroyed in the fire of 1823; a few that escaped are now set against the wall of the apse on each side of the Pontifical throne.

Temple of Janus.

Near the middle of the north-east side of the Forum, probably near the angles of the *Curia* and the *Basilica Aemilia*, stood the *Temple of Janus*, a small *aedicula* or shrine, which towards the end of the Republic, or perhaps earlier, was of bronze. It is shown with much minuteness on a First Brass of Nero, as a small cella without columns, but with richly ornamented frieze and cornice;[2] see fig. 29.

Fig. 29.
The Bronze Temple of Janus on a First Brass of Nero.

---

[1] Other bronze shields used to decorate the Forum are mentioned by Livy, ix. 40. Compare the Greek custom of decorating the architraves of temples with circular shields of gilt bronze, as was the case in the Parthenon, the Temple of Apollo at Delphi, and that of Zeus at Olympia. The Roman *clipei* appear to have been most frequently medallion portraits of historical personages, or, in some cases, of living men.

[2] The legend on this coin is PACE · TERRA · MARIQVE · PARTA · IANVM CLVSIT. Another bronze *aedicula* by the Forum was that dedicated to

THE TEMPLE OF JANUS

This curious little shrine is described by Procopius (*Bell. Goth.* i. 25) as being *in Foro pro Curia . . . templum totum aeneum exstructum quadratae formae est, eaque magnitudine quae vix legendo Jani simulacro sufficiat.* He then goes on to describe the statue of Janus with one face looking east and the other towards the west.

Temple of Janus.

The doors of the *Temple of Janus* were closed on those rare occasions when Rome was at peace with all the world.[1] From the time of its traditional founder, Numa, to that of Livy, it was only twice shut—once after the first Punic war, and secondly after the victory of Augustus at Actium; see Livy, i. 19; the *Res gestae* of Augustus in the *Monumentum Ancyranum*; and Suet. *Aug.* 22.

The "Gate of War."

The *Temple of Janus* contained a very ancient bronze statue, by an Etruscan artist, of the double-faced *Janus Bifrons* or *Geminus*. Pliny (*Hist. Nat.* xxxiv. 33) says that the figure indicated with its fingers the number 355—that is, the number of days reckoned in the Roman year. This miniature temple held another statue of Janus, brought from Egypt by Augustus, the sculptor of which, according to Pliny (*Hist. Nat.* xxxvi. 28), was either Scopas or Praxiteles. This uncertainty as to its author (Pliny says) arose partly from the thick gilding of the statue, and also because the enormous number of statues which had been brought to Rome, and the preoccupation of the people on matters unconnected with art, frequently caused the authorship of statues to be forgotten.

Statue of Janus.

Later statue.

The *Temple of Janus* gave its name to this part of the edge of the Forum, and from the row of shops of *argentarii* or bankers and money-lenders which were there, the word *Janus* came to mean the usurers' quarter—

Usurers' quarter.

Concord; see vol. i. p. 338. As the bronze was probably thickly gilt, the effect of these little shrines surrounded by white marble must have been very magnificent.

[1] Hence it was called πολέμου πύλη, "the Gate of War"; Plutarch, *Num.* 20.

*Postquam omnis res mea Janum
Ad medium fracta est. . . .* Hor. *Sat.* II. iii. 18.

Near the Temple of Janus was a group of sculpture representing the Three Fates; Procop. *Bell. Goth.* i. 25. It was from these that the Church of S. Adriano (the old *Curia*) was known throughout the mediaeval period as *in tribus Fatis.*

Venus Cluacina. Another small shrine near this point, probably in front of the *tabernae novae*, was the *aedicula of Venus Cluacina* or *Cloacina* (the *purifier*), which probably stood over the great *cloaca* (Livy, iii. 48); see vol. i. p. 350.

Livy (iii. 48) in describing the tragedy which in 450 B.C. caused the downfall of Appius Claudius, records that Verginia was stabbed by her father *prope Cloacinae ad tabernas quibus nunc novis est nomen.*

The central area of the Forum is now surrounded by basalt-paved roads (see *Plan*), rudely made of blocks badly fitting and carelessly relaid in late times; a great contrast to the one bit of old paving which still exists in front of the Temple of Saturn, see fig. 30.

Sacra Via. *Sacra Via.* On the south-west runs the *Sacra Via*;[1] this is the side known as *Sub veteribus*, from the old shops which once stood there. The ancient line of the *Sacra Via* was probably to some extent altered when the *Temple of Divus Julius* was built, but what its original line may have been it is now difficult to say. It was believed to have passed between the *Regia* and the *Temple of Vesta* and under the *Arch of Augustus* in the diagonal line which is indicated by the axis of the *Regia*. Recent excavations have, however, failed to find any trace of the *Sacra Via* along this line, and the space in front of the *Temple of Castor* is covered with large slabs of travertine, carelessly laid in the fourth or fifth century A.D.

After passing the *Basilica Julia* the *Sacra Via* begins to

[1] The course of the *Sacra Via* outside the Forum is described above, pp. 224 to 230.

ascend the *Clivus Capitolinus*, winding round the steps of the *Temple of Saturn*. At this point there is still remaining a piece of very ancient basalt-paving, probably of Republican date, the blocks of which are fitted with great care and accuracy (see fig. 30), quite unlike the rest of the roads in and

Ancient paving.

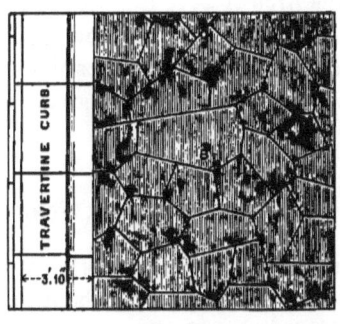

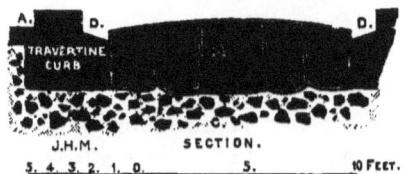

Fig. 30.

Example of early basalt road by the Temple of Saturn on the Clivus Capitolinus (see No. 14 on the *Forum Plan*).

A. Travertine paving.   C. Concrete bedding.
B. Polygonal basalt blocks.   D. Rain-water gutter.

The curb shown here is taken from another part of the road.

about the Forum, which have all had their paving roughly re-laid, probably in late Imperial times.[1] The road then passes upwards between the *Temple of Saturn* and the *Porticus of the XII Dii Consentes*, winding round the backs of these shrines, and so steeply upwards to the *Asylum* between the *Capitolium*

Clivus Capitolinus.

[1] Another well-preserved piece of paving in Rome is that which follows the curve round the hemicycle of Trajan's Forum ; see vol. ii. p. 33.

and the *Arx*, passing the great side doorway into the *Tabularium*, in front of which a piece of its paving is again visible.

Sub novis. The road which skirts the other side of the Forum *sub novis*, in front of the site of the *Basilica Aemilia*, also joins the *Clivus Capitolinus* behind the so-called *Graecostasis*, after passing through the Arch of Severus; see vol. i. p. 343. These two roads are joined by a short cross road opposite the *Temple of Divus Julius*; a junction which was possibly made when the line of the *Sacra Via* was altered on account of the building of this Temple.

EXISTING REMAINS IN THE FORUM.[1]

Later Rostra. The *Rostra* continued to be in their original position on the *Comitium* till 44 B.C., when they were rebuilt on a new site by Julius Caesar. Their removal is mentioned by Cicero, *Phil.* ix. 2; and Dion Cass. xliii. 49; see also Asconius ad Cic. *Pro Mil.* 5 : *Erant enim tunc Rostra, non eo loco quo nunc sunt, sed ad Comitium prope juncta Curiae.*

These *Rostra*, whether in their original position or as rebuilt by Caesar, were *the Rostra par excellence*, although there were several other platforms or tribunals in and round the Forum.

Rostra Julia. The only other *Rostra*, called the *Rostra Julia* to distinguish it, was the projecting *podium* of the *Heroon of Julius Caesar* built by Augustus, to which were affixed the beaks of the ships captured at Actium (see below).

Suetonius (*Aug.* 100) mentions both, distinguishing the *Rostra* rebuilt by Julius Caesar by the name *Rostra vetera*.

The recent removal of the road which crossed the Forum, close by the Arch of Severus, has exposed the very interesting remains of the *Rostra* of Julius Caesar, and has allowed the

[1] The number references given in this section refer to the numbers on the *Plan of the Forum* at the end of the book.

The existing remains of the *Curia* are described above at p. 238.

long-disputed question of its form to be at length decided; see figs. 31, 32, and 33.

The *Rostra* consists of a long rectangular platform about 80 Roman feet in length, and 11 feet high above the pave- *Existing remains.*

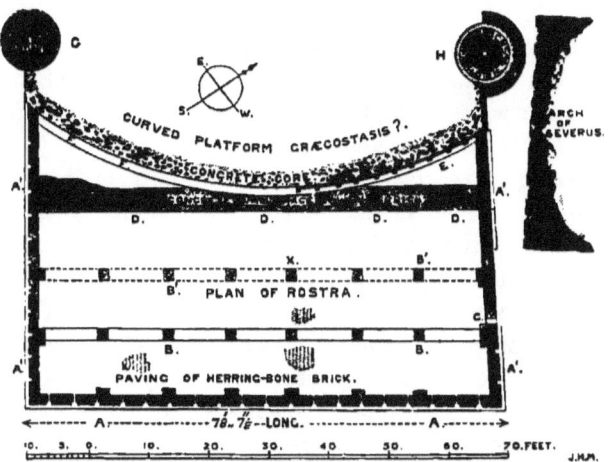

Fig. 31.
Plan of the Rostra and the curved platform behind it.

AA. Tufa wall with holes for rostra, and sinkings for the bronze pilasters.
A'A'. Tufa wall at the end with no holes for rostra.
BB. Travertine piers.
B'B'. Missing row of piers, of which one of the foundations (at X) has been discovered.
C. Probable position of the door to the under-space.
DD. Existing remains of the brick and concrete wall.
EE. Marble slabs lining the front of the curved platform.
FF. Concrete core of the platform.
G. Milliarium Aureum.
H. Umbilicus Romae.

ment of the Forum. Its end and side walls are of blocks of tufa, 2 Roman feet thick and 2 wide, but varying in length; each block was carefully fastened to the next with wooden dovetail dowels, all of which have decayed where they were exposed to the weather. A great part of this wall has been removed for building material, but at the west angle it is nearly perfect.

Floor of Rostra.
The upper floor or platform of the *Rostra* was supported on a series of travertine piers, of which there were originally two rows; on the top of these piers travertine lintels were laid, both longitudinally and across, forming a series of framed squares on which large travertine slabs were laid, thus forming a level floor for the orators.

Failure of piers.
Owing to the travertine piers being made of long blocks set on their ends, instead of on their "natural bed," most have given way through the stone splitting from end to end,[1] and at various periods in the third and fourth centuries the failing piers have been replaced or supported on each side by the addition of masses of brick-faced concrete in the form of piers or arches under the stone lintels. Only one isolated pier now remains perfect, and has fragments of its lintels still on it, but the positions of the others can mostly be traced. Many more remain of the piers or pilasters which are set against the tufa wall. One reason probably of the failure of the travertine piers was the weight of the statues with which the *Rostra* was crowded. Those shown on Constantine's relief (fig. 34) are large and heavy.

Back wall.
The back wall of the *Rostra* (D on fig. 31) is of concrete, faced with brick and studded with iron nails, in the usual Roman fashion, to form a key for its stucco coating. This brick facing is of especial interest, being the earliest example in Rome of known date (44 B.C.) The whole of the under space of the *Rostra* was thickly covered with stucco, including the travertine piers and lintels.

Under space.
The under floor is of "herring-bone" brickwork, laid on concrete; it is 2 feet 6 inches below the level of the Forum

[1] All stratified stone is stronger if laid in the same way that it was originally deposited, and travertine is especially weak when set on end, owing to its highly laminated structure.

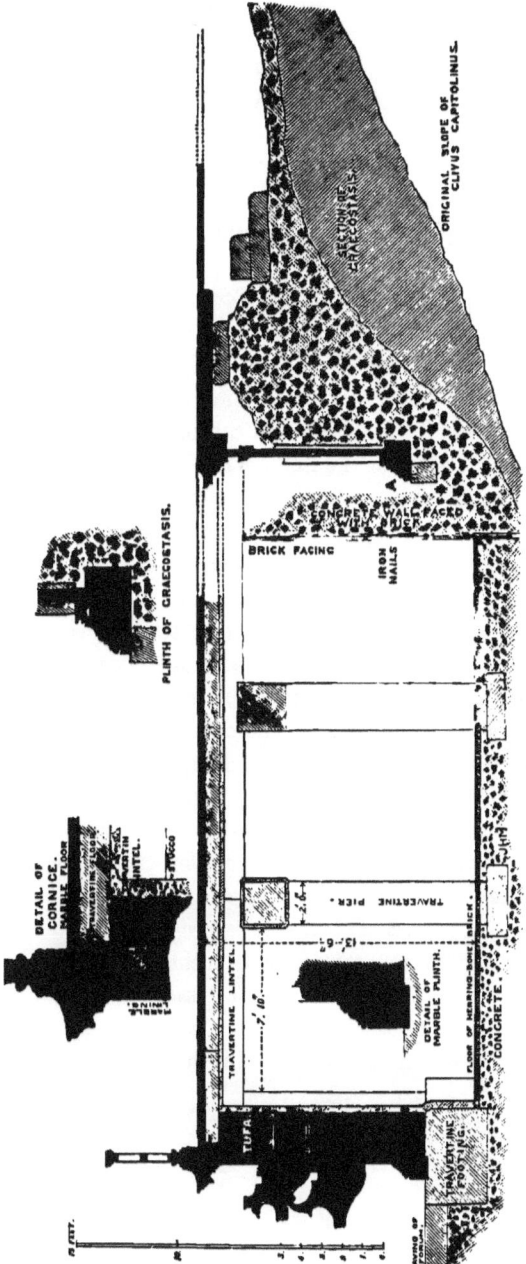

Fig. 32.

Section through front of Rostra and the curved platform behind it, showing the marble lining, screen, and a restoration of the bronze beaks, the positions of which are shown by the holes in the existing tufa wall. The details are to double scale.

256   THE ROSTRA   CHAP.

Under space. paving, probably to give headway under the lintels which carried the upper platform. At the end towards the Arch of Severus there are traces of a doorway forming an entrance to the space under the platform of the *Rostra*. No remains exist of any stairs, and the upper floor was probably reached from the curved platform behind, supposed to be the *Graecostasis* (see below).

Marble facing. The whole outside of the *Rostra* was most carefully and skilfully lined with marble slabs, with a richly moulded plinth and cornice. None of the latter is *in situ*, but many large pieces lie scattered near the column of Phocas; its mouldings are very graceful in design and carefully worked; see sections in fig. 32. All is of the finest white Pentelic marble.

Screen. Along the top of the cornice runs a groove, with holes for metal fastenings, showing where marble *cancelli* or balustrades were fixed to prevent people being pushed off the platform. Fragments also exist of the base moulding of these *cancelli*.[1] In one of the blocks of the cornice the groove in which the marble screen or balustrade fitted suddenly stops short, showing that the screen was not continuous, but had a break in the middle, so that the figure of the orator, standing in the middle of the platform, would be visible from head to foot to the crowd below; see fig. 33.

Rostra on a relief. *Ancient Relief showing the Rostra.* Additional proof of this is given by a relief on the Arch of Constantine, which, though worthless as a work of art, is of great antiquarian interest; see fig. 34. It represents these *Rostra* with a number of standing figures, and in the centre Constantine addressing the people. At the extreme ends are two colossal seated statues. The balustrade along the top of the platform is carefully shown, with its break in the centre. In the background appear, on

[1] Examples of precisely similar screens still exist in their places in the Basilica of the Flavian Palace and on the so-called "bridge of Caligula," an upper passage in his palace at the northern angle of the Palatine Hill.

Fig. 33.

Half of the front of the Rostra restored. A. Existing travertine pier and fragment of lintel. B. Bronze rostra restored. C. Plinth. D. Cornice. E. Screen along the top.

the left of the spectator, four of the arches of the Basilica Julia; next comes the Arch of Tiberius; in the centre are five columns with statues on them; and on the right the triple Arch of Severus is shown.

Bronze beaks. Bronze rostra. A special point of interest in the remains of the *Rostra* is the existence of some holes and metal pins, sufficient to show the number and position of the bronze beaks of ships (*rostra*) which gave this platform its name. These are visible in the most complete part of the front wall at the west angle, and show that there were two tiers of *rostra*, 19 in the lower, 20 in the upper tier, arranged alternately. The holes by which the beaks were fastened are about $2\frac{1}{2}$ inches in diameter, drilled through the whole thickness of the tufa wall, and even through the travertine piers, where one happened to come in the way; they of course also passed through the marble slabs which once lined the whole outside of the wall.

Pilasters. Where the lower tier of *rostra* were fixed there are also upright grooves (7 inches wide and 2 deep) sunk into the face of the tufa wall, probably made to hold bronze pilasters, which would appear at intervals along the marble facing. These upright grooves occur also on the end walls, though there are no holes for *rostra*.

An arrangement of upright pilasters, which is probably somewhat similar to that of the *Rostra*, still exists on the front of the curved platform behind.

Along the end of the *Rostra* by the Arch of Severus a considerable length of the moulded plinth of white Pentelic marble still remains *in situ*, though the tufa wall to which it was fastened is here wholly missing.

Fine workmanship. The great care and accuracy with which the various parts of the marble lining were fixed is very remarkable, and a great variety of clamps, pins, and dowels, both of bronze and iron, their ends run with lead, were used to fix each marble block to the adjacent ones, and also to the tufa wall behind. These can be well examined in the moulded plinth at the end

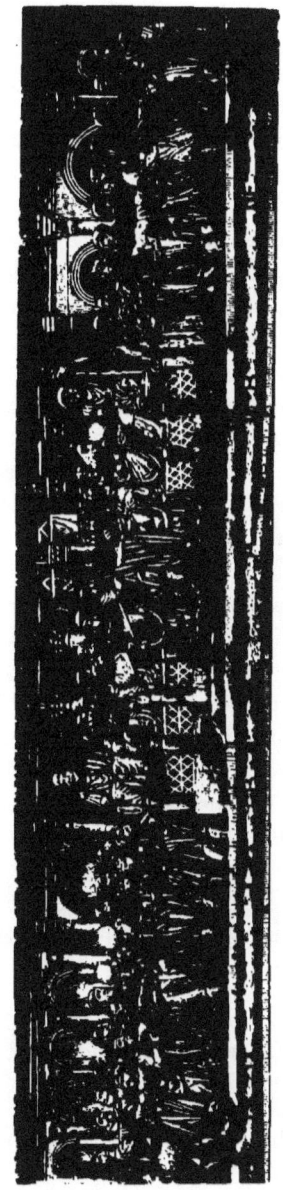

Fig. 34.

Relief showing—A. Constantine speaking from the Rostra; he stands in the middle of the break in the screen; the upper part of this central figure has been cut away. Behind the Emperor are two standard-bearers with ensigns. BB. Seated statues on high pedestals at each end of the Rostra. C. Arch of Tiberius with a single opening. D. Basilica Julia, four arches of which are shown. E. Arch of Severus with its three openings. On each side of the Emperor a crowd of eager listeners is shown, both on the Rostra and in the Forum below. Behind the Rostra are five statues on lofty columns. The square pedestals for these columns still exist; see p. 319 in the present volume.

and in the sub-plinth in front; and the whole face of the now exposed tufa wall is studded with iron fastenings, especially in the upright grooves mentioned above.[1]

The *Rostra* fastened on the front of this platform are said to have been the original beaks of the ships from Antium, which Caesar transferred (Florus, i. 11), together with some of the statues which stood in or near the ancient *Rostra*. Among the statues which Caesar transferred from the old to the new *Rostra* was a bronze equestrian portrait of Sulla, a statue of Pompey, and two of Caesar himself, see Dion Cass. xlii. 18, xliii. 49, and xliv. 4. Those of the ambassadors killed at Fidenae possibly were destroyed in the fire at the funeral of Clodius, as they do not seem to have been among those on the new *Rostra* of Julius Caesar—*Quorum statuae in Rostris steterunt usque ad nostram memoriam*, as Cicero says, *Phil.* ix. 2. It was on the existing *Rostra* that Julius Caesar went through the dramatic performance of having a crown offered him by the Consul M. Antony; Suet. *J. Caes.* 79, and Plutar. *Anton.* 12.

Statues.

Here too the bleeding body of Julius Caesar is said to have been shown by Antony to the crowd which thronged the Forum; and on the front of the *Rostra* Cicero's head and hands were fixed after his murder by Antony in 43 B.C.[2]

Coin of the Gens Lollia. Till the recent exposure of the remains of the *Rostra* it was usually thought that their form was curved or semicircular in plan, mainly on the evidence of a misunderstood *reverse* of a *denarius* of the *Gens Lollia*, with the legend PALIKANVS. It is more probable, however, that this coin represents a harbour with open arches, through which the beaks of ships at anchor are visible.

Coin type.

[1] Under the later Empire marble linings were of a less substantial kind; thinner slabs were used, and less complicated systems of dowels and clamps to fix them.

[2] Plutarch (*Cic.* 49, and *Anton.* 20) records that it was by Marc Antony's orders that Cicero's head and hands were fixed ὑπὲρ τῶν ἐμβόλων ἐπὶ τοῦ βήματος.

In any case, even if the *Rostra* are represented, it would be the original structure on the *Comitium*, not the existing one, as the coin is earlier than the end of Julius Caesar's reign.

Late extension of the Rostra. In addition to the late masses of brick and concrete which now obscure the remains of the *Rostra*, there is at one end, by the Arch of Severus, a prolongation of the platform of very late date, apparently of the fourth century A.D. Part of the original moulded plinth of the *Rostra* has been rudely refixed along this late extension, probably taken from the end which was concealed by this concrete addition; see No. 32 in the *Forum Plan*.

Rostra enlarged.

The *Graecostasis* (so called). Behind the Rostra, and coinciding with it in width, there are remains of a richly-decorated platform, curved in plan; see fig. 31. This is constructed of concrete made of tufa, pozzolana, and lime, with facing of Greek marbles, a great part of which still exists along about half its front. The moulded plinth is of Pentelic marble, and some of its blocks are incised with masons' marks, namely, the Greek letters Γ, Δ, Ԑ, Z, H, Θ, and K.

Curved platform.

Above this plinth there are slabs of "Porta Santa" marble, with narrow pilasters of the same material rebated to receive the adjacent slabs of marble at intervals of 3 feet. On the marble slabs are a number of metal pins, showing that they were decorated with metal *emblemata* or reliefs, probably of gilt bronze.[1] Above this there was once an entablature, probably of white marble like the plinth; none of it now remains, though the travertine blocks on which the cornice rested still exist along a great part of the curve.

Metal ornaments.

---

[1] The adornment of marble with *emblemata*, either of metal or of a different coloured marble, was a common practice among the Greeks, and largely followed by their Roman imitators. A notable example was the *zoophoros* or frieze of the *Erechtheum* in Athens; which is of dark Eleusinian marble, and had figures of white marble attached to it; see Otto Jahn, *Pausaniae descriptio Arcis Athenarum*, p. 51; Bonn, 1880. Part of the architrave of the Parthenon was decorated with ornaments of gilt bronze.

When the *Rostra* were complete it is evident that this richly-decorated front must have been wholly concealed; and this fact, together with many small points in the construction of the two structures, leaves little doubt that the *Rostra* were built subsequently to the curved platform, which, having perhaps been built by some party or individual hostile to Julius Caesar, was disregarded and its beauty concealed when he built the existing *Rostra*;[1] see fig. 32.

Early use of marble. The extensive use of various kinds of marble shows that this platform can be but little earlier in date than the *Rostra* (44 B.C.) It is the presence of this marble that has led Bunsen, Jordan, and others to pronounce it of late date, in spite of some known examples of the introduction of foreign marbles into Rome in the first half of the first century B.C.[2] Even Egyptian granite on a colossal scale was used in the portico of the Pantheon as early as 27 B.C.; see above, p. 23, on the early use of marble in Rome.

The level of this platform appears to have coincided with that of the *Rostra*, and the top of the two structures probably formed one unbroken floor, the access to which was from the higher ground behind, against the slope of which the curved platform is set; see section in fig. 32.

Graeco-stasis. The position of the ancient *Graecostasis*, near the original *Rostra*, is mentioned above (see vol. i. p. 237), and it is possible that this curved platform is the *Graecostasis* rebuilt on a second site, as is the case with the *Rostra* themselves.[3] The original

---

[1] Compare the reconstruction of the *Curia Cornelia* by Augustus, which, partly at least, resulted from hatred to Sulla and his party; see above, p. 238.

[2] This view as to the prior existence of the curved platform agrees with that of my friend Mr. Nichols, who has printed valuable papers on the subject in his *Notizie dei Rostri*, Rome, 1885; and in *Bull. Inst. Arch.* 1884, p. 85.

[3] It must, however, be admitted that there is very little evidence to connect this curved platform with the *Graecostasis*.

THE GRAECOSTASIS

Graecostasis is mentioned by Varro in the passage quoted (p. 237), and by Cicero (*Ad Quint. fr.* ii. 1), who mentions the noise made on it by the partisans of Clodius to disturb the Senate in the *Curia*.

The later structure was restored by Antoninus Pius (see Capitolinus, *Ant. Pius*, cap. 8), and again by Diocletian (*Catal. Imp. Vien.*, printed by Preller, *Regionen*, p. 143), in both cases after injury by fire, a fact which seems to show that, at least in later times, it had some sort of *Porticus*, roofed over to protect those on the platform from sun or rain. As, however, the whole of its marble floor is missing there are no existing proofs of this.

Pliny (*Hist. Nat.* vii. 212) tells us that in early times, before any sun-dial or clepsydra was set up in the Forum, the hour of noon used to be announced by the *accensus* of the Consuls, who watched for the moment when, *from the Curia*, he first caught sight of the sun between the (old) *Rostra* and the *Graecostasis*. In the same way the last hour of day was announced when the sun had sloped down *a columna Maeniana ad carcerem* (the Tullianum).

The *Columna Duilia* and (probably) the *Columna Maeniana* stood in the Forum somewhere near the *Rostra*. They are described below, in vol. ii. p. 309.

The *Umbilicus Romae*. At the north end of the supposed *Graecostasis* there is a curious cylindrical structure in concrete faced with brick, and lined with thin slabs of marble, evidently of late date, probably of the third century A.D. It is in three stages, each smaller than the one below. This is probably the *Umbilicus Romae*, or central point of the city, known only from its mention in the catalogues of the *Notitia* and the *Einsiedlen* MS.; see Preller, *Regionen*, Reg. viii. and Urlichs, *Cod. Top. Rom.* Its position is marked at H on fig. 31.

The notion of marking a central point with a cylindrical object was probably suggested by the sacred *Omphalos* in the

Umbilicus. Temple of the Pythian Apollo at Delphi, a conical stone covered with gold net-work ;[1] see Livy, xxxviii. 48.

Another theory is that the cylinder on the "*Graecostasis*" was the base of a gilt bronze statue of the *Genius Populi Romani*, set up by Aurelian, but its form is quite unlike that of the pedestal of a statue.[2]

Near the *Umbilicus* there are remains of some early *tufa* structure (Nos. 28, 28), but it is not known to what these blocks belonged. It is possible that they were part of the foundation of the *Columna Rostrata* of Duilius.

Milliarium Aureum. The *Milliarium Aureum.* The corresponding position at the opposite end of the curved platform was probably occupied by a much earlier monument, the *Milliarium Aureum*, a column sheathed with gilt bronze inscribed with the names and distances of the chief towns on the roads which radiated through the thirty-seven gates of Rome mentioned by Pliny, *Hist. Nat.* iii. 9; Dion Cassius (liv. 8) calls it τὸ χρυσοῦν μίλιον. See G on fig. 31.

It was erected by Augustus in 29 B.C., and its position is indicated by Tacitus (*Hist.* i. 27), who records that Otho and the Praetorian conspirators who killed Galba met, after passing from the Palace of Tiberius through the Velabrum, *ad Milliarium Aureum sub aede Saturni*; see Plutarch, *Galba*, 24, and Schol. ad Suet. *Otho*, 6.

It is also mentioned in the *Notitia*, Reg. viii., as being by the *Vicus Jugarius*. Its position, as shown on the *Forum Plan*, agrees with these indications, being near the start of the *Vicus*

---

[1] This is shown on many Greek coins, as, for example, on electrum *staters* of Cyzicus and on *tetradrachms* of the Seleucidae, especially of Antiochus III., and with more detail on various fine painted vases of the fourth century B.C. See a paper by the present writer in the *Jour. Hell. Stud.* vol. ix. p. 295.

[2] This view was supported by Becker, *Handbuch*, i. p. 360, who maintained that the *Milliarium* and *Umbilicus* were identical in spite of their being separately catalogued in the *Notitia*.

Jugarius, and close to the great flight of steps which led up to the *Temple of Saturn*. A fragment of the main part or pillar of the *Milliarium* still exists. It is studded with holes and stumps of the bronze pins which once fastened the sheathing of gold-plated bronze on which the inscription was cut. It was this casing of gilt bronze which gave it the name *Milliarium Aureum*. *Bronze casing.*

During excavations near this point, Canina also found some marble fragments which probably belonged to the pedestal of this pillar. These consist of a curved moulded plinth and frieze with floriated reliefs, and the base of a square pilaster, into which the curved part fits. The curve of the plinth shows that the diameter of the base, when complete, was about 10 feet 6 inches. The square base is now among a heap of fragments by the south end of the Rostra, and the curved fragments have recently been placed in their (supposed) original position. These fragments probably belong to a restoration in the reign of Severus. Their sculptured ornaments are very inferior to the work of the Augustan age.[1] *Remains of the base.*

The *Temple of Saturn* occupies the site of the prehistoric *Altar to Saturn*, mentioned above. It is clearly identified from the description of its position in the *Monumentum Ancyranum* (see below, vol. i. p. 384), and various passages in classical writings; and, moreover, it is shown on the *marble plan* (see *Forum Plan*). *Temple of Saturn.*

Varro (*Lin. Lat.* v. 42) speaks of it as being "*in faucibus Capitolii*"; and Servius[2] (ad *Aen.* ii. 115) says that it is in

---

[1] For detailed and illustrated accounts of the *Rostra* and the adjacent monuments see Jordan and Fabricius in *Ann. Inst.* for 1883, with plates in *Mon. Inst.*; Nichols, *Gli Avanzi dei Rostri*, etc., 1885; and a paper by the present author read in 1885 before the Society of Antiquaries, and printed in *Archaeologia*, vol. xlix., 1886.

[2] *Servius* is a name used to include many unknown early commentators on Virgil; an excellent edition has been edited by Thilo and Hagen, Leipsic, 1881-85.

Temple of Saturn. front of the *Clivus Capitolinus*, and near the *Temple of Concord*. The *Forum Plan* shows the manner in which the *Clivus Capitolinus* winds round it on its way up from the *Forum* to the *Capitolium*, on the lower outlying slope of which the temple is set. Its site is accurately described by Dionysius (i. 34)— παρὰ τῇ ῥίζῃ τοῦ λόφου, κατὰ τὴν ἄνοδον τὴν εἰς τὸ Καπιτώλιον φέρουσαν ἀπὸ τῆς ἀγορᾶς.

Chief treasury. The *Temple of Saturn* was one of especial importance, as it appears to have contained the chief public treasury—*Templum Saturni in quo et aerarium fuerat*, Servius, ad *Aen.* ii. 116; and Macrobius, *Saturn.* i. 8, *aedem vero Saturni aerarium Romani esse voluerunt*. These passages show clearly that the *Aerarium Saturni* was part of the temple, and not in the so-called *Tabularium*, as some archaeologists have asserted.[1]

Treasury officials. This treasury was presided over by *Quaestores* or *Praefecti*, with many subordinate officials; Suet. *Claud.* 24; and Tac. *Ann.* xiii. 28, 29. In several inscriptions these officials are mentioned. On the ground-floor of the Capitoline Museum is preserved a small marble pedestal of a statue of the elder Faustina, dedicated by a *viator* (a messenger) of a *Quaestor aerarii Saturni*;[2] see also Gudius, *Ant. Inscrip.* p. 125, and two inscriptions in the Vatican Museum, in the long gallery.

According to Varro (ap. Macrob. *Saturn.* i. 8) the original *Temple of Saturn* was founded by the last Tarquin, and dedicated by T. Lartius, the first dictator, in 501 B.C.; but Livy (ii. 21) and Dionysius (vi. 1) attribute it to the consulship of A. Sempronius and M. Minucius, three years later. In the reign of Augustus it was rebuilt on an enlarged scale by Munatius Plancus.

Existing remains. *Existing Remains of the Templum Saturni.* The only portion

[1] See also Livy, iv. 22; vii. 23; x. 46; xxiv. 18; xxvi. 36; and xxx. 39.

[2] This was the inscription found in the *aedicula* between the Temples of Vespasian and Concord, which caused the mistake of calling this little building the *Shrine of Faustina*; see vol. i. p. 341.

remaining of the *Temple of Saturn* of Augustus' time is part of the very lofty *podium* which towers above the *Vicus Jugarius*, built of massive blocks of travertine, and part of the lowest course of the facing of Pentelic marble with which the whole *podium* was once lined.

Treasure Chamber. It is interesting to note remains of a *Treasury.* small marble staircase which apparently led from the end of the *Sacra Via* into a chamber formed in the massive concrete substructure of the great flight of steps in front of the temple. The start of this little side entrance (No. 13 on the *Forum Plan*), with much-worn steps of white marble, rests on massive blocks of travertine. The chamber thus formed under the main staircase may have been used to store money or valuables, like the similar little room in the *podium* of the Temple of Castor, and elsewhere. At one side of this little staircase there is a large block of travertine projecting from the *podium* of the temple, and in it are large holes for metal fastenings, showing that on it once rested a statue or column, by the side of the steps into the little chamber.

Though not shown in the *Forum Plan*, it is probable that the very wide *Cella* of the *Temple of Saturn* was divided into a central space and aisles by two internal rows of columns, in the Greek fashion.

In the sixteenth century a fragment of the frieze was *Inscribed* found dating from the rebuilding of the temple in the time of *frieze.* Augustus; it was inscribed L · PLANCVS · L · F · COS · IMPER ITER · DE · MANIB . . . (*Cor. In. Lat.* vi. 1316). This important fragment is now lost.

The upper part of the temple now existing, with the eight *Last* columns and clumsily patched entablature, belongs to the last *rebuilding.* rebuilding by Diocletian after a fire. The columns, which are of grey and red Egyptian granite, are probably older than this, but were hurriedly reset in a very careless way, some being placed upside-down. On the existing rude entablature is part of the inscription which recorded the restoration of

Diocletian, once inlaid with bronze letters. . . . SENATVS
POPVLVS · QVE · ROMANVS · INCENDIO · CONSVMPTVM · RESTITVIT.

Temple of Ops. Adjoining or near to the *Temple of Saturn* was another treasury, the *Temple of Ops*, in which were stored the 700 million sesterces (about seven millions sterling) left by Julius Caesar at his death; see Cic. *Phil.* ii. 37.

Gold treasury. Livy (xxvii. 10) mentions another treasury called the *Aerarium Sanctius*, in which a reserve store of gold was kept for special emergencies; the hollow throne of *Jupiter Capitolinus* was for long used as a similar hiding-place for gold; see vol. i. p. 359.

Vicus Jugarius. The *Vicus Jugarius* (see *Plan of Forum*) started from the end of the *Sacra Via*, and passed between the *Temple of Saturn* and the *Basilica Julia* towards the river, under the *Tarpeian Rock*, which overhung this road, so that on one occasion, in 192 B.C., a fall of tufa rock from the cliff of the Capitolium killed several persons walking in the *Vicus Jugarius*; Livy, xxxv. 21; see also Livy, xxiv. 47, and xxvii. 37.

Thence the road passed on to the *Porta Carmentalis* in the Servian wall; by it stood an ancient altar to *Juno Juga* the patroness of marriage, from which its name was derived. Near the commencement of the *Vicus Jugarius* there are *Late arch.* remains of a brick and concrete arch or gateway, once faced with marble; see No. 2 on the *Forum Plan*. This arch is not earlier than the fourth century A.D., and was built abutting on one side against the marble-lined *podium* of the *Temple of Saturn*, while the other pier of this arch was set against one of the marble piers of the *Basilica Julia*, a perfect print of which still exists in the concrete of the gate, though the marble pier itself has disappeared.

Arch of Tiberius. The *Arch of Tiberius* probably stood near this point, spanning the adjacent *Sacra Via*. The *Plan of the Forum* at the end of this volume (No. 10) shows how the *Sacra Via* is contracted at this end, very possibly to bring it within the single opening of Tiberius' Arch. Tacitus (*Ann.* ii. 41) records that it was erected in 17 A.D. in honour of Tiberius, on account of the recovery by Germanicus of the standards lost by Varus in Germany. He describes it as *Arcus propter aedem Saturni, ob recepta signa cum Varo amissa ductu Germanici auspiciis Tiberii*.

The same event is recorded on a brass coin struck by Tiberius, with *obv.* Germanicus in a triumphal quadriga, GERMANICVS · CAESAR ; and *rev.* a Roman general standing holding an eagle standard, with the *legend* SIGNIS · RECE*ptis* DEVICTIS · GERM*anis* · S · C. *German victory.*

Several fragments of this arch made of Greek marble were found by Canina near the supposed site, and according to him traces of its travertine foundations were also discovered, but these are now difficult to trace. One fragment, a *voussoir* of the arch, now lies near the column of Phocas. A piece of the *attic*, with fragmentary inscription, is now in the *Sacra Via*, opposite the *Basilica Julia*, and another is on the platform of the *Porticus Deorum Consentium*; both have deeply-sunk matrices for bronze letters. *Traces of site.*

It is, however, doubtful whether these inscribed fragments really belong to the Arch of Tiberius; see Mommsen, *Monumentum Ancyranum*, 1883, p. 127 ; cf. also *Eph. Epigr.* iii. pp. 262, 274.

The Basilica Julia. Next in order of position comes the great *Basilica Julia* (see *Forum Plan*), bounded on the northeast side by the *Sacra Via*, on the north-west end by the *Vicus Jugarius*, and on the south-east by the *Vicus Tuscus*. As mentioned above, at p. 233, this site was partly occupied in early times by the row of shops first built by Tarquinius Priscus ; and according to some archaeologists by the first Roman Basilica called *Sempronia*. It is, however, more probable that the *Basilica Sempronia* (Livy, xliv. 16) stood farther away from the Forum towards the *Velabrum*.[1] *Basilica Julia.*

[1] The *Basilica Sempronia* was near the *Statue of Vortumnus*, see below, and the inscribed pedestal of this statue was found in the sixteenth cen-

The early history of the *Basilica Julia* is concisely given in a very important passage of the *Monumentum Ancyranum*, or Ancyrean copy of the inscription of Augustus, who says :—

Ancyrean inscription.

FORVM · IVLIVM · ET · BASILICAM · QVAE · FVIT · INTER · AEDEM
CASTORIS · ET · AEDEM · SATVRNI · COEPTA · PROFLIGATAQVE
OPERA · A · PATRE · MEO · PERFECI · ET · EANDEM · BASILICAM
CONSVMPTAM · INCENDIO · AMPLIATO · EIVS · SOLO · SVB · TITVLO
NOMINIS · FILIORVM · INCOHAVI · ET · SI · VIVVS · NON · PER-
FECISSEM · PERFICI · AB · HAEREDIBVS [MEIS · IVSSI]

According to these accounts the *Basilica* was begun by Julius Caesar, and completed by Augustus, who named it *Julia* after his adoptive father. It was soon after destroyed by fire, and rebuilt by Augustus on an enlarged scale in honour of his grandsons Caius and Lucius (the "filii" of the above inscription); see Dion Cass. lvi. 27, and Suet. *Aug.* 29.

Basilica Julia.

The *Basilica Julia* was one of the many buildings which were restored by Severus : an inscription found near it records that this was done in 199 A.D., after a fire. It was again burnt in 282 A.D., and restored by Diocletian ; and a final restoration is recorded on an inscribed pedestal which now stands in the exposed part of the *Vicus Jugarius*, at the end of the Basilica ; this. last restoration was the work of Gabinius Vettius Probianus, Praefect of the city in 377 A.D., who also gave or restored some statues, of which the bases still exist in the Basilica, with the following inscription :—

Inscribed bases.

GABINIVS · VETTIVS · PROBIANVS · V · C · PRAEF · VRB · STATVAM
FATALI · NECESSITATE · CONLAPSAM · CELEBERRIMO · VRBIS
LOCO · ADHIBITA · DILIGENTIA · REPARAVIT

The same inscription is repeated on another pedestal. A third runs thus :—

tury by the *Vicus Tuscus*, near the southern angle of the *Basilica Julia* ; see vol. i. p. 276.

GABINIVS · VETTIVS · PROBIANVS · V · C · PRAEF · VRBIS · STATVAM
QVAE · BASILICAE · IVLIAE · A · SE · NOVITER · REPARATAE
ORNAMENTO · ESSET · ADIECIT

During the Middle Ages this enormous building was treated as a marble quarry, and almost wholly removed for building material or burnt into lime on the spot. During the excavations of Canina three limekilns were found within the area of this one building, a fact which explains why so very little remains of this once massive and lofty *Basilica*.[1]

In plan the *Basilica Julia* was a large double *Porticus*,[2] with two tiers of columns one over the other; open, except for its low screens (*cancelli*), on three sides, and having a range of rooms two or three stories high on the south-west side— that away from the Forum. Some very interesting remains of these rooms, and traces of the staircase, still exist, and are partially excavated near the west corner. These are built of tufa, with bands of travertine at intervals, and travertine pilasters at the end of each division wall. This part possibly dates from the time of Julius Caesar. Augustus appears to have rebuilt the main building, with arches and engaged columns of Luna marble, two stories in height, the lower order being Tuscan in style.

Plan of Basilica Julia.

Parts of two of these piers have recently been exposed by the side of the *Vicus Jugarius*; they are built of massive blocks of marble, carefully jointed, and once covered with a

Existing piers.

[1] It has unhappily been much falsified by needless restoration; nearly all the brick piers are quite modern, and the one that has been restored in stone has been shown, by subsequent discoveries, to be unlike the ancient design.

[2] It should be noted that the word *Porticus* has a meaning quite different from that of the English word *Portico*. *Porticus* usually means a building with its roof supported by one or more rows of columns; either in one straight line or enclosing a space like a cloister. It is the same thing as the *Stoa* of the Greeks, from which the Roman *Porticus* was copied.

thin coat of *opus albarium* or fine stucco, to receive coloured decoration (No. 1, 1). The lower part of one of these piers is well preserved. The double aisle, which surrounded three sides, was vaulted in concrete, forming an upper floor, from which the public listened to the trials which were being conducted in the area below (see Pliny, *Ep.* v. 9, and vi. 33), where four separate tribunals of the *Centumviri* were held, including as many as 180 *Judices* or jurors. It was here that the younger Pliny practised as an advocate, and the Emperor Trajan held courts of justice; Dion Cass. lxxxviii. 10.

Court of Centumviri.

One of the late reliefs on Constantine's arch shows this or a similar *Basilica*, with its upper galleries (*maeniana*) crowded with people, who appear to be sheltered from the sun by curtains hung in the open arches.

It appears doubtful whether the large central space with paving of coloured marbles was roofed (Nos. 8 and 9). If not, it was probably sheltered by an awning stretched over it, as was sometimes the case with the whole central area of the Forum. Low marble screens or *cancelli* shut in the otherwise open arches on the ground-floor. A great number of fragments of these screens are scattered about the Forum, and the sub-plinth of one (No. 1) remains *in situ*, near the existing marble pier at the north-west end.

Low screens.

Without these screens to prevent public traffic, it would have been impossible to conduct judicial business in such buildings as the great Roman *Basilicae*. With them, and with the curtains which were frequently used to close the otherwise open rows of arches, the *Basilica Julia* must have been once a much more private and enclosed building than it now appears to have been, judging only from the existing remains.

Marble paving.

The space under the double aisles of the *Basilica Julia* is paved with massive slabs of white marble; and the central area had a very rich pavement of Oriental coloured marbles, namely, *pavonazetto, cipollino, giallo antico,* and *Africano,* arranged in concentric squares. On the white marble paving many *tabulae lusoriae* or gaming tables are incised : a few have inscriptions cut near them, with allusions to their use, *e.g.* VINCES · GAVDES PERDES · PLANGIS (No. 5). The dice-players of the Forum are mentioned by Cicero (*Phil.* ii. 23), *hominem nequissimum qui non dubitaret vel in Foro alea ludere.* *Gaming tables.*

Suetonius (*Cal.* 37) mentions that it was one of Caligula's amusements to throw money from the roof of the *Basilica Julia* among the crowd in the Forum below. The summit of this building was probably a link in the bridge by which this madman united the Palatine Palace to the *Temple of Jupiter* on the *Capitolium.* See also Josephus, *Ant. Jud.* XIX. i. 11. *Bridge of Gaius.*

The *Temple of Augustus*, which was begun by Tiberius and completed by Caligula (Suet. *Cal.* 21 and 22), is mentioned by Suetonius as forming part of this bridge—*Super Templum Divi Augusti, ponte transmisso, Palatium Capitoliumque conjunxit.*

A gallery which was possibly the starting-point of Caligula's bridge exists in the upper part of his palace (see vol. i. p. 194), and this bridge in its course towards the *Capitolium* must have passed over the stately building which is described below. Thence there was probably a wooden bridge to the roof of the *Basilica Julia*, and then a second wooden erection to bridge over the space from the *Basilica* to the *Temple of Jupiter Capitolinus.* No traces remain of these intermediate steps, which were probably removed at the death of the insane emperor.

There is very strong evidence to show that the large brick and concrete structure, once lined with marble, which stands at the foot of the Palatine, behind the Temple of Castor (see *Forum Plan*), is the *Temple of Augustus*, about the site of which so many theories have been invented. This building has recently been cleared from the modern workshops with which it was encumbered ; it is shown in a drawing by Ligorio in the Bodleian library in a far more perfect state than at present, with its lining of marbles and internal row of Corinthian columns set between the niches which still exist. *Temple of Augustus.*

Sketch by Ligorio.

Ligorio also shows a long porch or vestibule, occupying the whole of the long north-west side which is now missing; see fig. 35.

If the building was a temple, it was a very abnormal one in its whole design and plan.

Existing structure. On the other hand, in point of date and of position this great structure appears to agree with what we know of the *Temple of Augustus*. From its great height and size, its curious row of "buttress walls" at the north end, and the good preservation of its fine brick facing, it is worthy of more attention than it usually receives. Its position and the end with the "buttresses" are shown on the Plan of the Forum.

Record on coins. The founding of the *Temple of Augustus* by Tiberius and its completion by Caligula are recorded on various coins of these emperors. Its restoration in 159 A.D. by Antoninus Pius is recorded on silver and brass coins with the *legend*—TEMPLVM [or AEDES] DIVi AVGusti RESTitutum COS · IIII.

On all these coins the temple is represented in the usual conventional way as having a *hexastyle* front, but this cannot be taken as evidence with regard to its real form. Pliny (*Hist. Nat.* xxxv. 28 and 131) mentions a famous picture of Hyacinthus by the Athenian painter Nicias, which was dedicated by Tiberius in the Temple of Augustus. It had been brought from Alexandria by Augustus. This picture is described by Pausanias, iii. 19, 4.

Vicus Tuscus. The *Vicus Tuscus* starts from the *Sacra Via*, passing between the end of the *Basilica Julia* and the *Temple of Castor*, and so on through the *Velabrum* to the *Circus Maximus*. At many points along this line its basalt paving has been exposed at various times; but only the piece by the Forum is now visible, as the modern road is more than 12 feet above the old level.

Mythical story. According to a very doubtful legend it was called the *Vicus Tuscus*, or "Etruscan road," from the soldiers of the Etruscan chief Caelius Vibennus, the ally of Romulus, who

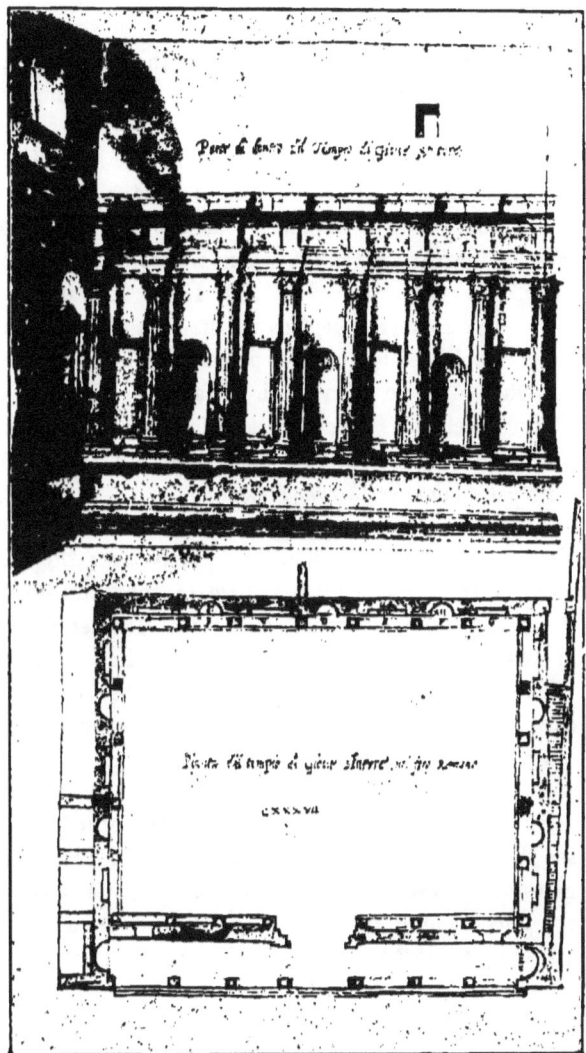

Fig. 35.

Sketch by Ligorio showing the "Temple of Augustus," with its internal range of marble columns resting on a dado. Below is a plan of the building. Ligorio himself thought this was the Temple of Jupiter Stator.

settled in the quarter through which this street was made. The suspicions of the Romans caused them to be transferred to this site from their original and more commanding settlement on the Caelian Hill, the name of which was said to be derived from their chief Caelius; see Varro, *Lin. Lat.* v. 46; Livy, ii. 14; xxvii. 37; xxxiii. 26; and Tac. *Ann.* iv. 65.

Vicus Thurarius. In later times a number of sellers of *thus*, perfume and incense, lived in this street, which was sometimes named after them, *Vicus Thurarius*; Hor. *Sat.* II. iii. 228, and *Epist* II. i. 269. The shameful neglect of the repairs of this important street, much used by religious processions, is one of the charges brought by Cicero (*Verr.* II. i. 59) against Verres, whose duty it had been as *Praetor urbanus* to keep it in good order. Cicero describes its whole length as being unfit for traffic, *a signo Vertumni in Circum Maximum.*

Ancient statue. Statue of *Vortumnus*. A very ancient bronze statue of Vortumnus, an early Italian deity, stood near the commencement of the *Vicus Tuscus*, a little to the south-west of the Basilica, where its pedestal (restored by Diocletian) was found in 1549. The part of its inscription then discovered was VORTVMNVS · TEMPORIBVS · DIOCLETIANI · ET · MAXIMIANI · · · (*Cor. In. Lat.* vi. 804). This interesting pedestal is now lost, but a drawing of it, with MS. note by Ligorio, exists in *Cod. Vat.* 3439, fol. 46. According to Propertius, the statue was the work of the mythical Volsinian sculptor Veturius Mamurius; see *Eleg.* IV. ii. 61. In the whole of this poem Propertius gives an interesting account of Vortumnus, and (l. 50) mentions the derivation of the name *Vicus Tuscus*; see also Livy, xliv. 16, and Pseudo-Ascon. ad Cic. *Verr.* II. i. 59, *signum Vertumni (erat) in ultimo vico thurario, sub Basilicae angulo flectentibus ad postremam dexteram partem.*

Temple of Castor. The *Temple of Castor*, on the south-east side of the *Vicus Tuscus*, is clearly identified by the *marble plan* (see *Forum Plan*); and its position is indicated by the passage in the *Ancyrean inscription* quoted above, p. 270.

The temple was originally founded to commemorate the apparition in the Forum of the twin brothers, Castor and Pollux,[1] who announced the victory of the Dictator Aulus Postumus at Lake Regillus,[2] in 496 B.C., and watered their horses at the *Fons Juturnae*, close by the site of the temple.

Temple of Castor.

The temple was dedicated, in 482 B.C., by the son of the victorious dictator, who was created *duumvir* for that special purpose; see Livy, ii. 20 and 42; Dionys. vi. 13; Plut. *Coriol.* 3; Ov. *Fast.* i. 707. Decrees and treaties cut on bronze plates were occasionally fixed to the walls of the Temple of Castor; see Livy, viii. 11. In front of the temple an equestrian statue of Q. Marcius Tremulus was placed in honour of his conquest of the Hernici in 306 B.C.; Livy, ix. 43.

Plutarch, *Pomp.* 2, records that a number of fine pictures and statues were dedicated in the Temple of Castor by Caecilius Metellus. Among them was a portrait of a famous Roman courtesan named Flora, who lived in the time of Pompey the Great.

Works of art.

In 119 B.C. the *Temple of Castor* was restored by the consul L. Metellus Dalmaticus (Ascon. ad Cic. *Pro Scaur.* 46). In the reign of Augustus, 6 A.D., it was rebuilt by Tiberius and Drusus out of the spoils taken in Germany; Suet. *Tib.* 20; Dion Cass. lv. 8, 27. To this period belong the three existing Corinthian columns[3] and rich entablature of the finest white Greek marble from the quarries of Mt. Pentelicus; they are very

Existing remains.

[1] Though dedicated jointly to both of the twin-brethren, the temple was usually called after Castor only; Suet. *J. Caes.* 10.

[2] Lake Regillus is now dried up, but traces of it are believed to exist in the plain between Gabii and the modern village of Colonna, about 13 miles from Rome.

[3] Other columns of the *Temple of Castor*, which had fallen, were used during the sixteenth century for various purposes, namely, to make the pedestal which Michelangelo designed for the equestrian statue of M. Aurelius, and for the marble statue of Jonah in the Church of S. Maria del Popolo which was designed by Raphael and executed by Lorenzetti; see Lanciani, *Anc. Rome*, p. 156.

graceful in design, and of most perfect workmanship, perhaps the most beautiful architectural fragment in Rome (No. 41).

The design is almost pure Greek in style and detail, but

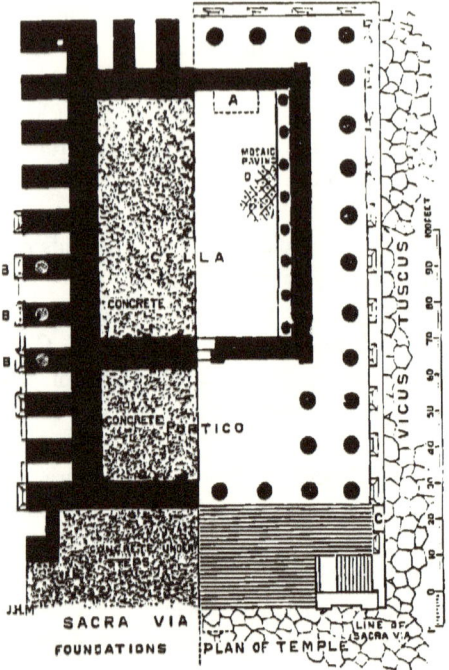

Fig. 36.
Plan of the Temple of Castor, showing construction of podium.

A. Pedestal of one of the two statues.
BBB. Spurs of foundation wall, of travertine and tufa, under the three existing columns; see fig. 37.
C. Steps to small chamber in the concrete core of the podium.
D. Existing bit of mosaic paving of earlier building.

one very curious constructional peculiarity shows the Roman timidity in the use of the flat marble lintel : the frieze is jointed so as to form a flat arch, throwing its weight, and that of the cornice, directly on to the columns—a needless precaution. It is also possible that the builders ran short of blocks which were long enough to reach from centre to centre of the columns, and so were obliged to build up the frieze with several separate pieces of marble.

The temple was *octastyle*, with about eleven columns on the sides; see *Forum Plan* and fig. 36. It stands on a handsome *podium*, 22 feet high, which was wholly lined with Pentelic marble, having a richly moulded cornice, and wide flat pilasters with moulded bases, one below each column of the *peristyle*. Fig. 37 shows the details of this *podium*, selected as a good example of Roman or rather Graeco-Roman mouldings during the best artistic period, the reign of Augustus.

Lofty podium.

Fine details.

The mouldings of the cornice and bases of the pilasters are well designed, with a judicious mixture of large and delicately small members, and are totally without enrichments, a pleasing contrast to the elaboration of the main Corinthian Order of the temple above.[1]

The marble facing of the stone core of the podium is very solid; it consisted of large slabs of marble 7½ inches thick, very unlike the thin veneers of the later Empire. Parts of the pilasters, which still exist below the three standing columns, are now exposed to sight, and bases of others exist on the opposite side in the *Vicus Tuscus*.

Marble facing.

In front was a wide flight of marble steps leading down in the direction of the *Sacra Via*, and there were also small stairs on each side (Nos. 43, 44).

By the side stair in the *Vicus Tuscus* there was a door, the

Treasure chamber.

---

[1] The best preserved pieces of this beautiful *podium* cornice are now lying near the foot of the wooden stairs which lead up from the Vicus Tuscus; near C on fig. 36. On the *podia* of Roman temples, see Vitruvius, iii. 4. 5. In this passage Vitruvius describes the subtle optical correction which gave a slight upward curve to the main horizontal lines of temples in order to prevent an appearance of sagging in the middle. This was one of the various applications of the principle of *entasis*, which were employed in the finest Greek buildings.

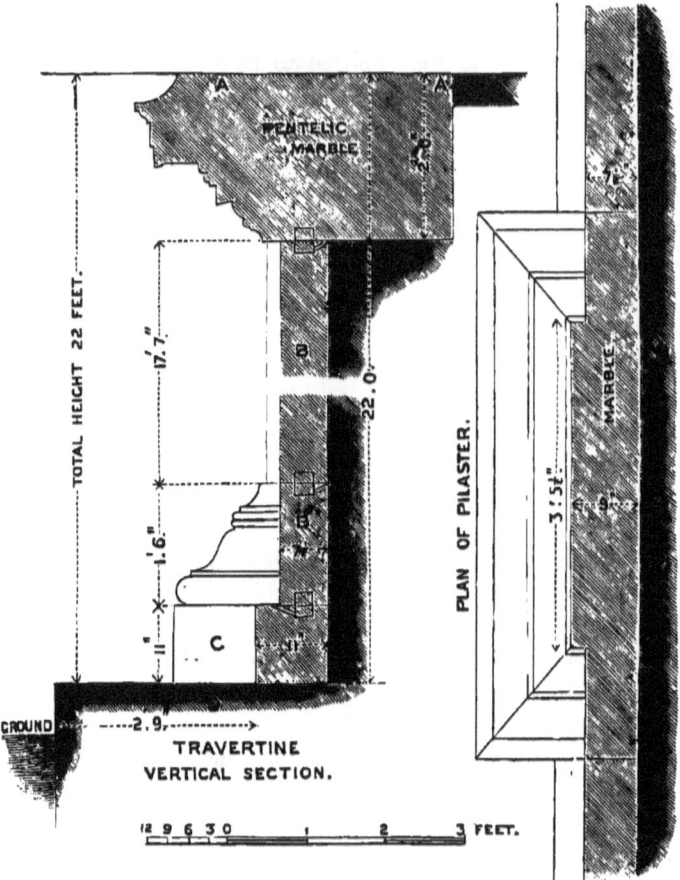

Fig. 37.

Details of the Podium of the Temple of Castor.

AA. Marble cornice at the level of the top of the podium.
BB. Marble slabs which line the plain part of the podium.
C. Moulded base of one of the shallow pilasters of the podium.
DD. Foundation of great blocks of travertine.
E. Core of the podium formed of concrete within a "box" of massive tufa blocks, as shown in plan on fig. 36.

worn marble sill of which still exists (C on fig. 36) leading into a small chamber formed in the concrete core of the *podium*, probably one of those strong rooms for storing plate and money which existed in many Roman temples;[1] the one in this temple is alluded to by Juvenal (*Sat.* xiv. 260).

Treasury.

The *Temple of Castor* was also used as an office for the verification of weights and measures. Many bronze weights exist with the inscription EX AD CASTOR, or, still more contracted, EX CA (*ex aede Castoris*).

Within the *Cella* fragments of a mosaic floor exist, evidently earlier in date than the rebuilding of 6 A.D., as is shown by the level of this mosaic being considerably below the marble bases of Tiberius' columns (No. 42, 42). The pattern is a simple series of lozenges of travertine and grey lava, with all the characteristics of late Republican mosaic, having *tesserae* smaller (about three to the inch) and much more neatly fitted than was usual in the mosaic of Imperial times. Similar mosaics of about the same date exist in the *Domus Publica* and in the so-called House of Livia on the Palatine; see vol. i. pp. 181 and 303.

Early mosaic.

Apart from its beautiful marble casing, the inner construction of the *podium* of this temple is a very interesting example of the wonderful care and solidity with which Roman temples of the best period were constructed; see fig. 36. Solid walls, 8 feet thick, of enormous blocks of the hardest tufa, each carefully clamped to the adjacent blocks, are built under all the walls of the *cella*, forming a sort of box with sides 22 feet high. The whole interior of this, with the exception of the small chamber above mentioned, was filled in solid with a dense mass of concrete, which set into one block like one immense stone. From these tufa walls other massive spur walls project at right angles, and on the ends of these the columns of the *peristyle* were set. The spur walls are of tufa,

Massive podium.

Stone and concrete.

[1] As for example in the Temples of Concord, Saturn, and that of Divus Julius.

282   TEMPLE OF CASTOR   CHAP.

Massive podium.   except the part immediately under each column, which is of travertine, the harder stone being used at the points of greatest pressure.[1]

These spur walls were also strengthened laterally by flat travertine arches, spanning the intercolumniations from wall to wall just below the columns.

The whole result of this elaborate and massive construction is an amount of strength far in excess of what was actually required, showing the most lavish expenditure of both labour and material.

Older temple.   The position of the present *Temple of Castor*, almost blocking up one of the three arches of the Arch of Augustus, suggests that the older temple, which was standing at the time when this arch was built, thirty-six years before, did not extend as far to the north as does the present structure built by Tiberius.

Fraud of Verres.   Cicero (*Verr.* II. i. 49 *seq.*) tells an interesting story of how Verres extorted money out of a pretended restoration of the Temple of Castor, pulling down and refixing some of the columns on the pretext that they were not absolutely perpendicular.

Stuccoed columns.   In his account of this transaction Cicero mentions that the columns were *dealbatae*—that is, covered with the hard white stucco made of pounded marble (*opus albarium*), which was usually applied as a ground for coloured decorations. The building referred to is of course the earlier one, which existed before the rebuilding by Tiberius and Drusus. The columns of this were probably not of marble but *peperino*, which, like the *tufa*, appears to have been always coated with stucco; see above, p. 78.

The Temple of Castor was occasionally used as a meeting-place for the Senate (Cic. *sup. cit.*), and its lofty podium was

[1] Parts of the very interesting foundation walls of the temple were in 1884 concealed and falsified by the most needless and senseless restoration of the substructure under some of the missing columns.

used, like the *Rostra*, as a tribunal for orators; see Plut. *Sulla*, 8, and Cic. *Pro Sest*. 15. It was the scene of many fierce political struggles, and even riots, especially in the time of Marius and Sulla, and when Julius Caesar, during his joint-consulship with Bibulus, advocated his Agrarian law; Dion Cass. xxxviii. 6. Again, shortly after, when the recall of Cicero from exile was proposed, Clodius and his party during a riot in the Forum fortified themselves in the temple, and broke up the steps to render access difficult; Cic. *In Pis*. 5.   *Political struggles.*

A door was broken in the back wall of the *Cella*, behind the statues of Castor and Pollux, by the insane Caligula, who connected the temple with his new palace at the north angle of the Palatine, and used to offer himself for worship, standing between the twins; Suet. *Cal*. 22.

Near the *Temple of Castor* was another *Tribunal* for orations, probably only a wooden *suggestum*, called the *Tribunal Aurelium*; Cic. *In Pis*. 5, and *Pro Sest*. 15.[1]

Close by the *Temple of Castor*, on its eastern side, towards the *Atrium Vestae*, are some remains of marble columns and entablature which are well worth close examination, as being among the most beautiful and delicately worked examples of marble architecture in Rome. The capitals of the columns are a sort of enriched Tuscan, and all the details are alike beautiful both in design and workmanship.   *Marble fragments.*

These very beautiful fragments are illustrated by Labacco, *Architettura*, 1557, pls. 17 and 18, as belonging to a temple, remains of which were discovered in the sixteenth century between the Church of S. Adriano and the Temple of Faustina. It seems probable that these remains belong to the Temple of Janus Quadrifrons mentioned in vol. ii. p. 23.

They are clearly of early Imperial date, probably of the

[1] This, or a similar tribunal, is shown on a bronze medal of Nero, with the legend—CONGIARIUM II · DATUM POPULO ROMANO; see Froehner, *Médaillons de l'Empire*, p. 14, Paris, 1878.

284 ARCH OF AUGUSTUS CHAP.

Augustan period, as is shown by the extreme delicacy and beauty of the work.

Fons Juturnae.   The *Fons Juturnae* existed in some form till Imperial times (Ov. *Fast.* i. 705, and Dionys. vi. 13), probably as a marble fountain or tank.[1] Remains of a circular travertine structure near the Temple of Castor (No. 45) have been supposed to belong to this; but their form— a sort of curb, with a channel for rain-water— makes it more probable that they belonged to the *Puteal Scriboni* or *Libonis* (Hor. *Ep.* i. 19, 8, and *Sat.* ii. 6, 35), a circular marble structure like a well-mouth, used to mark some spot where lightning had fallen, or where some sacred object was buried.[2] The *Puteal Scribonianum* is shown on a common *denarius* of the *Gens Scribonia*, of the first century B.C., ornamented with reliefs of lyres and hanging garlands; see fig. 38.

Puteal Libonis.

Fig. 38.
Denarius of the Gens Scribonia showing the *puteal Scribonianum.*

Arcus Augusti.   The *Arch of Augustus* was near the Temple of Castor, with one side touching the Temple of Julius; a late scholiast to the *Aeneid* describes it as being *juxta aedem Divi Juli*; its position is shown on the *Forum Plan*; see No. 46. It was set up in honour of Augustus' final victory at Actium in 30 B.C. (Dion Cass. li. 19). Its foundations were discovered in 1888, but the arch itself has wholly vanished. From the foundations, which consist of great blocks of travertine, we

---

[1] A shrine to the nymph Juturna was built in the Campus Martius by Q. Lutatius Catulus about 78 B.C.; see Ovid, *Fast.* i. 463.

[2] Another *putcal* (by the *Comitium*) enshrined the spot where the miraculous razor and whetstone of the augur Attus Navius were buried; Livy, i. 36; and Cic. *De Divin.* i. 17. It clearly was distinct from the *Puteal Scribonianum.*

A stone *puteal* set over a place that had been struck by lightning still exists *in situ* at Pompeii; it is close by the remains of the ancient Doric temple—the only relic in Pompeii of the pre-Roman colony.

see that it was a triple archway, the central arch being 14 feet wide. A marble inscribed block from its attic was found during the excavations of 1540-50 with this inscription, which is now lost :— *Arch of Augustus.*

SENATVS · POPVLVSQVE · ROMANVS · IMP · CAESARI · DIVI
IVLI · F · COS · QVINCT · COS · DESIG · SEXT · IMP · SEPT
REPVBLICA · CONSERVATA

The fifth consulship of Augustus was in 29 B.C., the year when he returned to Rome after his Egyptian victories in 30 B.C. ; see Lanciani, *Not. degli Scavi*, 1882, p. 227.

Temple of Divus Julius. Opposite the Temple of Castor stand the scanty remains of the Heroon or Temple of the deified Julius Caesar, built by Augustus in 42 B.C., as recorded in the Ancyrean inscription—AEDEM · DIVI · IVLI · · · FECI. Dion Cassius (xlvii. 18) says that this Heroon was built on the spot where Caesar's body was burnt, and Appian (*Bell. Civ.* ii. 149) records that Caesar's funeral pyre was placed on the site of the ancient *Regia*; see below, vol. i. p. 305. *Temple of Julius.*

Ovid (*Ep. ex Ponto*, II. ii. 85) mentions it as being near the Temple of Castor, and as facing towards the Forum and the Capitol; *Metam.* xv. 841. Further indications of its site are given by Statius (*Silv.* i. 22-66) in his description of the buildings near the statue of Domitian, so that no doubt whatever exists as to its identification.

Before the temple was built, a column of Numidian marble, 20 feet high, inscribed PARENTI · PATRIAE, was set by the Senate on the site of Caesar's funeral pyre (Suet. *J. Caes.* 85). According to Appian (*Bell. Civ.* ii. 148) an altar was also dedicated to Julius on this spot. *Column of Julius.*

Though only the concrete core of the *Podium* and a few marble fragments now exist, yet the plan of the temple can be fairly well made out, mainly from the voids in the concrete, which show the former position of the massive tufa walls in the *podium*, built as substructures to support the marble columns and walls of the upper temple. These were arranged on a similar system to that of the *Temple of Castor*, except that there were no projecting spur walls, as this temple had no *peristyle*. Prints of the great blocks are visible on the face of the concrete core, but all the stone itself has been removed for building material. Below the tufa walls there is a massive foundation made of large blocks of travertine.

Massive podium.

The plan of this temple is quite unique; it consisted of two parts—*first* a platform about 12 feet high, which projected in front of the temple, and was approached by two stairs.

Unique plan.

Secondly, a prostyle temple, which stood on the south-east side of the platform, and was reached by another flight of steps leading up to the portico from the front portion of the podium or platform.

The central part of the front of this *suggestus* or platform, once wholly lined with marble, is hollowed into a semicircular recess (No. 49); this is now filled up with late concrete and masonry, probably of the third or fourth century. Its original form is shown on the *Forum Plan*. To some part of this front were affixed the bronze beaks of the ships taken by Augustus at Actium (Dion Cass. li. 19); and hence this podium was known as the *Rostra Julia*, being so called to distinguish it from the original or *Rostra vetera*. Holes for the bronze rostra exist in the front of the apse-like wall.

Rostra Julia

It appears probable that this very unusual form for the *suggestus* was adopted in order that the apsidal recess might inclose the pre-existing column or altar, in which case the orator, when speaking from these *Rostra*, probably stood on one side of the recess.[1]

Curved recess.

Suetonius (*Aug.* 100) mentions that funeral orations in honour of Augustus were delivered both from the *Rostra Julia* and the ancient *Rostra—Bifariam laudatus est, pro aede Divi*

[1] In the *Forum Plan* the column is conjecturally shown in the middle of the recess, and the late filling up is omitted.

THE TEMPLE OF JULIUS

Julii a Tiberio, et pro rostris veteribus a Druso; see also Dion Cass. liv. 35.

Bronze coins of Augustus and Hadrian have representations of this building. On a second Brass of Hadrian the *podium* with the bronze *rostra* fixed to it is shown, and on it the emperor addressing people standing below. *Lofty cella.*

The *Temple of Julius Caesar* itself is raised considerably higher than the platform in front of it, from which it was reached by steps up to the prostyle portico. It was probably a Corinthian *prostyle hexastyle* building—that is, having a portico at one end, with six columns in front, and no free columns at the back and sides. According to Vitruvius, iii. 2, it was *pycnostyle*, having, that is, the columns closely set together. The cella appears to have been very small and shallow.

Fragments of the main cornice exist on and near the temple, including pieces of the horizontal part along the sides of the temple and the sloping part of the pediment in front. These fragments are, however, too poor in workmanship and design to belong to the time of Augustus. *Existing remains.*

They are probably portions of a later restoration or rebuilding of the temple.

Only one bit remains of the *Cella* floor, paved with simple marble mosaic.[1] A long piece of marble step, on the side towards the *Temple of Castor*, marks the old extent of the *podium*, and the start of one of the front stairs, with its step worn down by traffic, is still *in situ* (Nos. 47, 47, 48). *Mosaic floor.*

The rudely-worked plinth moulding against the late masonry, which now fills up the apsidal recess, was carelessly copied from the plinth of the original part, none of which now remains *in situ*, though some pieces are lying by the side of the road in front of the apse.

The appearance of this temple, first with its lofty *podium*,

[1] Since this was written in 1884 the last piece of mosaic pavement has crumbled away.

and then the temple proper rising high above that, must have been very strange. Several allusions to its abnormal height occur in classical writings, *e.g.* Ovid, *Ep. ex Pon.* II. ii. 85—

> *Fratribus*[1] *assimiles,*[2] *quos, proxima templa tenentes,*
> *Divus ab excelsa Julius aede videt.*

---

[1] Castor and Pollux.
[2] Germanicus and Drusus are alluded to.

CHAPTER VII

THE FORUM ROMANUM AND ITS ADJACENT BUILDINGS
(continued).

WE now come to a group of the most ancient and sacred buildings in Rome, the sanctity of which gave its name to the originally short piece of the *Sacra Via*, between the southern verge of the Forum and the *clivus* where the *Arch of Titus* now stands.

The *Temple of Vesta*, of which remains exist at the southern angle of the Forum (No. 51), was the most sacred of all the shrines of Rome. *Vesta* is the Latin form of the Greek goddess *Hestia*, to whom a sacred fire was kept always burning in the *Prytaneum* of every Greek city. Like the *Temple of Vesta*, the early Greek *Prytaneum* appears to have been a building of circular plan. The Greek fires were guarded by elderly widows, instead of by virgin priestesses, but in other respects the cult seems to have been very similar in Rome and in Hellenic cities. The Greek *Prytaneum* fires are described by Plutarch, *Numa*, 9, thus: Ἐπεί τοι τῆς Ἑλλάδος ὅπου πῦρ ἄσβεστόν ἐστιν, ὡς Πυθοῖ καὶ Ἀθήνῃσιν, οὐ παρθένοι, γυναῖκες δὲ πεπαυμέναι γάμων ἔχουσι τὴν ἐπιμέλειαν. Ἐὰν δὲ ὑπὸ τύχης τινὸς ἐκλίπῃ, . . . οὔ φασι δεῖν ἀπὸ ἑτέρου πυρὸς ἐναύεσθαι, καινὸν δὲ ποιεῖν καὶ νέον, ἀνάπτοντας ἀπὸ τοῦ ἡλίου φλόγα καθαρὰν καὶ ἀμίαντον. See also Plut. *Arist.* 20, and *Camil.* 20.

The ever-burning fire which these sacred edifices contained, symbolising the family hearth (Ϝεστία), or centre of home

The cult of Vesta.

Sacred fires.

Origin of Vesta.

life, was probably derived from some long-forgotten prehistoric period when the use of flint and steel was unknown, and fire could only be kindled by the slow and laborious use of the fire-drill.[1]

Prehistoric custom.

During this primitive time a village would naturally guard against the misfortune of finding itself without fire by combining to keep up and watch in some sheltered hut an ever-burning fire, from which the villagers might at any time relight their extinguished embers. This hut would for general convenience be set in the centre of the village, and would soon acquire a sacred character, and develop into the most important feature of a religious cult.

Guardians of the fire.

To watch this fire would naturally be the duty of women, especially of those who were not burdened with the cares of maternity. Hence may have arisen the institution of virgin priestesses, whose most important duty it was to feed the sacred fire. A survival of this prehistoric custom appears to have existed in the rule which enacted that, if the sacred fire ever did go out, it was to be rekindled by the primitive method of friction, and the negligent Vestal was to be punished by scourging. In later times the much easier method of relighting by a burning glass or concave mirror was permitted; Plut. *Numa*, 9. In either case the rekindling was done by the Pontifex Maximus.

In spite of the Vestals' care the sacred fire was sometimes allowed to go out; see Livy, xxviii. 11, who records that this happened in 206 B.C., and that the Vestal during whose night-watch the fire went out was scourged by command of the Pontifex P. Licinius.

New fire.

One of these methods was also adopted once a year, at the beginning of the new year, on the 1st of March, when the

---

[1] The fire-drill (ἀχάλκευτον τρύπανον) obtained a spark by the friction of a pointed stick of hard wood, which was made to drill a hole in a softer piece of wood by the help of a bow, a method still in use among some savage races.

Fire of Vesta was solemnly extinguished and relighted by the Pontifex; Ovid, *Fast.* iii. 137-145. The same practice also existed in Greece with regard to the similar sacred fire which was kept burning in the *Prytaneum*; see a very valuable paper on the Prytaneum and Vestal fires by J. G. Frazer, *Jour. Philol.*, 1886, vol. xiv. p. 146.

A similar custom still exists in the Roman Catholic Church. *Easter fire.* At Easter, on Holy Saturday, all the lights in each church are put out, and then a new flame is produced with flint and steel by the priest, who first lights the Paschal candle, and then, from it, the other lamps and candles in the church.

According to tradition the *Temple of Vesta* was founded by Numa, who transferred the centre of this cult from Alba Longa[1] to Rome, together with the four Vestal Virgins, its *Vestal Virgins.* priestesses; Plut. *Num.* 10; Dionys. ii. 65; Livy, i. 20; and Ov. *Fast.* iii. 46.

One of the later kings, Tarquinius Priscus or Servius Tullius, increased the number of the Vestals to six; see Dionys. ii. 67, and Plut. *Num.* 10.[2]

The conditions under which these highly honoured priestesses were selected, according to Aulus Gellius,[3] were these :—

1. The future Vestal had to be more than six and less *Qualifications.* than ten years old.
2. She had to be both *patrima* and *matrima*; having, that is, both parents alive, and of free birth.
3. Free from all physical or mental defects.
4. Not the sister of an existing Vestal, and not the daughter of an augur, flamen, or other important member of the priesthood.

---

[1] Alba Longa appears to have been the oldest of the Latin colonies in Latium.

[2] Very interesting accounts of the Vestals and their cult are given by Plutarch in his lives of *Romulus*, *Numa*, and *Camillus*.

[3] Aul. Gell. i. 12. 1 ; and Suet. *Aug.* 31.

Election of Vestals. She was chosen (*capta*) by the Pontifex Maximus, either by lot from a number of candidates in accordance with the (to us) unknown provisions of the *Lex Papia*, or, in exceptional cases, accepted as a gift from her parents.[1] How highly the honours and privileges of a Vestal Virgin were valued may be guessed from the fact that Tiberius in 19 A.D. gave to the daughter of Fonteius Agrippa a sum equal to over £80,000 to console her for her rejection by the Senate, when she was a candidate for this office.

At the *inauguratio* the child was robed in white, and her hair cut off; though, as appears from the recently discovered statues, it was allowed to grow afterwards. For a time her name was changed to *Amata*,[2] "the loved one."

Privileges of Vestals. The following were the principal privileges and advantages enjoyed by the Vestals:—

They possessed a large amount of endowed property;[3] and lived in a style of splendour and luxury.

The child-Vestal, immediately after her consecration (*inauguratio*), was free from the *patria potestas*, and gained the *jus testamenti faciundi*.[4] A duty, perhaps, rather than a privilege, was the power to give evidence *in foro et judicio*.[5]

They led by no means a cloistered or retired life; at the circus, theatre, and amphitheatre they enjoyed the post of honour by the side of the empress.[6] The Vestals, however, were usually excluded from the contests of nude athletes. This rule was broken through by Nero; see Suet. *Nero*, 12.

They were allowed the use of wheeled carriages, even when this was a rare privilege; on State occasions they rode in *plostra*,[7] but usually used the *currus arcuatus*, as well as the more humble sedan-chair.

If, while riding in the city, a Vestal met a criminal being

[1] See Tac. *Ann.* ii. 86.
[2] Aul. Gell. i. 12. 14, and 19.
[3] Livy, i. 20, and Tac. *Ann.* iv. 16.
[4] Aul. Gell. i. 12. 9.
[5] Tac. *Ann.* xi. 34.
[6] *Ibid.* iv. 16; Suet. *Aug.* 44.
[7] *Cor. In. Lat.* i. 121; and cf. Suet. *Tib.* 2.

led to death, she could set him free; but not unless the *Privileges of Vestals.*
meeting were an accidental one.¹

Their carriages and horses were free from tax; as is recorded on a bronze tablet, probably once fixed to a Vestal's carriage, with the inscription—

FLAVIAE · PVBLICIAE · V · V · MAXIMAE
IMMVNIS · IN · IVGO ²

The Vestals played an important part in all religious and State ceremonies, and possessed a considerable amount of patronage and much influence even in mundane matters, as is indicated on some of the inscribed pedestals of the statues of Chief Vestals found in the *Atrium Vestae*; see vol. i. p. 325. The Vestal Virgins were also the guardians of many important State documents, such as the emperor's will.³ *Influence of the Vestals.*

An offence against the person of a Vestal was punished by death, and they possessed the rare privilege of intramural burial.

The title of the Vestals was *Virgines et Sacerdotes*:⁴ on other inscriptions they are called *Castae Virgines perpetui nutrices et conservatrices ignis.*

The Vestal's vow was made for a period of thirty years, at the expiration of which she was free to resign her office, and even marry: this, however, was very rarely done. The thirty years were divided into three decades, during the first of which the novice learned her duties, during the second *Period of office.*

¹ Plut. *Num.* 10; and cf. Pliny, *Hist. Nat.* xxviii. 13.

² *Cor. In. Lat.* vi. 2147. This is the same lady to whom six of the pedestals mentioned below are inscribed.

Another similar bronze plate, recording that the carriage of Calpurnia Praetextata, Chief Vestal, was free from tax, is preserved in the Museum of the Collegio Romano (Museo Kircheriano).

³ See inscription of *Ancyra, Res gestae Augusti,* ed. Mommsen, Berlin, 1883.

⁴ *Cor. In. Lat.* vi. 2145.

practised them, and during the third taught them to her younger sisters. The senior Vestal was called *Virgo Vestalis Maxima*.[1]

Sacred relics. Serv. Aen. vii. 188. In the care of the Vestals were also some of the seven mysterious relics which formed the *fatale pignus Romani imperii*.[2] Dionysius[3] says, εἰσὶ δέ τινες οἵ φασιν ἔξω τοῦ πυρὸς ἀπόρρητα τοῖς πολλοῖς ἱερὰ κεῖσθαί τινα ἐν τῷ τεμένει τῆς θεᾶς· ὧν οἵ τε ἱεροφάνται τὴν γνῶσιν ἔχουσι καὶ αἱ παρθένοι. The seven relics were *the Palladium, the sceptre of Priam, the veil of Ilione, the Ancilia of Mars, the Ashes of Orestes*, the sacred *acus*, and *the terra-cotta Quadriga* made for the pediment of the Temple of Jupiter Capitolinus. The first three appear to have been guarded by the Vestals. The chief of them was believed to be the *Palladium*, the "signum de coelo delapsum" of Cicero,[4] brought by Aeneas from Troy.[5]

Burial alive. The penalty for a breach of chastity was the horrible one of being buried alive in a subterranean chamber at a place near the Colline Gate, known as the Campus Sceleratus; see Livy, viii. 15 and xxii. 57; Plut. *Num.* 10; Dionys. x. 40; and Suet. *Dom.* 8. Pliny (*Epis.* iv. 11) gives a most vivid and pathetic account of how the chief of the Vestals, named Cornelia, was treated in this way by order of Domitian, on bare suspicion, as a mere mad freak, and without a trial. Her supposed lover, a man of equestrian rank, was scourged to death on the *Comitium*;[6] see below, p. 305, note 1.

Temple of Vesta. The *Temple of Vesta or Hestia*, Ϝεστία, the personification of the Hearth, was an *aedes sacra*, not a *templum* in the strict sense of the word. It had never received *inauguratio* or consecration by the Augurs, probably on account of its excep-

---

[1] See Pliny, *Ep.* vii. 19, on the care taken of Vestals who were seriously ill, and who needed change of air.
[2] Livy, xxvi. 27.   [3] Dionys. ii. 66.   [4] *Phil.* xi. 10, 24.
[5] See also Dionys. i. 67; Plut. *Camil.* 20; and Ovid, *Trist.* iii. 1, 29—
"Hic locus est Vestae qui Pallada servat et ignem."
[6] For another similar case see Livy, xxii. 57.

tional sanctity and prehistoric antiquity of foundation. Its founder was said to have been the mythical Numa; Servius, *Ad Aen.* vii. 153; and Aul. Gell. xiv. 7.

The circular form of the shrine (*tholus*) symbolised the round earth, and its dome the canopy of heaven.[1] The sacred fire-altar of Vesta occupied the place of a statue of the goddess.[2] The fire was a sort of religious centre of Roman worship, the common hearth (*focus publicus*) of the whole Roman people; see Cic. *De Leg.* ii. 8, 20. The great Festival of Vesta, the *Vestalia*, was celebrated on the 9th of July.

Fire-altar.

The original temple was destroyed by the Gauls in 390 B.C., when the Vestals escaped to Caere in a waggon, having first buried the *Palladium* (*fatale pignus*) in a clay vessel or *dolium* in the Forum, a spot which afterwards became sacred under the name *doliola*; Livy, v. 40, and Plut. *Camil.* 20.

History of temple.

The temple was burnt again in 241 B.C., when Lucius Metellus, who was then Pontifex Maximus, saved the sacred relics from the flames at the expense of his own eyesight; Dionys. ii. 66, and Pliny, *Hist. Nat.* vii. 141.

The temple was again burnt in the great fire of Nero's reign (Tac. *Ann.* xv. 39-41, and Suet. *Nero*, 38), and lastly in 191 A.D., in the reign of Commodus (Herodian, I. xiv. 4); after which it was rebuilt by Severus, to which period the existing marble fragments belong.

[1] The word *tholus*, θόλος, was applied by the Greeks to circular buildings, like the Roman *Temple of Vesta*. The most important example was the magnificent *Tholus* in the *Asclepieion* of Epidaurus, built by the grandson (probably) of the famous Polycleitus in the first half of the fourth century B.C.; see Pausan. ii. 27. 3. In design it is like a magnified version of the Temple of Vesta with an *internal* as well as an *external* ring of columns. The important remains which still exist were excavated in 1887 to 1889.

[2] "Effigiem nullam Vesta nec ignis habet"; Ov. *Fast.* vi. 298. In the same way the Temple of Vesta at Hermione had a sacred fire, but no statue; see Pausan. ii. 35. 2.

practised them, and during the third taught them to her younger sisters. The senior Vestal was called *Virgo Vestalis Maxima*.¹

Sacred relics. Serv. Aen. vii. 188.   In the care of the Vestals were also some of the seven mysterious relics which formed the *fatale pignus Romani imperii*.² Dionysius³ says, εἰσὶ δέ τινες οἵ φασιν ἔξω τοῦ πυρὸς ἀπόρρητα τοῖς πολλοῖς ἱερὰ κεῖσθαί τινα ἐν τῷ τεμένει τῆς θεᾶς· ὧν οἵ τε ἱεροφάνται τὴν γνῶσιν ἔχουσι καὶ αἱ παρθένοι. The seven relics were *the Palladium, the sceptre of Priam, the veil of Ilione, the Ancilia of Mars, the Ashes of Orestes*, the sacred *acus*, and *the terra-cotta Quadriga* made for the pediment of the Temple of Jupiter Capitolinus. The first three appear to have been guarded by the Vestals. The chief of them was believed to be the *Palladium*, the "signum de coelo delapsum" of Cicero,⁴ brought by Aeneas from Troy.⁵

Burial alive.   The penalty for a breach of chastity was the horrible one of being buried alive in a subterranean chamber at a place near the Colline Gate, known as the Campus Sceleratus; see Livy, viii. 15 and xxii. 57; Plut. *Num.* 10; Dionys. x. 40; and Suet. *Dom.* 8. Pliny (*Epis.* iv. 11) gives a most vivid and pathetic account of how the chief of the Vestals, named Cornelia, was treated in this way by order of Domitian, on bare suspicion, as a mere mad freak, and without a trial. Her supposed lover, a man of equestrian rank, was scourged to death on the *Comitium*;⁶ see below, p. 305, note 1.

Temple of Vesta.   The *Temple of Vesta* or *Hestia*, Ϝεστία, the personification of the Hearth, was an *aedes sacra*, not a *templum* in the strict sense of the word. It had never received *inauguratio* or consecration by the Augurs, probably on account of its excep-

---

¹ See Pliny, *Ep.* vii. 19, on the care taken of Vestals who were seriously ill, and who needed change of air.
² Livy, xxvi. 27.   ³ Dionys. ii. 66.   ⁴ *Phil.* xi. 10, 24.
⁵ See also Dionys. i. 67; Plut. *Camil.* 20; and Ovid, *Trist.* iii. 1, 29—
"Hic locus est Vestae qui Pallada servat et ignem."
⁶ For another similar case see Livy, xxii. 57.

tional sanctity and prehistoric antiquity of foundation. Its founder was said to have been the mythical Numa ; Servius, *Ad Aen.* vii. 153 ; and Aul. Gell. xiv. 7.

The circular form of the shrine (*tholus*) symbolised the round earth, and its dome the canopy of heaven.[1] The sacred fire-altar of Vesta occupied the place of a statue of the goddess.[2] The fire was a sort of religious centre of Roman worship, the common hearth (*focus publicus*) of the whole Roman people ; see Cic. *De Leg.* ii. 8, 20. The great Festival of Vesta, the *Vestalia*, was celebrated on the 9th of July.

Fire-altar.

The original temple was destroyed by the Gauls in 390 B.C., when the Vestals escaped to Caere in a waggon, having first buried the *Palladium* (*fatale pignus*) in a clay vessel or *dolium* in the Forum, a spot which afterwards became sacred under the name *doliola* ; Livy, v. 40, and Plut. *Camil.* 20.

History of temple.

The temple was burnt again in 241 B.C., when Lucius Metellus, who was then Pontifex Maximus, saved the sacred relics from the flames at the expense of his own eyesight; Dionys. ii. 66, and Pliny, *Hist. Nat.* vii. 141.

The temple was again burnt in the great fire of Nero's reign (Tac. *Ann.* xv. 39-41, and Suet. *Nero*, 38), and lastly in 191 A.D., in the reign of Commodus (Herodian, I. xiv. 4); after which it was rebuilt by Severus, to which period the existing marble fragments belong.

[1] The word *tholus*, θόλος, was applied by the Greeks to circular buildings, like the Roman *Temple of Vesta*. The most important example was the magnificent *Tholus* in the *Asclepieion* of Epidaurus, built by the grandson (probably) of the famous Polycleitus in the first half of the fourth century B.C. ; see Pausan. ii. 27. 3. In design it is like a magnified version of the Temple of Vesta with an *internal* as well as an *external* ring of columns. The important remains which still exist were excavated in 1887 to 1889.

[2] "Effigiem nullam Vesta nec ignis habet"; Ov. *Fast.* vi. 298. In the same way the Temple of Vesta at Hermione had a sacred fire, but no statue ; see Pausan. ii. 35. 2.

In the time of the elder Pliny its dome was remarkable for its gilded tiles of Syracusan bronze; *Hist. Nat.* xxxiv. 13.

Palladium. The *Palladium* was only once seen by profane eyes; this happened during the reign of Commodus, when the Vestals with difficulty saved it from the fire which devastated this end of the *Forum Romanum* and the whole of Vespasian's *Forum Pacis*. On this occasion Herodian tells us (I. xiv. 4) γυμνωθὲν ὤφθη τὸ τῆς Παλλάδος ἄγαλμα.

Coin types. From its representations on coins the *Palladium* appears

Fig. 39.

First Brass struck by Antoninus Pius in memory of Faustina the Elder, with *rev.* Vesta holding the Palladium.

to have been a wooden *xoanon* of the usual stiff archaic type, a standing figure of Pallas holding a spear.

Fig. 39 shows the *rev.* of a First Brass struck by Antoninus Pius in honour of his dead wife, Diva Faustina. A Vestal is standing holding the *Palladium* with one hand, while with the other she pours from a *patera* a libation on to the sacred fire.[1] A very beautiful seated figure of Vesta is shown on the *reverse* of a gold coin (*aureus*) of Sabina. The goddess, draped in *stola* and *pallium*, and with veiled head, sits in a throne holding in one hand the *Palladium* and in the other a long sceptre (*hasta pura*); legend VESTA.[2]

[1] The specimen of this coin here represented was found by the present writer in the Forum close by the Temple of Vesta.

[2] Statues of Hestia or Vesta are hardly known to exist among the ex-

THE TEMPLE OF VESTA

The Temple of Vesta is shown on bronze medallions of *Form of the temple.* Faustina the elder, Lucilla, Crispina, and Julia Domna; see Froehner, *Médaillons de l'Empire Romain*, Paris, 1878, pp. 76, 96, 148, and 159. It is also represented on a marble relief now in the Uffizi at Florence. These, with the help of the existing concrete *podium*, and marble fragments of columns, entablature, and *lacunaria*, enable a fairly accurate restoration of the temple to be made; see fig. 40. It closely resembles the round temple in the *Forum Boarium* by the Tiber,[1] which used formerly to be mistaken for the *Temple of Vesta*, on account of Horace's lines, *Od.* I. ii. 13—

> *Vidimus flavum Tiberim retortis*
> *Littore Etrusco violenter undis*
> *Ire dejectum monumenta regis*
> *Templaque Vestae.*

The great flood of 1877 showed, however, that even now the waters of the Tiber could reach to this point in the Forum. Martial (*Ep.* i. 71, 3) clearly describes this site—

> *Quaeris iter? Dicam. Vicinum Castora canae*
> *Transibis Vestae, virgineamque domum.*

The "*virginea domus*" is the House of the Vestals or *Atrium Vestae.*

The existing architectural fragments are of poor workman- *Existing remains.* tant sculpture of the Graeco-Roman period. The celebrated "*Giustiniani Hestia*" (Torlonia Collection) has been so called on the slightest possible grounds. This very beautiful Greek statue has no attributes to distinguish it, and may possibly be a portrait statue of a priestess, not a deity at all. The treatment of the hair has a distinctly eikonic appearance.

[1] During the fifteenth and sixteenth centuries the *Forum Romanum* was often confused with the *Forum Boarium*; partly perhaps from its mediaeval name, the *Campo Vaccino*, which was taken to be a translation of *Forum Boarium*. The so-called *Tomb of S. Luke* at Ephesus, a Roman temple of about the time of Severus, was almost an exact copy of the Temple of Vesta; only scanty remains of it now exist.

Rex was near the *clivus* in the direction of the *Arch of Titus*; it is used to define the eastern end of the *Sacra Via* in its early limited sense; see above, p. 244.

The Domus given to the Vestals. When Augustus became Pontifex Maximus in 12 B.C. he preferred to live in his house on the Palatine, and he presented the *Domus Publica* to the Vestals because it adjoined their house—τὴν μέντοι τοῦ βασιλέως τῶν ἱερῶν (οἰκίαν) ταῖς ἀειπαρθένοις ἔδωκεν, ἐπειδὴ ὁμότοιχος ταῖς οἰκήσεσιν αὐτῶν ἦν; Dion Cass. liv. 27. In this passage again there appears to be a confusion between the house of the *Pontiff* and that of the *Rex Sacrorum*. It was the former which Augustus, as *Pontifex*, gave up to the Vestals, and yet Dion Cassius' phrase, τοῦ βασιλέως τῶν ἱερῶν οἰκίαν, suggests rather the house of the *Rex Sacrificulus*.

The Domus destroyed. The Vestal Virgins appear, soon after they received the gift of Augustus, to have pulled down the *Domus Publica*, and rebuilt their house on an enlarged scale, partly covering the site of the *Domus*. Thus the lower part of some of its walls and columns and some of its mosaic pavings have been preserved, owing to the fact that the house of the Vestals was built over it with floors at a rather higher level, thus covering and protecting the mosaics and other relics of the more ancient *Domus*.

The position of the very interesting remains of a house, which has been pulled down in order that the *Atrium Vestae* might be extended over its site, seems exactly to suit what we know of the position and history of the *Domus Publica*; see *Diagonal axis.* fig. 41. It will be seen that it is set at quite a different angle from the later buildings around it; its axis sloping diagonally towards the *Temple of Vesta*.

This diagonal axis coincides with that of the true *Regia*, the very interesting marble building the identification of which we owe to Mr. F. M. Nichols; see below, vol. i. p. 306. *Sacra Via.* Recent excavations have shown that the old line of the *Sacra Via* never passed, as had been thought, close by the *Temple of*

Vesta, between it and the true *Regia*; but there is reason to believe that it once did pass close by the north side of the marble *Regia*, and thus the diagonal axis both of the *Regia* and the *Domus Publica* was probably fixed by the older direction of the *Sacra Via*.

In later times, when the Temple of Divus Julius was built, the line of the *Sacra Via* was diverted at this place, and part of its original course built over; see above, p. 225.

Existing remains of the *Domus* are of several different dates, which can easily be distinguished; *first*, walls built of large blocks, 2 Roman feet thick, of soft tufa, the earliest building material used in Rome; these belong probably to the regal period. They are rapidly crumbling away. *Second*, walls of blocks of hard tufa, part perhaps of the rebuilding after 390 B.C. or after 210 B.C., the blocks are from 18 to 22 inches thick, and vary in length from 3 feet 6 inches to 4 feet; and *lastly*, concrete walls faced with brick, and columns of travertine, both free and engaged, with a large quantity of fine mosaic paving of the first century B.C.

The brick facing of this part is of special interest as being one of the earliest existing examples of the use of brick in Rome. The triangular bricks are from 1½ to 1¾ inch thick, and about 12 inches long. The joints average nearly ¾ inch in thickness. The concrete wall, which these bricks are used to face, is composed of lime, *pozzolana*, and fragments of broken brick. The fact that this house was apparently destroyed in the reign of Augustus gives it, at least in one direction, a date. All its constructional details agree with this supposition. The brickwork resembles that of the *Rostra* of 44 B.C., and of the Pantheon dated 27 B.C., these being the three earliest examples of brickwork in Rome to which a date can be given with any degree of certainty.

The existing remains are not sufficient to show more than fragments of the plan of this house, which is one of the earliest existing specimens of domestic architecture in Rome. At one

Remains of the Domus. point there is a small room, one side of which is open, with two travertine fluted columns, arranged like those in the *Tablinum* of the *Atrium Vestae*. In front of the engaged columns at another part of the house, a travertine channel or open gutter for rain-water is still preserved.

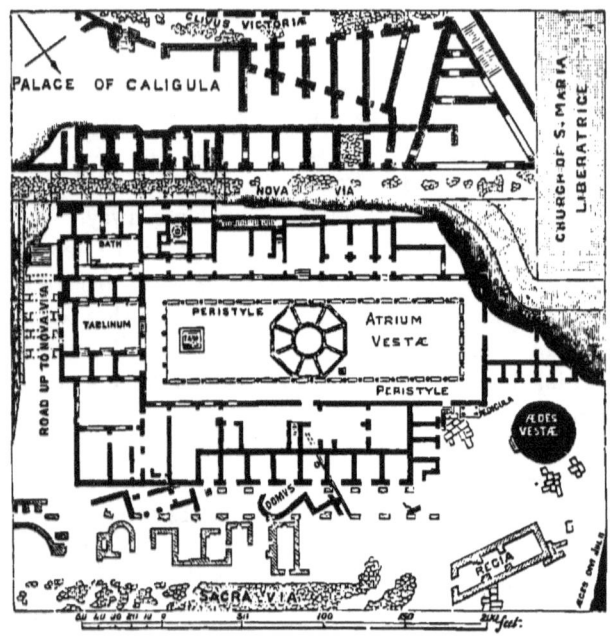

Fig. 41.

Plan showing the Remains of the Temple of Vesta, the Domus Publica, and the House of the Vestals, as rebuilt by Hadrian, excavated 1883-84.

Painted stucco. All the materials, tufa, travertine, or brick facing, were covered thickly with stucco, both inside and outside the house, and were coloured with bright tints and painted ornaments. The columns were coloured crimson, the rain-water channel bright blue, and the inner walls had simple paintings of leaf ornaments, wreaths, and flowers, the surface being divided into panels, with circles or garlands in the centre. Iron nails are driven into the joints of the brick facing all over the face of the walls, in the usual Roman way, to form a key for the painted stucco.

The mosaic floors, now rapidly disappearing, together with the paintings on the walls, were visible in many places, not only by the existing walls of the *Domus Publica*, but also in some of the line of shops which form part of one side of the House of the Vestals. These mosaics have simple patterns, lozenges, hexagons, or squares in white limestone and grey basalt. In the little brick-faced apse there is a graceful flowing scrollwork of foliage; other floors are made of hard white cement (*caementum marmoreum*) studded with irregular-shaped bits of the then rare Oriental coloured marbles.

Mosaic floors.

The fitting is very neat, and the *tesserae* of the mosaic patterns are very small, closely resembling the other early specimens of mosaic in Rome, namely, those in the *Temple of Castor*, and the so-called "*House of Livia*" on the Palatine. In the *Triclinium* of the latter the floor is similarly sprinkled with small irregularly-shaped bits of Oriental marbles and alabaster set on a white ground.[1]

These are all exceptionally interesting examples of mosaics of the time of Augustus, very rare among the existing mosaic

[1] Unhappily, these very interesting remains have already suffered much from exposure, the painted stucco has mostly fallen off, and the mosaics have been broken up wholesale, partly by the weather and also from injury done by visitors, both accidentally and wilfully. A paper by the present writer in *Archaeologia* (vol. xlix. 1886, pp. 391 to 422) is illustrated with a series of coloured plates showing the remains of the *Domus Publica* and the *Temple* and *Atrium Vestae*, with many details of the ornament and construction employed in these buildings. The greater part, both of the coloured decoration and of the mosaic pavings, have vanished since these drawings were made, so they have already become a record of some value. For example, no trace now remains of the red colouring on the engaged travertine columns, or of the brilliant blue pigment on the water channel.

Early mosaics. pavements of Rome, which in almost all cases belong to a later date and are very inferior in delicacy of workmanship. These early mosaics have rather more than three *tesserae* to the inch.

The fine, close-grained limestone which is used for the grounds in this and other early mosaics, occurs in thin beds among the travertine rocks all around Tivoli.

THE REGIA.

One of the most important discoveries of recent years with regard to this most interesting part of Rome has been due to the very able antiquary, Mr. F. M. Nichols, who was the first *The Regia.* to point out that remains still exist of the *Regia*[1] properly so called, that is, the official *Fanum* or "Chapter House"—not the residence of the *Pontifex Maximus*.[2]

Like the Temple of Vesta, the *Regia* was said to have been originally built by the mythical King Numa; see Plut. *Num.* 14. Ovid (*Trist.* III. i. 28) describes this part of the borders of the *Forum*—

> *Haec est a sacris quae via nomen habet,*
> *Hic locus est Vestae qui Pallada servat et ignem,*
> *Hic fuit antiqui Regia parva Numae.*

Site of the Regia. The *Regia* is recorded to have stood close by the Forum, at one end of that part of the road which was in early time more specially called the *Sacra Via*; see above, p. 224.

[1] See No. 50 on the *Forum Plan.*

[2] For a full account of Mr. Nichols' valuable discoveries see *Bull. dell' Imp. Istituto Arch. Germ.* vol. i. 1886, p. 94; and *Archaeologia*, vol. 50, 1887. Mr. Nichols' arguments as to the *Regia* proper being distinct from the *Domus Publica* or dwelling of the Pontifex are quite convincing.

In the same volume of the *Bullettino*, 1886, p. 99 *seq.*, there is a valuable paper on the *Regia* and its remains by the late Prof. H. Jordan, whose premature death has been so great a loss to the science of Roman archaeology.

Appian (*Bell. Civ.* ii. 149) tells us that the ancient *Regia* stood on the spot in the *Forum* where the body of Julius Caesar was burnt, and that the *Temple of Julius* was afterwards erected in the same place; see also Dion Cass. xlvii. 18. *Older Regia.*

In 36 B.C., after his triumph for victories in Spain, Cn. Domitius Calvinus rebuilt the *Regia* in a more magnificent way than before.

At this time its site was moved a little to the east, the old site being occupied by the *Temple of Julius*. As Mr. Nichols has pointed out, the existing remains of the *Regia* evidently belong to this rebuilding by Calvinus.

The *Regia*, which was the *Fanum* or sanctuary and public office of the *Pontifex*, consisted of the following parts—(i.) a "Chapter House" or council chamber for the *Pontifices*; see Pliny, *Epis.* iv. 11, 6;[1] (ii.) a *Tabularium* or record-office for the *Fasti* and other State documents; (iii.) a *Sacrarium of Mars*, in which the sacred spears of Mars were deposited; Aul. Gell. iv. 6; (iv.) a *Sacrarium* of the goddess *Ops-consiva*, which none might enter except the *Pontifex Maximus* and the *Vestal Virgins*; Varro, *Lin. Lat.* vi. 3. *Uses of the Regia.*

The *Regia* was a place of the very highest sanctity, and much important ritual was performed there. Thus, for example, on the Kalends of every month the *Regina Sacrorum*, the wife of the *Rex Sacrificulus*, offered in the *Regia* the sacrifice of a sow or a ewe-lamb to *Juno Lucina*, to whom the monthly Kalends were sacred.[2] *Ritual in the Regia.*

Though the *Domus Publica* or dwelling of the *Pontifex*, which appears to have closely adjoined the *Regia*, was given

---

[1] In this most interesting letter Pliny describes how an unhappy *Virgo Vestalis Maxima* was condemned to be buried alive. As an example of the illegality of the whole procedure Pliny notes that though Domitian condemned the chief Vestal *Pontificis Maximi jure*, yet he summoned the council of the *Pontifices* to meet, not in the *Regia*, but in his own Alban Villa, *reliquos Pontifices, non in Regiam, sed in Albanam villam convocavit.*

[2] On the *Rex Sacrificulus* see Livy, ii. 2.

up to the Vestals by Augustus and destroyed in or soon after his time, the *Regia* proper existed till long after. It is mentioned by Solinus (*Polyhis.* i. 21), *Regia quae adhuc ita appellatur*; and a fragment of the marble plan of Severus has on it the word [R]EGIA.

Existing remains. Existing Remains of the Regia. The remains of the building which Mr. Nichols has so skilfully identified as being those of the *Regia* are unfortunately very fragmentary, but with the help of excavation a great part of its plan has been made out; see Mr. Nichols' papers quoted above at p. 304. They consist mainly of one block, not quite rectangular in plan, but with one, the eastern end, set out of the square. This block, which measured about 25 feet by 65 feet 6 inches along the longest side, was divided into three rooms, about half the length being occupied by the larger room at the west end. To the north of this block are remains of a pavement of marble slabs which appear to have belonged to another chamber. At the west end of the block, near the *Temple of Julius*, there are scanty remains of a wall of *opus quadratum*, and another of concrete faced with *opus reticulatum*. The position of these remains is marked on the *Forum Plan*, see No. 50.

One portion only still exists to any great height above the ground; this is part of the parti-wall which separated the two smaller chambers at the eastern end. This wall, together *Marble wall.* with the jambs of its central doorway, is built of solid blocks of white Luna marble, with draughted joints, very neatly fitted, and bedded in a thin layer of lime mortar. The largest fragment which remains is 8 feet 7 inches high, and consists of five courses of these fine blocks of marble. They have fortunately been preserved by being worked into a later brick and concrete structure.

Plan of the Regia. The rest of the plan Mr. Nichols mostly discovered in 1886 by the help of excavation, which enabled him to trace the underground foundations of the missing marble walls.

The foundations consist of massive, well-jointed blocks of *tufa*. Within the chambers the pavement, part of which exists, was formed by large slabs of greyish marble.

The construction of this building, which consisted of solid blocks of marble from 22 to 23 inches deep, after the Greek fashion, is very exceptional in Rome, where, as a rule, marble is used rather in the form of facing slabs than of solid blocks. The circular temple by the Tiber in the *Forum Boarium* is one of the very few other examples of this more magnificent use of marble which still exist.

Marble blocks.

It is most probable, as Mr. Nichols has suggested, that the great marble blocks inscribed with the *Consular Fasti*, now in the Capitoline Museum, originally formed part of the walls of the marble *Regia*. This inscription is recorded to have been found at or near this spot in 1546; and the fact that it is cut, not on slabs, but on blocks of Luna marble, is strong evidence in favour of its having belonged to this exceptionally solid marble building; see MS. of Pirro Ligorio quoted by Fea, *Illustrazioni sui Fasti*, Rome, 1820.

Consular Fasti.

Mr. Nichols also suggests that the very beautiful marble fragments near the Temple of Castor (see above, p. 283) may have been part of the architectural decorations of the *Regia*; he shows the possibility of this by an illustration in his very valuable paper in vol. l. of *Archaeologia*, p. 247. But, according to the evidence of Labacco, writing in 1557, it appears that these fragments were found in or near the Forum of Nerva; if so, they can hardly have belonged to the *Regia*.

ATRIUM VESTAE.

The *Atrium Vestae*, or *House of the Vestals*, was excavated in 1883-84: it is on the whole the most important example of domestic architecture that has yet been discovered; in one respect, that of having a great part of the upper story

Atrium Vestae.

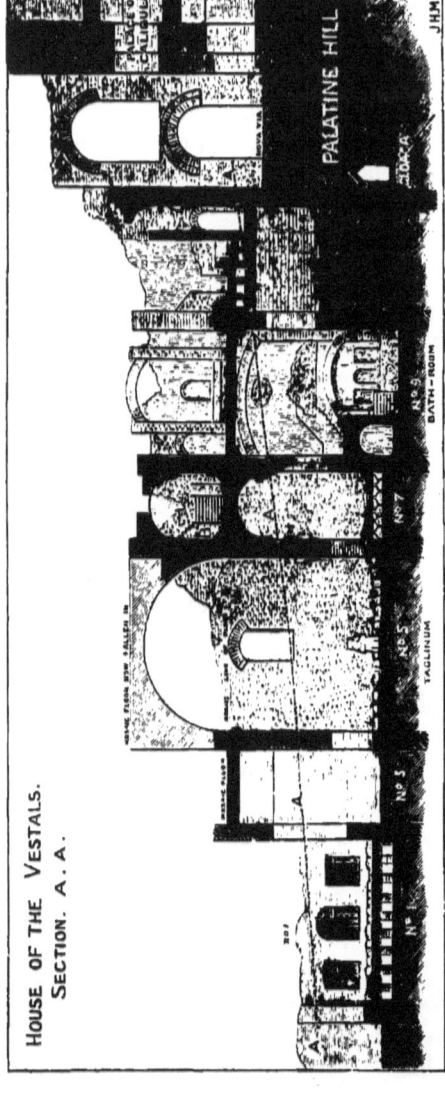

Fig. 42.

Section across the Atrium Vestae, taken through the Tablinum; see fig. 41

AAA. Line of road behind the Tablinum.
B. Stairs to upper rooms now destroyed.
1. Large hall with niches for statues.
3. Small room opening into Tablinum (5).
7 is the room with the floor supported on half Amphorae.
9 is the lower bath-room.

The upper bath-room, near the *Nova Via*, is shown to a large scale in fig. 66, vol. ii. p. 124.

preserved, it surpasses in completeness any of the Pompeian houses.

The House of the Vestals, the *Virginea domus* of Martial (*Ep.* i. 71, 3), was more than once burnt and rebuilt, usually sharing the fate of the Temple of Vesta. It is recorded to have been burnt in the great fire of 191 A.D., during the reign of Commodus, but it can have been only the upper stories that suffered seriously then, as the existing very extensive ground-floor of the *Atrium Vestae*, and even parts of the upper rooms, are shown by the character of the brick facing and by the stamps on the bricks to be of the time of Hadrian. Nothing now existing appears to be earlier than this, and the whole house was evidently rebuilt, probably on a much enlarged scale, during Hadrian's reign.

Atrium Vestae.

In order to gain increased space a great part of the lower slopes of the Palatine was then cut away, and an artificially levelled area of very large extent was formed at the foot of the hill. The amount of earth removed during this process must have been very great. The result is that the house is set against the side of the hill in such a way that its south-west side stands against an artificially scarped cliff, about 20 feet high, so that the upper floor of the house is about level with the *Nova Via*, which runs along the brink of this artificial cliff (see fig. 42). The *Tablinum* end of the *Atrium Vestae* is also set, as it were, into the side of the hill, in a similar way to the south-west side. Thus the sill of the end window, which is high above the *Tablinum* floor, is nearly level with the ground outside.

Hill cut away.

The whole of this side of the Palatine has been greatly altered from its natural contour. It is cut into the form of four gigantic steps or stages, the lowest being the ground-floor of the *Atrium Vestae*, the second the *Nova Via*, the third the *Clivus Victoriae*, and the fourth the summit of the hill.

Three stages.

The plan of the *Atrium Vestae* (see fig. 41) consists of a large open *Peristyle*, with rooms all round it, two or three

Plan of the Atrium.

Peristyle. stories high. The *Peristyle* itself was like a two-storied cloister; its lower range of columns were monoliths of *cipollino* marble, and the upper tier of columns were smaller monoliths of *breccia corallina*. Many of the columns from both tiers still exist in a more or less fragmentary state, and are still to be seen in or near their original positions. The upper story of the *Peristyle* has fallen down; when complete it formed a passage or gallery of approach to the bath-rooms and bed-rooms on the upper floor. On the north-east side is the principal entrance to the House, near the *Regia* and the *Temple of Vesta*, and by it, on the outside of the building, *Shrine of Vesta.* are remains of a small *aedicula* or shrine, the brick and concrete *podium* of which, 10 feet wide by 7 feet 6 inches deep, still exists, with parts of its marble lining and moulded plinth *in situ* (see *Forum Plan*, No. 52); on this stood four columns supporting an entablature, the front and side of which now lie near the spot: on the former is inscribed, in fine letters of the time of Hadrian—

SENATVS · POPVLVSQVE · ROMANVS · PECVNIA
PVBLICA · FACIENDAM · CVRAVIT

The existing pieces include only the architrave and frieze, the cornice being lost. It seems probable that this little shrine contained a statue of Vesta, there being none within the temple. The remains of this little shrine are marked AEDICVLA on fig. 41, p. 302.

Row of shops. On the north-east side of the Atrium is a row of small shops, which have no communication with the house; though the rooms which once existed above the shops did form part of the Vestals' House. Within these shops are considerable remains of the mosaic floors of the *Domus Publica* mentioned above. At the back of these shops, and opening on to the *Peristyle*, are a number of good rooms, once very handsomely decorated with floors of marble slabs or mosaics, and with walls lined with polished marble; see fig. 41.

In some of the rooms the design of the marble wall-linings can be clearly traced from the prints which the slabs have left on the cement backing. At the bottom was a marble skirting, from 18 inches to 2 feet high; and above that the wall was lined with two tiers of tall panels, separated by bands of differently coloured marbles about a foot wide.

Wall-linings.

In some cases the panels measured about 2 feet 10 inches wide by from 5 to 6 feet in height. The prints of the marble lining are specially clear in the last excavated room on the side towards the *Nova Via*; the room, that is, which is nearest to the Church of S. Maria Liberatrice; see above, p. 86.

The whole house, in fact, with the exception of the servants' offices, was once richly ornamented, with floors and walls wholly covered with rich Oriental marbles, and having moulded plinths and cornices cut in the rarer and more brilliant kinds, such as *rosso antico* from Greece, and even the very hard porphyry and green basalt. Among the many fragments which were found during the excavations are included almost all the fine Oriental marbles, granites, porphyries, and alabasters, which were used during the period of Rome's greatest magnificence, and in many parts the walls appear to have been further decorated with the brilliant jewel-like mosaics made with *tesserae* of coloured glass.[1]

Rich marbles.

On the north-east side are remains of stairs to the long range of upper rooms which on this side have fallen. At the south-east end of the *Peristyle* is the *Tablinum*, a sort of parlour, with a semicircular barrel vault, of which only part of the springing remains; see No. 5 on fig. 42.

Tablinum.

The front of the *Tablinum* was open, with two columns, at the end towards the *Peristyle*, whence it was approached by four steps between the columns. On each side of the steps

[1] The central room on the left of the *Tablinum* is used as a store-place for these rich fragments, as well as for a number of objects in bronze, ivory, fictile ware, and marble sculpture, which were found within the *Atrium Vestae*.

marble *cancelli*, placed between the columns and the wall, screened the Tablinum from the Peristyle. Part of the marble linings of this room and the moulded architrave of its side-doors are still *in situ*, as well as much of its marble paving, which is of three different dates. One small piece near the steps is of fine *opus sectile*, with patterns of red porphyry and green basalt let into a white marble matrix.[1] Another part has a simple but carefully fitted pattern of small squares and stars of Oriental marbles; and a third is of large rudely-set slabs of inferior marbles, evidently a late restoration.

Mosaic paving.

On each side of the *Tablinum* are three small vaulted rooms, the whole number of which corresponds with that of the six Vestals, probably not accidentally. The rooms on the right, being damp from their position against the side of the slope, were carefully warmed with hot-air flues.

Six small rooms.

As an additional precaution, the floor of the central room is protected from damp rising in a very remarkable way. A number of large amphorae were sawn in halves, and the whole area of the room covered with them; on these half vases the concrete *nucleus* and the marble paving-slabs were laid, leaving underneath the empty spaces in the sawn amphorae which support the pavement; see No. 7 on fig. 42.

Hollow floor.

Large Bath-room. The next room, at the back of the three small ones, is entered from a passage by the south angle of the *Peristyle*. This is a very curious room, and must have been almost without natural light when the floor over it existed. At one end it has a large bath, once marble-lined, with five small recesses for statuettes in the wall above the bath. An arch over this bath forms a bridge to reach three rooms on the south-west side of the room, the floors of which are at a higher level in the side of the hill (see No. 9 on fig. 42). This bridge was reached by steps ascending on to the top of a long, low, vaulted passage occupying one side of the

Bath-room.

Furnace.

[1] This piece of *opus sectile* is now lost.

room; this appears to have been a furnace to warm the rooms near it and over it. The top of this furnace is paved with herring-bone brickwork; one flue passes from it straight upwards; another passes horizontally under the floor of one of the small rooms by the Tablinum. It evidently did contain a fire, but its great length and size are quite unaccountable.[1]

On to the passage from which this bath-room is entered open several small vaulted rooms, which were kitchens, bakehouses, and other offices. One room has a corn-mill (*mola versatilis*) with a circular curb round it for the slaves to walk on who turned the upper grindstone with the help of wooden levers. The space is too small to admit a horse or ass, animals which were usually used for this arduous labour. Two reliefs, on sarcophagi in the *Galleria lapidaria* in the Vatican, show how this was done—by blindfolded horses yoked to a wooden framing fixed to the upper grindstone in a rather complicated way (see fig. 43). In the adjoining room are three low corn-bins, and behind is an oven, the flue[2] of which is visible on the face of the wall behind the mill.

Slaves' offices.

Next comes a staircase leading to the upper rooms which still exist in this part of the house, and beyond it are some handsomely decorated rooms on the south-west of the *Peristyle*, one of which has a moulded plinth of *rosso antico* and other marble linings, still *in situ*; the adjoining passage has a plinth of white marble, and above that painted stucco on the walls, the colours of which, especially the orange and crimson, were very brilliant when first discovered; the designs are simple floral patterns, wreaths, and garlands arranged in panels.

Handsome rooms.

[1] This exceptionally interesting room is now shut off by an iron gate, so as not to be accessible to visitors.

[2] The flue is of socketed clay pipes, 10 inches in diameter, set in a vertical channel formed in the brick facing of the wall, and then covered over with stucco.

Painted vault.

In the last room as yet excavated, at the west angle, lies a piece of its vaulted ceiling, richly decorated with painting of a similar character; it has a very high lustre, and was apparently executed by the methods described in vol. i. p. 94.

At the end of the *Peristyle*, opposite the *Tablinum*, is a large room with *hypocaust* floor for warming it under its pave-

Fig. 43.

Corn-mill (*mola versatilis*) worked by a blindfolded horse, driven by a slave who holds a measure of flour. Above is a lamp on a bracket. This relief is on a sarcophagus, now in the long gallery in the Vatican.

ment, which is formed of simple mosaic in white and grey. Part of this end of the house is still buried.

Peristyle.

The *Peristyle*, or large open court in the centre, was once very handsome. Its shape is unusual, being very long in proportion to its width, probably on account of the available site being narrow, limited as it was in the direction of the Palatine by the *Nova Via*. This court was surrounded with large columns of the wavy green and white *cipollino*, with white marble caps, bases, and entablature; very few fragments of these exist, and only one piece of column is *in situ*, though the position of the others is marked by their massive travertine foundation-blocks. The two-storied aisle round the *Peristyle* was lined with polished marble, some of which is still in place, and was paved with simple mosaic, except near the *Tablinum*, where there is a rudely fitted floor made of slabs of many kinds of fine Oriental marbles, evidently belonging to some late restoration. *Marble columns.*

Marble floor.

A number of small columns of the beautiful *breccia corallina* were found here; these belonged to the upper story of the *Peristyle*, and stood over the larger columns of *cipollino*.

Low parapet walls, covered with marble, were built between the main columns so as to screen off the colonnade from the central area.

In the open space near the *Tablinum* end is a large marble-lined tank for the water used by the Vestals in their lustral rites, and filled every day with fresh water brought from some sacred source, such as the Fountain of Egeria. *Water tank.*

For mysterious sacred reasons the Vestals were not allowed to have water brought in lead pipes, which were regarded as a modern and therefore unhallowed innovation; Tac. *Ann.* iv. 53. In the same way the use of iron tools was prohibited, both for the Temple of Vesta and for the other very sacred circular *Temple of the Dea Dia*, in the Grove of the *Fratres Arvales*.[1] Expiatory sacrifices had to be offered, *ob ferri inlationem et elationem*, if this rule were broken; a very inconvenient survival from the primitive Bronze Age. A similar prohibition existed with regard to the *Pons Sublicius*, in which no metal clamps or rivets were allowed; see vol. ii. p. 362. So also, at certain religious ceremonies, clay vessels of archaic form and make were used, instead of *Hieratic rules.*

No iron allowed.

[1] See Henzen's edition of the inscriptions of the *Fratres Arvales*, Berlin, 1874.

cups of gold or silver, both by the Arval Brothers and the Vestals.¹

Sewers. At another point is a small well-like shaft, which communicates with a large drain running under the whole building from south to north. Another large *Cloaca* runs from near the Tablinum direct to a sewer under the *Sacra Via*, which communicated with the so-called *Cloaca Maxima*. A third large drain runs at a higher level under the *Nova Via*, skirting the Palatine side of the *Atrium Vestae*; see fig. 42.

In the centre of the *Peristyle* are remains of a curious brick structure, a circle within an octagon (see fig. 41), which looks *Flower-bed.* like part of the low curbs or borders round flower-beds. Professor Jordan has suggested that this was a miniature garden, made instead of the extensive *Lucus Vestae*, which the Vestals once possessed.² This sacred grove, which contained several shrines and altars, extended up the slopes of the Palatine, and must have been destroyed when Caligula built his enormous palace on that part of the hill which overhangs the *Atrium Vestae*. Cicero, *De Div.* i. 45, mentions this *Lucus, qui a Palatii radice in Novam Viam devexus est.*

Upper floor. The upper story of the *Atrium Vestae*, a great part of which still exists on the side by the *Nova Via*, is one of the most interesting parts of this building. It consists of a series of small rooms, all once lined with marble, most of which contain baths, and are warmed very completely with flue-tiles covering *Methods of heating.* the walls, and *hypocausts*—floors built hollow, so that hot air could circulate under them. These were arranged with furnaces at the side, or below them, so that the hot air and smoke from the fire first passed under the floor, and then up

¹ Persius (ii. 59) alludes to this hieratic use of pottery,

Aurum vasa Numae Saturniaque impulit aera,
Vestalesque urnas et Tuscum fictile mutat.

Cf. the use of flint knives to kill sacrificial victims; see Livy, i. 24 and ix. 5.

² Comm. Lanciani regards this as the foundation of an *aedicula*, built to enshrine the *Palladium*.

the flue-tiles which lined the walls, and so escaped above the roof. These are among the very few examples which still exist of *hypocausts* in an upper story. The small pillars (*pilae*) which support the floors (*suspensura*) here rest on the vaults of the rooms below, which are filled in level with concrete.

Flue-tiles.

Fig. 66, in vol. ii. p. 124, gives a detailed drawing of one of these well-preserved little bath-rooms, showing its heating arrangements and its hot water bath lined with marble.

The floor of the room over the bath-room on the ground-floor with the bridge (mentioned above, p. 312) has fallen in, but remains of it exist at the edges, showing that it was a very remarkable instance of the bold way in which the Romans used concrete. The whole of this upper floor, about 20 feet in span, consisted simply of a great slab of concrete, 14 inches thick, merely supported at its edges by rows of travertine corbels, there being no intermediate support whatever. It is treated exactly as if it were one great slab of stone.

Concrete floor.

A large and handsome marble bath opened out of this upper room; it is now approached by a wooden bridge. It is lined with slabs of *pavonazetto*, *cipollino*, *Africano*, and white marble. In the top of one of the niches above this bath there are still remains of its lining of brilliant mosaics with *tesserae* of coloured glass.

Marble bath.

Farther on, there are remains of the stairs which led to a higher level still, a room over the barrel vault of the *Tablinum*; and behind the *Tablinum* there is a well-preserved mosaic pavement of a room on this upper floor, just above the cross road which led from the *Sacra Via* up to the *Nova Via*; see fig. 42, above, on p. 308.

Third story.

This road, unexpectedly discovered in September 1884, appears to have been constructed in the time of Hadrian; it is lined with piers and brick facing of his time. But at a later period it was disused, and its upper part blocked up by buildings erected over it. It was intended only for foot-passengers, and is paved with herring-bone brickwork.

Cross road.

The travertine steps at the upper end of this road, where it joins the *Nova Via*, are a later addition; the road originally sloped up without a break.

Late repairs. The upper story of the *Atrium Vestae* contains very little, except a few pieces of bare wall, that is as early as the time of Hadrian; the greater part of it belongs to the rebuilding in the reign of Severus, after the great fire under Commodus, in 191 A.D. There are also many alterations and patchings, which appear to date from the end of the third and even the fourth century A.D. Some of the upper rooms are paved with rudely shaped bits of marble, or even old tesserae re-used, and laid on their sides instead of end-ways as they were meant to go, sure signs of a late and architecturally degraded period.

It appears, in fact, that this house continued in use even after the last Vestal had died;[1] and at the north angle of the *Peristyle* remains were found of a house which had been built *Eighth century house.* in the seventh or eighth century A.D., in the then ruined House of the Vestals.

Two of the inscribed pedestals to the Vestals had been built into the walls of this house. These pedestals still stand at the north corner, turned the wrong way; unfortunately the mediaeval walling was all destroyed as soon as it was discovered, thus obliterating a very valuable piece of historical evidence. The walls too, while they existed, explained the curious position of the two pedestals, which is now quite unaccountable without a knowledge of what has been destroyed.

Peter's pence. *Hoard of English Coins.* In this interesting mediaeval building an earthen vessel was found containing a large hoard of English silver pennies of the ninth and tenth centuries; namely, 3 of Alfred the Great (871–900); 217 of Eadward I. (900–924); 393 of Athelstan (924–940); 195 of Eadmund I. (940–946); and a few of Sitric and Anlaf, Kings of Northumbria, and Plegmund, Archbishop of Canterbury, ranging be-

[1] The last of the Vestals is mentioned as being an old woman in 394 A.D.; see Zosimus, v. 38.

tween 900 and 946 A.D. In the same pot was found a bronze fibula with an inscription inlaid in silver, + DOMNO · MARINO PAPA + Marinus II. occupied the Pontificate from 942 to 946, and it appears probable that this interesting hoard was concealed during his reign.[1]

Pope Marinus II.

PORTRAIT STATUES OF VESTALS.

One of the chief points of interest in this most important excavation was the discovery of a number of portrait statues of the Vestals, at various points in the *Peristyle*, together with many pedestals belonging to the statues, each with a dedicatory inscription. Unfortunately the manner in which they were found leaves it uncertain which statue belongs to each pedestal. The statues, which are of heroic size, range from an almost complete figure to a mere fragment; they are of various dates, mostly of the third century A.D., though one or two date from the second.

Vestals' statues.

The finest as a work of art, dating probably from the time of Trajan or Hadrian, is a very noble portrait of a stately middle-aged lady, the upper half of which only exists; see fig. 44.[2] This figure is of especial value as having the only known ancient representation of the sacred vestment called the *suffibulum*, a sort of hood made of a piece of white woollen cloth with a purple border, rectangular in form; this was folded over the head, and fastened in front below the throat

Suffibulum.

---

[1] A detailed description of these coins is given by De Rossi as an appendix to the valuable work by Lanciani, *L'Atrio di Vesta*, Rome, 1883. De Rossi has suggested that this hoard may have been sent from England to Rome as *Peter's pence*.

[2] This statue has been removed to the Museum in the Thermae of Diocletian; the others still remain (in 1891) in the peristyle of the Vestals' House. About sixteen other busts from the *Atrium Vestae* are preserved in the same room in the Museum, together with the hoard of English pennies mentioned above.

by a *fibula*. Its use as a sacrificial vestment is mentioned by Varro, *Lin. Lat.* vi. 21; and it is described by Festus, ed. Müller, p. 340—*Suffibulum est vestimentum album oblongum quod in capite virgines vestales cum sacrificant semper habere solent, idque*

Fig. 14

Portrait statue of one of the chief Vestals, showing the *suffibulum* fastened in front by a brooch.

fibula comprehendebatur. In other respects the dress of this statue resembles that of the other Vestals, but it alone has this special sacrificial garment, which was peculiar to the Vestals.

The other statues also are of unusual interest, for though

many of the museums of Europe contain so-called statues of Vestals, yet these are the only authentic ones.

Various kinds of marble are used for these statues—the native marble from the quarries of Luna, Pentelic marble from Athens, and the brilliant crystalline marble from the island of Paros. In many cases the block has not been large enough for the whole figure; extended arms, projecting folds of drapery, and especially the heads, are frequently worked out of separate pieces of marble, and carefully fixed in their place with bronze or iron dowels run with lead. The junction of the head with the body is cleverly concealed, the joint coming where the top of the *stola* reaches the neck. The upper edge of the drapery is undercut, and the head and neck dropped down into it as into a socket, thus completely hiding the union. *Technique of statues.*

The folds of the *pallium* are, in many places, much undercut, and are worked to a very thin substance, giving great spirit and lightness of effect to the drapery, but in a manner more suitable for bronze than for marble. The portraits appear to be excellent, but little idealised; a vivid life-like expression is given to them, rather at the expense of sculpturesque dignity, by the way in which the artist has carved the eyebrows in relief and has indicated both the iris and the pupil of the eye. *Style of the statues.*

The costume of all is in the main the same, though some slight variations occur. On the whole, the design of the statues and the general arrangement of the drapery is superior to their execution, showing that the sculptors (*fictores*) followed older models. The costume is as follows: a *stola* or gown reaching from the neck to the feet, bound round the waist by a cord, the *zona*; usually it is without sleeves, but in some cases there are short sleeves fastened with a row of loops and buttons. Over this is worn the *pallium*, an ample garment, folded round the body in a great variety of ways, giving great scope to the sculptor for the arrangement of graceful folds and *Costume.*

the avoiding of monotony. In many cases the *pallium* is thrown over the head like a hood; in others it is simply looped in rich folds around and diagonally across the body.

Weighted robes. In many of these statues the *pallium* has weighted tassels at its corners, apparently to improve the disposition of the folds. Count Gozzadini of Bologna has suggested that this use of weights for such large garments as the pallium and the toga is alluded to by Horace (*Ep.* I. vi. 50) in the passage—

> *Mercemur servum qui dictet nomina, laevum*
> *Qui fodiat latus, et cogat trans pondera dextram*
> *Porrigere.*

Vittae. Round the head of each Vestal the *vittae* are twisted with a varying number of turns into a sort of coronet; these were fillets or rope-like rolls of linen, the ends of which in some cases, but not in all, appear falling in front over the shoulders. The Comm. Lanciani has suggested that different degrees of dignity are indicated by the more or less numerous twists in which the *vittae* encircle the Vestals' heads.

The hair is usually hidden by the *pallium* and the *vittae*, but in some of the statues enough is visible to show that it was allowed to grow long, although on entering the noviciate the hair of the child Vestal was cut off.

The feet are shod in boots, apparently of kid or other soft leather; some have a separate division for the big toe.

Necklace. One statue, that of a tall hard-featured lady, apparently a work of the end of the third century A.D., has on the breast a number of metal pins, which show where the pendant of a necklace was fixed, though the ornament itself is missing.[1]

[1] In 1591 a statue of a Vestal, with the necklace still attached, was found on the Esquiline, together with its inscribed pedestal (*Cor. In. Lat.* vi. 2145). It is now lost. Ulisse Aldroandi also mentions that in 1556 twelve pedestals, with dedicatory inscriptions to Vestal Virgins, were found by the Church of S. Maria Liberatrice; that is, near the west angle of the *Atrium Vestae*. Probably these twelve pedestals were all burnt into lime.

All the pedestals are inscribed to the *Virgo Vestalis Maxima*, Inscribed or chief of the Vestals, a rank usually gained in order of pedestals. seniority; the inscriptions on two of the pedestals of Flavia Publicia show that several lower grades were passed through before reaching this highest dignity (*Maximatus*).

The following are the inscriptions on the pedestals:—

1. TERENTIAE · FLAVOLAE
    SORORI · SANCTISSIMAE
    Virgini Vestali MAXIMAE
    Q · LOLLIANVS · Q · F
    POLL · PLAVTIVS · AVITVS
    COS · (Consul) AVGVR · PRaetor CANDidatus
    TVTELaris · LEGatus LEGionis VII
    GEMINAE · PIAE · FELICIS
    IVRIDICVS · ASTVRICAE · ET
    GALLECIAE · LEGatus AVGG · PROVinciae
    ASIAE · QVAESTor CANDIDATus TRIBunus
    LATICLAVIVS · LEGIONis XIII · GEMINae
    TRIVMVIR · MONETALIS · A · A · A
    (*auro argento aere flando feriundo*)
    F · F · * CVM *
    CLAVDIA · SESTIA · COCCEIA · SEVERIANA
    CONIVGE · ET · LOLLIANA · PLAVTIA · SESTIA · SERVI
    LIA · FILIA

This is a dedication to the chief Vestal, Terentia Flavola, by her brother Quintus Lollianus, and his wife and daughter. The year of his consulship is doubtful. Two other pedestals inscribed to this Vestal had previously been found; see *Cor. In. Lat.* vi. 2130 and 2144. One of these is dated 215 A.D.

The long list of honours and titles of Lollianus is an interesting one. He was *consul, augur, praetor, candidatus tutelaris; legate of the seventh legion;* governor of Asturia and Gallicia; *imperial legate* of the province of Asia; *quaestor candidatus; laticlave tribune* of the thirteenth legion; *triumvir of the mint*, with control over the coinage in gold, silver, and bronze.

    2.   TERENTIAE
                FLAVOLAE
                V · V · (*Virgini Vestali*)
                MAXIMAE
                CN · STATILIVS
                MENANDER
                FICTOR
                V̄ · V̄ · (*Virginum Vestalium*)
                CN · STATILI
                CERDONIS
                FICTORIS
                V̄ · V̄ · (*Virginum Vestalium*)
                ALVMNVS

Dedicated to the same chief Vestal by Cnaeus Statilius Menander, a *sculptor to the Vestals*, and pupil of Cnaeus Statilius Cerdo, also *sculptor to the Vestals*.

    3.   PRAETEXTATAE · CRASSI · FIL*iae*
                V*irgini* V*estali* MAXIMAE
                C · IVLIVS · CRETICVS
                A · SACRIS

Dedicated to the chief Vestal Praetextata, the daughter of Crassus, by C. Julius Creticus, one of the religious attendants of Vesta.

    4.   NVMISIAE · L · F · (*Lucii filiae*)
                MAXIMILLAE
                V̄ · V̄ · MAX
                C · HELVIDIVS · MYSTICVS
                DEVOTVS · BENEFICIIS · EIVS

To the chief Vestal Numisia Maximilla, dedicated by C.

H. Mysticus, "grateful for her benefits." Another inscription to this lady is dated 201 A.D.; see also vol. ii. p. 214.

The Vestals appear to have had considerable political influence, and probably controlled a good deal of patronage connected with religious offices. Next come six pedestals, all inscribed to the same chief Vestal, Flavia Publicia.

5.
FLAVIAE · L · FIL
PVBLICIAE · V · V · MAX
SANCTISSIMAE · PIISSIMAEQ
CVIVS · SANCTISSIMAM · ET
RELIGIOSAM · CVRAM · SACRORum
QVAM · PER · OMNES · GRADVS
SACERDOTII · LAVDABILI · ADMI
NISTRATIONE · OPERATVR · NVMEN
SANCTISSIMAE · VESTAE · MATRIS
COMPROBAVIT
AEMILIA · ROGATILLA · C · F · SORORIS · FIL
CVM · MINVCIO · HONORATO · MARCELLO
AEMILIANO · C · P · FILIO · SVO
OB · EXIMIAM · EIVS · ERGA · SE
PIETATEM

Dedicated to Flavia by her niece Aemilia Rogatilla, and her niece's son, on account of Flavia's remarkable kindness towards them. The inscription records that the goddess Vesta herself approved of Flavia's zeal and piety, and is also interesting for its mention of several grades of rank in the priesthood which were passed through before reaching the high dignity of *Virgo Vestalis Maxima.*

On the side of this pedestal is rudely scratched—

COL · V · ID · IVL
DDNN · · · AVG · II · ET
· · · CAES · COSS

The names are erased, but the only occasion in the third

century A.D. when the consuls were an "Augustus for the second time" and a "Caesar," was in the year 247 A.D., in the reign of Philip I., who in that year gave his son, the younger Philip, the title of Augustus; the inscription would be *Dominis nostris Imp. Caes. M. Julio Philippo Pio Felice Augusto II. et M. Julio Severo Philippo Caesare Consulibus.* The Senate after their death decreed a *memoriae damnatio*, and hence their names are erased.

 6. To the Same— FL · PVBLICIAE · V · V · MAX
    SANCTISSIMAE · AC · RELIGIOSIS
    SIMAE · QVAE · PER · OMNES · GRADVS
    SACERDOTII · APVT · (sic) DIVINA · ALTARIA
    OMNIVM · DEORVM · ET · AD · AETERNOS · IGNES
    DIEBVS · NOCTIBVSQVE · PIA · MENTE · RITE
    DESERVIENS · MERITO · AD · HVNC
    LOCVM · CVM · AETATE · PERVENIT
    BAREIVS · ZOTICVS · CVM · FLAVIA
    VERECVNDA · SVA · OB · EXIMIAM · EIVS
    ERGA · SE · BENIBOLENTIAM · (sic) PRAESTANTIAMQ

This contains a similar eulogy of Flavia's piety and careful guardianship of the eternal fires.

On the side of the pedestal is rudely incised—

    DEDICATA · PR · KAL · OCT
    DD · NN · VALERIANO · AVG · IIII · ET
    GALLIENO · AVG · III · COSS

This gives 30th Sept. 257 A.D. as the date of the dedication.

 7. To the Same— FL · PVBLICIAE
    SANCTISSIMAE
    AC · PIISSIMAE
    V · V · MAX

T · FL · APRONIVS
FICTOR · V · V (*Virginum Vestalium*)
LOCI · SECVNDI
DIGNISSIMAE
AC · PRAESTANTISSI
MAE · PATRONAE
CVM · SVIS

Dedicated to his patroness Flavia, by one of the sculptors of the Vestals; the phrase *loci secundi* probably refers to the position of his workshop in a row of others.

8. To the Same— FLAVIAE · L · F · PVBLICIAE
RELIGIOSAE
SANCTITATIS · V · V · MAX
CVIVS · EGREGIAM · MORVM
DISCIPLINAM · ET
IN · SACRIS · PERITISSIMAM
OPERATIONEM · MERITO
RESPVBLICA · IN · DIES
FELICITER · SENTIT
VLPIVS · VERVS · ET · AVREL
TITVS · 7 · 7 · DEPVTATI (*Centuriones deputati*)
OB · EXIMIAM · EIVS · ERGA · SE
BENIVOLENTIAM

On the moulded plinth the letters G · P (*Grati posuerunt*). The meaning of this is clear; it is dedicated jointly by Ulpius Verus and Aurelius Titus.

9. To the Same— FLAVIAE · PVBLICIAE
V · V · MAX
SANCTISSIMAE
AC · RELIGIOSISSIMAE
M · AVRELIVS · HERMES
OB · EXIMIAM · EIVS

ERGA · SE · BENEVOLENTIAM
PRAESTANTIAMQVE

Dedicated by Marcus Aurelius Hermes.

10. To the Same—FL · PVBLICIAE · V · V · MAX
SANCTISSIMAE · ET · PIISSI
MAE · AC · SVPER · OMNES
RETRO · RELIGIOSISSIMAE
PVRISSIMAE · CASTISSIMAEQVE
CVIVS · RELIGIOSAM
CVRAM · SACRORVM · ET
MORVM · PRAEDICABILEM
DISCIPLINAM · NVMEN · QVOQVE
VESTAE · CONPROVABIT (sic)
QVETVRIVS · MEMPHIVS · V · E (*Vir Egregius*)
FICTOR · V · V · DIGNATIONES (sic)
ERGA · SE · HONORISQVE · CAVSA
PLVRIMIS · IN · SE · CONLATIS
BENEFICIIS

This pedestal, unlike the others, is hexagonal in form, and was found, not in the Peristyle, but in a room near it. This also is dedicated by one of the sculptors to the Vestals, Queturius Memphius, with similar eulogies on this much-praised lady.

11.   COELIAE · CLAVDIANAE · V · V
MAX · SANCTISSIMAE · RELIGI
OSISSIMAE · AC · SVPER · OM
NES · PIISSIMAE · CVIVS · OPE
RA · SACRORVM · GVBERNAN
TE · VESTA · MATRE · MAXI
MATVS · SVI · XX · CONPLERIT
AVRELIVS · FRVCTOSVS · CLI
ENS · ET · CANDIDATVS · BENIG

NITATAE · (sic) EIVS · PROBATVS
SIC · XX · SIC · XXX · FELICITER

This is dedicated to Coelia Claudiana by Aurelius Fructosus her client, in honour of her reaching the twentieth year of her *Maximatus* or rank as *Virgo Vestalis Maxima* ; it concludes with a wish that as she has completed twenty years of this office, so she may happily complete thirty.

Four other inscribed pedestals to this lady have been found, one bearing the date 286 A.D. Only one of these now exists; it is in the *Palatine Stadium*, near the entrance; see *Cor. In. Lat.* vi. 2136 to 2139.

On one pedestal the Vestal's name has been erased; it is the latest in date, being of the year 364 A.D. About this time some of the Vestals became Christians (Pruden. *Peristeph. Hymn.* 2), and it may possibly be for this reason that the name on this inscription has been cut out.

OB · MERITVM · CASTITATIS
PVDICITIAE · ADQ · IN · SACRIS
RELIGIONIBVSQVE
DOCTRINAE · MIRABILIS
· · · E · V · V · MAX
PONTIFICES · V · V · C · C (*Viri Clarissimi*)
PROMAG · MACRINIO
SOSSIANO · V · C · P · M (*Vir Clarissimus, pro meritis*).

Dedicated by Macrinius Sossianus, *Promagister* of the College of the *Pontifices of Vesta*.

On the side is

DEDICATA · V · IDVS · IVNIAS
DIVO · IOVIANO · ET · VARRONIANO
CONSS

This gives the date as 9th June 364 A.D.[1]

[1] Varronianus, the second Consul, was the infant son of Fl. Jovianus, whose very brief reign ended early in the year 364 A.D.

OTHER BUILDINGS IN AND NEAR THE FORUM.

Arch of Fabius. The Arch of Fabius. The earliest triumphal arch erected in or near the *Forum Romanum* was that in honour of the victory of Q. Fabius Maximus over the Gaulish Allobroges, on account of which he received the honorary name *Allobrogicus* or *Allobrox*. This happened during his consulship in 121 B.C.; see Livy, *Ep.* lvi.; Schol. ad Cic. *In Verr.* i. 7; and Pliny, *Hist. Nat.* vii. 166. This arch marked the extreme limit of the Forum in this direction; see Cic. *Pro Plan.* 7, 17.

In 1540-50 excavations were made at this part of the Forum, and ruins of the Arch of Fabius were found close by the *Temple of Faustina*; on one of these fragments was inscribed — Q · FABIVS · Q · F · MAXSVMVS · AED · CVR · REST. Unfortunately the fragments which were then discovered were destroyed or used as building materials.

Existing remains. Again, in 1882, excavations at the same place brought to light about twenty-five fragments of this arch, which had escaped the limekilns of the sixteenth century.

Among these are massive travertine *roussoirs* which give the span of the arch, together with caps and other parts of the piers. The *soffit* or under-surface of the arch was of *peperino*, the outer facings of *travertine*, and the inner core of the masonry of *tufa*. These fragments are now lying not far from the *Temple of Faustina*, on the other side of the ancient road; see *Ann. Inst. Cor. Arch.* 1859, p. 307, and *Notizie degli Scavi*, 1882, p. 225.

Temple of Faustina. The *Temple of Faustina the Elder* stands at the east angle of the Forum, facing on to the present line of the *Sacra Via*. It was erected by Antoninus Pius in honour of his wife Faustina, who died in 141 A.D. After the death of the emperor it was dedicated by the Senate to him also, and an upper line added to the inscription on the architrave —

DIVO · ANTONINO · ET | DIVAE · FAVSTINAE · EX · S · C ; see
Capitolinus, *Ant. Pius*, 6.

The greater part of the Cella has been destroyed through *Existing remains.*
the conversion of the temple into the Church of *S. Lorenzo in
Miranda*, but the front is still well preserved, and is now
excavated down to its original level. It is Corinthian, *hexastyle,
prostyle*, with fine monolithic columns of *cipollino* (Carystian
marble), and a well-sculptured frieze in white Athenian marble,
with good reliefs of griffins and candelabra. This frieze is an
almost exact reproduction of one which has been found in the
Sanctuary of the Island of Delos. The *Cella* is built of massive
blocks of peperino, fitted in the most perfect way, and all was *Fine masonry.*
once lined with slabs of white marble. The lower part, which
has only been exposed within the last few years, is specially
worthy of note on account of the wonderful close fitting of the
blocks of masonry. The brick and concrete foundations of the
marble steps in front still exist, and in the centre of the flight
there is a pedestal for a statue, which is a later addition.

This temple is shown on various coins both in silver and *Coins.*
bronze struck in honour of the deified Faustina by Antoninus
Pius, with the legend DEDICATIO · AEDIS or DIVAE · FAVSTINAE.
Two statues of seated figures, Antoninus and his wife, are
represented as if seen through the *Cella* door.

By the south-east side of the temple, which is now *Marble paving.*
excavated, are remains of a very fine pavement, made of large
slabs of Hymettian marble; this appears to be part of the
paving of a *peribolus* or enclosure which once surrounded the
temple, probably extending in front of the steps close up
to the line of the *Sacra Via*. This *peribolus* and its low
enclosing screen are indicated on some of the coins which
show the Temple of Faustina.

In later times, in the fourth or fifth century A.D., some *Late baths.*
baths appear to have been built over this fine massive pavement. A small bath, with thin marble veneer, is actually
sunk into a hole cut through the marble slabs.

End of the circuit. This brings us again to the site of the great *Basilica Aemilia*, which faced on to the north-east side of the Forum, and completes the circuit of the buildings round it.

THE TEMPLE OF CONCORD AND BUILDINGS NEAR IT.

We now pass to the other end of the Forum, near the Capitoline Hill. The space between the *Tabularium* on the Capitoline Hill and the north-west end of the Forum is mostly occupied by a very important range of buildings. The chief *Temple of Concord.* of these is the *Temple of Concord*, in itself one of the most magnificent in Rome, and remarkable above all for the wonderful collection of works of art which it contained; see *Forum Plan* and *Marble Plan* on do.

The *Temple of Concord* was founded by Camillus in 367 B.C. (Plut. *Cam.* 42); rebuilt by L. Opimius in 121 B.C. (Plut. *Grac.* 17; and Appian, *Bell. Civ.* i. 26); and again *Rebuilt under Augustus.* rebuilt, on an enlarged scale with great splendour, in the reign of Augustus, like the Temple of Castor, by Tiberius and Drusus out of the spoils won in Germany; Suet. *Tib.* 20, and Ovid, *Fast.* i. 637 *seq.*

The *Temple of Concord* appears to have been used as a place of sacrifice of special sanctity. A newly discovered fragment of the inscriptions of the *Fratres Arvales* records that a sacrifice was offered to the *Dea Dia* in the Temple of Concord by T. Licinius Cassius Cassianus, Promagister of the Arval College. The inscription states that he offered the sacrifice *manibus lautis, velato capite.* This important fragment was found in 1886, and is published in *Bull. Com. Arch.* 1886, p. 361.

Meeting of Senate. The Senate frequently met in this temple; and it was here that Cicero delivered two of his orations on the Catiline plot: here too, on the Portico, Cicero and the Senate, supported by the Roman knights, withstood the partisans of Antony after the murder of Caesar; see Cic. *Phil.* vii. 8. It appears possible that this extensive portico took the place and name of the ancient *Senaculum* or preliminary place of meeting used by the Senate before entering the *Curia*.

Ovid, *Fast.* i. 638, alludes to the position of the Temple of Concord close by the *gradus Monetae*, a long flight of steps leading from the Forum up to the Temple of *Juno Moneta* on the *Arx*. These steps appear to have descended past the Tabularium and the Temple of Concord down to the *Tullianum* or *Carcer*, now called the "Mamertine Prison."

Gradus Monetae.

The lower flight of steps mentioned above, p. 154, from the prison to the Forum was known as the *scalae gemoniae*, or, as Pliny calls them, "the stairs of sighs" (*gradus gemitorii*). On these were exposed the bodies of criminals who had been killed in the prison or near it; the corpses of Sabinus, Sejanus, Vitellius, and many other distinguished persons were flung on these ill-omened stairs.[1]

Scalae Gemoniae.

The existing remains of the *Temple of Concord*, like those of the *Temple of Castor*, date from the rebuilding under Augustus. Though at first sight it seems that little besides the rough concrete of the *podium* now remains, yet a careful examination will reveal much that is interesting, and enable a satisfactory restoration to be arrived at. The modern road covers part of the great flight of steps which led down to the Forum, and part of the *Cella* is still concealed by the steeply ascending road which slopes up past the end of the *Tabularium*.

Existing remains.

The lower part of the *podium* wall consists of large, closely fitted, and well-clamped blocks of hard tufa, once lined with

---

[1] Pliny (*Hist. Nat.* viii. 145) tells a pathetic story of how, when in the reign of Tiberius the bodies of Titius Sabinus and his servants were thrown on the *gradus gemitorii*, the corpse of one of them was watched by his faithful dog day and night. The dog also stole some bread and tried to force it into its dead master's mouth, and finally, when the bodies were thrown into the Tiber, the dog swam after them and tried to bring his master's corpse to land. Sabinus was one of the victims of Sejanus, whose body soon after was flung on the same stairs.

slabs of white Greek marble, and having a moulded plinth and cornice of solid marble.

Plan of temple.
In plan the *Temple of Concord* is very unusual (see *Plan of the Forum*), consisting of a large *Cella*, much wider than its depth, and an extensive projecting Portico, forming a large covered platform capable of holding a considerable crowd of people. From this Portico a wide and lofty flight of steps sloped down towards the back of the "*Graecostasis*" and the *Rostra*.

Within the great *Cella* were rows of columns set against the walls; these columns rested, not on the floor of the *Cella*, but on a projection, like a low wall, forming a continuous dado or shelf to hold some of the numerous statues which crowded this temple. A similar surbase or dado supporting an internal range of columns is shown in Ligorio's sketch of the "Temple of Augustus"; see fig. 35, p. 275.

Construction of temple.
The construction of this low projecting wall, built of mixed materials, shows the positions of the missing inner columns. At the place where each column came the low dado wall is built of hard travertine, while the intermediate part, which only had the weight of the statues to bear, is constructed of concrete and blocks of tufa, used very much at random. On one of these travertine piers can be seen marks of the column which once stood there, and the holes for its metal clamps. These internal columns had bases of

Beauty of detail.
white marble, sculptured with the utmost richness and beauty of workmanship; several of these bases (unlabelled) are now in a passage on the ground-floor of the Capitoline Museum, and are worthy of study as being among the most beautiful architectural fragments in Rome, dating from the time of Augustus, which was the period of the greatest artistic refinement in matters of detail. All these details are evidently the work of a Greek architect.

Marble linings.
Some of the internal marble lining of the *Cella* is still in place, and is well preserved, especially at one point where it has been protected by the addition of a large pedestal for a

statue; No. 25 on the *Forum Plan.* There is a well-moulded *Moulded plinth.* plinth (see fig. 15, vol. i. p. 87) of yellow Numidian marble; above it are large slabs of the beautiful purple-stained *pavonazetto* from Phrygia, and below the moulding, *cipollino* and other marbles. These linings are fixed with great care by clamps and hooks of bronze and iron, run with lead. The floor is paved with large neatly-jointed slabs of *Porta Santa* marble, *pavonazetto* and *cipollino,* of which many fine pieces exist.

All the marble linings in this temple and in others of the Augustan period, are much thicker than the scanty veneers used in the buildings of the later Empire.

The threshold of the central door into the *Cella* is formed *Great threshold.* of two enormous monoliths of *Porta Santa* marble, 21 feet 6 inches long; in the centre are two deep socket-holes for bronze bolts; and near them is the sunk matrix in the marble, in which was once inlaid a small bronze *caduceus*—symbol of Concord; No. 27 on the *Forum Plan.*

The main cornice of the exterior of the temple is very *Details of cornice.* large and beautiful, both in design and workmanship.[1] A portion of it has been pieced together very cleverly out of existing fragments, and is preserved under the upper arcade of the *Tabularium.* In workmanship and almost wholly in design it is a fine specimen of Greek art; it differs, however, from the best Hellenic work in having its members more overlaid with surface enrichments than was usual among the Greeks of the best time. The large acanthus leaves, which cover the main *cymatium,* are carved with great delicacy and spirit, and the whole is a perfect model of an elaborate Corinthian cornice, probably the finest of this great size that exists, either in Rome or out of it.[2]

---

[1] The *Einsiedlen* MS. gives part of an inscription on the architrave, now wholly lost, which recorded a restoration of the temple, S · P · Q · R AEDEM · CONCORDIAE · VETVSTATE · COLLAPSAM · IN · MELIOREM · FACIEM OPERE · ET · CVLTV · SPLENDIDIORE · RESTITVERVNT.

[2] The entablature of the temple of Olympian Zeus in Athens, though

Massive podium. Like the Temple of Castor and other temples in Rome, the whole *podium*, with the exception of a space left for a treasure chamber, is filled in solid with concrete made of tufa, poured in between the massive walls built of carefully clamped tufa blocks. A long narrow chamber was formed in the concrete, leading from the front of one wing of the *podium* toward the *Tabularium*, with which it has been supposed once to have communicated, but this never was the case, as may be seen from the fact that the cavity in the concrete stops short before reaching the *Tabularium* wall. This chamber was probably used for a secret strong-room to hold some of the treasures in which the *Temple of Concord* was so rich; like the similar chamber in the *podium* of the *Temple of Castor.*

Treasure chamber.

It will easily be seen that when the temple was complete it must have concealed a large part of the wall of the *Tabularium*, against which it abuts, and even have blocked up some of its arches. On the face of the *Tabularium* wall is an interesting piece of evidence which shows that the older *Temple of Concord*, which was in existence when the present *Tabularium* was built in 78 B.C., was considerably smaller than the temple rebuilt by Augustus, of which remains now exist. Part, and part only, of the wall concealed by the temple is left somewhat rough on the face, not neatly dressed as the rest is; and this rough part is precisely that extent of wall which was concealed by the older temple, the builders of the *Tabularium* naturally not thinking it worth while to dress to a smooth surface that portion of their wall which would not be seen. The end of the rough surface can easily be traced just under the middle of the last window on the right, in the lower story of the *Tabularium.*

Older temple.

There were, moreover, no windows in that part of the *Tabularium* basement which was concealed by the older *Temple* less elaborate in detail, must have been equally fine in point of design and workmanship.

of Concord, as they would, of course, have been useless; this is shown on the *Forum Plan*; see No. 23, 23.

The general design of the *Temple of Concord* is well shown on the *obverse* of a *First Brass* of Tiberius, dated *Trib. Pot.* XXXIIX. (*i.e.* 36 A.D.) It is much more carefully and minutely executed than is usual with representations of buildings on Roman coins. This coin gives a front view of the great Portico, with the *Cella* projecting like a wing on each side; and in each wing a large window, probably introduced by the architect to give light to the many works of art within.[1] Through the open door the principal statue of the interior is shown, a large seated figure of Concord on the massive pedestal which still exists in the *Cella*; No. 24 in the *Forum Plan*. Statues grouped under the Portico and at its sides are shown, and also the pedimental sculpture; and a group of three figures embracing, as a symbol of Concord, at the apex, with others up the slope of the pediment, including, on each slope, a winged figure of Victory. On each side of the great flight of steps there is a colossal standing figure. That on the left is shown to be Mercury by the caduceus in its hand.

Coin of Tiberius.

Statues.

Fig. 45.

First Brass of Tiberius showing the Temple of Concord.

The Cella of this temple appears to have been a sort of museum of ancient works of Greek painting and sculpture, engraved gems, gold and silver plate, and other objects.

Works of art.

The following are the chief of those mentioned by Pliny: statues of *Apollo* and *Juno* by Baton, *Hist. Nat.* xxxiv. 73; a group of *Latona* with the infants *Apollo* and *Diana* by Euphra-

Statues.

---

[1] The occasional use of windows is an important point of difference between Greek and Roman temples. No example of a window is known to exist in any Greek temple. Those in the Athenian Erechtheum are late insertions of the time of Constantine.

Works of art. nor, *ib.* 77 ; statues of *Aesculapius* and *Hygeia* by Niceratus, *ib.* 80 ; *Mars* and *Mercury* by the sculptor Piston, *ib.* 89 ; and statues of *Ceres, Jupiter,* and *Minerva* by Sthennis, *ib.* 90. Also the following paintings : *Marsyas* bound by Apollo, the work of Zeuxis, *Hist. Nat.* xxxv. 66 ; *Liber Pater* or Bacchus by the Athenian Nicias, *ib.* 131 ; and a picture of *Cassandra* by Theorus, *ib.* 144.

Lastly, four elephants cut in the very hard Aethiopian obsidian which were presented as curiosities by Augustus (*Hist. Nat.* xxxvi. 196); and, greatest treasure of all, the *Ring of Polycrates.* sardonyx signet of Polycrates, king of Samos, which, after being thrown into the sea to propitiate his Nemesis, was, by means of a fish, brought back to the doomed tyrant; this relic was enclosed in a golden horn; *Hist. Nat.* xxxvii. 4. Pliny is, however, incredulous as to the authenticity of this celebrated signet.[1]

Other shrines of Concord. Another *Temple of Concord,* founded in 219 B.C., stood on the Capitoline *Arx* (Livy, xxii. 33, and xxvi. 23); and there was a bronze *Aedicula of Concord* in the *Area Vulcani,* probably near the great *Temple of Concord*; this was dedicated by Cn. Flavius in 305 B.C.; Livy, ix. 46 ; according to Pliny (*Hist. Nat.* xxxiii. 19) it stood *in Graecostasi, quae tunc supra Comitium erat.*

There was also a Temple of Concord, dedicated by Livia the wife of Augustus, near the *Porticus Liviae,* not far from the *Thermae of Titus* on the Esquiline Hill ; see Ovid, *Fast.* vi. 637.

Temple of Vespasian. The *Temple of Vespasian* stands close by that of Concord, and abuts on to the *Tabularium* in a similar way, blocking up the archway at the foot of the long flight of steps which led from the base of the Capitoline Hill to the rooms in the *Tabularium* which faced on to the *Asylum* ; see vol. i. p. 376.

[1] According to Herodotus (iii. 39) and other ancient writers the famous gem of Polycrates was not a *sardonyx* but an emerald ; see Middleton, *Ancient Gems,* 1891, p. 35.

TEMPLE OF VESPASIAN

This temple was built by Domitian, about 94 A.D., in honour of his father; it underwent important restoration in the reign of Severus, as was recorded on the entablature, the inscription on which is quoted in the *Einsiedlen* MS.—DIVO · VESPASIANO AVGVSTO · S · P · Q · R [1] · IMPP · CAESS · SEVERVS · ET · ANTONINVS PII · FELIC · AVGG · RESTITVERVNT; part of the last word only now exists.

The existing three columns (No. 20 on the *Forum Plan*), with their finely sculptured frieze and cornice, evidently belong to the original temple; the work is far too well executed for the time of Severus. These columns were taken down and more securely refixed by the French at the beginning of this century. *Existing remains.*

The *Temple of Vespasian* was *Corinthian, hexastyle,* and *prostyle*, with a nearly square *Cella* containing a very large marble-lined platform or pedestal at the end opposite the door. The interior had ranges of columns against the walls, set on a projecting dado, as in the *Temple of Concord*. The construction of this dado below the columns is similar to that of the *Temple of Concord*, with travertine piers and intermediate filling-in of concrete. Holes for fixing the marble base of one of these columns are visible on the top travertine block, at one point in this low internal wall or dado; and some of the slabs of white marble which rested on the dado are still in their place. *Internal columns.*

What exists of the Cella wall is built of massive blocks of travertine, very finely jointed, without mortar and clamped with iron run with lead. This was lined outside with white Pentelic marble; a good deal of the richly moulded plinth of the *podium* still remains *in situ*, and indications of the *podium* cornice can be traced against the wall of the *Tabularium*. The inside of the Cella had its walls covered and its floor paved *Cella wall.*

---

[1] To this point the inscription is the original one of the time of Domitian; the rest is the addition recording the restoration by Severus and his son Caracalla (Antoninus).

with coloured Oriental marbles in a similar way to the *Temple of Concord*; some of this lining still exists.

Details of cornice. The rich details of the entablature can best be studied in the arcade of the *Tabularium*, where a piece has been preserved and restored. It is equal in beauty of workmanship to that of the *Temple of Concord*, but is less pure in style, being somewhat overloaded with ornament; the *corona* is fluted, and no plain flat surfaces are left as a relief to the eye. The great egg and dart moulding is undercut, almost with the skill of a Chinese puzzle, and minute ornaments are introduced which must have been quite invisible when the work was in its place at a great height above the eye. The beautiful floriated patterns, which cover each egg of the lower egg and dart member, are worked with the delicacy of a cameo brooch, although not a trace of these patterns could be visible from below.

Frieze. On the frieze are sculptured ox-skulls and sacrificial instruments, worked with great care and richness of design; on the *praefericulum* or ewer is a minute relief of a battle between a bull and a rhinoceros; the *patera* or libation-plate is fluted, *Priestly badges.* and has a well-modelled head in the centre. Other objects, no less carefully sculptured, are the *aspergillum* or holy-water sprinkler, the *securis* or axe with which the *Popa* killed the sacrificial victim, the *culter*, a straight-edged knife; a *cochlear* or spoon for pouring the libations of blood, and a *galerum* or flamen's woollen cap with the *apex*, a wooden spike, at its top.

These sacred objects were used as the symbols or badges of the various priestly Collegia in Rome. Together with the Augur's *lituus* or crozier they are very frequently represented on the *reverses* of coins of the early Imperial period.

Small shrine. *Aedicula*, wrongly called *of Faustina*. In the narrow space, scarcely 7 feet wide, between the *Temples of Vespasian* and *Concord*, a small brick and concrete shrine was built against the wall of the *Tabularium*; this was a little vaulted room apparently two stories high, once lined with marble; marks of its vault are visible against the *Tabularium* wall; see No. 21 on the Forum Plan.

Owing to the discovery at this point of a marble pedestal dedicated to Faustina,[1] it has sometimes been assumed that this little shrine was an aedicula erected in her honour. This is, however, a mistake, as the chamber is contemporary with the adjacent *Temple of Vespasian*; and is therefore many years earlier than the time of either of the two Faustinae. This is proved by the fact that the moulding on the marble plinth of the Temple of Vespasian is not worked, but the block is left in the rough, at that part where the wall of this *aedicula* comes upon it. If the *aedicula* had been a later addition the moulding would of course have been worked, as that part of the plinth would in that case have been visible till the *aedicula* was added. *Base of statue. Proof of date.*

It appears possible that this little shrine was dedicated to Titus, whose name does not appear jointly with Vespasian's in the inscription (given above) on the entablature of the large temple. And yet the *Notitia, Reg.* IX., mentions dedications to both Vespasian and Titus; which seems to show that some building in honour of the latter did exist; see Preller, *Regionen der Stadt Rom.*

When the *Temple of Vespasian* was built, the level around it was artificially lowered (at Nos. 18 and 22 on the *Forum Plan*); traces of the older level are visible at the side of the tufa substructions of the *Temple of Concord*, where a line of travertine, built into the tufa, shows the position of the former travertine paving, which was hacked away when a new pavement of travertine slabs was laid, about 2 feet 6 inches below the earlier level. Parts also of the concrete foundation and rough footing stones of the *Tabularium* were laid bare by the same alteration, as is shown in fig. 48, vol. i. p. 376. *Older level.*

Porticus of the Dii Consentes and the *Schola of Xanthus. Dii Consentes.*

[1] See above, p. 266.

Dii Consentes.

Next comes the *Porticus of the Dii Consentes*; this conjunction of twelve chief deities was of Etruscan origin; they were six of each sex, and were called the *Senatus Deorum*; see Varro, *Lin. Lat.* viii. 70, and *De re rust.* I. i. In the latter passage Varro mentions twelve gilt statues of these deities as existing in his time; and in the former he remarks that these shrines were popularly called *Deum Consentum*, instead of the more correct form *Deorum Consentium*. The *Forum Plan* shows these little chambers set against the slope of the Capitoline Hill, near the bend of the *Clivus Capitolinus*, the paving of which is recorded by Livy (xli. 27) to have been laid down in 174 B.C.

At this point the hill was quarried away to make room for some of the shrines; the bare tufa rock is visible at the back of two of them. Others have a back wall of tufa masonry, or brick-faced concrete; the latter appears to date from the Flavian period; the tufa wall is probably of the Republican period.

Restored porticus.

The *Porticus* with Corinthian columns of *cipollino* (much restored by Canina) is late in date, as is recorded on the entablature. This inscription records a restoration by Vettius Praetextatus, Praefect of the city in 367 A.D.

These shrines are built on a large marble-paved platform (No. 15), set against the slope of the hill; and under it, towards the Temple of Vespasian, is a row of small rooms, seven in number, which were used as the offices (*schola*) of the scribes and *praecones* of the aediles. These chambers are usually

Schola Xanthi.

known as the *Schola Xanthi* from an inscription (now lost) which recorded their restoration, and the erection of seven silver statues of gods by A. Fabius Xanthus and another; Gruter, *Inscrip.* 170, 3.

The inscription was *Bebrix Aug. L. Drusianus A. Fabius Xanthus cur imagines argenteas Deorum septem post dedicationem scholae et mutulos cum tabella aenea de sua pecunia dederunt.* Another inscription recorded that the same Drusianus and

Xanthus restored the *schola* for the *scribis, librariis et praeconibus aedilium curulium*, and ornamented it with marble statues and bronze seats. Both these inscriptions were cut on the frieze of the marble entablature.

Schola Xanthi.

Clerks of the Clivus Capitolinus are mentioned in more than one inscription; cf. Cicero, *Phil.* ii. 7. These clerks were probably occupants of a similarly placed row of offices, which existed before the present ones were built. The brick facing of the concrete walls of the existing rooms is of the Flavian period. The rooms were lined outside with white marble and have fine marble thresholds; inside they were stuccoed and painted.

The *Arch of Severus* stands to the north of the *Rostra*, across a basalt-paved road, the line of which appears to have been slightly altered when the arch was built. Remains of the ancient travertine curb, at several places along the northeast side of the Forum, give the older direction of this road; see *Forum Plan*. The Arch of Severus was erected in 203 A.D., after victories in Parthia and other eastern countries, in honour of Severus and his sons Caracalla and Geta.

Arch of Severus.

Representations of this arch on coins of Severus[1] show that its attic was surmounted by a bronze chariot drawn by six horses, in which stood a figure of Severus, crowned by Victory; at the sides of the chariot were statues of Caracalla and Geta; and an equestrian statue stood at each angle.

Statues.

The arch is built of massive blocks of white Pentelic marble, except the base, which is of travertine faced with slabs of marble. The steps cut under the two side arches are a late addition, as is also the basalt-paved road under the central arch.

According to Fea, marble steps were found by him under the late basalt paving of the central arch, and similar steps are said to have been discovered under the central archway of

Steps in the arch.

[1] A rare denarius in the British Museum with this type is figured by Stevenson, *Dict. of Roman Coins*, p. 78.

others of the Roman triumphal arches. This being the case, it is difficult to see how the chariots in triumphal processions could have passed through it, unless temporary wooden planking was laid over the steps for use on the occasion of each triumph.

Sculptured reliefs.

Sculpture on the Arch of Severus. The four large reliefs over the side arches, though poor works of art, are very interesting for their representations of scenes of battle and sieges in the east. The one on the left, on the side towards the Forum, represents victories in Mesopotamia; the relief of Nisibis by Severus after the defeat of his rivals Pescennius Niger and Aemilianus in Pontus, in the year 195 A.D. Another part of this relief represents the siege of Carrae. Over the right hand arch, on the same side, is represented the siege of Hatra on the Tigris, and the submission of Abagarus King of Osrhoene. On the side towards the Capitol, over the right hand arch, is the taking of Babylon, and the flight thence of the Parthians; and also another siege of Hatra in 199 A.D. Over the left arch is the siege of Seleucia and Ctesiphon; the defeat of the Parthian King Artabanus, and his Arabian allies, in 201-202 A.D. In the spandrels of the central arch are winged Victories bearing trophies, and four small figures representing the four seasons. In the spandrels of the side arches are the river gods of the conquered countries, the Euphrates, Tigris, and two tributaries.

Victories of Severus.

Rivers.

On the pedestals of the columns are life-sized reliefs of captives driven by Roman soldiers, the same design being mechanically repeated. The large panel on the attic is occupied with a long inscription repeated on both sides, announcing the titles and honours of Severus and Caracalla, and that the arch was erected *ob rempublicam restitutam imperiumque Populi Romani propagatum.* After the death of Severus, when Caracalla had murdered his brother, he ordered all statues and reliefs of Geta to be destroyed, and his name to be erased from all inscriptions. Additional titles after the name

Inscription.

of Caracalla (who is here called *M. Aurelius Antoninus Pius*) occupy the place of the erased names of Geta. That is, the words OPTIMIS · FORTISSIMISQVE · PRINCIPIBVS have been cut over the obliterated name P · SEPT · LVC · FIL · GETAE · NO-BILISS · CAESARI, which can still be made out from the holes by which the bronze letters were fixed to the marble.

Name erased.

The large reliefs are very much overcrowded with figures, and have but little decorative effect; instead of being framed in panels, with mouldings round them, as in arches of a better period, they are crowded close up to the columns and entablature. The capitals of the Order are of debased *Composite* style. The *soffits* of the three arches are richly decorated with *lacunaria*, sunk coffers with enriched mouldings and centre flowers, all coarsely executed, but of good decorative effect.

Debased style.

THE CENTRAL AREA OF THE FORUM.

Pavement. This irregularly-shaped space (see *Forum Plan*) is paved with massive slabs of travertine, a great many of which are evidently late in date. On the earlier part, where the slabs are laid more evenly and more closely jointed, are incised the series of lines [1] mentioned above; see p. 236.

Stone paving.

Sculptured Plutei. One curious structure of unknown use, but on account of its reliefs of the highest interest, stands in this central area, near the *Column of Phocas*. It consists of two short marble walls, or *plutei*, each with its plinth and cornice returning round the ends, showing that it is not part of a longer wall, but complete in itself (No. 36). These are set on travertine blocks, evidently of late date, and there are no indications to show what the use of these marble walls was, or even where they were meant to stand. On the insides of these screens, as they are now placed, repeated twice over, are very spirited reliefs of a sacrificial boar, ram, and bull, the Roman

Marble walls.

[1] These marks are shown by the blue lines on the *Forum Plan*.

Suovetaurilia,[1] each decorated with fillets and wreaths. On the other sides are very interesting reliefs of scenes in the reign of Trajan, to whose time the sculpture belongs. They are of special interest for the views in the background of buildings in the Forum, most of which can be clearly identified.

Scene in the Forum. On the left of the relief towards the Capitol, the emperor is standing on the *Rostra*, the beaks of which, in two tiers, are represented. Behind him are a number of attendant figures, and in front, standing on the ground, a crowd of men holding up their hands in acclamation. Behind the *Rostra* a triumphal arch is shown, and a temple raised on a lofty *podium*. These are probably the *Temple of Castor* and the *Arch of Augustus.*

Trajan's asylum. On the right the emperor appears again, seated on a platform, with male figures behind him; in front stands a female carrying a baby, and leading an infant by the hand (much broken). This represents the institution in 99 A.D., by Trajan, of a charity for destitute children; the same scene occurs on one of his first brasses, with the legend ALIM[ENTA] · ITALIAE;[2] see Cohen, ii. 303-305. Behind the main group is a long row of arches, evidently the lower story of the *Basilica Julia.*

Marsyas and fig tree. On the extreme right is the *Statue of Marsyas* (Hor. *Sat.* I. vi. 120, and Pliny, *Hist. Nat.* xxi. 9) and the sacred *fig tree*, probably that mentioned by Pliny (*Hist. Nat.* xv. 78), as having sprung up in the Forum on the site of the gulf of Curtius, not the *Ficus Ruminalis* on the *Comitium.* The fig tree is surrounded at its base by a sort of square marble *puteal*. Marsyas is represented as an aged faun bearing a wine-skin.[3] The statue of Marsyas, which appears to have stood near the *Rostra* and the *Comitium*, was a conspicuous object in the Forum, and is frequently mentioned in classical writings; see

---

[1] *Suovetaurilia* is compounded of *sus, oves,* and *taurus.*

[2] The full legend would be "*Alimenta ingenuorum puerorum et puellarum Italiae.*"

[3] This statue of Marsyas is also shown on the *reverse* of a common denarius of about 100 B.C., with the *legend* L · CENSORI*nus.*

Mart. *Ep.* ii. 64. Seneca, *De Ben.* vi. 32, and Pliny, *Hist.* *Marsyas.*
Nat. xxi. 9, mention it as the spot where Julia, the daughter of Augustus, used to meet her lovers.

On the other *pluteus* the emperor is again represented on the *Rostra*, seated; the greater part of his figure is missing. In front a number of men bring tablets, and pile them in a heap before him, ready for burning. This records Trajan's remission of certain arrears of taxes due to the Imperial treasury. Trajan's successor, Hadrian, gained much popularity by a similar act of liberality; Spartian. *Hadr.* 7. *Remission of taxes.*

This is recorded on an interesting *First Brass* of Hadrian, with on the *rev.* the emperor setting fire with a torch to a pile of documents in the presence of three citizens, who raise their hands in acclamation. The *legend* is RELIQVA · VETERA · HS NOVIES · MILL[IES] · ABOLITA.

On the left of this scene in the relief the *fig tree* and *Marsyas* are again shown, and next to them the lower arches of the *Basilica Julia* are repeated. On the right are an *Ionic hexastyle* temple, evidently that of Saturn; and a *Corinthian hexastyle* temple, clearly that of Vespasian: the Ionic and Corinthian capitals are distinctly shown on both these temples; between them is an arch, probably that of Tiberius, across the *Sacra Via.* *Forum buildings.*

Other explanations of these reliefs have been given, but the above are the most satisfactory.[1] In representations like these of Roman buildings, or those that appear on coins, accuracy must not be expected; and too much stress should not be laid on the relative positions of objects shown in these reliefs, since most certainly the sculptor would take any liberties that suited his space or composition. It will be observed that the temple on the first relief is shown with the impossible number of five columns on its front.

Whatever the use of these marble walls may have been, it

[1] See Brizio, *Ann. Inst.* 1872, p. 309; Henzen, *Bull. Inst.* 1872, p. 81; and Jordan, *Marsyas auf den Forum*, Berlin, 1883.

is at least certain that they are not in their original place. One possible suggestion is that they formed a sort of gangway or passage through which voters had to pass to reach the ballot boxes on the Comitium, in order to facilitate the onward movement of the crowd of citizens in an orderly stream.

Statues. Statues. An immense number of statues were set up in and around the area of the Forum at different times, till at last they must have encumbered the space to a very inconvenient extent. As early as 158 B.C. the Censors P. Cornelius Scipio and M. Popilius removed all the statues of magistrates which had been set up round the Forum with the exception of those which had been placed there in accordance with a decree of the Senate or of the Roman people; see Pliny, *Hist. Nat.* xxxiv. 30.

In early times the honour of a statue in the Forum was but rarely granted, as Livy remarks (viii. 13) when he records that in 339 B.C. equestrian statues of the Consuls L. Furius Camillus and C. Maenius were erected in the Forum in honour of their victories in Latium.

Base of statue. *Existing pedestals.* Towards the other end of the Forum, immediately over the line of the "*Cloaca Maxima*," are remains of a large concrete and brick pedestal (No. 38), which is sometimes supposed to be that of the equestrian statue of Domitian, described by Statius (*Silv.* i. 22) as standing in front of the Temple of *Divus Julius*. But this statue was destroyed immediately after the death of Domitian, and the materials of the concrete and the character of its brick facing show that it is very much later in date than his time. It is therefore more probable that it was the base of the bronze equestrian statue of Constantine, mentioned in the *Notitia*, *Reg.* VIII.

Marble pedestal. Near the Arch of Severus there is a fine marble pedestal of an equestrian statue, which has been treated in an extraordinary way (No. 35). It is set up standing on its end, and across it is incised an inscription, of the year 383 A.D., in honour of Arcadius and Theodosius, a striking example of the artistic barbarism of the end of the fourth century.

Another great marble pedestal (No. 31) near the Arch of Severus appears to have once supported an equestrian statue; it is now set up on one end on a cubical block of travertine, and on its side is cut crossways an inscription in honour of Fl. Julius Constantius, c. 340 A.D. *Other bases.*

Of almost equally late date is the square pedestal of a column near this point, sculptured on all four sides with rude reliefs of sacrificial scenes, and inscribed on a shield held by Victories, CAESARVM · DECENNALIA · FELICITER.

Though worthless as a work of art, the sacrificial scene is interesting; it shows the emperor pouring a libation from a *patera* on to an altar. By him stand a flute-player, a boy with a box of incense, and a Flamen wearing the *galerum* and *apex*. The emperor is crowned by Victory assisted by a male figure. *Late reliefs.*

These reliefs are a striking example of the utter degradation of Roman art during the fourth century, sunk into hopeless and ignorant copyism, and absolutely devoid of life and vigour such as often exist during periods of technical unskilfulness, when a people are struggling out of artistic barbarism towards a growing sense of beauty.

The seven cubical brick and concrete structures which line the *Sacra Via* opposite the *Basilica Julia* are also not earlier than the time of Constantine. They were once faced with marble, with heavy moulded plinths and cornices, many pieces of which are strewn around. These cubical structures were pedestals for statues mounted on tall columns, such as those shown behind the *Rostra* in the relief on Constantine's Arch; see fig. 34, vol. i. p. 259. Some broken pieces of these columns lie near. They are of Egyptian granite, and some of them appear to have been decorated with bronze reliefs; the metal pins to fasten the bronze ornaments still remain embedded in the granite. It is probable that these seven columns stand opposite and parallel to the site of the old line of shops *Bases of columns.*

called *tabernae veteres*, which must have been removed to make room for the *Basilica Julia*.

Column of Phocas. The most conspicuous monument of the mid-Forum (No. 39) is the Corinthian column with an inscription on its pedestal in honour of the bloodthirsty tyrant Phocas; the inscription was cut on the pedestal by Smaragdus, in the eleventh year of his exarchate, 608 A.D. The name of Phocas is erased, but the date shows that it was erected in his honour by the servile Exarch of Ravenna. It is a fine fluted column, stolen from some building of a good period, and is raised on a rudely heaped-up pile of steps, partly of marble and partly of blocks of tufa.

Mr. F. M. Nichols has recently pointed out (*Archaeologia*, vol. lii.) that there are good reasons for thinking that this column was not originally erected in honour of Phocas, but of some personage in the fourth century A.D., and that Smaragdus merely altered the dedicatory inscription to that which now, in part at least, exists.

Small shrines. Remains of various small marble structures (shown on the Forum Plan) exist along the north-east part of the central area. Their use is not known; but they look like small *aediculae*. Near the marble *plutei* there are also traces of a nearly square building with rudely moulded plinth. These are all of late date, not earlier than the third or fourth century A.D.

Venus Cluacina. Close by the point where the great *cloaca* passes under the road on the north-east side of the Forum, some marble blocks remain (No. 37 on the *Forum Plan*) which may perhaps be part of the small shrine of *Venus Cloacina* (the purifier), which is known to have stood in this part of the Forum. This shrine appears to be alluded to on the *rev.* of a denarius of the Gens Mussidia, with two citizens standing on a railed platform, approached by steps at one end, probably one of the platforms for voting and other purposes which stood on *the Comitium*. On the base of this platform is the word CLOACIN, and above, the *legend* L · MVSSIDIVS · LONGVS; see also Livy, iii. 48.

A strip of the whole narrow south-east end of the Forum was occupied in the fourth century A.D. by a long brick and concrete building, lined with marble (No. 40 on the *Forum Plan*). This was, unfortunately, nearly all destroyed by Comm. Rosa, who excavated this part of the Forum; but its extent can be traced by the remains of its moulded marble plinth, a great part of which is still *in situ*. {*Late building.*}

Numerous fragments of other buildings, statues, and reliefs are scattered about the Forum. Among them are some of the fine tiles of Parian marble, which under the Empire, and even earlier, were commonly used for roofing; see Livy, xlii. 3. There are also many pieces (near the *Rostra*) of the marble gutters or channels to carry off rain-water, which were commonly set outside of Roman temples and other buildings, usually along the whole of the sides, just below the lowest step of the *stylobate*. {*Fragments.*}

Fragments of two inscribed pedestals are of much interest as recording the existence of two statues by famous Greek sculptors. One of these has the inscription OPVS · POLYCLIT[I]; and the other has the name of *Timarchus*. These fragments are now placed in the *Basilica Julia*. Other pedestals have been found inscribed with the names of *Bryaxis* and *Praxiteles*; see *Bull. Com. Arch. Rom.* ii. p. 176. {*Bases of Greek statues.*}

A very interesting relief is set against the *Temple of Castor*, by the small side steps at the east angle. It appears to be part of the capital of a Corinthian pilaster. Among the acanthus foliage there is a winged Victory sacrificing a bull before the statue of some female deity. Behind is a reclining figure of the goddess *Tellus* or the Earth, holding a cornucopiae; an infant is climbing on her lap.[1] {*Sculptured capital.*}

Countless pieces scattered around of all the rich Oriental {*Costly materials.*}

[1] This allegorical figure of Mother Earth occurs frequently on the *reverses* of Roman coins.

Costly materials. marbles, alabasters, porphyries, and granites, which were imported into Rome, show how magnificent the *Forum Romanum* must once have been; the rich colours of these being set off by the vast masses of polished white marble of which the buildings were mainly constructed, and contrasting with the metallic gleam of the many statues in silver and gold-plated bronze, which at its time of greatest splendour thickly crowded the whole of the *Forum* and its surroundings.[1]

[1] Pliny mentions several trees which grew in or close round the Forum, such as the sacred fig tree near the *puteal* on the *Comitium*, and another fig tree in the central area, on the spot where the Gulf of Curtius had opened (*Hist. Nat.* xv. 77, 78); an enormous lotus tree in the *Vulcanal*, the roots of which extended across the *stationes municipiorum* as far as the Forum of Julius (*Hist. Nat.* xvi. 235); and in the central part of the Forum a large and ancient cypress which lived till the reign of Nero (*Hist. Nat.* xvi. 236).

CHAPTER VIII

THE CAPITOLINE HILL.[1]

IN prehistoric times this hill was called the *Mons Saturnius* (see Varro, *Lin. Lat.* v. 41), its name being connected with that legendary "golden Age" when Saturn himself reigned in Italy. One record of these primitive traditions still exists in the *Temple of Saturn* at the foot of the *Clivus Capitolinus*, which was fabled to stand on the site of the altar erected to Saturn by the companions of Hercules;[2] see vol. i. p. 232.

Mons Saturnius.

The *Capitoline Hill*, which, like the other hills of Rome, has had its contour much altered by cutting away and levelling, consists of a mass of tufa rock harder in structure than that of the Palatine Hill. It appears once to have been surrounded by cliffs, very steep at most places, and had approaches only on one side—that towards the Forum; first, by means of the winding continuation of the *Sacra Via*, which led past the *Tabularium* up to the *Asylum*, and thus to the yet higher levels of the Arx and the *Temple of Jupiter Capitolinus*; and secondly by the *Gradus Monetae*, past the other end of the *Tabularium*, leading straight up to the Arx. Both these approaches are still in use, and others were added in mediaeval times on the side of the hill which faces towards the *Campus Martius*, one leading up to the Church of Ara Coeli, and

Capitoline rock.

[1] The existing remains of the very ancient wall which surrounded the Capitol are described in the section on the wall of Servius; see vol. i. p. 127.

[2] In the Capitoline Museum there is a marble pedestal inscribed *Herculi Primigenio Sacrum.*

another, the principal approach, by a broad stairway to the central depression between the two peaks.

Double peak. The top of the hill consists of a lower central part, flanked by two peaks of about equal height. The south-western peak was known as the *Capitolium*,[1] and the north-eastern one was called the *Arx* or Citadel. These parts of the Capitoline Hill are clearly distinguished in many passages of classical writers, especially by Livy (vi. 20), who in this chapter repeatedly speaks of the two summits as being distinct portions of the hill.[2] Strabo also (v. 3) describes the intermediate valley or *Asylum* as being between the *Arx* and the *Capitolium*—μεταξὺ τῆς ἄκρας καὶ τοῦ Καπιτωλίου; see also Aul. Gell. v. 12.

Asylum. It was in this valley that Romulus was said to have established his *Asylum* or refuge for fugitives from the neighbouring towns in order to increase his little settlement. The Capitoline Hill is said to have become the great stronghold of the Sabines under their king Tatius, who from that secure fortress frequently harassed and even defeated the Latins of the Palatine, till the two village-forts were united by alliance and finally under the rule of one king, the mythical Romulus. As a stronghold it must have been even more impregnable than the Palatine, being more completely surrounded by nearly perpendicular cliffs, and so much smaller as to be more easily defended by a small garrison.[3]

Mons Tarpeius. The *Capitolium* was also in early times known as the *Mons Tarpeius*, so called from the familiar legend of the treachery of Tarpeia, told by Propertius, *El.* iv. 4; see also Varro, *Lin. Lat.* v. 41. Dionysius (ii. 40) adopts a different tradition,

---

[1] In late times the whole hill is sometimes loosely spoken of as the *Capitolium*.

[2] See also Livy, ii. 34; vi. 15; viii. 37; and xl. 44.

[3] The *Arx* on the Quirinal Hill, where the Sabine Numa lived, was also called *Capitolium*, and was named *Capitolium Vetus*, to distinguish it. It also possessed a primitive triple Temple to Jupiter, Juno, and Minerva.

which makes Tarpeia fall a victim to her heroic attempt to deceive the Sabine assailants.

In later times the name *rupes Tarpeia* was applied, not to the whole peak, but to a part of its cliff which faced towards the *Vicus Jugarius* and the *Forum Romanum*. The identification of that part of the Tarpeian rock, which was used for the execution of criminals according to a very primitive custom, is now impossible owing to the great changes which have taken place in the shape of the Capitoline cliffs on the side towards the Vicus Jugarius. *Tarpeian rock.*

At one place the cliff of the *Capitolium* is quite perpendicular, and has been cut very carefully into an upright even surface. A deep groove, about a foot wide, the use of which is not apparent, runs up the face of this level cutting.

This cliff is popularly though erroneously known as the *Tarpeian rock*, and the little alley which leads to the foot of it is called the *Vicolo della rupe Tarpeia*.

The Capitoline Flavissae. There are many rock-cut chambers excavated in this part of the cliff; some openings into them appear in the face of the rock. These rock-cut chambers and passages extended under the great Temple of Capitoline Jupiter. They were used by the Capitoline *aeditui* as secret treasuries (θησαυροί), and also to contain any fragments of the very sacred and archaic Etruscan sculpture, made of *terra cotta*, which by accident fell from the exterior of the temple. *Treasure chambers.*

Aulus Gellius (*Noc. Att.* ii. 10) describes these subterranean chambers as *cellas quasdam et cisternas quae in area sub terra essent, ubi reponi solerent signa vetera quae ex eo templo collapsa essent, et alia quaedam religiosa e donariis consecratis*. The name *flavissae*, or *favissae* in old Latin, was given to these treasure-chambers. Aulus Gellius (*loc. cit.*) says, *Q. Valerium Soranum solitum dicere quos "thesauros" Greco nomine appellaremus, priscos Latinos "flavissas" dixisse*. *Flavissae.*

He goes on to explain that the word *flavissa* is derived *a flando*, because in these early treasuries was stored the archaic bronze money, such as the *As libralis*, which was *cast* in a mould, not struck by dies.

The perpendicular cliff was once very much higher than it is at present, as there is a great accumulation of rubbish at its foot. At the top several courses of the tufa blocks of the very primitive circuit wall of the hill can be seen from below. These remains appear to be earlier in date than the wall of Servius; the blocks are composed of the soft reddish tufa which forms the Capitoline Hill, and their rough workmanship resembles that of the so-called Wall of Romulus. They probably belong to that very primitive period when the Capitoline Hill was an independent fortress, with complete circuit wall of its own.

Ancient wall.

That this cliff cannot be the *Tarpeian rock* where criminals were executed is shown by Dionysius (viii. 78, and vii. 35), who expressly says that this took place in the sight of people in the *Forum Romanum*, so that the popular "Rupes Tarpeia" is on the wrong side of the hill.

Tarpeian rock.

The side towards the Forum and the *Vicus Jugarius* is now closely built over, and its contour has been completely altered, but it is evident that it was once a steep cliff, probably quite as abrupt as on the western side.

The Capitolium and the Arx. Few points in the topography of Rome have been so much disputed as the question of the relative positions of the *Arx* and the *Capitolium*, Canina and the Italian antiquaries[1] taking one view, and Bunsen with other able German writers the other. Now, however, the point may be regarded as practically settled, owing to a series of discoveries which have been made on the south-western peak.

Two peaks.

Apart from these discoveries, evidence from classical writings is not wanting to support the view that this south-

---

[1] The learned Roman antiquary, the Comm. Lanciani, was one of the first to accept Bunsen's attribution of these names; see an interesting paper by him in the *Bull. Comm. Arch. Rom.* iii. 1875, p. 165.

western part of the hill is the *Capitolium*. For example, *Capitolium.*
Livy (xxxv. 21) mentions the fall, in 192 B.C., of a mass of
rock from the *Capitolium* into the *Vicus Jugarius*, by which
several people were killed. This road passed close under the
Capitolium, while it is a long way from the other peak of the
hill; see also Livy, vii. 10.

Again, steps are mentioned by Ovid (*Fast.* vi. 183) as leading from the *Temple of Concord* up to the *Temple of Juno Moneta*, which was on the *Arx*; see p. 333; this can only apply to a staircase on the north-eastern side.

TEMPLES ON THE CAPITOLINE HILL.

The earliest Roman temple mentioned by any classical *Jupiter Feretrius.*
writer was built on the *Capitolium*; this was the Temple to
Jupiter Feretrius, vowed by Romulus after hanging the *Spolia
Opima*, taken from the defeated Acron, King of the Caesinenses, on a sacred oak which grew on the Capitolium; Livy, *Sacred oak.*
i. 10; Dionys. ii. 34; and Plut. *Marcell.* 8.

The worship of a sacred tree, especially the oak, appears
to be one of the oldest and most widely spread of primitive
cults. A great deal of interesting matter with regard to the
worship of the oak is given by Mr. J. G. Frazer in his valuable
Golden Bough, 1890; see vol. ii. pp. 291-370, and other places
in the same volume.

It may, however, be presumed that *Roma Quadrata*, from *Triple temple.*
the date of its founding, possessed that joint Temple to
Jupiter, Juno, and Minerva (*Tinia, Thalna,* and *Menrva*),
which, according to the religious rites of the Etruscans, was
erected in every new-built town. It was to this triad of
deities that the great temple on the *Capitolium* was consecrated, though it is usually spoken of as the Temple of *Jupiter
Capitolinus* alone.

Temple of Jupiter Capitolinus. Its *cella* was divided into
three chambers, each containing a statue of one of these

358   CAPITOLINE JUPITER   CHAP.

Three deities. deities, that of Jupiter in the centre, of Minerva on the right hand (Livy, vii. 3), and Juno on the left. In the roof of the Cella of Jupiter there was a hypaethral opening, for religious reasons, in order that the sky might be visible, *ut libero coelo frueretur*, as Lactantius says. So also Ovid, *Fast.* ii. 671 *seq.*—

*Nunc quoque se supra, ne quid nisi sidera cernat,
Exiguum Templi tecta foramen habent.*

From its combined antiquity, size, and magnificence this may be regarded as the most important of all the temples in Rome. In the Cella of Minerva a bronze nail (*clavus annalis*) was driven into the wall once a year in the Ides of September, the anniversary of the dedication, as a sort of sacred calendar (Livy, vii. 3); in late times this survived as a ceremony of great importance and sanctity. Dictators even were appointed *clavi figendi causa*; Livy, vii. 3, viii. 18, and ix. 28. This temple was the goal of triumphal processions, and in front of it a solemn sacrifice was offered by the victorious general or emperor, in the presence of the chief members of the Roman hierarchy, the Pontifex Maximus, the Flamen Dialis, the Vestal Virgins, and others. The scene is one frequently represented on the large bronze coins of the Empire.[1]

Clavus annalis.

Founder of the temple. The original building was founded by Tarquinius I., built by his son Tarquinius Superbus (Livy, i. 38, 53, and 55), but not consecrated till after his expulsion from Rome, when it was solemnly dedicated by M. Horatius Pulvillus, Consul-Suffectus, in the year 509 B.C.; see Livy, ii. 8, and vii. 3; Dionys. v. 35; Plutarch, *Public.* 15; Tac. *Hist.* iii. 72; Val. Max. v. 10; *Cor. In. Lat.* i. 487; and Pliny, *Hist. Nat.* xxviii. 15.

Stuccoed stone. The original *Temple of Capitoline Jupiter* was built of peperino and hard tufa, coated in the usual way with fine marble-dust stucco or *opus albarium*. Livy (xl. 51) records that in the year 179 B.C. this cement coating was renewed, *aedem Jovis in Capitolio columnasque circa poliendas albo locavit*

[1] See fig. 47 on p. 364.

[*Censor Lepidus*]. The temple was in the Etruscan style, with widely-spaced columns and wooden architraves.

Its *cultus* statues in the three Cellae, as well as the sculpture in and on the pediment, were of painted terra cotta, the usual material for Etruscan architectural sculpture.

The statue of Jupiter, according to one story, was modelled by Turianus, an Etruscan sculptor from Fregenae, as was also the terra-cotta Quadriga which stood on the top of the pediment; Livy, x. 23. Pliny (*Hist. Nat.* xxxv. 157) attributes the statue of Jupiter to a sculptor from Veii named Volca; cf. *Hist. Nat.* xxviii. 6. The Quadriga, according to another legend, is said to have been made for Tarquinius Superbus at Veii; it was numbered among the seven sacred relics, on the preservation of which the welfare of Rome depended.[1] Any fragments of this terra-cotta sculpture which got broken off were carefully preserved; see above, p. 355. *Terra-cotta sculpture.*

The gold and ivory throne of the seated statue of Jupiter was used as a sacred and, to some extent, secret depositary for the State store of gold coin and bullion. *Throne of Jupiter.*

As early as 390 B.C. this store of gold had amounted to no less than 2000 pounds weight when the whole of it was given up to the victorious Gauls as a general ransom for the city; see Pliny, *Hist. Nat.* xxxiii. 14, and Livy, v. 48, v. 50, and vii. 15. *Store of gold.*

In later years, when the throne treasury was again plundered by C. Marius the Younger in 82 B.C., the weight of gold, Pliny tells us, amounted to 13,000 pounds weight. This, however, seems to have included gold stolen from other shrines.

Pliny (*Hist. Nat.* xxxiii. 15) relates how the temple guardian (*aedituus*) committed suicide with the poison contained in a hollow ring, to avoid torture, when the gold was stolen, *Theft of gold.*

---

[1] The seven sacred relics are mentioned above, vol. i. p. 294; see Pliny, *Hist. Nat.* vii. 141, xxviii. 6, and xxxv. 157; Plut. *Publ.* 14; and Cancellieri, *Le sette cose fatali*, Roma, 1812.

probably by M. Crassus, in the second consulship of Cn. Pompey, 55 B.C.

Annual painting. On certain festivals every year it was the custom, even as late as the Imperial period, to renew the gaudy vermilion paint (γάνωσις) with which the statue of Jupiter had been decorated in the usual primitive fashion; see Pliny, *Hist. Nat.* xxxiii. 112, and xxxv. 157; and Plut. *Quaes. Rom.* 98; in this passage Plutarch tells us that the annual γάνωσις with red pigment (*minium*) was one of the chief duties of the Roman Censors.

Lofty podium. The temple was built on an enormous platform (Livy, vi. 4), partly constructed of the native tufa of which the hill itself is formed, and partly of *peperino*; this extended over the slope of the hill, making a lofty *podium*; ἐπὶ κρηπῖδος ὑψηλῆς, as Dionysius says.

Three cellae. In consequence of its three Cellae being set side by side, the temple was nearly square in shape. It is described with some minuteness by Dionysius (iv. 61); and Vitruvius (iv. 7) gives a technical account of its proportions and details.[1] It is also mentioned by Vitruvius (iii. 3) as an example of *araeostyle* (wide-spaced) intercolumniation, and as having *signa fictilia* (clay statues), *more Tuscanico* (after the Etruscan fashion).

Destruction by fire. This ancient building survived the Gaulish invasion in 390 B.C., and lasted till the year 83 B.C., when it was burnt by an incendiary, probably some one of the faction of Marius. Among other things this fire destroyed a gold shield (*clipeus*) ornamented with reliefs, which had been dedicated from the spoils of Hasdrubal, and placed over the entrance to the central *Cella*; see Pliny, *Hist. Nat.* xxxv. 14. Other gilt bronze shields were fixed on the pediment by L. Aemilius Paullus out of fines imposed by him as Aedile; see Livy, xxxv. 10.

Votive offerings. The Capitoline Temple of Jupiter was enormously rich in

[1] The Temple of Jupiter Capitolinus was taken by all writers on architecture as the typical example of the Tuscan style.

votive offerings; among them was a gold crown weighing 246 pounds given by King Attalus; see Livy, xxxii. 27; and again Livy, xxviii. 39, mentions another gold crown dedicated out of the Punic spoils in 205 B.C.; cf. Livy, x. 23, xxxv. 41, and xxxviii. 35.

The reconstruction of the temple was begun in 82 B.C. by Sulla, on its old foundations and plan, but with increased magnificence both of material and design. A number of columns were taken by Sulla from the Corinthian *Temple of Olympian Zeus*[1] in Athens to adorn the Capitoline Temple (Pliny, xxxvi. 45); it was, however, left incomplete by Sulla, and finished by Q. Lutatius Catulus, who also appears to have rebuilt the so-called *Tabularium* of the Capitol; see Plut. *Publ.* 15. Augustus assisted in the restoration of the temple, but the name of Catulus appeared alone on the frieze of the building. *Rebuilding by Sulla.*

This second temple lasted till 70 A.D., when it was again burnt, with other buildings on the Capitoline Hill, during the attack of the rioters who were supporting Vitellius against Sabinus, Vespasian's brother; Suet. *Vit.* 15. *Second fire.*

Immediately on succeeding to the throne Vespasian began the rebuilding of the temple with great enthusiasm, even labouring at clearing the site with his own hands—τὸν τε νεὼν τὸν ἐν Καπιτωλίῳ εὐθὺς οἰκοδομεῖν ἤρξατο; Dion Cass. lxvi. 10; see also Suet. *Vesp.* 8; Aur. Victor, *Caes.* 9; and Tac. *Hist.* iv. 53. In this third temple, which was consecrated in A.D. 71, the old plan was still, for religious reasons, strictly adhered to, but Vespasian was allowed by the priests to increase its height; Tac. *Hist.* iv. 53. *Rebuilding by Vespasian.*

Two interesting inscriptions relating to this rebuilding are published by Henzen, *Acta Frat. Arval.* 91, 118. These in-

[1] Mr. Penrose has shown in his interesting account of the excavation of the Olympicion in Athens (*Athen. Arch.* ed. of 1888) that it was probably not the columns of the peristyle, but the monolithic columns of coloured marble from the interior of the *Cella*, that Sulla moved from Athens to Rome.

scriptions record that on the 7th of the Ides of December the Fratres Arvales met in the Temple of Ops to record their vows, AD · RESTITVTIONEM · ET · DEDICATIONEM · CAPITOLI · AB · IMP T · CAESAR · VESPASIANO · AVG.

Third fire. During the reign of Titus, in 80 A.D., the temple was burnt again, for the third time, during a fire which raged for three days. It was rebuilt by Domitian, with greater splendour than ever, with Corinthian columns of Pentelic marble; Suet. *Dom.* 5; Dion Cass. lxvi. 24; and Plut. *Public.* 15. In the last-mentioned passage Plutarch says that he saw in Athens the columns of Pentelic marble which were being prepared for Domitian's new temple of Capitoline Jupiter, and that they were of excellent design, but that, after they were brought to Rome, they were much injured by being re-cut and polished, which to some extent spoilt their proportion.

Fourth temple.

Bronze tiles. The roof was covered with bronze tiles,[1] which were gilt; and, according to Plutarch, no less than 2½ millions sterling were spent on the gilding or gold plating of this most magnificent temple. The doors of the three *Cellae* were covered with gold reliefs, which remained intact till about the year 390 A.D., when they were stripped off by Stilicho; see Zosim. v. 38. The gold-plated bronze tiles were partly taken from the roof by the Vandal Genseric in 455; Procop. *Bell. Vand.* i. 5; and the rest by Pope Honorius, who removed them in 630 A.D. to cover the roof of the Basilica of S. Peter; see Marliani, *Topog.* ii. 1. The floor of the temple was paved with a variety of *sectile* mosaic made of shaped pieces of marble, which Pliny calls *opus scutulatum*; *Hist. Nat.* xxxvi. 185.

Gold reliefs.

Mosaic floor.

Sculptured reliefs. Many interesting representations of this triple temple and its sculpture exist on coins and reliefs. The pedimental sculpture is shown on a relief published in the *Ann. Inst.* 1851, p. 289. In the centre is Jupiter enthroned, with his feet on an eagle; on his left is Minerva, and on his right

[1] The older temple, when restored by Catulus, also had bronze tiles; see Pliny, *Hist. Nat.* xxxiii. 57.

Juno; the angles of the *tympanum* or *aetos* are filled up by figures of Vulcan making armour, Ceres, and other deities.

A relief from the *Arch of Marcus Aurelius*, now on the

Fig. 46.

stairs of the *Palazzo dei Conservatori*, has a good representation of the front of the temple, though it is shown with only four columns; see fig. 46. The three gold-plated doors of the Cellae are represented, and the sculpture in the pediment is

Marble relief.
shown with much minuteness, including the three chief deities in the centre, and others on each side, very like the relief mentioned above. A richly designed row of bronze *antifixae* runs up the slope of the pediment; on its apex is the famous terra-cotta Quadriga, or a copy of it; and there are remains of other groups at each angle of the gable.

A third marble relief in the Louvre shows the front of the Capitoline Temple very clearly, with its three folding doors, each partly open.

Coin types.
The whole front of the temple is shown on two republican denarii; one of the *gens Volteia* has it as a *tetrastyle* building, with three doors; another with the legend *Petillius Capitolinus* shows it as *hexastyle*.[1]

Fig. 47.
The Emperor offering sacrifice in front of the Temple of Capitoline Jupiter, on the reverse of a First Brass of Caligula.

Fig. 47 shows the *reverse* of a *First Brass* of Caligula, with the emperor offering sacrifice, with veiled head, in front of the Capitoline Temple. The Quadriga is shown on the top of the pediment, and other statues are vaguely indicated. On a *First Brass* of Vespasian and a Second Brass of Domitian the temple is represented as *hexastyle*, and the three statues of the deities are shown in front, though they were really of course within the three *Cellae*. A bronze *medallion* of Hadrian shows the three statues only—in the centre Jupiter, with an eagle above his head; on

---

[1] Representations of buildings on coins are usually treated in a very conventional way, and are no guide as to the number of columns on the front of a temple, or anything except a very rough notion of its form. The statue within the *Cella* is frequently shown outside; and a statue is introduced even when there was none within, as in the case of the *Temple of Vesta*; cf. fig. 45 on p. 337.

his right Minerva, in helmet and armour; and on his left Juno, with outstretched hand.[1]

At various times, from 1835 to 1880, extensive remains have been discovered under and near the Palazzo Caffarelli, on the western peak of the hill. These consist chiefly of a very large platform built of blocks of tufa, like those used in the Servian wall, forming a large *podium* on which the temple stood; the full extent of this has not been discovered, and it has not therefore been possible to test the accuracy of Dionysius' description of the temple (iv. 61).[2]

Existing remains.

In 1875 part of an enormous drum of a fluted column was found upon this platform; it is nearly 7 feet in diameter, too large, that is, for any Capitoline Temple except that of *Jupiter Capitolinus*; moreover, this fragment is of Pentelic marble, the material which is recorded to have been used in the last rebuilding by Domitian.

By the south side of the large tufa platform, a small platform similarly constructed was discovered in 1875. This is possibly the foundation of the primitive *Temple of Jupiter Feretrius* founded by Romulus, and rebuilt by Augustus, as is recorded in the inscription of Ancyra. The *flavissae* or subterranean treasure-chambers excavated in the rock below the Temple of Jupiter are mentioned above, see p. 355.

Smaller podium.

The following inscription was found in the fifteenth century in the building usually called the *Tabularium*, a name given to it mainly on the authority of this inscription; it is

Tabularium inscription.

---

[1] The three *cultus* statues in the Capitoline temple are represented, seated in thrones, on the *reverse* of a fine medallion of Antoninus Pius; see Froehner, *Méd. Rom.* p. 49. In his text Froehner wrongly takes these to be the statues in the pediment, which are always represented as standing figures. Seated figures would not so well have fitted the higher, central part of the pediment.

[2] See *Mon. Inst. Arch. Rom.* v. Tav. 36; and x. Tav. 30ª; *Ann. Inst.* 1851, p. 289, and 1876, p. 145; and *Bull. Comm. Arch. Mun.* iii. 1875, p. 165.

Tabular-ium.

quoted by Poggio of Florence, writing c. 1450, in his work titled, *De Fortunae Varietatibus*—Q · LVTATIVS · Q · F · CATVLVS COS · SVBSTRVCTIONEM · ET · TABVLARIVM · EX · S · C · FACIENDVM COERAVIT · EIDEMQVE · PROB.

The Comm. Lanciani suggests (*Bull. Arch. Mun.* iii. p. 165 *seq.*) that the *substructionem* mentioned in this inscription is the great platform of the *Temple of Jupiter Capitolinus*, though one would expect some distinct mention of the temple if that were the case.[1] In any case the inscription is very vague and puzzling, the word *Tabularium* being also used without any explanatory qualification.[2] Q. Lutatius Catulus was Consul in the year 78 B.C., which gives the date of the above record.

Juno Moneta.

The Temple of Juno Moneta. The peak of this hill opposite to the *Capitolium* was called the *Arx* or Citadel, and on it stood a large Temple to *Juno Moneta* or the *Adviser*; part of it was used as the mint, and hence *Moneta* came to mean *money*; Livy, vi. 20, vii. 28, and xlii. 7. It appears to have occupied the site of the present Church of Ara Coeli, the floor of which is about 14 feet higher than the summit of the opposite peak.

Founded in 344 B.C.

The original *Temple of Juno Moneta* was founded by L. Fur. Camillus, Dictator in 344 B.C. (Livy, vii. 28), on the site of the house of the Sabine King Tatius, and also on the site of the house of Manlius Capitolinus; Livy, vi. 20; Plut. *Rom.* 20; and Ovid, *Fast.* vi. 183.[3] It is this latter passage in which the close neighbourhood of the *Temple of Juno* to the great *Temple of Concord* appears to be clearly established, showing that the *Arx* cannot have been on the opposite peak—

---

[1] Valuable accounts of the *Temple of Jupiter Capitolinus* are given by Hirt, *Der Capit. Jupiter Tempel, Abhandl. der Berl. Akad.* 1813; Niebuhr *Rom. Gesch.* i. 55-58; Bunsen, *Besch.* 3A, 5-14; and Becker, *Handbuch,* i. p. 387.

[2] *Tabularium* was a generic name for a place where records were kept, and there were many *Tabularia* in Rome.

[3] From Plutarch (*Camil.* 36) it would appear that the Temple of Juno was founded by Camillus in 384 B.C., but this is evidently a mistake.

Candida, te nives posuit lux proxima templo   Ovid, Fast.
Qua fert sublimes alta Moneta gradus :   vi. 183.
Nunc bene prospicies Latiam, Concordia, turbam.

The steps mentioned are those which led from the Forum up to the "*Carcer imminens foro*," now called the Mamertine prison, and thence past the side of the *Temple of Concord* and the so-called *Tabularium* up to the *Temple of Juno Moneta* on the summit of the *Arx*; see Forum Plan. Certain important records were deposited in the *Temple of Juno Moneta*. Among them was the book written on linen, which is mentioned by Livy, iv. 7. Another ancient MS. on linen (*liber linteus*) is mentioned by Livy, x. 38. *Scalae Monetae.*

MS. records.

The whole of this peak of the Capitoline Hill was covered by the Church and Monastery of Ara Coeli. It now appears probable that the *Temple of Juno Moneta* occupied the site of the present church, not that of the adjoining monastery, since during the recent destruction of the monastic buildings of Ara Coeli to make room for the new monument to Victor Emmanuel, no remains of the Temple of Juno have been discovered. The only discoveries made during this extensive demolition have been some further remains of the ancient Capitoline wall. *Site of Temple of Juno.*

Other Temples on the Capitoline Hill. A large number of other temples and shrines crowded the summit of the whole Capitoline Hill, which must, under the Empire, have been one enormous group of great architectural splendour, decorated with countless statues and other works of art, including great quantities of the spoils of earlier art from Hellenic cities, and also a number of statues by the Graeco-Roman sculptors of the Imperial period. *Smaller temples.*

Two of these temples were large enough to hold meetings of the Senate, namely, the *Temple of Fides*, founded by Numa[1] *Temple of Fides.*

[1] It need hardly be said that such a statement as "founded by Numa" simply means that the origin of the temple was lost in the mists of pre-

and rebuilt in the first Punic war (Livy, i. 21, and Plut.
Temple of Honos and Virtus. Num. 16), and the *Temple of Honos and Virtus*, built by Marius; Cic. *Pro Sest.* 54; *De Divin.* i. 28. The latter was designed by the Roman architect C. Mutius, and is highly praised for the symmetry of the proportions of its Cella and columns by Vitruvius (vii. *Praef.* 17), who expresses a regret that it had not been built of marble; he mentions (iii. 2. 5) that it was *peripteral*.

An inscription quoted by Nardini, *Roma Antica*, ed. Nibby, 1819, iii. p. 138, records that Marius built this temple out of spoils taken from the Teutons and Cimbrians; see also Orelli, *Inscrip.* 543.[1] Both these temples stood on the west or Capitoline peak.

Vejovis. In the intermediate valley was an *Aedes Vejovis*, Aul. Gell. v. 12. The positions of other and less important shrines on the Capitoline Hill are unknown; among them were *aediculae* dedicated to *Jupiter Custos, Venus Victrix, Venus Capitolina, Beneficium*, and *Ops*.

Jupiter Tonans. In commemoration of an escape from death by lightning, Augustus built a small temple to *Jupiter Tonans* near the great Temple of *Jupiter Capitolinus*; see Suet. *Aug.* 29; and Pliny, *Hist. Nat.* xxxvi. 50;[2] in this passage Pliny mentions the Temple of Jupiter Tonans as an example of the use of marble in solid blocks. Its building is recorded in the Ancyrean inscription, and the same inscription mentions that Augustus rebuilt the ancient Temple of *Jupiter Feretrius*.

historic antiquity. An analogous case is the frequent Greek attribution of archaic statues to the mythical sculptor Daedalus.

[1] Marius was obliged to build this temple of very moderate height, in order that it might not be in the way of the augurs' observations from the *Auguraculum*; Festus, ed. Müller, p. 322.

[2] *Jupiter Capitolinus* appeared in a dream to Augustus, and expressed jealousy of the Temple to *Jupiter Tonans*; upon which Augustus hung bells on the shrine of the latter, and explained to *Jupiter Capitolinus* that *Jupiter Tonans* was only there as his doorkeeper; Suet. *Aug.* 91.

On the opposite side, near the *Temple of Juno Moneta*, was a *Shrine to Concord*,[1] vowed, during a mutiny among his soldiers in Gaul, by the Praetor L. Manlius, in 215 B.C., and dedicated two years later; Livy, xxii. 33. *Shrine of Concord.*

A triumphal arch in honour of Nero, which was erected on the Capitol, is shown on some of his coins; see fig. 94, vol. ii. p. 302. *Arch of Nero.*

One structure of great religious importance upon the *Arx* was the *Auguraculum*, an elevated platform from which the *Augurs*[2] observed the signs of the heavens (see Festus, ed. Müller, p. 18); an Etruscan custom dating from prehistoric times. It appears to have been transferred by Augustus to the Palatine, and is catalogued in the *Notitia* under the name *Auguratorium*; see vol. i. p. 158. *Auguraculum.*

Works of Art on the Capitoline Hill. Chief among the crowd of statues on the Capitoline Hill was the colossal bronze statue of Apollo, 45 feet high, brought from Apollonia in Pontus, by M. Lucullus; see Pliny, *Hist. Nat.* xxxiv. 39. This colossus was the work of the famous Athenian sculptor *Kalamis*, who flourished in the generation before Pheidias. Pliny also mentions (*ib.* 40) a colossal bronze statue of Hercules, brought from Tarentum (Livy, ix. 44), which was set on the Capitol by Fabius Verrucosus; and (*ib.* 43) a bronze colossal Jupiter erected by Sp. Carvilius out of the bronze armour taken as spoils from the Samnites. This statue was so large that it was visible from the Alban Hills, and Car- *Colossal statues.*

---

[1] Another *aedicula* to Concord, made of bronze, existed near the Forum; see above, p. 338.

[2] Under the Empire the *Collegium of Augurs* consisted of sixteen members, of whom the emperor usually was one. They offered sacrifice with veiled head, holding in one hand a *lituus*, which, except in having a short handle, resembled the *crozier* of a twelfth-century bishop.

The importance of the Augurs is indicated by the Imperial title *Augustus*, which, according to the common interpretation of the word, means "consecrated by augury."

vilius had a statue of himself made out of the waste bronze filings; the latter small statue in Pliny's time stood before the feet of the colossus. He mentions also two bronze busts (*ib.* 44), which were greatly admired, the work of the sculptors Chares and Decius, presented by the Consul P. Lentulus.

Bronze busts.

Among the most costly votive offerings on the *Capitolium* were golden quadrigae dedicated in 204 B.C. by the Curule Aediles; see Livy, xxix. 38.

Kings of Rome.

Among the most ancient of the works of art on the Capitoline Hill were statues of all the kings of Rome, mentioned by Pliny (*Hist. Nat.* xxxiii. 9) in his discussion on the antiquity of the custom of wearing rings. Pliny thinks it strange that only two of the kings, Numa and Servius Tullius, were represented with rings.

Statue from Praeneste.

In 380 B.C. a statue of Jupiter Imperator was brought among the spoils of Praeneste and placed *inter cellam Jovis ac Minervae*, with an inscription on a bronze tablet to record that it had been dedicated by the Dictator T. Quinctius after the conquest of nine cities; see Livy, vi. 29.

Bronze dog.

In the *Cella of Juno*, in the *Temple of Jupiter Capitolinus*, there was a wonderful realistic statue in bronze of a dog licking its wound, which was valued so highly that a special official was appointed, under penalty of death, to guard it. This statue perished during the fire caused by the Vitellian rioters; see Pliny, *Hist. Nat.* xxxiv. 38.

Jupiter Tonans.

The statue of *Jupiter Tonans*, according to Pliny (*ib.* 79), was the finest of the statues on the Capitoline Hill. It was the work of Leochares, who, about the middle of the fourth century B.C., was one of the sculptors employed on the Mausoleum at Halicarnassus.

Capitoline Jupiter.

The terra-cotta statue of Jupiter Capitolinus, dedicated by Tarquinius Priscus, was a notable example of Etruscan Art, as were also the terra-cotta reliefs in the *tympanum*, and the quadriga on the apex of the pediment of the temple. These were all painted red with *minium*, and the colouring was renewed at regular intervals as it faded. The statues on the pediment are mentioned by Cicero, *De Div.* i. 11. In later times the statue of Jupiter appears to have been of gold; see *Gold statue.* Mart. xi. 4. It was a seated figure holding a thunderbolt; see Ovid (*Fast.* i. 202), who is speaking of the original clay statue. Jupiter's head was crowned with a gold wreath of oak leaves; Plaut. *Trinum.* I. ii. 93.

There were also a number of fine pictures on the Capito- *Paintings.* line Hill, the work of many of the great Greek painters; Pliny (*Hist. Nat.* xxxv. 69) mentions a picture of Theseus by Parrhasius; one of Proserpine carried away by Pluto, the work of Nicomachus, the son and pupil of Aristiacus, in the *Cella* of Minerva (*ib.* 108); and a Victory in a quadriga, painted by the same artist, which was dedicated by the Consul Plancus.

The first *myrrhine vases*[1] brought to Rome were dedicated *Votive* in the Temple of Capitoline Jupiter by Pompey the Great; *treasures.* and there Livia Augusta offered the largest crystal cup ever seen in Rome, weighing about 150 pounds; Augustus dedicated in the *Cella* of Jupiter 16,000 pounds weight of gold, and pearls and gems to the value of fifty millions of sesterces, at one offering; Suet. *Aug.* 30; Pliny, *Hist. Nat.* xxxvii. 18 and 27.

Servius (*Ad Aen.* iii. 29) records that Augustus, after his *Bronze* victory over the Egyptian fleet, used the captured *rostra* to *columns.* make four bronze columns, which were afterwards dedicated by Domitian on the Capitoline Hill.

There is a mediaeval tradition that these are the columns which for many centuries past have stood at the sides of one of the altars in the Lateran Basilica. Whether this be true or not, they are very large and magnificent fluted columns with Corinthian capitals, of bronze thickly plated with gold, and are well worthy of examination as being among the most important examples of ancient metal-work on a large scale which still exist. Their fine workmanship shows that they

[1] See vol. i. p. 22.

were cast during a good artistic period. They now stand in the left transept as one faces the High Altar in the Lateran Church.

THE CAPITOLINE TABULARIUM.

Tabularium. The *Tabularium* (so called) occupies nearly the whole front of the *Asylum* or central depression in the Capitoline Hill, facing towards the Forum; this is in some respects the most interesting of the existing buildings of Rome, and much the most extensive and perfect example of Republican date. But little is known of its use or history; the most important document relating to it is the inscription, quoted in vol. i. p. 366, *Building of* which records the building of a *Tabularium* by Q. Lutatius *Catulus.* Catulus, Consul in the year 78 B.C., the same man whose name appeared as the rebuilder on the front of the Temple of *Capitoline Jupiter*; see Tac. *Hist.* iii. 72.

With regard to the name *Tabularium*, the difficulty is that there were many *Tabularia* in Rome; see Livy, iii. 55, and xliii. 16; and Virgil (*Geor.* ii. 502) uses the word in the plural; nor have we any mention by any classical writer of a building in Rome which was known as *the Tabularium, par excellence*. Mommsen's suggestion that this was the *Aerarium* is contradicted by the many passages which show that the Public Treasury was in or adjoining the *Temple of Saturn*; see vol. i. p. 266. In default of a better name the *Tabularium* is a convenient one to adopt, and certainly to some extent appears to be authorised by the above-quoted inscription.

Existing The building stands on the slope of the Capitoline Hill, *remains.* the tufa rock of which is cut away to receive it. Its front, facing the Forum, reaches nearly to the foot of the hill, while its back, at a much higher level, faces on to the *Asylum*, or valley between the *Arx* and the *Capitolium*. The Forum front consisted of an open arcade with engaged Roman-Doric columns of *peperino*, having capitals and architrave of *travertine*; the rest of the entablature is missing. According to Poggio there was in his time (the fifteenth century) another story above the existing arcade. Each bay of the arcade is vaulted with tufa concrete, once covered with stucco ornaments; only one of the arches is now open and visible outside, and it is mostly a modern restoration.

One main entrance, still in use, is from the *Clivus Capito-* *linus* at the south-west end of the building, a very fine specimen of masonry, with a remarkable flat arch nearly 17 feet in span, beautifully jointed.[1] The whole external walls are of *peperino* built with very accurately worked blocks, each exactly 4 Roman feet long by 2 wide and 2 thick, laid in alternate courses of headers and stretchers, with a very thin coat of pure lime mortar in all the joints—a very beautiful example of Republican *emplecton* masonry. The inner walls are of similar blocks, but of *tufa* instead of *peperino*, or else of concrete made of broken tufa, pozzolana, and lime, in the usual early fashion, without any admixture of brick or travertine. *Fine masonry.*

The opposite (eastern) corner of the building has been destroyed, but there was evidently another entrance there, probably from the *Gradus monetae*. This entrance led into the open arcade of the *Tabularium*, which appears to have been a thoroughfare, so that foot-passengers could enter from one side and pass out at the other, from the *Gradus monetae* to the *Clivus Capitolinus*. A row of rooms opened into this public arcade, and at a higher level behind, facing on to the *Asylum*, was a large hall, now reached by a wide flight of stairs from the main arcade. *Eastern angle.* *Great hall.*

This hall occupies the whole length of the *Tabularium*; it is roofed with concrete quadripartite vaulting supported on rows of piers. These piers, however, appear to be later in date than the time of Catulus, 78 B.C., but have been so much restored that it is very difficult now to judge of their age.

[1] This is now the entrance by which the visitor is admitted to the very interesting series of chambers described below. The arch is now so much restored that it is difficult to trace the original *voussoirs*.

374   THE TABULARIUM   CHAP.

Long stairs. From near the south angle of this great hall the long steep staircase of 67 steps (mentioned below) leads down to the doorway in the front of the Tabularium which is shown on fig. 48. The position of these stairs is shown on the *Forum Plan*, No. 17.

More immediately at the back of the arcade, at the northeast end of the building, there is a well-preserved room, to which access is now given by some wooden stairs, through a doorway broken in the wall of the room; the original entrance was at the other end by a flight of travertine steps resting on tufa foundations, which still remain. This chamber was originally in two stories, but the intermediate concrete vaulting and floor are now gone, and only the stone springers of the barrel vault exist. In the middle of the floor of this *Other stairs.* room is the well-hole of a large staircase descending to the very interesting lower story. The steps and travertine curb round the well-hole are well preserved. The descent is easy, and the steps are varied, as was usually the fashion in Roman stairs when space allowed, by an intermediate inclined plane; thus diminishing the labour of the ascent; see *Forum Plan*.

A very massive flat arch supports the wall above where the stairs pass under it; they then turn to the left and lead *Lower chambers.* to a succession of small rooms, or rather a long passage under the arcade with windows, one in each bay, opening on to the Forum; see No. 23, 23 on the *Forum Plan*. This is all built of solid tufa masonry, faced outside with *peperino*, with vaults above of tufa concrete, supporting the road which runs *Windows.* along the upper arcade. The windows were originally only 2 Roman feet wide, but have all been enlarged, except one. As is mentioned above, p. 336, these windows do not extend along the north-eastern part of the *Tabularium* wall, where the back of the older *Temple of Concord* abutted against the front of the *Tabularium*.

Behind this long passage is the solid tufa rock, so there are no other rooms at this level. The front wall here is very massive, being 11 feet 3 inches thick, with a series of arched recesses or *embrasures*—on plan, mere rectangular apertures, 5 feet 6 inches high—into which the small windows opened. The arches of these recesses are formed of tufa concrete. *[Long passage.]*

This passage does not extend to the north-east end of the *Tabularium*, and its opposite end is now blocked up. It appears to have had six bays with windows, each under the centre of an arch of the upper arcade; and then at this same level, a little beyond the place where the seventh window would come (counting from the staircase end), there is an archway, opening down to the original floor of the passage, which must have led out on to some building which does not now exist. *[Blocked archway.]*

This may possibly have been a *Porticus of the Dii Consentes* earlier than that of Flavian times which now exists. The present *Porticus* blocked up the archway, but the earlier structure may have been lower, so that the opening led out on to its roof.

This archway can be traced, though with difficulty, on the outside of the building; the vault of the first of the chambers of the XII Dii Consentes cuts across it. It is blocked up, and only two or three of its *voussoirs* exist; it is shown on the *Forum Plan*, No. 16.

One of the most interesting features of the *Tabularium* is a very long and rather steep staircase of sixty-seven steps, without a break or landing, which leads from the outside of the building, at its lowest point towards the Forum, up to the great hall facing on the *Asylum* at the back; see *Forum Plan*, No. 17. These stairs are partly cut through the rock of the hill, and have no communication with any other part of the building. The walls are of neat tufa masonry in 2 feet courses, like the rest of the building, and are vaulted over by a series of concrete barrel vaults, supported on massive tufa flat arches, set at regular intervals over the stairs, and following its rise. *[Long stairs.]*

The exit at the foot of the staircase was by a very beautifully jointed peperino doorway, with a flat arch of travertine, and over it a semicircular relieving arch of peperino; see fig. *[Doorway blocked.]*

48. It seems probable that this was one of the points at which the Vitellian rioters, in 70 A.D., broke into the Capitol —*tum diversos Capitolii aditus invadunt juxta lucum asyli et qua*

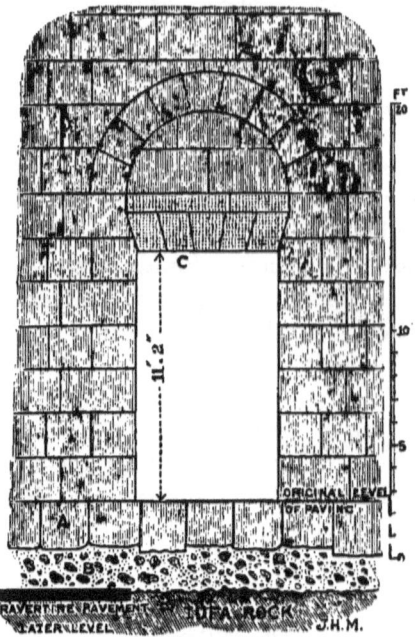

Fig. 48.
Example of Opus Quadratum, 78 B.C. Arch at foot of the stairs of the Tabularium.
The flat arch C is of travertine, the rest of peperino.
A. Footing-course of rough stones.
B. Concrete foundation, exposed by the lowering of the paving when the Temple of Vespasian was built. Each block is 4 Roman feet long by 2 wide and 2 thick ; a thin stratum of mortar is used.[1]

Tarpeia rupes centum gradibus aditur. Inprovisa utraque vis; propior atque acrior per asylum ingruebat; Tac. *Hist.* iii. 71.

When Domitian built the Temple of Vespasian he set it

[1] This drawing shows the doorway as it was before it was blocked up by the Temple of Vespasian.

against the front wall of the *Tabularium* in such a way as completely to block up this doorway, and it was possibly about the same time that the Porticus of the XII gods was rebuilt, which blocked up the other archway near this, but at the higher level.[1]

The noble mass of Republican masonry which forms this front wall is built *battering* or sloping on its outer face; that is to say, each course of *peperino* recedes nearly an inch behind the face of the course below. The foundations, made of tufa concrete, are exposed near the Temple of Vespasian by the lowering of the pavement on each side of it, as is shown in fig. 48. The fine layer of lime-mortar in all the joints of this wall is not thicker than stout paper, and is not primarily intended to act as a holding cement or mortar, but simply to make the two adjacent surfaces of the blocks fit together with absolute completeness of contact.

Fine masonry.

Unfortunately, much damage has been done to this very interesting building during mediaeval times, especially about the year 1300, in the reign of Pope Boniface VIII., and later by Nicholas V., when both angles towards the Forum were destroyed and the whole front built up to make it into a fortress, with towers at the corners. Inside much damage was done to the tufa walls behind the arcade by the place being made into a salt store—always a Government monopoly—by which the soft tufa masonry and even the *peperino* have been seriously corroded.[2]

Mediaeval alterations.

[1] The architectural effect of the Forum front of the *Tabularium* was wholly disregarded when the two lofty Temples of Concord and Vespasian were built against it. These buildings, when complete, blocked up and hid nearly all the open arches of the Doric arcade; that the older Temple of Concord was smaller than the existing one is shown by indications on the face of this wall; see vol. i. p. 336.

[2] At present the arcade is used as a museum of architectural fragments, many of which are well worth study, especially the great entablatures of the *Temples of Concord* and *Vespasian*. See Righetti, *Descrizione del Campidoglio*, 1833; Azzurri, *L'Antico Tabulario*, 1839; Supham, *De Capitolio Romano*, 1866; Jordan, *Topogr. Roms*, and *Ann. Inst.* for 1881.

CHAPTER IX

THE ARCHITECTURAL GROWTH OF ROME.

BEFORE passing on to a description of the Imperial Fora it may be well to give some account of the architectural state of Rome immediately before the Christian era.

It had long before then very largely outgrown the limits of the Servian enclosure; in fact the most architecturally magnificent portion of Rome was then outside the ancient wall. This was the *Campus Martius*, originally called the *Ager Tarquiniorum*, from its owners the Tarquin kings,[1] after whose expulsion it was known as the Field of Mars, from a prehistoric altar and temple dedicated to that deity. The construction of several great *cloacae* redeemed it from a marshy plain to firm ground.

Campus Martius.

A long list of magnificent public buildings which stood here is given by Pliny (see vol. ii. pp. 215-218) and by Strabo (v. 3. 8); who describe the *Campus Martius* as the most splendid quarter of Rome. This was owing to the fact that, being unencumbered with old houses and streets, at the close of the Republic there was nothing to hinder the whole of its vast area from being laid out with new streets, *porticus*, and open spaces, with much regularity and symmetry, when the great building era set in during the reigns of Augustus and his successors.[2]

[1] See Plutarch, *Public.* 8.
[2] During mediaeval times the reverse was the case. The *Campus Martius* was the most thickly populated quarter of Rome, inhabited largely

Three large theatres, an amphitheatre, many temples, the *Pantheon* and great *Thermae of Agrippa*, the splendid group of buildings which were clustered round the *Porticus Octaviae* and the great *Circus Flaminius* were some of the chief architectural splendours which grew up in the *Campus Martius* through the munificence of Augustus and his friends ; see vol. ii. chap. vi.

Public buildings.

Outside the *Porta Capena*, and over the extensive Esquiline Hill, and in other directions, new and populous quarters of the city had extended beyond the limits of the regal walls. And yet, up to the time of Augustus, there had been no *Regiones* added to the four primitive ones of Servius; see vol. i. p. 124.

Rome, in the first century B.C., was too powerful and too safe from external enemies to need a wall of fortification, but for political, social, and religious reasons, Augustus planned and carried out a complicated division of the whole intramural and extra-mural city into *Regiones* and *Vici*, each with its set of officials, both municipal and priestly.

Regiones of Augustus.

Fourteen Regiones. The main divisions were into fourteen *Regiones*; and each *Regio* was subdivided into *Vici* (or parishes), varying in number from seven in the smallest, the *Regio Caelimontana*, to seventy-eight in the largest, the *Regio Transtiberina*. The whole 14 *Regiones* contained 265 *Vici*. Each *Vicus* formed a religious body with its *aedicula Larium* or *Compitalis*; and they were presided over by *Magistri vicorum*, the lowest in rank of the Roman magistrates.[1]

265 Vici.

An interesting marble altar was found in 1888 near the new Ponte Garibaldi which had been dedicated to the Lares of Augustus in 3 A.D. by the *Vico-Magistri* of the *Vicus Aesculeti*. On one side there is a relief representing four Vico-Magistri offering sacrifice, and on two other sides there is a relief of one

Vicus altar.

by the poorer classes ; with here and there the castle of some powerful feudal lord, such as were the Orsini and Colonna Counts.

[1] A valuable paper on the limits of the *Regiones* of Augustus is published by Comm. Lanciani in *Bull. Com. Arch.* 1889. pp. 115 to 137.

of the *Lares*, represented as a graceful youth, wearing a short tunic, and holding a large branch of laurel.

A similar altar exists in the Vatican, and another in the Uffizi in Florence, both dedicated in the reign of Augustus.

These three are the only examples of altars dedicated by *Vico-Magistri* which are known to exist.

Vigiles. A large body of police, who also combined the office of firemen, was reorganised by Augustus after a serious fire in 6 B.C.; see Suet. *Aug.* 30. They were divided into seven *Cohortes Vigilum* of about a thousand men each, and each cohort was presided over by a *Tribunus Vigilum* with seven *Centuriones* under him; their barracks (*stationes*) were very extensive and handsome buildings; see below, vol. ii. p. 255.

Magistrates. A superior class of magistrates (*Curatores* and *Denunciatores*), chosen annually from the Tribunes, Aediles, or Praetors, with a number of subordinate officials, had the supervision of the *Regiones*, assisted by the *Praefectus Vigilum*, who, in addition to his other responsibilities, performed the duties of a very dignified sort of Police Magistrate, whose district included the whole fourteen *Regiones* of Rome.

Fourteen Regiones. The following is a list of the fourteen *Regiones*[1] of Augustus, taken from the *Regionary Catalogues*, which were mainly compiled in the reign of Constantine :—

Porta Capena. I. PORTA CAPENA, extending beyond the fork of the *Via Appia* and *Latina*, as far (probably) as the later circuit wall of Aurelianus.[2] It was divided into ten *Vici*.

Principal buildings, etc., contained in Regio I.[3] — Two

[1] The fourteen *Rioni* (a corruption of *Regiones*) into which Rome is still divided do not follow the ancient lines of these districts.

[2] It seems probable that the line of the great wall of Aurelianus was (partly at least) determined by the boundaries of the *Regiones* of Augustus, being mostly planned so as to include the whole of these.

[3] Our chief knowledge of the contents and limits of each *Regio* is derived from the catalogues of the *Notitia* and *Curiosum*, two lists, varying slightly, which were drawn up in the fourth century. They are published by Preller, *Regionen der Stadt Rom*, Jena, 1846; and by Nardini,

FOURTEEN REGIONES

Temples of Mars, the sacred Grove and Spring of Egeria, the Sepulchre of the Scipios, Arches of Drusus, Trajan, and Lucius Verus, the Baths of Severus, and the Baths of Commodus.

II. CAELIMONTANA, including the Caelian Hill. *Caeli-*
Principal Contents.—*The Temple of Claudius, the Macellum* *montana.*
Magnum (great market of Nero), *the Caput Africae, the Castra peregrina* (barracks of the foreign legion), *the Domus Vectiliana* (Palace of Commodus), *Temples of Bacchus and Faunus*. This is the smallest *Regio*, containing only seven *Vici*.

III. ISIS ET SERAPIS, contained eight *Vici*. It included the *Isis et* valley of the Colosseum, and the adjacent part of the Esquiline *Serapis.* Hill.

Principal Contents.—*The Flavian Amphitheatre, the Ludus Magnus, the Baths of Titus, the Baths of Trajan, and the Porticus Liviae.* In the reign of Nero the greater part of this *Regio* was occupied by his *Golden House*. Its name was derived from the *Temples of Isis and Serapis*.

IV. TEMPLUM PACIS, contained eight *Vici*. It included *Templum* the *Velia*, most of *the Subura, the Fora of Vespasian and Nerva*, *Pacis.* *the Sacra Via*, and buildings along the north-east side of the *Forum Romanum*.

Principal Contents.—*The Great Temple and Forum of Peace*, whence came its name; *the Temple of Pallas and all Nerva's Forum, the Temple of Romulus and of Jupiter Stator, the Templum Urbis Romae, Hadrian's Temple of Venus Felix and Roma Aeterna, the Temple of Tellus, the Basilica of Constantine, the Basilica of Aemilius Paulus, the Vulcanal and the Sacra Via, the Meta Sudans and the Colossus of Nero.*

V. ESQUILINA, contained fifteen *Vici* and included the *Esquilina.* northern part of the Esquiline, and the Viminal Hill.

Principal Contents.—*The Nymphaeum of Sev. Alexander, the Gardens and Villa of Maecenas, the Amphitheatrum Castrense, the*

Roma Antica, ed. Nibby, 1818-20, whose work is arranged in the order of these lists. See also Urlichs, *Codex Topogr. Urbis Romae*, Würtzburg, 1871, and Jordan, *Forma Urbis Romae*, Berlin, 1875-82.

Barracks of the second Cohors Vigilum, the Temple of Minerva Medica, and the Macellum Liviae.

Alta Semita.
VI. ALTA SEMITA, contained seventeen *Vici*, and included the Quirinal Hill as far as the Praetorian Camp, which was afterwards included in the Wall of Aurelian.

Principal Contents.—*The Capitolium Vetus, the Temple of Venus and the Horti Sallustiani, the Baths of Diocletian and the Baths of Constantine, the Barracks of the third Cohors Vigilum, the Temple of Quirinus, with a statue 20 feet high.*

Via Lata.
VII. VIA LATA, contained (according to the *Notitia*) fifteen *Vici*. It was bounded on the west by the street called Via Lata (part of the modern Corso), which issued from the *Porta Ratumena* and skirted the Campus Martius, where, at the distance of about a third of a mile from the gate, it was continued northwards under the name of the *Via Flaminia*. A record of this main street is preserved in the title of the Church of *S. Maria in Via Lata* in the Corso. On the east this *Regio* extended to the foot of the Quirinal Hill.

Principal Contents.—*The Tomb of Poblicius Bibulus, the Campus and Septa Agrippae,*[1] *the Temple of the Sun, the Forum Suarium* (pig market), *the Arches of M. Aurelius, and Lucius Verus, and Temples of Spes, Fortuna, and Quirinus.*

Forum Romanum.
VIII. FORUM ROMANUM, contained thirty-four *Vici*. It included not only the Forum from which it took its name, but also the Fora of Julius Caesar, Augustus, and Trajan, and the whole of the Capitoline Hill.

Circus Flaminius.
IX. CIRCUS FLAMINIUS, contained thirty-five *Vici*. It included *the Campus Martius*, and was bounded by the Capitoline Hill, *the Via Lata* and *Flaminia*, and the Tiber.

Principal Contents.—*The Forum Olitorium, the Theatres of Pompey, Marcellus, and Balbus, the Amphitheatre of Statilius Taurus, the Pantheon and Baths of Agrippa, the Porticus Argonautarum, the Mausoleum of Augustus, the Porticus Octaviae, and various Temples adjoining; the Temples and Columns of Antoninus*

[1] More correctly called the *Septa Julia*.

Pius and *Marcus Aurelius, the Baths of Sev. Alexander;* the Temple *of Minerva Chalcidica* (built by Pompey), *the Iseum and Serapeum* adjoining it, and a large number of other magnificent buildings.

X. PALATINA, contained twenty *Vici.* It included the whole of the Palatine Hill. *Palatina.*

XI. CIRCUS MAXIMUS, contained eighteen *Vici.* It included the whole valley between the Aventine and the Palatine Hills, with the *Velabrum* and the *Forum Boarium;* being bounded on that side by the line of the Servian wall. *Circus Maximus.*

Principal Contents.—The Circus Maximus, the Temples of Ceres (S. Maria in Cosmedin), *Mercury and Hercules, the Arch of Constantine, and the Servian Porta Trigemina.*

XII. PISCINA PUBLICA, contained fourteen *Vici.* It included the space between the Caelian and the Aventine, extending beyond the *Via Appia.* *Piscina Publica.*

Principal Contents.—The Baths of Caracalla, the Barracks of the fourth Cohors Vigilum, a Villa of Hadrian, and other buildings, of which little is known.

XIII. AVENTINA, contained seventeen *Vici.* It included the whole of the Aventine Hill, and its slopes down to the river. *Aventina.*

Principal Contents.—Temples of Diana, Minerva, Jupiter Libertatis, and *Juno Regina, the Horrea Galbae* (by the river), *and the Forum Pistorium* (bakers' market).

XIV. TRANSTIBERINA, contained seventy-eight *Vici,* and included the whole transpontine city, with the Janiculan and Vatican Hills, and also the island in the Tiber. *Transtiberina.*

· *Principal Contents.—The Circi of Caligula and Hadrian, the Mausoleum of Hadrian, the Barracks of the seventh Cohors Vigilum, the Nemus Caesarum, the horti Getae and the Temple of Aesculapius,* and others on the island.

Besides these important improvements in the internal organisation of the city, Augustus spent immense sums of money in building and restoring the temples and other public buildings of Rome. Of the enormous extent of his benefactions to the city a most important record exists, engraved on the walls of a temple at Ancyra. For topographical purposes this is the most valuable of all existing Roman inscriptions.[1]

THE MONUMENTUM ANCYRANUM.

Temple at Ancyra. Ancyra was a city in the province of Galatia; more anciently it was included in Phrygia. It contains a Corinthian, hexastyle, peripteral temple dedicated to *Roma and Augustus*. The columns of the peristyle are all gone, but the *cella* remains, built of large blocks of marble.[2] On the walls of the cella and the pronaos are engraved, in both Latin and Greek, long lists of the deeds of the Emperor Augustus.

Inscription. This inscription, commonly known as the *Monumentum Ancyranum*, is a copy, together with a Greek translation, of the sepulchral inscription which was engraved on two bronze columns or pilasters, which stood one on each side of the entrance to the *Mausoleum of Augustus* in the *Campus Martius* of Rome.

Suetonius, who quotes largely from this inscription, calls it, in his life of Augustus, an *index rerum a se gestarum*; see *Aug.* 101. The original manuscript of the inscription, together with his will, and the written directions about his funeral, which Augustus prepared before his death, were all placed under the care of the Vestal Virgins.

Three sections. Like all Roman sepulchral inscriptions, *the Monumentum Ancyranum* is divided into three sections; the first gives a list

---

[1] It has been published by Zumpt (in 1845, with Supplement in 1869) and by Mommsen; the latter's edition of 1883, Berlin, which has photographic facsimiles of the slabs, is by far the best.

[2] An interesting article on the Ancyrean inscription by L. Cantarelli is printed in *Bull. Com. Arch.* 1890, pp. 1 and 57. The writer tries to prove that this is not a copy of the *titulus sepulcralis*, but an inscription *sui generis*, of a quite exceptional kind.

of the *cursus honorum* or titles and honours which had been conferred on Augustus.

The second part records his *impensae*, all his various gifts and acts of munificence, the buildings he restored or founded, the public spectacles he provided for the amusement of the Romans, and the precious offerings dedicated by him in the temples of the gods. *Gifts.*

The third section deals with his acts or *res gestae*.[1] The title of the whole is, "*Rerum gestarum Divi Augusti, quibus orbem terrarum imperio populi Romani subjecit, et impensarum quas in rempublicam populumque Romanum fecit, incisarum in duabus aheneis pilis, quae sunt Romae positae examplar subjectum.*" *Acts.*

The following is a list of the buildings in Rome recorded in the second part of this inscription to have been built or restored by Augustus :—*The Curia and the Chalcidicum adjoining it; the Temple of Apollo and its Porticus on the Palatine ;*[2] *the Temple of Divus Julius, the Lupercal, the Porticus Octavia,*[3] *a pulvinar or state box at the Circus Maximus.* *Buildings of Augustus.*

Temples of Jupiter Feretrius and Jupiter Tonans on the Capitol; a Temple of Quirinus; Temples of Minerva, Juno Regina, and Jupiter Libertatis on the Aventine.

The Temple of the Lares on the Summa Sacra Via, and of the Dii Penates on the Velia; a Temple of Juventas, and a Temple of the Mater Magna (Cybele) on the Palatine Hill.

The Temple of Capitoline Jupiter, and the Theatre of Pompey "*restored at a great expense without the inscription of my name.*"

[1] Drawings of the *Temple of Augustus* at Ancyra are published by Texier and Pullan, *Ruins of Asia Minor*, 1865, plates 22-25; and still better by Perrot et Guillaume, *Explor. Arch. Galatie et Bithynie*, Paris, 1872.

[2] In this very brief way is recorded the construction of the magnificent group of buildings included in the *Area of Apollo*; see vol. i. p. 183.

[3] Founded by Cn. Octavius, and rebuilt by Augustus; it must not be confounded with the new *Porticus Octaviae*, built by Augustus in honour of his sister.

New springs of water collected, and the Aqueduct of the Aqua Marcia restored.

Buildings of Augustus.
"*The Forum Julium, and the Basilica Julia, both begun by my (adoptive) father (J. Caesar), I completed, and the Basilica Julia I rebuilt, after it had been burnt, on an enlarged scale.*" These buildings, the inscription records, *though not finished during the life of Augustus, were completed by his heirs, in accordance with the provisions of his will.*

"*During my sixth Consulship*" (28 B.C.), Augustus says, "*I restored (refeci) eighty-two temples of the gods.*"

"*In my seventh Consulship (27 B.C.) I repaved at my own expense the Via Flaminia and its bridges.*"

The Temple of Mars Ultor and the Forum Augustum were built by Augustus on a site which he bought from private persons. The theatre by the Temple of Apollo he built in the name of his nephew Marcellus.

He offered precious gifts out of spoils of war in the Temples of Capitoline Jupiter, Divus Julius, Apollo Palatinus, Vesta, and Mars Ultor.

Then follows a list of the public spectacles provided for the people of Rome at the expense of Augustus.

Public shows.
Gladiatorial fights in his own name . . . times (the number is broken out of the slab), *and in his grandsons' and nephews' names five times, in which about 10,000 gladiators fought.*

Two contests (certamina) of athletes in his own name, and three in his nephews' names. Games (ludi) four times in his own name, and twenty-three times in that of other officials.

Fights with African beasts in the Circus Maximus, in the Forum, and in the Amphitheatre (of Statilius Taurus), in his own name and that of his grandsons and nephews twenty-six times; in which fights about 3500 beasts were killed.

Naval battles in the Naumachia[1] *in the Nemus Caesarum across the Tiber, in which thirty beaked ships with three and four*

---

[1] This Naumachia was an enormous tank or lake excavated in the ground; it was 1800 feet long and 1200 feet wide.

tiers of oars, and many other smaller ships were engaged, with about 3000 *fighting men, besides the rowers.*

He also offered spoils of war in all the Temples of Achaia and Asia (*Minor*).

The inscription then records the *melting of his* 80 *silver statues, and with the money thus obtained golden gifts being offered in the Temple of Apollo Palatinus.*

This wonderful catalogue gives some notion of the architectural splendour that was added to the city of Rome in the reign of Augustus.

It must also be remembered that indirectly, by his example and encouragement, Augustus induced many rich citizens to spend enormous sums in the construction of magnificent public buildings, such as the Pantheon and Baths of Agrippa, the Bridge of Agrippa, the Aqueduct of the *Aqua Virgo*, the Amphitheatre of Taurus, the Libraries of Asinius Pollio, the Theatre of Balbus, and countless other improvements of all kinds; see Suet. *Aug.* 29 and 30.

Gifts of citizens.

The saying, recorded by Suetonius, of Augustus having turned Rome into a marble city was certainly not without foundation. The old days of stern Republican simplicity suddenly came to an end under the auspices of Augustus, and the whole city, both in its public buildings and private houses, burst out, as it were, into a sudden blaze of splendour, glowing with the brilliance of richly veined marbles, poured into Rome from countless quarries in Africa, Greece, and Asia Minor.

Sudden splendour.

The next chief era of building in Rome was during the time of the Flavian emperors. During the reign of Vespasian an immense deal of building was done to repair the ravages of the burning of Rome in Nero's reign. Tacitus (*Ann.* xv. 41) describes Vespasian's munificence, *in tanta resurgentis urbis pulcritudine*; and this is also recorded on the *rev.* of a *First Brass* of the same emperor, which represents him raising by

Flavian epoch.

the hand a kneeling female figure, by whom is standing the goddess *Roma*, with the *legend* ROMA · RESVRGES[1] · S · C.

THE AGE OF SEVERUS.

Reign of Severus. Only one other period in the history of Rome can fully compare with the age of Augustus in its architectural activity; that was during the reign of Septimius Severus and his sons, a few years before and after 200 A.D. At that time, however, though Rome was even richer than during the reign of Augustus in quantity and variety of costly marbles, alabasters, and porphyries, yet purity of design and delicacy of workmanship had woefully fallen off; and so the large and numerous buildings which, with unflagging energy, were erected during the whole reign of Severus, can in no way have rivalled in artistic beauty those of the more polished and Hellenised age of Augustus.

Buildings of Severus. The following is a list of buildings in Rome founded anew or reconstructed during this second period of extraordinary architectural activity, between 196 and 215 A.D.[2]

The Marcian Aqueduct, restored and extended to the *Thermae Severianae*, 196 A.D.

The Paedagogium puerorum, on the Caelian Hill, 198 A.D.

The Temple of Cybele on the Palatine, rebuilt in 200 A.D.

The Claudian Aqueduct and that of the *Anio Novus*, restored in 201 A.D.

The Theatre of Pompey, the Pantheon, and Thermae of Agrippa, the Amphitheatrum Castrense, and the Praetorian Camp, all restored in 202 A.D.

The great Palace of Severus, and the Septizonium on the Palatine, built in 203 A.D.

In the same year were restored *the Stadium of the Palatine,*

---

[1] This is probably a contraction for RESVRGENS.
[2] See a valuable article on this subject by Comm. Lanciani, *Bull. Comm. Arch. Rom.* 1882.

the *Porticus Octaviae, and the whole Forum Pacis with its Temples of Peace and Sacrae Urbis Romae.*

In various years before 211 A.D., *the Temple of Vespasian and the Temple of Fortuna Muliebris, the Schola Scribarum, the Baths* near the transtiberine *Porta Septimiana, the Horti of Geta, and a Porticus* decorated with sculpture of the deeds of *Divus Severus*, also on the right bank of the Tiber. *Buildings of Severus.*

The Antonine Aqueduct, and the enormous *Baths of Caracalla* were mainly built between 210-215 A.D.

The devastation caused by the great fire in the reign of Commodus, 191 A.D., was one of the causes for these extensive reconstructions. Denarii and quinarii of Sept. Severus record his extensive building operations by the *legend* on the *rev.* RESTITVTORI VRBIS and a standing figure of Severus pouring a libation on an altar. The quinarius with this type is very rare. A specimen is published in Sambon's *Catalogue*, 1883, No. viii. p. 73, No. 619.

WORKS OF ART IN ROME.

In spite of the Romans being a thoroughly inartistic people, the city of Rome under the later Empire must have contained a most enormous accumulation of works of art of different schools and dates, far beyond that which can ever have been collected in any other city of the world.

Under the Republic an immense number of bronze statues were brought to Rome from one after another of the conquered Etruscan cities. *Etruscan statues.*

From Volci alone Pliny tells us (*Hist. Nat.* xxxiv. 34) no less than 2000 statues were brought, probably at the time of its capture in 280 B.C.

In later times almost every Hellenic city, first those of Magna Graecia and Sicily, and then those of Greece itself, contributed its quota to the rapidly growing crowd of statues in Rome. An enormous quantity of works of art of all kinds *Greek statues.*

was brought to Rome by L. Mummius after his capture of Corinth in 146 B.C.

Greek spoils. Similar spoliation was carried on by Lucius and Marcus Lucullus during the Mithradatic and Macedonian wars, and their example was followed by every subsequent Roman conqueror; see Pliny, *Hist. Nat.* xxxiv. 36, and Livy, xxxi. 26.[1] Under the Empire the finest works of Greek art, including many archaic statues whose interest must have been mainly antiquarian, were constantly being transported to Rome.[2]

From Delphi alone, at one time, Nero is recorded to have taken 500 bronze statues, which were mostly used by him to decorate the endless rooms and courts of his *Golden House.*

In addition to this almost inconceivable crowd of statues in gold and ivory, in bronze, in marble, in terra cotta, and other materials which were collected from all the principal cities of the Greeks, there were under the Empire an immense *Graeco-Roman sculpture.* number of new statues made by contemporary Greek or Graeco-Roman sculptors, such as Pasiteles and his pupils[3] Stephanus and Menelaus, and by Arcesilaus, Zenodorus, and countless other artists.

The imagination fails to realise one tithe of the artistic treasures which must have been accumulated in Rome before the days of Constantine. Every Greek artist of note seems to

[1] Plutarch (*Paull. Aem.* 32) describes the 250 waggons of pictures and statues which were carried off by Paullus Aemilius after his conquest of Macedonia.

[2] Caligula even ordered Pheidias' colossal gold and ivory statue of Zeus at Olympia to be removed to Rome. It was, however, found that the statue could not be moved without destroying it, the thin facing of ivory and the gold drapery being too delicate to stand any jar; see Josephus, *Antiq. Jud.* XIX. i. 1.

[3] Pausanias (v. 20, 1) mentions Colotes the Parian, as having been a pupil of Pasiteles.

In the *Amer. Jour. of Arch.* (vol. iii. 1887, pp. 1-13), Dr. Waldstein has published an interesting paper on Arcesilaus, Pasiteles, and other Graeco-Roman sculptors of the first century B.C.

have been represented, not by one or two specimens, but in some cases by the great bulk of the results of his life's work. A considerable part of Pliny's encyclopaedic work is devoted to a mere outlined description of the Greek spoils which in his time adorned this all-devouring city; see especially *Hist. Nat.* xxxiv. to xxxvi.

In the same way all other classes of art were represented in enormous profusion among the spoils which enriched Rome. Mural paintings cut off walls, easel pictures painted on panels, gold and silver plate, tapestry and gold embroideries, engraved gems, jewelry and crystal vases, objects in ivory and amber; everything, in short, that was precious from its antiquity, its sanctity, its materials, or its workmanship, was brought to swell the accumulated treasures of the Capital of the World.

Varied spoils.

PLAN OF THE FORUM ROMANUM

REFERENCES TO THE FIGURES AND PAGES IN VOL. I.

		PAGE
1, 1.	(*Basilica Julia*) existing marble piers and fragment of screen	269
2.	Impression of marble pier in the late archway of brick-faced concrete.	268
3.	Only remaining one of the ancient travertine piers	271
4, 4.	Chambers of tufa and travertine, with traces of the stairs	271
5.	*Tabula lusoria*, with an inscription, cut on the paving of the Basilica	273
6.	Opening into the *Cloaca Maxima*	143
7.	Massive travertine pedestal.	
8, 8.	Paving of *porta santa* and *Africano* marbles	272
9, 9.	Paving of various Oriental marbles	272
10.	Probable position of the Arch of Tiberius	268
11, 11.	Existing granite columns of the Temple of Saturn	267
12.	Main flight of steps, of which only the concrete core remains	267
13.	Start of the small side stairs to the chamber under the main flight of steps.	267
14.	The only piece existing of the ancient basalt paving	251
15.	Platform of the *Porticus of the Dii Consentes*	342
16.	Upper door in the *Tabularium* blocked up by the *Porticus of the Dii Consentes*.	375
17.	Door at foot of stairs of the *Tabularium* blocked up by the Temple of Vespasian	376
18.	Travertine paving of the time of Domitian.	341
19.	Pedestal of Vespasian's Statue	339
20.	Three existing columns of the Temple of Vespasian	339
21.	*Aedicula* built by Domitian	340
22.	Travertine paving of the time of Domitian.	341
23, 23.	Long passage and windows in the lower story of the *Tabularium*.	374
24.	Pedestal of the Statue of Concord	337
25.	Pedestal added by one of the Flavian Emperors.	334

PLAN OF THE FORUM 393

		PAGE
26.	Fragment of a later pedestal	334
27.	White marble door-jamb and massive threshold of *porta santa* marble	335
28.	Remains of some early structure in tufa	365
29.	Three travertine steps down to lower paved level, probably that of the *Comitium*	242
30.	Marble steps to this lower level	242
31.	Large marble pedestal (not *in situ*) inscribed to Fl. Julius Constantius	349
32.	Late addition to *Rostra*	261
33.	Remains of a small marble structure	350
34.	Marble pedestal of a column, with rude reliefs of the fourth century A.D.	349
35.	Marble pedestal of an Equestrian Statue, set on end, and inscribed to Arcadius and Theodosius	348
36.	Marble screen walls (*plutei*) with reliefs of the time of Trajan (not *in situ*)	345
37.	Remains of a small marble structure, possibly the Shrine of *Venus Cloacina*	350
38.	Large concrete core of a late pedestal	348
39.	Steps to the column of Phocas, part marble and part tufa .	350
40.	Late building of brick and concrete lined with marble .	351
41.	Existing three columns of the Temple of Castor . . .	277
42, 42.	Existing pieces of mosaic pavement	281
43.	Main steps of the Temple of Castor	279
44.	Side steps; only the three lowest remain	279
45.	Part of circular travertine curb; *Puteal Scriboni?* . .	284
46.	Foundations of the Arch of Augustus	284
47.	Line of side steps of *Aedes Divi Julii*	287
48.	Small front stairs up to podium of *Aedes Divi Julii* .	287
49.	Curved recess in podium, which probably once contained an altar to Divus Julius; now blocked up by late masonry .	286
50.	Remains of the Regia identified by Mr. F. Nichols . .	306
51.	Concrete core of the podium of the Temple of Vesta . .	298
52.	Small *Aedicula* by the entrance to the *Atrium Vestae* .	310
53, 53.	Shops adjoining the *Atrium Vestae*	310
54.	Stairs from the *Nova Via* up to the *Clivus Victoriae* and Palace of Caligula	191
54A.	Stairs shown on a fragment of the Marble Plan leading up from the level of the Forum to that of the *Nova Via* .	222
55, 55.	Windows in the *Curia* of Diocletian (S. Adriano), now below the ground level; see fig. 27	239
56.	Marble doorway shown by Du Perac (now missing) . .	239

www.ingramcontent.com/pod-product-compliance
Lightning Source LLC
Chambersburg PA
CBHW020539300426
44111CB00008B/722